"This wide-ranging book, with contributions from well-known scholars, provides a timely reminder that food marketing, by focusing on pleasure (not health!) can, in fact, be the ally of healthier eating."

– Pierre Chandon, The L'Oréal Chaired Professor of Marketing—Innovation and Creativity at INSEAD. Director of the INSEAD-Sorbonne Université Behavioural Lab

"This book brings together an impressive range of international experts in consumer research to explore the connection between food and wellbeing. We know that the over consumption and under consumption of food impacts on consumers' wellbeing. But in this collection of essays, researchers focus on the pleasure of food to highlight the central role that consumers' experiences play in promoting health and wellbeing."

– Julie L. Ozanne, Professor of Marketing, University of Melbourne

"Professor Batat with her book "Food and Experiential Marketing" offers an incredible collection of insights related to food, pleasure, and marketing in promoting healthy eating behaviors. With 14 chapters this book reveals the importance of different theoretical and methodological perspectives if the goal is to help consumers achieve personal and social wellbeing. This book is a must read for anyone interested in food marketing, the role of pleasure in eating, and consumers' wellbeing."

–Paula C. Peter, Professor of Marketing, San Diego State University

"Food and Experiential Marketing addresses an important and timely issue for societies worldwide: How can we integrate experiences of food pleasure with the need to adopt healthy eating habits? This book provides important research to help move societies towards enhanced individual and societal food wellbeing."

–Sonya A. Grier, Professor of Marketing, American University

Food and Experiential Marketing

Pleasure plays a significant but often neglected role in the creation of consumer wellbeing and the relationship between the food consumption experience and healthy eating. This innovative collection focuses on the experiential and hedonic aspects of food and the sociocultural, economic, ideological, and symbolic factors that influence how pleasure can contribute to consumer health, food education, and individual and societal wellbeing.

Food and Experiential Marketing uses a holistic perspective to explore how the experiential side of food pleasure may drive healthy eating behaviors in varied food cultures. It questions: Is food pleasure an ally or an enemy of developing and adopting healthy eating habits? Can we design healthy offline and online food experiences that are pleasurable? What are the features of food consumption experiences, and how do they contribute to consumer wellbeing?

Providing an overview of experiential and cultural issues in food marketing, this book will be invaluable for consumer behavior and food marketing scholars, public policy professionals, and the food industry in understanding the importance of pleasure in promoting healthy eating behaviors.

Wided Batat is Professor of Marketing and Founder of B&C Consulting Group. She is also an internationally renowned expert and speaker on experiential and digital marketing, specializing in the fields of retail, luxury, food, wellbeing, youth cultures, generation Z and Y, Millennials and post-Millennials, and tourism.

Routledge Interpretive Marketing Research

Edited by Stephen Brown University of Ulster, Northern Ireland

Recent years have witnessed an 'interpretive turn' in marketing and consumer research. Methodologies from the humanities are taking their place alongside those drawn from the traditional social sciences.

Qualitative and literary modes of marketing discourse are growing in popularity. Art and aesthetics are increasingly firing the marketing imagination.

This series brings together the most innovative work in the burgeoning interpretive marketing research tradition. It ranges across the methodological spectrum from grounded theory to personal introspection, covers all aspects of the postmodern marketing 'mix', from advertising to product development, and embraces marketing's principal sub-disciplines.

Digitalizing Consumption
Tracing how devices shape consumer culture
Edited by Franck Cochoy, Johan Hagberg, Magdalena Petersson McIntyre and Niklas Sörum

Taste, Consumption, and Markets
An Interdisciplinary Volume
Edited by Zeynep Arsel and Jonathan Bean

Consumption, Psychology and Practice Theories
A Hermeneutic Perspective
Tony Wilson

Gifts, Romance, And Consumer Culture
Edited by Yuko Minowa and Russell W. Belk

Food and Experiential Marketing
Pleasure, Wellbeing and Consumption
Edited by Wided Batat

For more information about this series, please visit: www.routledge.com/Routledge-Interpretive-Marketing-Research/book-series/SE0484

Food and Experiential Marketing

Pleasure, Wellbeing, and Consumption

Edited by
Wided Batat

Routledge
Taylor & Francis Group
LONDON AND NEW YORK

First published 2019
by Routledge
2 Park Square, Milton Park, Abingdon, Oxon OX14 4RN

and by Routledge
605 Third Avenue, New York, NY 10017

First issued in paperback 2020

Routledge is an imprint of the Taylor & Francis Group, an informa business

British Library Cataloguing in Publication Data
A catalogue record for this book is available from the British Library

Library of Congress Cataloging-in-Publication Data
Names: Batat, Wided, editor.
Title: Food and experiential marketing : pleasure, wellbeing and consumption / edited by Wided Batat.
Description: 1 Edition. | New York : Routledge, 2019. |
Series: Routledge interpretive marketing research | Includes bibliographical references and index.
Identifiers: LCCN 2018059983 (print) | LCCN 2019008815 (ebook) |
ISBN 9781351182201 (E-Book) | ISBN 9780815396352 (hardback : alk. paper)
Subjects: LCSH: Branding (Marketing) | Direct marketing. |
Customer relations. | Food--Marketing.
Classification: LCC HF5415.1255 (ebook) | LCC HF5415.1255 .F66 2019 (print) | DDC 664.0068/8--dc23
LC record available at https://lccn.loc.gov/2018059983

ISBN 13: 978-0-367-72717-8 (pbk)
ISBN 13: 978-0-8153-9635-2 (hbk)
ISBN 13: 978-1-351-18220-1 (ebk)

Typeset in Bembo
by Taylor & Francis Books

Contents

Illustrations

Figures

Tables

Boxes

Preface

This book results from several years of joint research and practice on experiential marketing, food consumption, and consumer wellbeing conducted by the editor who has gathered eminent scholars and food actors to explore the food experience realm. The book offers a deep examination of experiential and cultural issues in food marketing to help scholars, public policy, and the food industry to study the important role of pleasure in promoting healthy eating behaviors which is a general approach to eating, where the diet may be more appropriately described as balanced/varied, is pleasurable, and does not enhance anxieties (controlling calories, carbs, etc.). The contributions in this book seek to expand the research conducted to date, and approach the relationship between food consumption experience and wellbeing through a broad lens – focusing on experiential and hedonic food consumption as well as other sociocultural, economic, ideological, and symbolic factors that influence the experiential pleasure of food and its contribution to consumer health, food education, and individual or societal wellbeing. Therefore, the objective of this book is to deliver a comprehensive framework to examine how the experiential aspect of food that is shaped by different food cultures modifies the research agenda of scholars investigating the role of healthy eating in promoting food wellbeing.

The contributions support the logic that pleasure plays an important, but often neglected role in the making of personal and social wellbeing. Applying pleasure to future educational food programs and campaigns calls for synergistic, theoretical, practical, and methodological approaches that will lead to interesting new ideas related to food experiential marketing and wellbeing. The book develops this new perspective by exploring the experiential aspects of food, such as discovering novelty, nostalgia, epicurean eating, tasting, experimenting, hedonism, estheticism, and symbolism. This new approach seems particularly relevant, since it finally helps to provide a more practical and applied vision of the food experience: How do we define a food experience? How can we structure and build a pleasurable and healthy food experience? What are the determinants of the experiential pleasure of food? Chapter 1 provides the reader with a conceptual introduction to a new paradigm: the experiential pleasure of food and its contribution to wellbeing. This chapter examines how the experiential pleasure of food may offer key insights into new approaches to promoting healthy eating amongst contemporary societies by considering an experiential approach to food consumption. In this chapter, Wided Batat identifies and discusses how the determinant of the experiential pleasure of food can enhance consumer wellbeing and explore public policy implications and future research areas through a perspective that views food pleasure as a source, rather than a deterrent, of health.

Chapter 2, written by Michela Addis and Morris B. Holbrook, deals with the shift from food service to a food experience logic. The authors underline that, nowadays, the food industry is subject to the new widespread trend toward a big interest in experiences, which promises to revolutionize the whole industry. On one hand, consumers search for enjoyable and pleasurable offers that evoke strong emotions not only through the quality of food but by means of a broad range of components. On the other, brands and companies experiment with new formats, offers, and business models in an effort to reach these experience-seeking consumers. The trial-and-error approach that has been adopted so far indicates a few recurring mistakes by firms and raises two key strategic issues that they must solve. Specifically, in order to transform food services into successful food experiences, companies should (1) design holistic experiences, focusing on the integration of all relevant elements instead of searching for an excellent level on just a single driver, and (2) balance the two opposing goals of any food-experience investment – namely, scalability and perceived authenticity of the consumption experience. Only by offering consumers memorable food experiences can providers produce higher levels of individual and societal food wellbeing and thereby create increased happiness.

In Chapter 3, Anne T. Byrne and David R. Just explore food consumer trends and their contributions to food experience, pleasure, and public policy in the United States (US). This chapter uses seven current trends to explore how Americans eat for pleasure and wellbeing. The US is a geographically large country that is ethnically, racially, and economically diverse; the experience of one American can look quite different from the experience of another. Rather, the two authors have focused on phenomena and behavior that are of particular interest given the current policy climate and challenges.

Chapter 4, written by Julie Andrieu and Wided Batat, explores the rise of TV cooking programs, their typologies, and their evolution. In this chapter, the two authors explore how culinary journalism contributes to food pleasure and wellbeing by analyzing three successful French culinary programs led and produced by the French iconic culinary journalist and food critic Julie Andrieu herself to show how these shows are constructed in a way to provide viewers with closeness, simplicity, and the pleasure of cooking and developing a healthy approach to food.

In Chapter 5, Nancy N. Chen explores the cultural pleasure of eating and healing. In this chapter, the author shows that the pleasures of food are deeply embedded in cultural life and social engagement. The first part addresses new spaces of engagement with food for Chinese middle-class consumers. In the second part, the chapter considers medicinal foods as a critical intervention to address the connections rather than divide between food and medicine as separate categories. Through recent ethnographic research on contemporary Chinese foodways, this chapter will examine how pleasure through nourishing bodies may offer key insights into new formations of thinking, aging, and being well.

Chapter 6 by Danielle L. Eiseman, highlights the coffee-drinking experience and consumer pleasure and engagement. This chapter is a conceptual piece that explores the potential of experiential marketing approaches for engaging the public on the issue of climate change. More specifically, the chapter examines the coffee-drinking experience as the mechanism for communicating the potential risks and need for action on mitigating and adapting to climate change. The coffee-drinking experience is a pleasurable, emotive, and multisensory activity that enhances feelings of wellbeing. These elements of the coffee-drinking experience could potentially break through tightly bound political ideologies and identities when discussing polarizing topics. Furthermore, given that coffee is often consumed between work and home, the notion of "third place" is discussed. This chapter first examines the emotions and senses activated during the coffee-drinking experience, the coffee house as third place, as well as potential avenues for connecting the consumer with the impacts of climate change through the coffee-drinking experience with links to social marketing.

In Chapter 7, Zafeirenia Brokalaki and Jeff B. Murray introduce creative ethnography as a research method to exploring food consumption and pleasurable experiences. In this chapter, the two authors explore ethnography as a method to research food consumption and pleasurable experiences. Through a play consisted of three acts, authors discuss the genealogical development of creative ethnography. First, they review the meaning, role, and purpose of classical ethnography in relation to food culture, family, and identity. Classical ethnography is designed to help the researcher engage cultural contexts through participation with the ultimate purpose of achieving empathetic understanding. Due to market demands for quick turn-around and practical implications, classical ethnography has been adapted by market research firms and used in a corporate context. Thus, the second act presents contemporary ethnography using illustrative examples from the food retail industry. Ethnography has also been used recently to help researchers comprehend sensual stimuli, emotion, and movement. This third type of ethnography focuses on embodied approaches to food-related market research. The chapter concludes by discussing some of the strengths, challenges, and evaluation criteria for ethnographic food research.

Chapter 8 by Ghina Chammas and Nadine A. Yehya, on cooking, food experiential learning, and connectedness explores the dynamic experiential food learning and socialization processes of traditional Lebanese cuisine among 60 mothers living in rural Lebanon. Cooking is more than just healthy food provision, it is an activity, which allows women to become more than just mothers with regards to sociocultural expectations. Women essentially take up cooking after marriage as a life-long skill to bring about and fuel family happiness and wellbeing. The chapter positions cooking as grounds to juggle modernity, traditions, and lessons learned from mothers. Rather than focusing solely on old traditional recipes, mothers tend to add a Westernized touch to cater to current food trends. Through the understanding of the chapter, the contribution of food cooking experience to consumer wellbeing and food marketing is also discussed.

In Chapter 9, Emily M. Moscato examines bicultural (Japanese and American) food experiences. This chapter explores food practices and their implications for pleasure and wellbeing through the perspective of a bicultural Japanese and American family. It seeks to understand what food practices increase experiences of pleasure and how elements of these practices enhance wellbeing. Special attention is paid to the contrast of cultural orientations towards food in the situated lives of the participants. Aesthetics, appreciation, and engagement are identified as three areas in which practices foster pleasure; the cultural antecedents and mechanisms of these practices are examined. The US has poorer health outcomes and less pleasure-based food orientation than Japan. Pleasure-enhancing routines in Japan can illuminate ways to infuse greater pleasure and wellbeing into American food practices.

Chapter 10, written by Adrienne F. Muldrow and Jamie L. Grigsby, explores food storytelling and narratives from food cultural experiences. For authors, storytelling is an important part of individuals' lives. Telling stories about food is a normative part of US culture. The chapter begins with a discussion about the origins of storytelling and narrative structures. In the next part of the chapter, an in-depth discussion about the importance of telling stories and current storytelling research in the marketing discipline are discussed, including the benefit of narrative transport and the use of brand biographies. The next section explores the many ways that food stories can be told and by whom. The latter section is followed by a discussion on how food consumers can use stories to improve the wellbeing of those around them.

In Chapter 11, Steven Chan examines the fusion between East and West by discussing how the Asian epicurean experience evolves and embraces wellbeing by asking the question: Do Asian cultures present a unique perspective for understanding epicurean experience? The chapter tackles this question by applying cultural psychology research findings to reveal how East Asian cultures, as compared to Western cultures, interpret their world as a more holistic, interdependent, and changing environment. These differences influence the epicurean experience in myriad ways, ranging from food aesthetics to food nostalgia. Ultimately, the effect of these differences results in enjoyment and food wellbeing more defined by a collective interdependent group self-identity, versus a more independent individual self-identity. Understanding these cultural differences allows us to segment the marketplace and cater to each segment more effectively, ultimately elevating epicurean enjoyment and wellbeing for all.

Chapter 12, written by Gwarlann De Kerviler, deals with the French food gastronomy experience and its contribution to wellbeing. This chapter provides an in-depth understanding of the features of French gastronomy and the unique association that French consumers attach to food and wellbeing. The study identifies the specificities as well as considering the explanatory factors for French consumers' approach to cuisine and healthy eating behaviors. The chapter also includes interviews with renowned French chefs with three Michelin star restaurants to explore how they contribute to consumer well-being in the gastronomy sector.

In Chapter 13, Ana Babić Rosario examines the food-shopping experience on the periphery of the supermarket and wellbeing. Indeed, understanding the effects of food consumption on health and consumer wellbeing has been identified as a topic of significance in recent years, both amongst scholars and food marketers. This chapter adopts a practice theory approach, and is based on ethnographic accounts of the Whole30 dietary program in North America from 2015 to 2018. Of specific interest in this chapter is the influence of social media affordances on consumers' shopping habits and sensemaking of marketplace discourses, as well as interactions with the various spaces of the market – in the supermarket and online. Additionally, attention is paid to food pleasure and ways in which consumers negotiate the meanings of hedonic food consumption in the pursuit of wellbeing.

Finally, Chapter 14, written by Anthony Patterson, Robert Kozinets, and Rachel Ashman, closes the book by taking a deep look at food porn and the way it affects consumer wellbeing. From a netnography of consumer self-representations of food consumption, this chapter uses theory derived from Lacan to conceptualize the iMirror to explore how people seek self-development and the cultivation of their wellbeing through the practice of digital culinary voyeurism, vicariousness, and adventurism. Contrary to what some extant literature suggests, we assert that consumers can "have their cake and eat it," that creating, sharing, and viewing food images online allows them to eat incessantly, virtually at least, while never gaining an ounce of weight. This study also shows that food photo fans gain almost as much nourishment from their practices as they do from eating the actual food. They enhance their wellbeing by catering to basic human needs to be involved in competition, collaboration, the tendency to gather in consumer tribes, and the universal appetite to be appreciated by peers for making valued contributions to that tribe.

This book was part of a great experience involving contributors working on the topic of food from different perspectives. I would like to thank the authors who have contributed with very insightful and inspiring chapters to this edited book. Thanks!

Contributors

Michela Addis is Full Professor of Management at Università di Roma Tre, Italy where she teaches cultural marketing, market research, and management. She was also adjunct senior faculty member of the SDA Bocconi School of Management, Marketing Department. She received a PhD in Business Administration and Management from Bocconi University, Milan in 2001. She has been a visiting scholar at the Helsinki School of Economics (2000) and at the Columbia Business School (2000, 2004, 2005). Her areas of expertise include experiential marketing, customer engagement, and hedonic consumption. She is the author of two books on experiential marketing and many papers in national and international journals such as the *Journal of Consumer Research, Journal of Cultural Economics*, and *Psychology and Marketing.*

Julie Andrieu is a food critic and has been a television/radio journalist in the field of food for more than 20 years. Julie runs a consulting and audiovisual production company. She is the presenter and producer of culinary TV programs broadcast on French national channels such as France 3: "Les Carnets de Julie." In this program, Julie introduces the viewers to the regions of France through stories around terroir products and regional local food cultures. Julie has strongly contributed to democratizing traditional French cuisine in her daily practice by opening it to foreign influences, thanks to her show "Fourchette et sac à dos" (in English Fork and backpack) on the French national channel France 5. Julie also hosted a radio show on Europe 1 from 2005 to 2007 through which she proposed a discovery of personalities and their relationship to food. She is the author of 27 cookbooks.

Rachel Ashman is Lecturer in Marketing and an early career researcher at the University of Liverpool. She holds a BSc in Fashion and Textile Retailing, and a PhD in Digital Consumption from the University of Manchester. Her research interests include fashion retailing, digital marketing, and cultural aspects of consumption. In addition to other outlets, her work has been published in the *Journal of Consumer Research, Journal of Business Research*, and *Computers in Human Behavior.*

Ana Babic Rosario is Assistant Professor of Marketing at the Daniels College of Business, University of Denver. She received her PhD in Marketing from HEC Paris. Her research focuses on technology-mediated consumption practices, electronic word of mouth, consumer nostalgia, and the sociology of food. Her research appears in the *Journal of Marketing Research*, among others, and was recognized with the Emerald/EFMD Outstanding Doctoral Research Award and the International Society of Service Innovation Professionals (ISSIP) Best Conference Paper Award. Ana currently serves on the Editorial Review Board of the *International Journal of Research in Marketing* and is an active member of the American Marketing Association, the Association for Consumer Research, and the Consumer Culture Theory Consortium.

Wided Batat is a marketing professor and an internationally renowned expert and speaker on experiential and digital marketing specializing in the fields of retail, luxury, food, wellbeing, youth cultures, generations Z and Y, Millennials and post-Millennials, and tourism. She has published dozens of books in English and French and articles in top-tier academic journals that have received several awards. Professor Batat introduced an innovative and disruptive approach to global and digital customer experience by providing a strategic framework of the customer experience offline and online and the new experiential marketing mix (7Es). An entrepreneur, Batat is also a bilingual (French and English) international professional trainer and the founder of B&C Consulting Group, an innovative market research and consumer insights company specializing in global and digital customer experience design, buying behavior, and consumer trends. Follow her on LinkedIn and Twitter.

Zafeirenia Brokalaki is a cultural scholar working at the intersections of consumer research, cultural studies and performance studies. She joined the University of Leicester, School of Business, as a Lecturer in Marketing, after having completed a PhD in Culture, Media and Creative Industries at King's College London. Her broad research areas coalesce around the experiential, symbolic and political dimensions of cultural consumption, and the historical transformative dynamics of the arts market. Zafeirenia works on topics that concern the politics of aesthetics with a particular focus on participatory art and non-institutional creativity, the genealogy of the body and embodied/arts-based epistemologies. She has been involved in a range of funded research projects, and has served as a consultant for numerous cultural organizations in the United Kingdom, Greece, and Cyprus. She is a Fellow at the Royal Society of Arts (RSA).

Anne T. Byrne is a PhD student in the Charles H. Dyson School of Applied Economics and Management. Her research focuses on food and agricultural economics, with current projects in food assistance programs and consumer food choice. Prior to her studies at Cornell University, she received her MS in Agricultural and Resource Economics at Colorado State University.

Ghina Chammas is a project coordinator and researcher at the Nature Conservation Center at the American University of Beirut. She received a

Master's in Environmental Engineering from Imperial College London and a BS in Environmental Health with a minor in Public Health from the American University of Beirut.

Steven Chan is Assistant Professor of Marketing at the Sy Syms School of Business at Yeshiva University. His work focuses on marketing psychology, consumer behavior, decision making, comparison biases, and culture. Chan's research has been published in academic journals such as the *Journal of Public Policy and Management, Behavioral and Brain Sciences*, and *Advances in Consumer Research*. He has participated in past Transformative Consumer Research conferences on the mindful consumer (2015) and on the experiential pleasure of food (2017).

Nancy N. Chen is Professor and Chair of Anthropology at the University of California at Santa Cruz. She is the author of *Food, Medicine, and the Quest for Good Health* (2009) and *Breathing Spaces: Qigong, Psychiatry, and Healing in China* (2003). She has also co-edited four volumes: *Bioinsecurity and Vulnerability* (2014); *Asian Biotech: Ethics and Communities of Fate* (2010); *China Urban: Ethnographies of Contemporary Culture* (2001); and *Bodies in the Making: Transgression and Transformation* (2005).

Danielle L. Eiseman is Postdoctoral Research Fellow and Program Manager at the Cornell Institute for Climate Smart Solutions and the Center for Conservation Social Sciences in the Departments of Earth and Atmospheric Sciences and Natural Resources, Cornell University. She obtained her PhD in Marketing from Heriot Watt University, Edinburgh and is on the editorial board for the journal *Interdisciplinary Perspectives on Equality and Diversity*. Her research interests include sustainable consumer behavior, the nexus of food and climate change, and food experiences as an engagement tool for climate change action.

Jamie L. Grigsby is Assistant Professor of Marketing at Missouri State University, Springfield. She obtained her PhD from Kent State University in 2017. Her dissertation explored storytelling and narrative transportation in advertising. Her other research interests include the effectiveness of advertising messages, consumer decision making, and impulse purchasing behavior.

Morris B. Holbrook is the Dillard Professor Emeritus of Marketing, Graduate School of Business, Columbia University. From 1975 to 2009 he taught courses at the Columbia Business School in marketing strategy, consumer behavior, and commercial communication. His research has covered a wide variety of topics with a special focus on issues related to communication in general and to aesthetics, semiotics, hermeneutics, art, entertainment, music, motion pictures, nostalgia, and 3D stereography in particular. He pursues such hobbies as playing the piano, attending concerts, going to movies and the theater, collecting musical recordings, taking stereographic photos, and being kind to cats.

David R. Just is the Susan Eckert Lynch Professor of Science and Business in the Charles H. Dyson School of Applied Economics and Management, Cornell University. He received his PhD in Agricultural and Resource Economics from the University of California, Berkeley in 2001. His research focuses on behavioral economic applications to food choice and food policy, with a particular focus on food assistance programs. Other research interests include behavioral models of risky choice and analysis of biofuel policy.

Gwarlann De Kerviler is Associate Professor of Marketing and is currently Head of Marketing and Negotiation Department at the IÉSEG School of Management. She holds a PhD from Paris-Dauphine University, an MBA from Harvard Business School, and an MSc from ESSEC Business School. Her research focuses on four main areas: customer relationship management (satisfaction and loyalty management); luxury marketing (brand and experience management in luxury); social media/new technologies (blogs, online reviews, and mobile services management); and matching market mechanisms. She has published several papers in top French and international journals such as the *Journal of Retailing and Consumer Services, Journal of Business Research*, and *Recherche et Applications en Marketing*. She teaches courses related to her research interests to master's students, MBA students, and executive professionals.

Robert Kozinets is the Jayne and Hans Hufschmid Chair of Strategic Public Relations at the USC Annenberg, a position he shares with the USC Marshall School of Business. Rob is a globally recognized expert on social media, marketing, branding, and innovation. Besides having invented netnography in 1995, he has authored and co-authored over 150 pieces of research on the intersection of technology, media, brands, and consumers His research examines topics such as social branding, word-of-mouth marketing, themed retail spectacle, media consumption, technology ideologies, brand archetypes, utopian consumer culture, capitalist emancipation, and consumer activism through investigating sites such as Star Trek and Star Wars fandom, ESPN Zone, the American Girl brand, Walmart, Volkswagen, mobile device use, food porn, digital social networks, and the Burning Man project. This research has been published in a wide variety of widely cited top-tier academic articles, book chapters, popular press articles, case studies, videographies, and even poetry.

Emily M. Moscato is Assistant Professor of Food Marketing and Gerald E. Peck Fellow at Saint Joseph's University in Philadelphia. She focuses her research on consumer wellbeing with particular interest in social and environmental food sustainability and using alternative data-gathering methods for collecting consumer insight and motivating change. Her research has been published in the *Journal of Public Policy and Marketing, Appetite, Qualitative Market Research*, and *Journal of Business Research*.

Adrienne Muldrow is an Assistant Professor of Communication at East Carolina University. She uses quantitative and qualitative research techniques to ascertain psychological and behavioral effects resulting from representations present in various forms of marketing communications. Specifically, she explores content from: (1) social media, (2) digital media, (3) health contexts (including how food is represented in the marketplace), and (4) content containing an intersectionality of gender, body image, and race. Her work has been published in the *Journal of Health Communication, Health Communication*, and *Journal of Business Research.*

Jeff B. Murray is Department Chair and R.A. and Vivian Young Professor of Marketing in the Department of Marketing, Walton College, University of Arkansas. He has taught courses and doctoral seminars in Australia, Denmark, Finland, France, Germany, Scotland, Shanghai, Sweden, and the United Kingdom. His research focuses on ethnography, semiotics, critical marketing, and the sociology of the body. Jeff's research appears in the *Journal of Marketing, Journal of Consumer Research*, and *Journal of Marketing Management*, among others. He remains active in the American Marketing Association, the Association for Consumer Research, the American Sociological Association, and Consumer Culture Theory Consortium. He resides in Fayetteville, Arkansas with his wife and son.

Anthony Patterson is Professor of Marketing at the University of Liverpool Management School. Much of his research focuses on providing a snapshot of current cultural practice and theorizing how these phenomena impact on consumer behavior. Recently, Tony's research projects have investigated components of technocapitalism, service ecosystems, and entrepreneurship as a manifestation of neoliberalism. He is the recipient of the University of Liverpool's Sir Alistair Pilkington Award for Teaching Excellence and his publications have appeared in the *Journal of Consumer Research, Journal of Service Research*, and *Journal of Business Research*, among others.

Nadine A. Yehya is a Senior Communications Specialist and Science Writer at University of California, Davis. She was an Assistant Professor of Marketing at Suliman Olayan School of Business at the American University of Beirut. She received her PhD from the Brian Lamb School of Communication at Purdue University. Her research focuses on strategic communication, health communication, and media studies in developing country contexts. She published in many business, health, and communications journals including *Business Horizons*, *Communications Research*, *Health Communication*, and *International Journal of Communication.*

1 Introduction to the experiential pleasure of food

How does pleasure advance consumer wellbeing and promote healthy eating behaviors?

Wided Batat

The introduction of the "experiential pleasure of food" is a new paradigm that promotes the epicurean consumption of food and its contribution to healthy eating, thus improving consumer wellbeing. The logic in this chapter goes beyond a visceral food approach based on biological needs to provide scholars, public policy, food industry, and marketers with a new epicurean approach based on enduring pleasure by identifying the key determinants of the experiential pleasure of food and their contributions to promoting healthy eating behaviors and consumer wellbeing. The prevailing dominant paradigm driving research and recommendations for promoting healthy eating behaviors is a visceral and rational eating pleasure. Cornil and Chandon (2016) define visceral eating pleasure as the short-lived hedonic relief created by the satisfaction of eating impulses. Visceral eating pleasure is the by-product of relieving a visceral urge, often beyond eaters' volitional control, and it can be summarized by its valence (pleasant or unpleasant) regardless of the rich aesthetic experience of eating.

The existing rational and normative model of the relationship to food pleasure and health does not take a holistic and sociocultural perspective to explore the role of pleasure in food consumption and reveal how the experiential side of food may drive healthy eating habits. Indeed, food pleasure that can drive healthy eating behaviors depends on the sociocultural context and the food culture where it has been shaped. For example, in the North American food culture, the notion of pleasure (Alba and Williams, 2013) is separated from an individual's daily life and is limited to special times where guilty pleasures (e.g., indulging in chocolate) are a moral failing. In the European food culture, especially in the French context, food education is based on everyday pleasurable food experiences. Besides, the concept of epicurean eating is applicable to consumers of all ages. Thus, instilling this type of approach amongst families with young children and adolescents who are developing their independence with significant discretionary spending on food and drink would seem really valuable for the future wellbeing of society. In this chapter, I propose a fundamental restructuring of the dominant paradigm from "food visceral pleasure" to "food as experiential pleasure." Through a multi-disciplinary analysis of the literature in human sciences as well as in marketing and consumer research on contemporary food behaviors, this chapter examines how the experiential pleasure of food may offer key insights into new approaches to promoting healthy eating and food wellbeing amongst contemporary societies by answering two major questions: What does the experiential pleasure of food mean? And how does it contribute to consumer wellbeing?

Food pleasure in consumer research

The analysis of the literature on food pleasure (carried out by using the database Web of Science Core Collection including only literature in English from 1995 to 2017 and the keywords combining "pleasure," "experience," "health," and "food" in psychology biological; psychology clinical; psychology applied; sociology; business; psychology experimental; psychology; psychology social; or business finance) showed that amongst a total of 695 articles about food pleasure, published from 1995 to 2017, only 109 articles focused on food pleasure as it relates to the psychology, sociology, and business fields. Three of the articles focused on exploring food pleasure and its influence on purchase intentions (Nowlis and Shiv, 2005; Shiv and Nowlis, 2004), one analyzed food pleasure as it relates to eating intentions, while the remaining article focused on the relationship of food pleasure and portion control (Cornil and Chandon, 2016).

In their research on the relationship between food pleasure and purchase intentions, Nowlis and Shiv conducted experiments to test whether distractions affect the pleasure experienced during food sampling, and thus have a subsequent effect on consumer purchase intentions of the sampled product. Nowlis and Shiv found that the ultimate pleasure that a consumer derives from the taste of a food sample depends on two components, an informational component and an affective component. The findings suggest that distraction affects the subsequent choice of the sampled item by increasing the impact of the affective component on subsequent choice or by decreasing the impact of the informational component on subsequent choice (Nowlis and Shiv, 2005). Other research on the effect of food pleasure on eating intentions conducted by Moore (2014), who examined whether individual differences in affect intensity predict consumer's responses to food advertisement, revealed three mediators (i.e., emotional memories, weak impulse control, and the intensity of pleasure anticipation) that indirectly link affect intensity to food cravings and behavioral intentions and two moderators (i.e., vividness of advertisement, dieting status of participants) of the relationship between affect intensity and consumption-related outcomes. The study conducted by Cornil and Chandon (2016) on the role of sensory pleasure on portion size choice had two main goals. The first objective was to explore ways to make people who have already decided to eat a hedonic food actually prefer (not just choose) smaller food portions, at no hedonic cost to themselves and no economic cost to producers. A second aim was to test whether sensory imagery increases the influence of sensory pleasure expectations over hunger satiation expectations in portion size choice. However, little is known about the experiential pleasure of food, and how it influences consumer preferences. Further, psychological studies of food choices and eating habits typically focus on the individual consumer, with bodily experiences conceptualized as separate events, underestimating the role of food consumption to the feeling of pleasure (Wiggins, 2002).

An experiential perspective on food pleasure

Although food meets a basic human need, it also has a strong influence on human emotion. It is commonly known to trigger positive emotions of nostalgia, comfort, and pleasure. For example, the sudden exposure to an enticing aroma can activate specific memories associated with the pleasures of food consumption (Moore, 2014). Yet, the same olfactory stimuli can also activate visceral impulses like a sudden urge to eat or drink, and in the absence of the restraining influence of cognitive deliberations, these visceral impulses can have a powerful impact on eating behavior that can lead to a wide range of psychological disorders such as anorexia nervosa, bulimia, overeating, and depression (Wong and Qian, 2016). Thus, the impact of food on consumers' physical and emotional health is significant. In contrast to an information-processing view of a consumer as an objective rational thinker, the experiential perspective focuses on a consumer's subjective experience (Holbrook and Hirschman, 1982). That subjective experience may not conform to the goals of economic rationality, where consumers maximize preferences or outcomes. Instead, consumers can value more subjective outcomes such as wellbeing or enjoyment. Holbrook and Hirschman (1982) outline an experiential research approach that examines more subjective variables. For the domain of food, the multiple modes of sensory experience provide rich data for examining food consumption. In examining food consumption, the enjoyment of food can be an end goal: A gourmand savors the taste of each bit. Or a Chinese family may enjoy both the preparation of and eating of dumplings for the spring festival as a symbol of prosperity. In each case the consumption serves hedonic goals more than a basic utilitarian need of hunger.

The experiential approach can apply such hedonic meanings to construct or shift existing meanings for food. In this way hedonic meanings can serve as a bridge in achieving more utilitarian goals such as health or moderation in eating. Hedonic consumption is defined as "facets of consumer behavior that relate to multisensory images, fantasies, and emotive aspects of product usage experience" (Holbrook and Hirschman, 1982: 82); consumption that "is (and is expected to be) pleasurable" (Alba and Williams, 2013: 4). While Holbrook and Hirschman emphasize subconscious and less accessible mental constructs in the experiential approach, why should thoughts and concepts easily accessible in memory be excluded from our view of experience? Both conscious and subconscious mental formations work together to give meaning to hedonic outcomes. Even in the case of consuming chocolate for a sensual experience, both conscious and subconscious thoughts derive meaning for the consumer. We can see this experiential approach applied to the eating experience in recent literature where eating for hedonic goals diverges into two categorically different types called visceral and epicurean (Cornil and Chandon, 2016). Because these two types rely on different subjective meanings, an information processing approach would not easily identify their patterns. An experiential approach to food and pleasure employs this appreciation of symbolic meaning to decipher different consumer paths and outcomes.

Evidence shows that positive emotions can lead to an enhanced eating experience and choice of healthier foods (Macht, 1999). When discussing the experiential pleasure of food, it is valuable to take into account key determinants, food experiences, and activities; from production and distribution to eating and disposal that are embedded within a particular food culture and shaped by its history, social norms, values, beliefs, etc. Therefore, the experiential pleasure of food can be related to all food activities, is influenced by individual, micro, and macro determinants, and driven by both utilitarian and hedonic motives. For example, growing food can be a passion or an occupation, likewise cooking can be a beloved hobby or an undesirable obligation. There is no simplistic way of separating or examining the relative strength of these motives. What does endure is food consumption's experience association with pleasure. To increase the opportunity for greater food wellbeing, pleasurable nature of these activities must be increased by identifying the key determinants that can enhance the experiential pleasure of food and thus help consumers achieve their food wellbeing goals. Thus, I define the experiential pleasure of food as: the cognitive and emotional value that a consumer perceives from the multisensory, symbolic, and sociocultural determinants of food experiential activities. As Table 1.1 shows, I identified seven primary determinants that characterize the experiential pleasure of food framework: food aestheticism, food socialization, food sharing, food storytelling, food memory and nostalgia, food symbolism, and food taste and sensory.

These determinants will help scholars, marketers, food industry, and policymakers to develop new educational programs and marketing actions based on the promotion of healthy eating by considering one or several key determinants of the experiential pleasure of food. The following section will introduce and explain how each determinant of the experiential pleasure of food can contribute to consumer wellbeing.

Key determinants of the experiential pleasure of food

Food aestheticism

The sight of food causes a myriad of responses in consumers, ranging from the release of insulin and heart rate shifts to preparing the body for food ingestion (Wallner-Liebmann et al., 2010), to emotional responses compelling the consumer to ingest the food (Ouwenhand and Papies, 2010), to the retrieval of memories associated with the food and expectations of flavors based on prior experiences (Shin et al., 2009). Thus, food can provide experiential pleasure even before it is consumed, explaining why practitioners of the culinary arts

Table 1.1 Key determinants of the experiential pleasure of food

Determinants	*Focal concepts*	*Contribution to consumer wellbeing*	*Policy implications*	*Marketing and business implications*
Food aestheticism	Food appearance Food as art Multisensory food perception Food pleasure vs. food disgust	Positive relationship with food Opportunities for social connection More mindful choices	Enhance the appearance/taste congruence of healthy, socially responsible, and sustainable foods	Position healthy and sustainable food based on multisensory food aesthetics that is appealing to consumers
Food socialization	Modeling Explicit (e.g., family) and implicit (e.g., school) means of learning about food Cultural norms	Taste preference development Personal relationship to food Social norms	Consider how media portray specific foods to vulnerable consumers (e.g., low-literate consumers and kids) Formalized taste education	Position healthy and sustainable foods through marketing as socialization agent for food activities
Food sharing	Commensality Collaborative consumption Sharing economy	Enjoyment Affiliation Learning	Support community and school activities Initiate food safety laws Support alternative food networks Support family mealtime	Develop food sharing apps Involvement with consumption communities Increase of healthy, family-friendly eateries
Food storytelling	Food meanings Food symbolisms Food semiotics Food interactionism	Community Pleasure Comfort Kinship	Build food narratives that promote intersectionality in order to promote healthy and sustainable foods	Pursue more beneficial health alternatives and increase food wellbeing based on focal concepts related to food storytelling
Food memory and nostalgia	Positive and negative food memories (Gastro) nostalgia	Conscious awareness of food memories and nostalgia	Increase children's food preferences for healthier alternatives in adulthood	Increase use of nostalgia to promote healthier food products in adulthood

Determinants	*Focal concepts*	*Contribution to consumer wellbeing*	*Policy implications*	*Marketing and business implications*
Food symbolism	Food meaning as subjectively constructed but still embedded in a sociocultural context	New associations are formed related to the promotion of healthy and sustainable food	Initiate communications to change food meanings to complement school lunch programs	Promote healthier food choices consistent with new food meanings
Food taste and sensory	Individual senses Multisensory experiences	Interdisciplinary approach to understanding the pleasure of food	Inform healthy eating initiatives and food socialization interventions	Inform food marketing practices

spend much time and energy on developing skillful plating and food presentation (Carafoli, 2003). The ways in which food aesthetics can influence how much pleasure consumers experience can be explained by three factors comprising food appearance: optical properties of the food (like color), the physical form of the food (its shape), and its mode of presentation (arrangement) (Hutchings, 1977). Most of the studies on food aesthetics examine the first and last factor. There is some evidence that the presentation and arrangement of food can elicit pleasure on its own even before consumption, as a piece of art would elicit pleasure through the visual system. Consistent with the metaphor of food arrangement as visual art, scholars have examined whether there are parallels between what makes non-food art beautiful and what makes food arrangements beautiful, and whether that beauty translates to increased willingness to try or increased liking of the food.

One factor that contributes to the perceived pleasantness of still-life art is balance. A composition is said to have achieved balance when "its elements and their qualities are poised or organized about a balancing center so that they appear anchored and stable," and the weight of an element is driven by its "size, shape, color, location within the composition, and implied directionality" (Zellner et al., 2010: 575). Another visual factor hypothesized to increase the pleasantness of an image is color; there is an "inverted U" relationship between complexity of visual stimuli and liking of visual stimuli, so moderate complexity from adding some color should increase liking for visual art (Cox and Cox, 2002). Likewise, among practitioners of culinary arts, balance and color are considered important components of food presentation (Hutchings, 1999). In a large-scale naturalistic dinner setting, Michel et al. (2015) replicated the positive effect that balance has on food perceptions by showing that diners were willing to pay more for an appetizer if it was presented in the center of a plate (balanced) versus if the food was placed off-center (unbalanced). Participants also indicated enjoying the food more and rated it as more artistic when it was presented in a balanced versus unbalanced manner.

The appearance of food can also provide information to consumers that influences their consumption expectations and experience. For instance, consumers use visual cues such as luminance to judge how fresh vegetables are (Wada et al., 2010) and use color to judge how refreshing a beverage will be (Zellner and Durlach, 2003). Also, Morrot, Brochet, and Dubourdieu (2001) found that when white wine was colored with an odor-free red dye, participants used descriptors for the wine that were more appropriate for red wine than for white wine, illustrating the ability of visual cues such as color to influence flavor perception. There is some evidence in the beverage literature that consumers enjoy beverages more if they are able to accurately versus inaccurately predict the flavor. Some anecdotal evidence for the potential of this effect to extend from beverages to the food realm comes from Carlson who, after biting into a tomato he thought was an apple, wrote "the disgusting, disagreeable effect on me of that fluid, insipid, warm mass that filled my mouth was something very striking, and I have not forgotten it in forty years" (1930: 89). Cornil and Chandon's (2016) epicurean perspective suggests wellbeing can be increased by focusing on multisensory food aestheticism. They provide an example of Japanese bento lunchboxes as a reflection of the epicurean perspective. This same example can provide insight into the perils of taking aesthetics to the extreme and the power of cultural pressure. Thus, food aesthetics can increase the positivity of an eating experience by enhancing taste perceptions of the food and by providing accurate information about taste expectations. The study of food aesthetics suggests that the appearance of food should be considered an external emotional factor that influences consumer food choices and wellbeing.

Food socialization

Socialization is the process by which we learn about the values, norms, and attitudes of our own culture (Rozin, 1987). As an extension, food socialization includes the cultural and familial values, traditions, and rituals that influence our food consumption beliefs and practices (Block et al., 2011). Socialization occurs from infancy by implicit means and later incorporates explicit means (Monnery-Patris et al., 2016). Although socialization occurs throughout one's lifespan, childhood is a particularly important time for acculturation. For example, rules as to the appropriateness of breakfast foods during other dayparts is found to be implicitly recognized by three- to five-year-old children (Birch et al., 1984). Later research finds that these rules of appropriateness do not, however, influence the evaluation of enjoying these foods (Kramer et al., 1992). Yet, cultural norms are persistent through institutions including schools. Teachers influence perceptions of healthy and epicurean eating through implicit socialization, such as monitoring healthy, culturally normative foods and explicit socialization, and curriculum-based programs in which teachers promote experiential learning and model consumption of novel foods (Gatenby et al., 2011).

Three areas of socialization are of particular sociocultural influence on how individuals are exposed to and interpret food pleasure: parents, modeling behavior, and agency (micro level), culturally situated attitudes and norms regarding food (macro level), and marketing and media (macro level). Family, especially parents, play a critical role in food socialization, influencing their children's food preferences and how their children associate food with emotions and certain behaviors (Mitchell et al., 2013). These influences shape long-term food relationships, for example, research indicates individuals who have positive childhood mealtimes are more likely to have balanced diets as adults (Ainuki et al., 2013). Substantial evidence exists of parenting practices – including restrictive feeding, parental pressure, modeling of food intake, and availability or repeated exposure to foods – influencing a child's eating and relationship to food (Guidetti and Cavazza, 2008). For instance, highly restrictive approaches to feeding, which negate a child's ability to make decisions on what and how much to eat, are found to diminish the degree to which children learn to use their own internal hunger and satiety cues to determine consumption (Carper et al., 2000).

Media and marketing also serve as socialization agents for food activities by transmitting norms, values, and attitudes and constructing the social reality of those who use them (Bryant and Oliver, 2009). Marketing and media have long been associated with creating aspirational health and beauty standards and offering products to help individuals towards obtaining such standards. Media selection and use among children and adolescents can lead to the internalization of a distorted view of the world and can rival the influence of other socialization agents including family, school, and peers (Shrum, 2009). Within this great sociocultural context, however, opportunities exist to formalize and influence consumers' relationship with food to encourage healthier eating by connecting these foods to epicurean consumption. Therefore, food socialization influences the experiential pleasure of food, and thus contributes to consumer wellbeing. Through explicit and implicit learning of cultural values, norms, and attitudes to food, individuals acquire taste preferences and positive or negative associations with food which shape their experiential pleasure of food. By focusing on food socialization, scholars can extend research and suggest future directions for research on food wellbeing by offering a means to examine and understand the sociocultural context that shapes food associations and behaviors.

Food sharing

Sharing is a pervasive everyday activity that rejects a precise definition. Sharing can be distinguished from gift giving and marketplace exchanges by its resistance to reciprocity, its shared ownership, and its communal nature (Belk, 2010). Sharing of food has been studied extensively in archeology, anthropology, and sociology due to its perceived critical evolutionary and sociocultural link to human development and socialization (Jones, 2007). Through its social engagement, sharing provides an opportunity to reinforce values and norms and strengthen communal ties such as intimacy (Miller et al., 1998). For example, participation in a shared community garden allows for the dissemination of healthy recipes, tips on growing, preparing, and storing vegetables, and exchange of healthy foods among the community (Teig et al., 2009). However, food sharing has not been directly addressed within consumer research literature. While it is associated with food socialization, it is an area that deserves individual attention because of its participatory nature and its ability to influence the exposure, tastes, and associations individuals have with different foods and food activities.

Food storytelling

Storytelling is a fictional or non-fictional oral performance told by a teller to an audience to disseminate information. Storytelling in the marketing literature exists to uncover and translate greater meaning behind a consumer's experience. Food storytelling uses narratives as representations of experience. Therefore, the audience does not need to undergo physical and social risks as one who has first-hand experience. In narratives, the storyteller is allowed to compress time as the audience should receive more information than they would if they had to experience the event themselves (Sugiyama, 2001). For example, Wallendorf and Arnould (1991) illustrate this compression of time when family members at Thanksgiving tell old family narratives that have been rehearsed and retold such that newer family members are invited into the first-hand experience. Storytelling about food in the marketing literature seems to come from an anthropological or structuralist perspective. Block and colleagues state that "anthropologists have long studied cultural attitudes toward food not simply as a combination of nutrients, but as community, pleasure, comfort, and kinship" (2011: 6). Food carries experiential signs along with often signaling of community and comfort. Similarly, Bourdieu (1990) states that food is a vessel for family. From Mick's (1986) conception of semiotics, stories about food and community seem to be about how consumers use food and stories about consumer mythology that employ elements of symbolic interactionism.

In food storytelling, flexible discourses are used to describe differing food items that cannot be separated from cultural meanings. Families communicate about food in overt and covert manners (Moschis, 1985). Parents can explicitly state what food the family will have or children can learn food socialization by observing others (Moschis, 1985). Interestingly, family communication, arguably a form of storytelling, happens through various mechanisms that include a process, structure, pattern, frequency, and content (Moore and Moschis, 1981). Information about food between family members can be communicated through a conscious or unconscious modeling of norms and expectations, positive and negative reinforcement, or a combination of modeling and reinforcement that, over time, lead to explicit pronouncements of attitudes, values, and behaviors (Moschis, 1985). Moore (2012) found that telling a story using more explaining language with hedonic products, such as food reviews, led to less positive and less negative reviews and decreased the chance the individuals would spread news about the product. Conversely, explaining langue with utilitarian products polarizes positive and negative evaluations and increases the chance that individuals will share information about the positive product experiences. Experiential versus utilitarian nature of products can have moderating effects.

Storytelling about food, and the experiential pleasurable nature therein, is linked to food wellbeing because such stories help individuals create "positive, emotional, and social relationships with food at the individual, societal" (Block et al., 2011: 6), familial, and group level (Price and Arnould, 2000). Specifically, food storytelling contributes to consumer wellbeing by helping consumers accomplish symbolic and hedonic goals by fostering and strengthening social connections in the maintenance of cherished rituals, the sharing of sensory ingredients, and the preservation of established traditions. These elements ultimately lead to the continuation of society's food culture (e.g., Bublitz et al., 2013).

Food memory and nostalgia

Memory is the most determinant factor in how we learn to eat (Wilson, 2015). What and how we eat shapes the meaning of our lives so much that memories of food and our eating experiences become central to how we remember our past experiences. When we experience nostalgia, a longing for a past period in our lives, what we ate stands saliently in representing the time and feelings of that past. No human experience surpasses using more of our human senses than the act of eating food: Sight, smell, touch, sound, and of course taste combine to provide each of us vivid eating experiences. Prior research has defined pivotal development periods for the formation of taste preferences. Coined the *flavor window* representing the age of four to seven months old, babies are most open to adopting new flavors during this period (Wilson, 2015). But that does not preclude changes to tastes across childhood and adulthood. True of all behaviors, humans are prone to develop habits, which are then difficult to change without systematic regimen (Duhigg, 2012). Eating habits are similarly resistant to change, but applying the findings about their meanings can most effectively shift existing patterns. Memories of food can be both positive and negative. Positive memories of food can form nostalgia and evoke a longing for the past. Eating foods linked with those positive memories can connect us to that past in a fond manner. Negative memories of food can produce food aversions and inhibit us from enjoying those foods.

Food memories are formed with many layers of our senses and interpretations of those sensations. Having a flavor profile stored in memory is enough to activate it in the brain and begin to experience the associated pleasure. Because words and categories link to these memories, the semantic meanings impact our responses to food. While nostalgia for food means that our current food preferences are influenced by our memories of eating, food memories from infancy and childhood stand as the strongest memories given that they represent critical development periods in life. Helping infants and children develop healthier food memories will promote healthier eating choices in adulthood. Rather than help food brands profit by selling consumers unhealthy alternatives, prior research has led to empowering consumers to make healthier choices. Nostalgic comfort foods are traditionally unhealthy. However, we show how the processes of food nostalgia can work towards developing healthier food memories and choices.

Food symbolism

Food is more than just eating. It has significant symbolic meaning and incorporates much more than the physical consumption of nutrients (Bourdieu, 1984). Foodways can only be understood holistically, with every aspect of the human taken into account. Daily practice brings together many desperate determinants, from the need for vitamin A to the desire to emulate the rich and famous. Unity is provided by the fact that people must integrate into one meal, or one snack, or one shopping trip, the satisfaction of many needs: health, portability, social and sexual life, the sense of control, and enjoyment. The use of food as a symbol to represent human experience, whether a birthday cake or a ceremonial feast, allows symbolic meaning to serve as a key variable. In extending the pioneering work of Holbrook and Hirschman, Schmitt precisely defines consumer experiences as perceptions, feelings and thoughts that consumers have when they encounter products and brands in the marketplace and engage in consumption activities – as well as memory of such experiences (Schmitt, 2011). Food symbolism research reveals that food preferences are not wholly fixed on the objective chemistry of a food item. Rather, the meanings people infuse onto food greatly contribute to food preferences. We can apply those processes for forming food meanings to form positive meanings and associations for healthier food alternatives. Prior works have highlighted how food marketing does not have the health of consumers in mind. We change that paradigm with food symbolism by offering development of meanings that can be used to market healthier options to consumers, while also maintaining the place of food businesses.

Food taste and sensory

Taste and sensory properties have been shown to influence food consumption experiences that drive pleasure. Mental images derived from different types of narratives can prompt smell responses. Krishna, Morrin, and Sayin (2014) found that the greatest salvation happens when people see an image of food and smell the actual food scent. Furthermore, Elder and Mohr (2016) found that food sound salience acts as a monitoring cue for consumption where listening to the sound of a crunch decreased consumption. Irmak, Vallen, and Robinson (2011) found that people use the appearance of words to determine the healthfulness of different foods, such that dieters become more sensitive to the visual word versus consciously looking for more information about the actual healthfulness of different foods. For Deng and colleagues (2016), listening to music with lyrics drive a more global-oriented construal where listening to lyrical music leads people to choose restaurants with superior primary features. Further, Zhang, Wadhwa, and Chattopadhyay (2016) showed that dark color packaging is associated with pleasure as it increases indulgent choice.

Although food meets a basic human need, it also has a strong influence on emotions, including pleasure. These emotional reactions to food can be elicited through sensory properties. For example, exposure to smells can not only contribute to the activation of specific memories associated with the pleasures of food consumption, they can also activate visceral impulses like a sudden urge to eat or drink that can have a powerful impact on eating behavior. Research suggests that pleasure must be sacrificed for the sake of good health. Developing an understanding of how the sensory properties of food impact consumers' physical and emotional health is significant. Focusing on the sensory approach to the pleasure of food can extend current research by contributing to existing literature on food wellbeing related to food marketing and food consumption experiences.

Conclusions

This chapter shows that each of the seven key determinants has a direct or indirect impact on the formation of the experiential pleasure of food that contributes to consumer wellbeing. In contrast to visceral food pleasure, the experiential pleasure of food is the kind of indulgence that is unrelated to impulses and within people's volition. It can be pursued as an end in itself (i.e., it is not the by-product of relieving an urge), and it cannot be summarized by its valence because it is intrinsically linked to differentiated aesthetic, social, sensory, and symbolic eating experiences. Further, whereas the "visceral" view assumes that eating for pleasure is the enemy of healthy eating and must be controlled or suppressed to avoid overeating, even at the expense of wellbeing, the experiential perspective holds that eating for pleasure drives food control and helps consumers to achieve their wellbeing by focusing on one or multiple key determinants of the experiential pleasure of food.

References

Ainuki, T., Akamatsu, R., Hayashi, F., & Takemi, Y. (2013). Association of enjoyable childhood mealtimes with adult eating behaviors and subjective diet-related quality of life. *Journal of Nutrition Education and Behavior*, 45(3), 274–278.

Alba, J.W., & Williams, E.F. (2013). Pleasure principles: A review of research on hedonic consumption. *Journal of Consumer Psychology*, 23, 2–18.

Belk, R. (2010). Sharing. *Journal of Consumer Research*, 36(5), 715–734.

Birch, L.L., Billman, J., & Richards, S.S. (1984). Time of day influences food acceptability. *Appetite*, 5(2), 109–116.

Block, L.G., Grier, S.A., Childers, T.L., Davis, B., Ebert, J.E., Kumanyika, S., … Pettigrew, S. (2011). From nutrients to nurturance: A conceptual introduction to food wellbeing. *Journal of Public Policy and Marketing*, 30(1), 5–13.

Bourdieu, P. (1984). *Distinction: A Social Critique of the Judgement of Taste*. Cambridge, MA: Harvard University Press.

Bourdieu, P. (1990). *The Logic of Practice*. Cambridge: Polity Press.

Bryant, J., & Oliver, M.B. (2009). *Media Effects: Advances in Theory and Research* (3rd ed.). New York: Routledge.

Bublitz, M.G., Peracchio, L.A., Andreasen, A.R., Kees, J., Kidwell, B., Miller, E.G., … Vallen, B. (2013). Promoting positive change: Advancing the food wellbeing paradigm. *Journal of Business Research*, 66, 1211–1218.

Carafoli, J.F. (2003). Tempting the palate: The food stylist's art. *Gastronomica*, 3(2), 94–97.

Carlson, A.J. (1930). Physiology of hunger and appetite in relation to the emotional life of the child. In *The child's emotions: Proceedings of the Mid-West conference on character development*. Chicago: University of Chicago Press, pp. 81–90.

Carper, J., Orlet Fisher, J., & Birch, L. (2000). Young girls' emerging dietary restraint and disinhibition are related to parental control in child feeding. *Appetite*, 35(2), 121–129.

Cornil, Y., & Chandon, P. (2016). Pleasure as a substitute for size: How multisensory imagery can make people happier with smaller food portions. *Journal of Marketing Research*, 53(5), 847–864.

Cox, D., & Cox, A.D. (2002). Beyond first impressions: The effects of repeated exposure on consumer liking of visually complex and simple product designs. *Journal of the Academy of Marketing Science*, 30(2), 119–130.

Deng, X., Yang, X., Jia, L., & Lee, H. (2016). Strumming the chords of your mind: The effects of lyrical music versus instrumental music on construal level and choice. In P. Moreau & S. Puntoni (Eds), *NA Advances in Consumer Research*. Duluth, MN: Association for Consumer Research, pp. 275–276.

Duhigg, C. (2012). *The Power of Habit: Why We Do What We Do in Life and Business*. New York: Random House.

Elder, R.S., & Mohr, G.S. (2016). The crunch effect: Food sound salience as a consumption monitoring cue. *Food Quality and Preference*, 51, 39–46.

Gatenby, L.A., Donnelly, J., & Connell, R. (2011). Cooking communities: Using multicultural after-school cooking clubs to enhance community cohesion. *Nutrition Bulletin*, 36(1), 108–112.

Guidetti, M., & Cavazza, N. (2008). Structure of the relationship between parents' and children's food preferences and avoidances: An explorative study. *Appetite*, 50(1), 83–90.

Holbrook, M.B., & Hirschman, E.C. (1982). The experiential aspects of consumption: Consumer fantasies, feelings, and fun. *Journal of Consumer Research*, 9(2), 132–140.

Hutchings, J.B. (1977). The importance of visual appearance of foods to the food processor and the consumer. *Journal of Food Quality*, 1(3), 267–278.

Hutchings, J.B. (1999). *Food Color and Appearance*. Gaithersburg, MD: Aspen.

Irmak, C., Vallen, B., & Robinson, S.R. (2011). The impact of product name on dieters' and nondieters' food evaluations and consumption. *Journal of Consumer Research*, 38(2), 390–405.

Jones, M. (2007). *Feast: Why Humans Share Food*. Oxford: Oxford University Press.

Kramer, F., Rock, K., & Engell, D. (1992). Effects of time of day and appropriateness on food intake and hedonic ratings at morning and midday. *Appetite*, 18(1), 1–13.

Krishna, A., Morrin, M., & Sayin, E. (2014). Smellizing cookies and salivating: A focus on olfactory imagery. *Journal of Consumer Research*, 41(1), 18–34.

Macht, M. (1999). Characteristics of eating in anger, fear, sadness and joy. *Appetite*, 33(1), 129–139.

Michel, C., Velasco, C., Fraemohs, P., & Spence, C. (2015). Studying the impact of plating on ratings of the food served in a naturalistic dining context. *Appetite*, 90, 45–50.

Mick, D.G. (1986). Consumer research and semiotics: Exploring the morphology of signs, symbols, and significance. *Journal of Consumer Research*, 13(2), 196–213.
Miller, L., Rozin, P., & Fiske, A.P. (1998). Food sharing and feeding another person suggest intimacy: Two studies of American college students. *European Journal of Social Psychology*, 28(3), 423–436.
Mitchell, G.L., Farrow, C., Haycraft, E., & Meyer, C. (2013). Parental influences on children's eating behaviour and characteristics of successful parent-focussed interventions. *Appetite*, 60, 85–94.
Monnery-Patris, S., Marty, L., Bayer, F., Nicklaus, S., & Chambaron, S. (2016). Explicit and implicit tasks for assessing hedonic-versus nutrition-based attitudes towards food in French children. *Appetite*, 96, 580–587.
Moore, D.J. (2014). Is anticipation delicious? Visceral factors as mediators of the effect of olfactory cues on purchase intentions. *Journal of Business Research*, 67(9), 2045–2051.
Moore, R.L., & Moschis, G.P. (1981). The effects of family communication and mass media use on adolescent consumer learning. *Journal of Communication*, 31(fall), 42–51.
Moore, S.G. (2012). Some things are better left unsaid: How word of mouth influences the storyteller. *Journal of Consumer Research*, 38(6), 1140–1154.
Morrot, G., Brochet, F., & Dubourdieu, D. (2001). The color of odors. *Brain and Language*, 79(2), 309–320.
Moschis, G.P. (1985). The role of family communication in consumer socialization of children and adolescents. *Journal of Consumer Research*, 11(4), 898–913.
Nowlis, S.M., & Shiv, B. (2005). The influence of consumer distractions on the effectiveness of food-sampling programs. *Journal of Marketing Research*, 42(2), 157–168.
Ouwehand, C., & Papies, E.K. (2010). Eat it or beat it: The differential effects of food temptations on overweight and normal-weight restrained eaters. *Appetite*, 55(1), 56–60.
Price, L.L. & Arnould, E.J. (2000). The meaning and production of "homemade." In *AMA Winter Educators' meetings*. San Antonio, TX: American Marketing Association, pp. 5–8.
Rozin, P. (1987). Sweetness, sensuality, sin, safety, and socialization: Some speculations. In J. Dobbing (Ed.), *Sweetness*. London: Springer, pp. 99–111.
Schmitt, B. (2011). Experience marketing: Concepts, frameworks and consumer insights. *Foundations and Trends in Marketing*, 5(2), 55–112.
Shin, A.C., Zheng, H., & Berthoud, H.R. (2009). An expanded view of energy homeostasis: Neural integration of metabolic, cognitive, and emotional drives to eat. *Physiology and Behavior*, 97(5), 572–580.
Shiv, B., & Nowlis, S.M. (2004). The effect of distractions while tasting a food sample: The interplay of informational and affective components in subsequent choice. *Journal of Consumer Research*, 31(3), 599–608.
Shrum, L.J. (2009). Media consumption and perceptions of social reality: Effects and underlying processes. In J. Bryant & M.B. Oliver (Eds), *Media Effects: Advances in Theory and Research* (3rd ed.). New York: Routledge, pp. 50–73.
Sugiyama, M.S. (2001). Food, foragers, and folklore: The role of narrative in human subsistence. *Evolution and Human Behavior*, 22(4), 221–240.
Teig, E., Amulya, J., Bardwell, L., Buchenau, M., Marshall, J.A., & Litt, J.S. (2009). Collective efficacy in Denver, Colorado: Strengthening neighborhoods and health through community gardens. *Health and Place*, 15(4), 1115–1122.
Wada, Y., Arce-Lopera, C., Masuda, T., Kimura, A., Dan, I., Goto, S., … Okajima, K. (2010). Influence of luminance distribution on the appetizingly fresh appearance of cabbage. *Appetite*, 54(2), 363–368.

Wallendorf, M., & Arnould, E.J. (1991). We gather together: Consumption rituals of Thanksgiving day. *Journal of Consumer Research*, 18(1), 13–31.

Wallner-Liebmann, S., Koschutnig, K., Reishofer, G., Sorantin, E., Blaschitz, B., Kruschitz, R., … Mangge, H. (2010). Insulin and hippocampus activation in response to images of high-calorie food in normal weight and obese adolescents. *Obesity*, 18(8), 1552–1557.

Wiggins, S. (2002). Talking with your mouth full: Gustatory mmms and the embodiment of pleasure. *Research on Language and Social Interaction*, 35(3), 311–336.

Wilson, B. (2015). *First Bite: How We Learn to Eat*. New York: Harper Collins.

Wong, M., & Qian, M.Y. (2016). The role of shame in emotional eating. *Eating Behaviors*, 23, 41–47.

Zellner, D.A., & Durlach, P. (2003). Effect of color on expected and experienced refreshment, intensity, and liking of beverages. *American Journal of Psychology*, 116(4), 633–647.

Zellner, D.A., Lankford, M., Ambrose, L., & Locher, P. (2010). Art on the plate: Effect of balance and color on attractiveness of, willingness to try and liking for food. *Food Quality and Preference*, 21(5), 575–578.

Zhang, K., Wadhwa, M., & Chattopadhyay, A. (2016). The color of indulgence: How dark color influences indulgent consumption. In P. Moreau & S. Puntoni (Eds), *NA Advances in Consumer Research*. Duluth, MN: Association for Consumer Research, pp. 275–276.

2 From food services to food experiences

Eating, wellbeing, and marketing

Michela Addis and Morris B. Holbrook

Even if food had never been anything but fuel for an individual's body, more and more today, as never before, people consume food in their efforts to find satisfaction and wellbeing, not only through nutritional sustenance but also through the holistic experiences they enjoy. Food consumption has recently evolved and now presents an opportunity more for memorable experiences than for mere physical nourishment (Batat et al., 2018; Scott and Vallen, 2019). Almost any business report about the new trends in food includes experiences as the key drivers for the future of the industry. According to analyses performed by Innova Market Research and reported by *Forbes* (Lempert, 2017), the new food world in 2018 will be cooler than ever, with consumers looking for offerings with many specific features. Specifically, the food industry products will be sustainable and green for the whole planet; multisensory, with special attention to the sense of touch; directly connected with producers, putting consumers in direct contact with farmers so as to build food communities; positively affecting individuals' brains and health; enriched by technology and artificial intelligence in ways that will make food easy to choose, plan, and consume; informative to consumers about the paths food travels from the ground to their plates; designed in ways that enhance individuals' safety; relevant to the whole society, highlighting the political dimension of food; and offered in exciting physical and virtual environments with big investments made by food retailers. Similarly, Euromonitor International (2018) recognizes five megatrends in this industry, namely, experience more; healthy living; shopping reinvented; pre-minimization; and connected consumers.

In short, everyone agrees that the food industry is witnessing a revolution as it evolves from serving utilitarian needs to providing hedonic pleasures. However, despite the widespread awareness of concrete examples and cases, scholars have only begun to scratch the surface, with what remains a limited attention to the vital role of experiences in this industry (Mossberg and Eide, 2017).

The development of consumption experiences

The traditional focus on utilitarian value has been integrated with and sometimes even replaced by attention to the role of hedonic value. Beginning with ancient origins that blossomed during the 1980s (Hirschman and Holbrook, 1982; Holbrook and Hirschman, 1982), an emphasis on consumption experiences has spread into all areas of marketing and consumer research. Indeed, the experiential view of consumer behavior has slowly become one of the most dominant perspectives in explaining the attitudes and preferences of individuals and organizations. Over the years, consumption experiences have gained much attention both from scholars and managers.

Scholars have studied consumption experiences via an intense and broad debate about their definition, antecedents, and consequences, focusing on several facets of this complex construct and highlighting the role of fantasies, feelings, and fun as drivers of hedonic value (e.g., Holbrook, 1991; Holt, 1995; Huffman et al., 2000; Rook, 1987). At the beginning, these aspects were regarded as restricted to specific product categories such as films, plays, music, the visual arts, literature, and any other consumption activities in which emotions constitute the main drivers of their value. More recently, they have been recognized as common and widespread in most – if not all – forms of consumption, where the entertainment factor (Wolf, 1999) has been widely and profitably adopted to explain all sorts of consumption phenomena. Today, nobody seriously questions the dual nature of consumer value – partly utilitarian (extrinsically motivated) and partly hedonic (intrinsically motivated) (Holbrook, 1999; Spangenberg et al., 1997).

In the recent past, many studies have contributed to a better analysis of consumption experiences by giving special attention to specific aspects (Alba and Williams, 2013). One body of studies of key relevance to our present concerns involves the domain of service marketing, with special attention to experiential shopping. By focusing on the environmental contexts in which experiences take place, these studies have highlighted the general and specific features of servicescapes that should be designed and managed with great care by any retailer, especially by those who directly interact with customers physically or virtually (e.g., Bitner, 1992; Chebat and Dubé, 2000; Kumar and Karande, 2000; Mehrabian and Russell, 1974). Over the years, regardless of their original function, servicescapes have become places to experience pleasure, enjoyment, and entertainment (Chronis, 2005; O'Dell and Billing, 2005). Another useful stream of research on consumption experiences focuses on emotions and their role in driving consumer behavior.

Based on a solid psychological stream of research, a broad range of studies has addressed the link between individual emotions and market performances in the areas of advertising, customer satisfaction, or branding and even just as antecedents that explain consumer attitudes and decisions (e.g., Bagozzi et al., 1999; Holbrook and O'Shaughnessy, 1984; Richins, 1997; Thomson, 2001). Further, another stream of research that has greatly contributed to a deeper understanding of consumption experiences has concerned itself with postmodern marketing. Such studies explore the holistic complexity of individuals via phenomena that cannot be reduced to a simplistic set of rules and models. If marketing management as a reductive set of codified procedures is limited in its interpretation of reality, an experiential perspective provides both scholars and managers with more comprehensive tools. Indeed, the links between the experiential view and postmodernism (Brown, 1995; Firat and Venkatesh, 1993, 1995) include:

- an emphasis on both the emotional and the rational sides of consumption;
- enlarging the temporal scope of consumption;
- starting from what happens before a purchase and continuing until a memory of the experience;
- adopting a holistic framework instead of breaking up the experience into useless specific drivers;
- taking the consumer's perspective;
- focusing on the interaction with consumers acting as prosumers;
- and finally, neglecting the traditional emphasis on the utilitarian goals of consumption.

Meanwhile, the more managerial literature has emphasized more pragmatic applications of consumption experiences in an effort to provide managers with useful models (Berry et al., 2002) and toolkits (Carbone and Haeckel, 1994; Pine and Gilmore, 1999; Schmitt, 1999). This latter perspective – operating, as it does, in something of an intellectual vacuum – might not have contributed much to the advancement of knowledge on the topic, but it has built a relevant bridge between academics and professionals. Indeed, these managerial self-help approaches have popularized the relevant concepts and models, helping to make them appealing to broader audiences. As a result, in recent years, we find an increasing number of firms investing in experiential marketing strategies that aim to enrich their offerings and to engage their customers in strong, long-lasting, happiness-inducing relationships.

Though worldwide economic and political crises generate a high level of uncertainty as measured by the Economic Policy Uncertainty Index (www.policyuncertainty.com), firms keep on investing more and more in experiential marketing. In a world where it is very difficult to succeed through traditional advertising and communication – partly because the individual's attention span averages about six seconds – finding new ways to create the "wow" effect is often the starting point for one-to-one connections with consumers. Indeed, the 2017 Freeman Global Brand Experience Study recently found that, in five years, approximately 30 percent of chief marketing officers are expected to allocate between 21 and 50 percent of their budgets to brand-experience marketing (Freeman, 2017). As the 40th anniversary of the experiential view approaches, creating emotional and engaging connections with brands in the long term has become a key challenge both for professionals and for scholars. Indeed, progress toward designing and delivering successful consumption experiences has appeared in many industries, nowhere more conspicuously than in food-related services.

Old and new challenges for food experiences

Despite the current promising state of the art, a few key aspects of experiential marketing still need further theoretical development in order to achieve higher returns on firms' investments in the future. In this scenario, the food industry represents a key context whose investigation promises big advances due to three key factors as shown in Figure 2.1:

- The food industry is highly service-based. The food industry is by definition one of the main industries in which services represent the main element. This point refers not only to the places where people usually "consume" food (full-service and fast-food restaurants, cafés and bars, self-service cafeterias, and street stalls/kiosks) but also to places where people "buy" food. Indeed, according to a recent study by Euromonitor International (2018), the link between service and retailing will be stronger than ever in the future.
- The food industry has high symbolic value. By well-established customs, food links individuals to others, and it affects the relevant human environments and behavioral situations (Block et al., 2011; Kniazeva and Venkatesh, 2007). Indeed, cultural anthropology is the discipline most useful to understanding the value of food consumption (Counihan and Van Esterik 2013). Collective imagination shapes food consumption and its symbolic value, so that people communicate by way of food, which thereby turns into a general semiotic system that itself becomes a situational context (Barthes, 2013).
- The food industry is highly fragmented. According to the most recent estimates, the worldwide consumer food-service industry is worth USD 2.8 trillion, representing a major share of overall global consumer spending (Euromonitor International, 2018). But this huge economic contribution

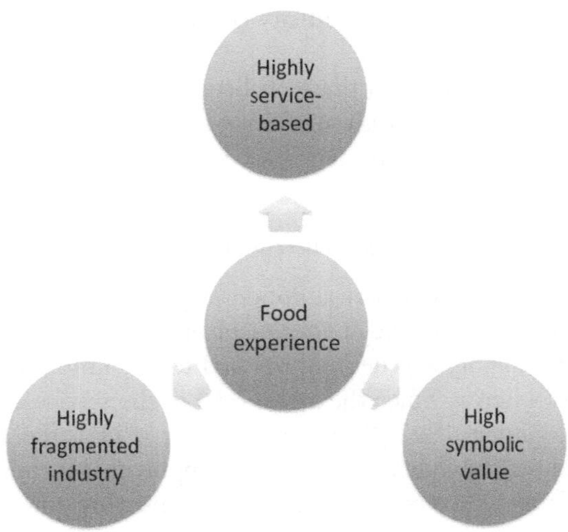

Figure 2.1 From food services to food experiences

comes from several diverse segments, ranging from full-service dining to online delivery and generated by satisfying a broad set of customer needs. Everywhere, local markets are highly fragmented, interconnected with other industries (including retailers), and strongly linked to the recent development of logistics and delivery platforms such as Amazon and UberEats. Thus, in any country, experimentation and innovation typify the search for original formats to differentiate competitive offerings. (For some salient examples, please see the Appendix).

Because of these three factors, food consumption offers important opportunities to create memorably innovative experiences. As a consequence, experiential marketing emerges as a key differentiation strategy both for online and for offline purchases and consumption (Batat et al., 2018). Online experiences must rely on aggressive investments in platforms and deliveries (based on efforts to learn from data and to interpret them properly so as to customize in accord with customers' individual preferences), and offline experiences should also be uniquely targeted (based on strong branding and customer engagement). In general, creating memorable food experiences that provide profitable returns cannot be taken for granted, as the relevant knowledge still needs further development. We believe that anyone interested in providing customers with memorable consumption experiences must deal with two key challenges that require further analysis. These are especially relevant for food-related experiences because of the high complexity and intense competition involved. Thus, success in marketing food-related experiences depends more and more on a company's competences to deal with the following two challenges (turning them into opportunities):

- designing integrated holistic experiences as opposed to single-driver experiences;
- balancing scalability and authenticity of the consumption experience.

In what follows, we focus on these challenges by relying both on theoretical knowledge and on the case study of Eataly, which in approximately ten years has revolutionized the food industry.

Designing integrated holistic experiences as opposed to single-driver experiences

One of the topics related to consumption experiences that has gained much attention refers to the role of the environments in which they occur. The physical environments in retailing – sometimes referred to as "atmospherics" – have long attracted scholars' interest. Since the key model of the servicescape was originally developed (e.g., Bitner, 1992; Booms and Bitner, 1981), the relevant environments in any industry have been designed to support the organizational goals and requirements of the service process. Indeed, demonstrably, physical environments exert direct and strong effects on consumers' attitudes and behaviors (Reimer and Kuehn, 2005).

Thus, servicescapes have attracted much scholarly attention, and over the years this stream of research has evolved via attempts to assess the links between specific investments and consumers' reactions. In environmental psychology, belonging to the broad category of stimulus-organism-response (S-O-R) models, the servicescape has been linked to the pleasure-arousal-dominance (P-A-D) paradigm, as initially developed by Mehrabian and Russell (1974). Through the strong connection between the S-O-R and P-A-D frameworks, the impacts of specific elements of environments have been studied by assessing their direct and mediated effects in the global service framework. Environmental stimuli define the retail atmosphere and thereby shape the consumer's emotional and behavioral reactions. Especially during the 1990s, this stream of research proliferated by designing and analyzing innovative cases that at that time defined the high-quality standard for retailers.

Many typologies of atmospheric stimuli have been proposed over the years. Perhaps the most comprehensive appeared in the rich literature review by Turley and Milliman (2000). According to their classification, atmospheric variables can be usefully analyzed via the following framework:

- **External variables**, such as the architectural style, the colors of the building, and so on. Even if only a few studies have addressed this category of variables, they represent the initial set of cues, starting with the purchase experience.
- **General interior variables**, including lighting, music, aroma, and so on. Many studies test the impact of these stimuli on consumers, assessing their influence on both emotions and cognitions.
- **Layout and design variables**, such as the waiting queues, department locations, and so on. Though this area has seen limited studies, these stimuli directly affect purchases.
- **Point-of-purchase and decoration variables**, such as shelf space and price displays. A clear understanding of the effects of these elements on consumers' reactions is necessary for companies that must define and negotiate the use of space in the environments for their products.
- **Human variables**, which have been repeatedly found to affect customers' and employees' reactions. This category includes both variables related to staff and those related to consumers.

In the food industries, many cases have been studied to highlight the role of specific elements as drivers of successful shopping and consumption experiences. Regarding the shopping environment, the PAD model has been widely applied in the past, and many food stores nowadays reflect this strategy. Historically, theme restaurants and bars offered the perfect context in which experiences could be designed. In the 1990s, theme restaurants were innovative, and they soon became popular, raising consumers' and firms' expectations (Brown and Patterson, 2000). Perhaps the most successful such creation – the Rainforest Café, a jungle-theme restaurant – reached USD 13.5 million at the end of 1994 for its first opening in the Mall of America.

The retailing history abounds with successful themed establishments. Other well-known international examples include Chuck E. Cheese, the Fox Sports Grill, the Hard Rock Café, Planet Hollywood, the Buddha Bar, the Harley-Davidson Café, and the T-Rex Café. Even if, in some cases, they have been downsized (as for the Hard Rock Café and Planet Hollywood), the format of the theme restaurant remains a viable marketing approach. Indeed, as the recent investments by Steven Schussler on Puff the Magic Dragon indicate, it still promises a strong market appeal. Significantly, these restaurants and bars offer complete themed experiences by bundling all elements together – from the décor to the menu itself – to offer a combination of dining and entertainment. And it appears that, by contrast with traditional restaurants, good food is not the main driver that appeals to the prospective patron (Fleming et al., 2007). Rather – like theme parks and theme hotels – these restaurants immerse consumers in contexts that are intentionally very rich in symbols.

Through themed experiences, these establishments provide customers with a path to escape from their ordinary lives. Thus, the environmental atmosphere of restaurants becomes part of their offering, actually the key part of it, shaping what becomes a memorable experience. And, to generate extraordinary food experiences, marketing must work with other fields in ways that take advantage of excellent specialized competences. Indeed, anyone who owns specific competences able to make a differentiating contribution now tends to become a "star." For instance "starchitects" as well as "starchefs" proliferate, celebrating these contributors to meaningful food-related experiences. But the food experience shows that excellence in any isolated competence is not enough – no matter how superior a food experience is in any one of these relevant aspects – architecture, interior design, cuisine, sensorial marketing, or whatever. To generate memorable food-related experiences, firms do not have to offer more music, provide customers with more light, offer them more high-quality food, or provide other kinds of "more." Rather, a successful food experience offers a holistic bundle of elements that provide a unique and consistent experience across numerous criteria. One such case that has attracted attention on the world stage is Eataly. Since its foundation in 2007, Eataly has grown rapidly in terms of revenue, number of stores, and market size while always providing its customers with a unique integrated experience. Indeed, the Eataly experience offers a few relevant insights of interest to anyone striving to design holistic experiences. Specifically, the Eataly food experience appears notably well integrated with respect to at least six main features, as shown in Figure 2.2.

- **Positioning: broad concept**. The first aspect of the highly integrated experience that Eataly offers to its customers refers to its vision – a carefully designed and implemented strategy based on a highly abstract concept that emphasizes the appeal of food "made in Italy." A positioning based on the "Made in Italy" of Eataly is so strongly linked to the symbolic value and heritage of the country of origin that one could easily argue that Eataly actually sells Italy itself by capitalizing on this highly effective extrinsic

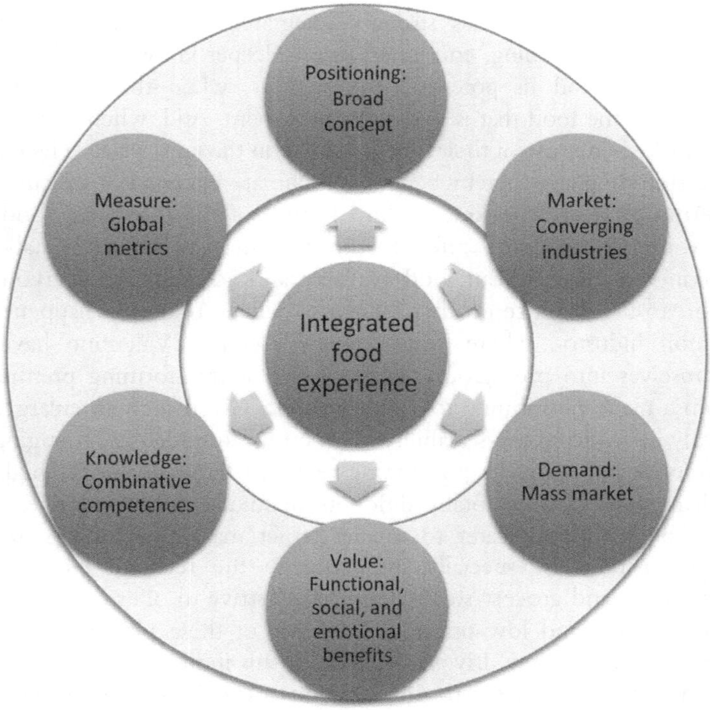

Figure 2.2 Integrated food experience at Eataly

quality cue (Becker, 1999). Such quality cues and signals tend to drive consumers' preferences toward experience goods because they reduce their typical evaluative ambiguity and uncertainty (Caves, 2000). In short, the theme of Eataly is Italian food, with no specific boundaries or limits. This Made-in-Italy theme is highly appreciated both in Italy and abroad, increasing the value of anything that refers to this label. Indeed, recent data indicate that exports of food made in Italy equal USD 38 billion worldwide (Promos, 2017). The innovation launched by Eataly builds on this phenomenon by including an extended range of product categories.

- **Market: converging industries**. The broad Made-in-Italy positioning works toward the emergence of a meta-market. Since its foundation, Eataly has developed a unique formula based on the combination of three traditionally separate industries: restaurants, retailers, and education. Typically, these three industries satisfy three different sets of customer needs – namely, eating, shopping, and learning – leading to the creation of three separate industries with distinct players and different business models. But Eataly has introduced a disruptive innovation by combining and mixing all three, offering a unique and holistic experience based on food. Anything that refers to food refers to Eataly as well, no matter which specific need the consumer might have. Such a positioning builds on the synergies that link the three industries and appears as strongly integrated in consumers' perceptions. Indeed, while learning, consumers gain a deeper knowledge about food, its preparation, and its potential uses so that, when they eat, they better appreciate the food that is sold all around them. And, when they shop, they can make better use of their time by eating in the same place. The concept of one-stop shopping thereby benefits all who are interested in Italian food.

- **Demand: mass market**. A third feature of the integrated food experience offered by Eataly refers to the mass market. Indeed, Eataly aims at making excellent Italian food available and accessible to everyone, in an effort to democratize quality. Similar to what has already happened in the fashion industry, where houses like Gucci and Valentino have turned themselves into prestigious brands, Eataly is transforming premium food from a niche positioning to a mass market. Given such an enlarged target, Eataly can expand the scalability of its business model by leveraging on the economies of scale. Its positioning refers to the domain of "high-quality Italian food," which totally differs from luxury or premium experiences that, by definition, cater to smaller target markets. This big size of the target markets is especially important in the retailing industry, where superstores and grocery stores traditionally strive to offer customers variety, convenience, and low prices. The ability of these players to target mass markets is thus a key driver of success in this industry.
- **Value: functional, symbolic, and emotional benefits**. From the qualitative viewpoint, Eataly proposes to its customers an integrated offering that provides them with functional, symbolic, and emotional benefits. People visiting Eataly can obtain satisfaction of their utilitarian needs (nutritional sustenance), but they can also benefit from an experience devoted to hedonic rewards (positive and favorable emotions). The cultural and symbolic value of Italian food is also emphasized, thanks to the exclusivity of the aspirational value of high-quality Italian food and its surrounding social environment. Indeed, according to the most recent data, 1.2 billion individuals buy at least one agricultural Made-in-Italy product, while the Italian share of €60 billion accounts for approximately 50 percent of the total revenue of the whole industry (Federalimentare, 2015).
- **Knowledge: combinative competences**. To create an integrated offering, Eataly proposes a customer journey that relies on several touch points. Despite the high number and variety of these touch points, Eataly's food experience stands out for its consistency. In line with the broad stream of research on combinative capabilities, the success of an engaging and memorable customer experience depends on the ability to align all the relevant touch points and to offer a uniquely harmonious theme. In the case of Eataly, such a theme is represented by the concept of high-quality Italian food, which is then realized by a full range of touch points that attain consistency across the whole customer journey. In order to achieve such an integrated experience, Eataly focuses more on the general fit among its full range of competences than on having excellent capabilities in isolated areas.

- **Measures: global metrics.** The last feature referring to the integrated food experience offered by Eataly pertains to its control approach. Here, results cannot be assessed by a metric such as sales per square foot that is traditionally measured. Eataly avoids such a measure because it focuses only on a limited area of the experience – i.e., shopping – neglecting other aspects (eating, learning) that equally contribute to creating the overall experience. Thus, Eataly prefers to assess its performance by measuring two global indicators – gross revenue and earnings before interest, taxes, depreciation, and amortization – both of which adopt a global perspective and are therefore better able to assess the performance of the whole experience.

All the above elements are aligned to give rise to a memorable Eataly food experience, thanks to another key strategic element pursued by the company – namely, storytelling. Following its long history, extending back to ancient times, storytelling has recently emerged as a major focal point in marketing because it represents the means to encouraging consumers' transportation into brand-related narratives (Green and Brock, 2000; Van Laer et al., 2014). Today, storytelling is regarded as the main communication strategy for building brand equity, especially for products that are rich in symbolic value (Mossberg, 2008). Thanks to storytelling, companies build a complex environment by engaging customers and shaping their experiences. Thanks to storytelling, people can have memorable experiences that help them escape from their ordinary life. As Oscar Farinetti, the founder of Eataly, once said, "If a fact is not narrated, it does not exist."

Balancing scalability and authenticity of the consumption experience

Joan Miró once said: "I get my ideas from the simplest things. I prefer a plate out of which a peasant is eating his soup to the ridiculously ornate plates wealthy people use." Miró was referring to his own masterful artistry and did not know that he was anticipating one of the biggest trends in food consumption and actually in any industry. Specifically, the quest for authenticity is a pervasive trend in all aspects of everyday consumption, a cornerstone in driving consumers' preferences (Mak et al., 2013; McCarthy, 2009). For example, the Indian unorganized food-services market is expected to go up to USD 58 billion by 2020 (Technopak Advisors, 2017) by satisfying the desires of travelers who look for authentic experiences.

Following a long tradition (Phillips, 1997), authentic products have recently started to gain the attention of companies – including those in the food industry (Lu and Fine, 1995) – as a point of difference in their positioning strategy (Bruhn et al., 2012; Fritz et al., 2017; Grayson and Martinec, 2004). Indeed, the quest for real products and authentic food experiences is increasing on all sides (Beverland, 2006; Brown et al., 2003; Grayson and Martinec, 2004; Peñaloza, 2000). But, with the increasing pace of competitive dynamics, providing customers with authentic experiences represents a difficult challenge.

The nature of mass-market products typically drives customers to question their authenticity (Rose and Wood, 2005).

As the consumer-research literature has pointed out, authenticity in experiences can be interpreted as both a product feature and an experience outcome, but in both cases it entails the participation of customers as active players co-creating a credible staging for the relevant experience (Carù and Cova, 2007; Chronis and Hampton, 2008; Gottdiener, 1998; Hollenbeck et al., 2008; Kozinets et al., 2002). Indeed, perceived authenticity depends on both marketers and consumers: The former engineer the environments and their constituting elements, and the latter continually craft their own narratives (Beverland and Farrelly, 2010; Munoz et al., 2006). Thus, if consumers want to experience food, they help to create the resulting outcome. This feature poses a major challenge to anyone wanting to participate in the food industry (Beverland, 2006). As previously discussed, successful food experiences rely on the integration and convergence of industries, giving birth to experimental and innovative meta-markets.

The resulting themed environments based on food – narratively based social processes (Gottdiener, 2001) – are marked by high levels of experimentation and innovation, asking companies to pay great attention to the synergies they hope to orchestrate. Firms must deal with the risk of failure in shaping how consumers perceive authentic food experiences. Such risks are especially emphasized by another feature of these new business models referring to their scalability: To be successful as a start up, a company must be prepared for upward scaling. Thus, perceived authenticity and scalability are two different and potentially opposed objectives. Eataly again illustrates the need to balance scalability and authenticity. In this connection, Eataly's history can be divided into three stages, as follows.

- **The start-up stage**. After its foundation in 2007, Eataly spent the first years fixing its business model, designing the integrated food experience, and putting it into operation in an old vermouth factory in Turin. By 2009, Eataly had opened 12 stores in Italy and internationally, establishing the standard for their food experience.
- **The strengthening stage**. In 2010, Eataly entered a new stage with the opening of its New York store and started to exploit its model internationally on a much grander scale. Entering the United States market, Eataly began to exploit its standard, to find partners, and to adapt its formula to the international environment. The joint venture with Mario Batali and Joe Bastianich's hospitality group contributed to the success of the New York store, which in its first year generated USD 70 million in revenue, far above all expectations.
- **The exploitation stage**. In 2017, Eataly entered its current stage, focusing on the search for new business opportunities to enrich its value proposition and to exploit the brand built over the past ten years. From growth through the opening of replicated stores, it started to invest in a new emerging market, attracting tourists to a theme park devoted to food. Indeed, its slogan has blossomed into "eating Italian food, living the Italian way,"

opening a full range of possibilities. As of May 2018, Eataly World operates 14 stores in Italy, nine stores in the biggest worldwide capital cities, and another eight venues that present formats different from the traditional stores in which people eat, shop, and learn.

In the historical stages just described, Eataly has tried to deal with the need to balance scalability and authenticity differently over time. If such an issue was not a priority during the initial start-up stage – because the company strived to perfect the formula to set up for the future – it later became quite important. In the second strengthening stage, the necessary balance was generally found with great efficacy because it lay at the core of the business model. Specifically, Eataly's stores were conceived as spaces where people eat, shop for, and learn about high-quality Italian food. This unique and distinctive positioning has been successful, as shown by the increasing number of stores opened around the world and by the various control measures mentioned earlier.

Despite such success, some might argue that the formula is adapted to the specificities of the country hosting the store so that its perceived authenticity cannot be taken for granted. In that connection, the import and export regulations in any country, plus that country's supply-chain characteristics, play a big role. These conditions reduce the concrete opportunities for small producers of high-quality Italian food to sell abroad, with the consequence of decreasing the perceived authenticity of Eataly World spaces. Eataly World must deal with the relevant constraints if it wants to feature everything that would be found at a typical fancy grocery store but on a larger scale so as to benefit from the aforementioned scale-based economies.

In the third exploitation stage, the balance between authenticity and scalability has become even more difficult. Indeed, Eataly World must deal with this issue not only with regard to its typical business model. Beyond that, Eataly World is not only "a bigger Eataly" but is something else, something different. What is really innovative is the new meta-market that it aims to develop by enlarging its business model to create a tourist attraction. In November 2017, Eataly opened FICO, which stands for "Fabbrica Italiana Contadina" or "Italian farming factory." FICO is the biggest Eataly project yet, a massive themed Italian-food food park, an investment to valorize and recreate gastronomic knowledge of the food presented at the stores. FICO, with an investment of USD 120 million, has been presented as the "Disneyland of food." For the first time, Eataly World presents the whole production processes of many food products sold (through 48 shops) and consumed (through 42 restaurants). Visitors can watch the production process of cheese, truffles, tomato sauce, chocolate, or pasta and can visit a pigsty, a chicken coop, or a vineyard.

It might be too early to assess the ultimate success of this massive food experience. If initially 17,000 visitors were expected on a daily basis, an average of only 1,100 visitors per day have actually appeared. Further, the business plan estimates revenues of €90 million in the first three years. But this business model relies not on the price of an entrance ticket but only on a mark-up on the revenues of the 150 companies that participate (20 percent for food sales and 30 percent for food consumption). However, it is not too early to assess the perceptions of Eataly World's authenticity. With regard to this issue, Eataly World appears to face some troubles in that many perceive it as just another themed amusement park – that is, standard and fake. In this connection, the theoretical framework developed by Chronis and Hampton (2008) to analyze a site's perceived authenticity provides a useful perspective. According to their model, authenticity is articulated in five different ways:

1 *object-related authenticity* that refers to tangible objects and artifacts;
2 *factual authenticity*, which encompasses the accuracy of the proposed narrative;
3 *locational authenticity*, which refers to the physical landscape and to the actual locations that embody the proposed narrative;
4 *personage authenticity*, related to the characters of the proposed narratives;
5 *contextual authenticity* that depicts individuals' perception of the context of the narrative, which should be unmanaged by human intervention, faithful to the environment, and free from any kind of commercialization.

Object-related authenticity has been attained by the huge efforts of the involved companies to recreate the contexts in which food is produced. At the same time, *factual authenticity* is guaranteed by the long tradition and heritage of the companies invited to take part in this project. But other kinds of authenticity appear questionable at Eataly World. Indeed, many wonder whether the Eataly World formula can provide an authentic narrative, especially with regard to the staging of the productive processes. Despite the level of investment, Eataly World can only mimic original productive plants located in different geographical areas. Producing the Italian products that embody the Made-in-Italy theme entails competences, skills, heritage, networking, and cultural aspects that cannot easily be reproduced. Places are part of that culture and cannot be replicated.

For example, truffles do not actually grow there but are just buried there for demonstration. By separating locations of origin from the location of demonstration, Eataly World seems to ignore the effective power of what is called the "belief of contagion" – namely, the "belief that objects can acquire a special aura or essence of a particular source through physical contact" (Newman and Dhar, 2014: 372). Thus, the various controversial perceptions of Eataly World are not surprising. From the beginning, it has been described by the *Guardian* as "a US-style megamart, a Wholefoods on steroids" (Seymour, 2017); by the *New York Times* as "a food court that had metastasized into an entire mall" (Rail, 2017); and by *Der Spiegel* as "a Disneyworld of food … affected by the syndrome of giantism" (Mayr, 2018). Thus *locational authenticity* appears to be threatened.

Further, *personage authenticity* relies on the competences and skills of employees engaged to contribute to the narrative, as certified by a partnership with the University of Gastronomic Sciences founded by Slow Food. Eataly World pays great attention to these roles. However, a similar level of attention seems to be lacking with regard to such temporary workers as sales staff and check-out assistants that Eataly World employs only for the peak seasons. Finally, *contextual authenticity* appears limited in the case of Eataly World. Indeed, the aspiration of all involved companies to achieve commercial success of the site is manifest throughout its offering. The whole experience is devoted to increasing revenues by encouraging visitors not only to learn, to shop, and to eat food but also to park their cars, to take buses, to watch videos, and so forth. Eataly World clearly comprises a bundle of elements that aim at generating cash flows. Its commercial nature appears quite plainly insofar as the imperatives of scalability must not be denied.

Food experience and its contribution to wellbeing and food marketing

Many obstacles threaten the transformative path of food from services to experiences. But, for those who are not easily discouraged, the potential results promise attractive opportunities. Small entrepreneurs and even global companies will achieve higher levels of market performance that should be measured through a holistic perspective, as in the above case of Eataly.

However, below the aggregated commercial measures, significant improvements also promise to benefit single consumers. Block et al. (2011) explore the individual returns of food to food-related wellbeing, which is a very complex construct – emotional, psychological, physical, and social – referring to the strength of the relationship between food and wellbeing at both the individual and collective levels. By adopting the more general perspective of food as a wellbeing provider, food departs from its narrow role as a source of energy to enter an expanded world of pleasurable activities. Indeed, such a destiny is shared by many kinds of consumption that have recently become vehicles to increase individual subjective wellbeing. The latter refers to individuals' evaluations of a plethora of objects related to their lives, such as events, identities, contexts, and so on (Diener, 1984). It is part of the quality of life as perceived by individuals (Keyes et al., 2002), which is comprised of three main aspects: (1) the individual evaluation of the general life or part of it; (2) the individual's affect; and (3) eudaimonia, which is a sense of purpose in life (Diener et al., 2006; Stutzer and Frey, 2010).

As clearly indicated, wellbeing is subjective in nature, being different from the objective circumstances in which the individuals actually find themselves. Such a difference lies at the basis of the widespread debate about the search for a correlation between objective conditions – e.g., income – and subjective wellbeing at both the individual and aggregate levels. Indeed, starting with the initial resolution on happiness and holistic development adopted by the Government of Bhutan, through the French commission led by the Nobel Prize winner Stiglitz, the debate about wellbeing has produced a stampede in search of what has been called the "happiness imperative" of our times (Stearns, 2012). Many political scientists, social psychologists, and economists debate the correct definitions and proper measures of national success on the aggregate level and its relations with other economic indicators (Fox, 2012). Such a topic is highly complicated, mainly because of the changing nature of the concept, the difficulties in gathering and analyzing data properly, and interferences from many uncontrollable variables (Diener, 2000; Easterlin, 1974; Kahneman et al., 1999; Stevenson and Wolfers, 2008). At the individual level, many dispute the meanings of this antique but abstract concept (Diener and Seligman, 2002; Kahneman et al., 2004), with marketing and consumer research trying to better understand the contributions of consumption activities to wellbeing and happiness (Mogilner, 2010; Mogilner et al., 2011; Shah and Alter 2014).

Though many discuss the measuring system in an effort to increase the validity and reliability of the methodological tools needed to track and control the situation of individuals as well as societies, the potential contribution of consumption experiences to the general wellbeing is something that no one questions. Positive experiences drive happiness more than rewarding purchases of material objects do (Nicolao et al., 2009; Van Boven and Gilovich, 2003). Food is no exception to this rule. Specifically, we believe that turning food services into positive food experiences generates value with regard to all dimensions constituting wellbeing. First, having a pleasurable food experience drives a better evaluation of that event – eating – in an individual's life, so that the first component of wellbeing should get a higher assessment. Second, food-related pleasure makes individuals feel better, with a stronger and wider range of positive emotional reactions. Third, it also encourages a healthier psychological functioning. In this sense, an old Chinese proverb says: "Eating is one of the four aims of life. What the other three are, no one knows."

However, those three positive returns should not be taken for granted by companies. Only through proper marketing analysis, strategies, and policies can food experiences increase food-related wellbeing and, thereby, overall individual subjective wellbeing so as to build a better aggregate level of national happiness. In the end, "one cannot think well, love well, sleep well, if one has not dined well" (Virginia Wolf).

Conclusions

Any player in the food industry must deal with the new trend toward offering not just services but rather service-based experiences. Designing and implementing gustatory experiences is generally regarded as a key requisite to success in the food-services industry. But creating a superior food experience is not an easy task. Our chapter has addressed two key challenges that still require companies to find innovative solutions. Specifically, successful food experiences should be holistic, requiring companies to create an integrated bundle of services and elements. A high level of synergy among all these components is mandatory for firms aiming at producing memorable food experiences. A well-projected theme might contribute more to a superior food experience than would excellent levels on just one or a few of these elements. Second, customers must perceive food experiences as authentic. But, unfortunately, the high level of investment usually required to gain economies of scale may threaten the achievement of perceived authenticity.

Only through successful experiences can food marketers build strong long-term relationships with their customers. Customer engagement represents a relevant aspect to be pursued by managers in order to transform potential consumers into loyal customers. As a consequence, only a well-organized program of customer-relationship management can provide companies with the competences and processes to sustain highly valued food experiences over time. Too often in the food industry, such a strong foundation has not appeared. Will food-service providers rise to these challenges? Only a deeper understanding of food-related consumption experiences will tell.

Appendix: examples of experience-related promotional communications for food, drink, and restaurants

For the past few years, the second author has collected examples of experience-related themes that appear in television commercials, radio advertisements, print ads, store signs, and other promotional messages. By now, his collection has grown to over 650 examples, many of which reflect various experience-based marketing strategies for food, drink, and restaurants. A sampling of these food-related communications would include the following items.

Food

Baileys Coffee Creams (candy) – "The taste could only be Baileys. The experience could only be yours"
Dorritos (tacos) – "A taste experience like no other"
Fish Farm (French gourmet foods) – "Food as pleasure … The Experience"
Ghiardelli (chocolate) – "All the ingredients for the most intense chocolate experience"
Hillshire Farm Deli Select (premium lunch meat) – "Made with special touches for a delectably different taste experience!"
Lindt Lindor (chocolate truffles) – "Like nothing you have ever experienced"
Matador (beef jerky) – "A Revolutionary Snacking Experience"
Oro Dioliva (olive oil) – "Experience Complimentary Tasting"
Seabear (wild salmon) – "Seafood Experiences to Share"

Drink

Braun Tassimo (hot beverage system) – "Experience all the irresistible hot drinks you could ever wish for"
Coca-Cola BlaK^{TM} – "Experience BlaK^{TM} … Every sip is an experience"
Critics' Choice (wine tastings) – "Part of the New York Wine Experience"

Frontgate Estate (wine club) – "Introducing a Rewarding New Way to Experience Wine"
Geerlings & Wade (wines) – "The Vineyard Experience"
Gevalia (coffee) – "All You Need for the Perfect Coffee Experience"
Jablum (coffee from Jamaica) – "Experience Jablum's Blue Mountain Coffee" and "The Coffee Experience Beyond Compare"
LavAzza (Italian coffee) – "Experience an Italian Classic Since 1895"
Mojito Lab (Paris) – "The Mojito Experience"
Mountain Road (Wine country, VA) – "Mountain Road Wine Experience … cooler by several degrees"
Smartwater Sparkling (bottled water) – "Elevate Your Experience"
Wine Spectator – "New York Wine Experience … Celebrate the Good Life!"
Wine Spectator wine-tasting event – "*Wine Spectator*'s New World Wine Experience"
Zagat Wine Club – "Share the Zagat Wine Club experience with friends" and "Wouldn't it be great to share your wine experiences with fellow wine lovers and be able to buy wine with greater confidence?"

Restaurants

American Girl Place – "Experience dining designed with girls in mind!"
B.R. Guest restaurants – "Tell us … about your experience today"
Barbao – "Barbao has closed. We are grateful to all who experienced the restaurant with us. Please consider visiting our other restaurant"
Ben & Jack's Steakhouse – "A true New York Experience"
Boucherie – "We would appreciate your feedback about your experience"
Caribbean Xpress – "A Tasty Island Experience"
Chazz Palminteri Ristorante Italiano – "Experience the Taste of Italy!"
Ciao by the Beach – "Our passion here at Ciao by the Beach is to help you create special memories with our intimate family dining experience"
CIBO Express (gourmet markets) – "An OTG experience™"
Coffee Bean & Tea Leaf – "We Apologize for the Inconvenience. We Are Closing at 2:00 P.M. Today in Order to Improve the Coffee & Tea Leaf Experience! The Store will Reopen Tomorrow Morning at 6:30 A.M."
Dirty Dog Jazz Cafe – "Detroit's Best Jazz Experience"
Eléa (Greek restaurant) – "Experience Eléa … True Greek"
Empire Steak House – "Experience the Taste"
Georgia's Café – "Experience a Taste of Europe"
Great Steak Houses of North America – "The Ultimate Steak Experience!"
Limani – "A dining experience like no other"
Megu – "Imperial Oyster Experience"
New Ciao Montauk – "The Ultimate Dining Experience"
Pizza Hut – "Experience the flavor of now"
Red Lobster – "Creating an Experience that's not just a meal"
Riverboat Bar & Grill (Newton, MA) – "Experience Our New Menu"

Soda Fountain (Rosie's Chicken Salad Sandwich) – "This will be a 'riveting' experience"
Spring House Restaurant, Kitchen & Bar – "The Spring House experience is gracious and authentic"
Sushi Yasaka – "Moderate Price, Extraordinary Experience"
Swallow East – "A New Kind of Dining Experience"
Ted's Montana Grill – "Experience Nacho Nirvana"
Telecharge (Broadway ticket sales) – "Book a dining experience today to enjoy before or after the show!"
Two Rivers Grille – "A New Dining Experience"

Notice a couple of salient features of these examples. First, "experience" appears as both an approbative verb ("Experience Blak™" or "Experience the Taste of Italy!") and a favorable noun ("The Vineyard Experience" or "The Mojito Experience"). Second, in either usage, an "experience" is presented – often without further qualification – as something good in itself. Nobody bothers to claim that the relevant experience is pleasant or beneficial rather than distasteful or malevolent. Apparently, many marketing managers subscribe to the gospel found in the aforementioned managerial self-help books without bothering to assert that the experiences in question are positive as opposed to negative in nature. This strikes us as a potentially dangerous symptom of the extent to which the experiential view has come to dominate our thinking without sufficient circumspection of a self-critical nature.

References

Alba, J.W., & Williams, E.F. (2013). Pleasure principles: A review of research on hedonic consumption. *Journal of Consumer Psychology*, 23(1), 2–18.

Batat, W., Peter, P. C., Moscato E. M., Castro I. A., Chan, S., Chugani, S., & Muldrow, A. (2018). The experiential pleasure of food: A savoring journey to food well-being. *Journal of Business Research)* (In press).

Bagozzi, R.P., Gopinath, M., & Nyer, P.U. (1999). The role of emotions in marketing. *Journal of the Academy of Marketing Science*, 27(2), 184–206.

Barthes, R. (2013). Toward a psychosociology of contemporary food consumption. In C. Counihan & P. Van Esterik (Eds), *Food and Culture: A Reader*. New York: Routledge, pp. 23–30.

Becker, T. (1999). "Country of origin" as a cue for quality and safety of fresh meat. In *67th Seminar, October 28–30, 1999, LeMans, France* (No. 241034). Wageningen: European Association of Agricultural Economists.

Berry, L.L., Carbone, L.P., & Haeckel, S.H. (2002). Managing the total customer experience. *MIT Sloan Management Review*, 43(3), 85–89.

Beverland, M. (2006). The "real thing": Branding authenticity in the luxury wine trade. *Journal of Business Research*, 59(2), 251–258.

Beverland, M., & Farrelly, F.J. (2010). The quest for authenticity in consumption: Consumers' purposive choice of authentic cues to shape experienced outcomes. *Journal of Consumer Research*, 36, 838–856.

Bitner, M.J. (1992). Servicescapes: The impact of physical surroundings on customers and employees. *Journal of Marketing*, 57–71.

Block, L.G., Grier, S.A., Childers, T.L., Davis, B., Ebert, J.E., Kumanyika, S., … Pettigrew, S. (2011). From nutrients to nurturance: A conceptual introduction to food wellbeing. *Journal of Public Policy and Marketing*, 30(1), 5–13.

Booms, B.H., & Bitner, M.J. (1981). Marketing strategies and organisation structures for service firms. In J. Donnelly & W.R. George (Eds), *Marketing of Services*. Chicago, IL: American Marketing Association.

Brown, S. (1995). *Postmodern Marketing*. London: Routledge.

Brown, S., & Patterson, A. (2000). Knick-knack paddy-whack, give a pub a theme. *Journal of Marketing Management*, 16(6), 647–662.

Brown, S., Kozinets, R.V., & Sherry, J.F. (2003). Teaching old brands new tricks: Retro branding and the revival of brand meaning. *Journal of Marketing*, 67(3), 19–33.

Bruhn, M., Schoenmüller, V., Schäfer, D., & Heinrich, D. (2012). Brand authenticity: Towards a deeper understanding of its conceptualization and measurement. In Z. Gürhan-Canli, C. Otnes, & R.J. Zhu (Eds), *Advances in Consumer Research*. Duluth, MN: Association for Consumer Research, pp. 567–576.

Carbone, L.P., & Haeckel, S.H. (1994). Engineering customer experience. *Marketing Management*, 3(3), 9–19.

Carù, A., & Cova, B. (2007). Consumer immersion in an experiential context. In A. Carù & B. Cova (Eds), *Consuming Experience*. London: Routledge, pp. 34–47.

Caves, R.E. (2000). *Creative Industries: Contrasts between Art and Commerce*. Cambridge, MA: Harvard University Press.

Chebat, J.C., & Dubé, L. (2000). Evolution and challenges facing retail atmospherics: The apprentice sorcerer is dying. *Journal of Business Research*, 49(2), 89–90.

Chronis, A. (2005). Coconstructing heritage at the Gettysburg storyscape. *Annals of Tourism Research*, 32(2), 386–406.

Chronis, A., & Hampton, R.D. (2008). Consuming the authentic Gettysburg: How a tourist landscape becomes an authentic experience. *Journal of Consumer Behaviour*, 7(2), 111–126.

Counihan, C., & Van Esterik, P. (2013). Why food? Why culture? Why now? Introduction to the third edition. In C. Counihan & P. Van Esterik (Eds), *Food and Culture: A Reader*. New York: Routledge, pp. 1–15.

Diener, E. (1984). Subjective wellbeing. *Psychological Bulletin*, 95(3), 542–575.

Diener, E. (2000). Subjective wellbeing: The science of happiness and a proposal for a national index. *American Psychologist*, 55(1), 34–43.

Diener, E., & Seligman, M.E. (2002). Very happy people. *Psychological Science*, 13(1), 81–84.

Diener, E., Tamir, M., & Scollon, C.N. (2006). Happiness, life satisfaction, and fulfillment: The social psychology of subjective wellbeing. In P.A.M. van Lange (Ed.), *Bridging Social Psychology: The Benefits of Transdisciplinary Approaches*. Hillsdale, NH: Erlbaum.

Easterlin, R.A. (1974). Does economic growth improve the human lot? Some empirical evidence. In P.A. David & M.W. Reder (Eds), *Nations and Households in Economic Growth*. Cambridge, MA: Academic Press, pp. 89–125.

Euromonitor International. (2018). *Passport: Consumer Foodservice Global Industry Overview*.

Federalimentare. (2015). Atlante Geografico del food Made in Italy. Retrieved from: www.federalimentare.it

Firat, A.F., & Venkatesh, A. (1993). Postmodernity: The age of marketing. *International Journal of Research in Marketing*, 10(3), 227–249.

Firat, A.F., & Venkatesh, A. (1995). Liberatory postmodernism and the reenchantment of consumption. *Journal of Consumer Research*, 22, 239–267.

Fleming, C.A., Miller, R.K., Washington, K.D., & Miller, R.K. (2007). *The 2007 Restaurant and Foodservice Market Research Handbook*. Loganville, GA: Richard K. Miller & Associates.

Fox, J. (2012). The economics of wellbeing. *Harvard Business Review*, 90(1–2), 78–83.

Freeman. (2017). *Freeman Global Brand Experience Study*. Retrieved from: www.freeman.com/resources/brand-experience-a-new-era-in-marketing

Fritz, K., Schoenmueller, V., & Bruhn, M. (2017). Authenticity in branding: Exploring antecedents and consequences of brand authenticity. *European Journal of Marketing*, 51(2), 324–348.

Gottdiener, M. (1998). The semiotics of consumer spaces: The growing importance of themed environments. In J.F. Sherry (Ed.), *Servicescapes*. Chicago, IL: NTC Business Books, pp. 29–54.

Gottdiener, M. (2001). *The Theming of America: American Dreams, Media Fantasies, and Themed Environments* (2nd ed.). Boulder, CO: Westview Press.

Grayson, K., & Martinec, R. (2004). Consumer perceptions of iconicity and indexicality and their influence on assessments of authentic market offerings. *Journal of Consumer Research*, 31, 296–312.

Green, M.C., & Brock, T.C. (2000). The role of transportation in the persuasiveness of public narratives. *Journal of Personality and Social Psychology*, 79, 701–721.

Hirschman, E.C., & Holbrook, M.B. (1982). Hedonic consumption: Emerging concept, methods and propositions. *Journal of Marketing*, 46, 92–101.

Holbrook, M.B. (1991). Romanticism and sentimentality in consumer behavior: A literary approach to the joys and sorrows of consumption. *Research in Consumer Behavior*, 5, 105–180.

Holbrook, M.B. (1999). Introduction to consumer value. In M.B. Holbrook (Ed.), *Consumer Value: A Framework for Analysis and Research*. London: Routledge, pp. 1–28.

Holbrook, M.B., & Hirschman, E.C. (1982). The experiential aspects of consumption: Consumer fantasies, feelings, and fun. *Journal of Consumer Research*, 9, 132–140.

Holbrook, M.B., & O'Shaughnessy, J. (1984). The role of emotion in advertising. *Psychology and Marketing*, 1(2), 45–64.

Hollenbeck, C., Peters, C., & Zinkhan, G. (2008). Retail spectacles and brand meaning: Insights from a brand museum case study. *Journal of Retailing*, 84(3), 334–353.

Holt, D.B. (1995). How consumers consume: A typology of consumption practices. *Journal of Consumer Research*, 22, 1–15.

Huffman, C., Ratneshwar, S., & Mick, D.G. (2000). Consumer goal structures and goal-determination processes: An integrative framework. In S. Ratneshwar, D.G. Mick, & C. Huffman (Eds), *The Why of Consumption: Contemporary Perspectives on Consumer Motives, Goals, and Desires*. London: Routledge, pp. 9–35.

Kahneman, D., Diener, E., & Schwarz, N. (Eds). (1999). *Wellbeing: Foundations of Hedonic Psychology*. New York: Russell Sage Foundation.

Kahneman, D., Krueger, A.B., Schkade, D.A., Schwarz, N., & Stone, A.A. (2004). A survey method for characterizing daily life experience: The day reconstruction method. *Science*, 306(5702), 1776–1780.

Keyes, C.L., Shmotkin, D., & Ryff, C.D. (2002). Optimizing wellbeing: The empirical encounter of two traditions. *Journal of Personality and Social Psychology*, 82(6), 1007–1022.

Kniazeva, M., & Venkatesh, A. (2007). Food for thought: A study of food consumption in postmodern US culture. *Journal of Consumer Behaviour*, 6(6), 419–435.

Kozinets, R., Sherry, J., DeBerry-Spence, B., Duhachek, A., Nuttavuthisit, K., & Storm, D. (2002). Themed flagship brand stores in the new millennium: Theory, practice, prospects. *Journal of Retailing*, 78(1), 17–29.

Kumar, V., & Karande, K. (2000). The effect of retail store environment on retailer performance. *Journal of Business Research*, 49(2), 167–181.

Lempert, P. (2017). 10 food trends that will shape 2018. *Forbes*, December 13. Retrieved from: www.forbes.com/sites/phillempert/2017/12/13/10-food-trends-that-will-shape-2018/#7455cfc04104

Lu, S., & Fine, G. (1995). The presentation of ethnic authenticity: Chinese food as a social accomplishment. *Sociological Quarterly*, 36(3), 535–553.

Mak, A.H., Lumbers, M., Eves, A., & Chang, R.C. (2013). An application of the repertory grid method and generalised Procrustes analysis to investigate the motivational factors of tourist food consumption. *International Journal of Hospitality Management*, 35, 327–338.

Mayr, W. (2018). Der unheimliche erfolg einer feinkostkette. *Der Spiegel*, January 11. Retrieved from: www.spiegel.de/spiegel/eataly-das-erfolgsgeheimnis-einer-feinkostkette-a-1186754.html

McCarthy, E.D. (2009). Emotional performances as dramas of authenticity. In P. Vannini & J.P. Williams (Eds), *Authenticity in Culture, Self, and Society*. Ashgate Publishing: Farnham.

Mehrabian, A., & Russell, J.A. (1974). *An Approach to Environmental Psychology*. Boston, MA: MIT Press.

Mogilner, C. (2010). The pursuit of happiness: Time, money, and social connection. *Psychological Science*, 21(9), 1348–1354.

Mogilner, C., Aaker, J., & Kamvar, S.D. (2011). How happiness affects choice. *Journal of Consumer Research*, 39(2), 429–443.

Mossberg, L. (2008). Extraordinary experiences through storytelling. *Scandinavian Journal of Hospitality and Tourism*, 8(3), 195–210.

Mossberg, L., & Eide, D. (2017). Storytelling and meal experience concepts. *European Planning Studies*, 25(7), 1184–1199.

Munoz, C.L., Wood, N.T., & Solomon, M.R. (2006). Real or blarney? A cross-cultural investigation of the perceived authenticity of Irish pubs. *Journal of Consumer Behaviour*, 5(3), 222–234.

Newman, G.E., & Dhar, R. (2014). Authenticity is contagious: Brand essence and the original source of production. *Journal of Marketing Research*, 51(3), 371–386.

Nicolao, L., Irwin, J.R., & Goodman, J.K. (2009). Happiness for sale: Do experiential purchases make consumers happier than material purchases? *Journal of Consumer Research*, 36(2), 188–198.

O'Dell, T., & Billing, P. (2005). *Experiencescapes: Tourism, Culture, and Economy*. Copenhagen: Copenhagen Business School Press.

Peñaloza, L. (2000). The commodification of the American West: Marketers' production of cultural meanings at the trade show. *Journal of Marketing*, 64: 82–109.

Phillips, D. (1997). *Exhibiting Authenticity*. New York: Manchester University Press.

Pine, J.B.II, & Gilmore, J.H. (1999). *The Experience Economy*. Boston, MA: Harvard Business School Press.

Promos. (2017). Export agroalimentare nel mondo. Retrieved from: www.promos-milano.it

Rail, E. (2017). In Eataly, an Italian amusement park for foodies. *New York Times*, December 5. Retrieved from: www.nytimes.com/2017/12/05/travel/eataly-world-fico-bologna-italy.html

Reimer, A., & Kuehn, R. (2005). The impact of servicescape on quality perception. *European Journal of Marketing, 39*(7/8), 785–808.

Richins, M.L. (1997). Measuring emotions in the consumption experience. *Journal of Consumer Research*, 24(2), 127–146.

Rook, D.W. (1987). The buying impulse. *Journal of Consumer Research*, 14(September), 189–199.

Rose, R., & Wood, S. (2005). Paradox and the consumption of authenticity through reality television. *Journal of Consumer Research*, 32, 284–296.

Schmitt, B. (1999). *Experiential Marketing: How to Get Customers to SENSE, FEEL, THINK, ACT and RELATE to Your Company and Brands*. New York: Free Press.

Scott, M. L. & Vallen, B. (2019). Expanding the Lens of Food Well-Being: An Examination of Contemporary Marketing, Policy, and Practice with an Eye on the Future. *Journal of Public Policy & Marketing*, 38(2), 127–135.

Seymour, S. (2017). Eataly World opens but leaves a bad taste in Bologna. *Guardian*, November 17. Retrieved from: www.theguardian.com/travel/2017/nov/17/eataly-world-bologna-megamarket-betrayal-italian-gastronomy

Shah, A.K., & Alter, A.L. (2014). Consuming experiential categories. *Journal of Consumer Research*, 41(4), 965–977.

Spangenberg, E.R., Voss, K.E., & Crowley, A.E. (1997). Measuring the hedonic and utilitarian dimensions of attitude: A generally applicable scale. *ACR North American Advances*.

Stearns, P.N. (2012). The history of happiness. *Harvard Business Review, 90*(1/2), 104–108.

Stevenson, B., & Wolfers, J. (2008). *Economic Growth and Subjective wellbeing: Reassessing the Easterlin Paradox* (No. w14282). Cambridge, MA: National Bureau of Economic Research.

Stutzer, A., & Frey, B.S. (2010). Recent advances in the economics of individual subjective wellbeing. *Social Research: An International Quarterly*, 77(2), 679–714.

Technopak Advisors. (2017). *Indian Food Services Industry: Engine for Economic Growth and Employment*. Report. Retrieved from: www.ficci.in

Thomson, K. (2001). *Emotional Capital: Maximising the Intangible Assets at the Heart of Brand and Business Success*. Mankato, MN: Capstone.

Turley, L.W., & Milliman, R.E. (2000). Atmospheric effects on shopping behavior: A review of the experimental evidence. *Journal of Business Research*, 49(2), 193–211.

Van Boven, L., & Gilovich, T. (2003). To do or to have? That is the question. *Journal of Personality and Social Psychology, 85*(6), 1193–1202.

Van Laer, T., de Ruyter, K., Visconti, L., & Wetzels, M. (2014). The extended transportation imagery model: A meta-analysis of the antecedents and consequences of consumers' narrative transportation. *Journal of Consumer Research*, 40, 797–815.

Wolf, M.J. (1999) *The Entertainment Economy. How Mega-Media Forces Are Transforming Our Lives*. New York: Times Books.

3 Food consumer trends: food experience, pleasure, and policy in the United States

Emerging trends to watch for in American food consumption for researchers, policymakers, and consumers

Anne T. Byrne and David R. Just

People make decisions about food frequently throughout the day, often from the moment they wake up. This includes decisions made for their own consumption and in many cases decisions about what or when their family members will eat. These decisions take place in a wide variety of settings, at work, home, in a store, or other venues. Decisions about whether to eat and what to eat are driven by a multitude of factors. Some meals may be carefully planned to emphasize nutrition, while others are the result of an impulse to eat something that looked too delicious to pass up. This chapter uses seven current trends to explore how Americans eat for pleasure and wellbeing. Given the vast nature of the topic (even when restricting ourselves to the United States (US)), we do not claim our treatment to be comprehensive. In considering US food culture, it's important to remind ourselves of the vast variation in subcultures around the US. The US is a geographically large country that is ethnically, racially, and economically diverse; the experience of one American can look quite different from the experience of another. Rather, we have focused on phenomena and behavior that are of particular interest given the current policy climate and challenges. We begin with an overview of food consumption in the US and then discuss several trends in US food culture.

An overview of food consumption in the United States

The United States Department of Agriculture (USDA) gathers comprehensive data on American food production and consumption which are widely used to document Americans' eating habits. The USDA reports several major facts or trends in the US that provide a necessary backdrop for any discussion of food pleasure and wellbeing in the US. First, Americans are not eating diets that align with federal nutritional recommendations. They fall short in their consumption of fruits, vegetables, and dairy (USDA Economic Research Service, 2017). Indeed, only about 40 percent of Americans consume the recommended servings of fruit and vegetables on any given day (Guenther et al., 2006). The most commonly consumed vegetables are potatoes and tomatoes, which are often consumed in the form of French fries and pizza, respectively (USDA Economic Research Service, 2017). Among fruit, Americans prefer apples and oranges which are most frequently consumed in juice form. Americans have changed the way they consume dairy; in 1975 the most common source of dairy was fluid milk, but cheese consumption doubled between 1975 and 2015 and is now the most common source of dairy in the American diet. While Americans used to fall short in their consumption of grains, they now eat slightly more than recommended (~110 percent of recommended consumption), which has largely been driven by an increase in the consumption of corn products. Americans have consumed more than the recommended amounts of meat, eggs, and nuts for decades and 2015 data show they are consuming almost 140 percent of the recommended amounts of these items. However, the types of meat Americans consume has changed over the last several decades; beef consumption has declined since the 1970s while chicken consumption has increased tremendously (over 300 percent increase since 1970) and is now the most common meat in the American diet, comprising 40 percent of all meat consumed (USDA Economic Research Service, 2017).

The US diet has been widely associated with the relatively high prevalence of obesity in the US relative to other countries. Almost two thirds of US adults are overweight, and roughly one third are obese (OECD, 2017). This high rate of obesity results from a dramatic rise from the 1970s through the early 2000s. Attempts to address this high prevalence of obesity using food policy have been hotly debated. Implemented policies include required posting of nutrition information or calorie counts, dramatic changes to the school lunch program meal requirements, and a handful of cities in the US implementing a tax on added sugar in beverages. Other policies that have been debated include general taxes on fat or sugar, restrictions on locations of fast-food restaurants, restrictions on advertising of various unhealthy foods, or restrictions on the size of foods or beverages that can be served.

The USDA also reports on where Americans are spending money on food. They note that the share of American household budgets devoted to food has gone down from 17.5 percent in 1960 to 9.8 percent in 2014 (USDA Economic Research Service, 2018a). However, Americans are eating out more than ever before; in 2014 food away from home was a greater share of total food expenditure than food at home, marking the first year Americans spent more on food out than at home. As Americans spend more money on food out, more of the "food dollar" is spent on services. In 2016, for every dollar spent on food, 36.3 cents were spent on services at food-service establishments (USDA Economic Research Service, 2018a). While there are a wide variety of restaurant and fast-food options in the US, it can be helpful to consider which chains dominate the market. Subway has the most stand-alone locations (26,887 stores) and is distributed widely across the country (Nations's Restaurant News, 2017). It should be noted, however, that this number does not include the many Subway locations in gas stations.

McDonald's has slightly more than half as many locations (13,813), followed by Starbucks (10,138), which are typically only located in urban areas, and Pizza Hut (7,581). By sales, McDonald's is the largest restaurant chain with $36.4 billion in annual US sales, followed by Starbucks ($17.9 billion), Subway ($11.3 billion), Taco Bell ($9.4 billion), and Burger King ($9.3 billion) (Nations's Restaurant News, 2017). The fastest-growing chain is Raising Cane's Chicken Fingers, a Texas-based fast-food chicken restaurant, followed by Jersey Mike's Subs, Marco's Pizza, and Wingstop Chicken (Ruggless, 2017). Two of the top four fastest-growing chains in the US specialize in chicken, reflecting the growing demand for chicken reported by the USDA. In addition, chicken has taken a much more prominent role in the menus of the more established fast-food restaurants in the past two decades. Food away from home is generally understood to be more calorie-dense (USDA Economic Research Service, 2010), and thus a contributor to obesity. While there are many studies that demonstrate that higher intakes of food away from home contribute to increased weight at an individual level, the overall impact on the distribution of overweight status in the US is not well understood.

Finally, although the US has the highest gross domestic product in the world and has the third largest food production of any country in the world, there are still many Americans who struggle with food insecurity. Most American households are food secure, meaning they do not miss meals for lack of food. Yet, 12.3 percent were food insecure at some point in 2016 (USDA Food and Nutrition Service, 2018b). There is some evidence this percentage has declined mildly over the last year, though no official numbers are available. These rates are highest among households with single mothers as well as Black and Hispanic households. Households with children have higher rates of food insecurity in general, with 16.5 percent reporting food insecurity during some time in 2016. Food insecurity affects Americans in every state but rates are highest in the southern states, with Mississippi reporting the highest rate of any state at 18.7 percent. The USDA has several programs to address food insecurity; the largest program is the Supplemental Nutrition Assistance Program (SNAP, formerly referred to as food stamps) in which the USDA spends over $65 billion each year. This program provides participants a transfer of money to an electronic benefits card that functions something like a debit card. Participants can use this money at participating stores to purchase most food items.

Federal food assistance expenditures have increased dramatically in the past 20 years; they totaled less than $35 billion in 2000 and totaled close to $98.6 billion in 2017 (USDA Food Security and Nutrition Service, 2018b). Notably, food insecurity increased over this period. Food assistance programs have also been suggested as a policy tool to address obesity. For example, reforms in the school lunch program were designed specifically to reduce calorie counts and increase fruit and vegetable consumption. Efforts to restrict access to calorie-dense foods on SNAP have also been debated, often facing significant pushback from food security advocates.

Approaches and assumptions in understanding food pleasure and wellbeing

In this section, we explore the key considerations in understanding food pleasure and wellbeing, paying careful attention to food and eating in the US. We first discuss modeling approaches and how obesity and overeating can be integrated into a behavioral model. We then describe the special considerations necessary to understanding childhood food behavior, including reasons for targeting policies at childhood food consumption and common pitfalls. Finally, we describe important considerations in understanding American food pleasure and wellbeing that change with income and how low-income Americans may experience food consumption differently than those with higher incomes and more wealth.

Pleasure, overeating, and obesity

While there are several studies that argue the prevalence of obesity is the direct result of Americans' habit of overeating (e.g., Ruhm, 2012), it is difficult to find a clear definition of "overeating." The ambiguity in the meaning of overeating has long been a source of contention, with the definition having important implications for how the concept can be used. For example, some have defined overeating as when one consumes a greater mass than is excreted by the body (Dole, 1959). However, defining the word this way means that associations between overeating and weight gain are an identity and not the subject of study. An alternative definition would classify eating more than the average amount for an individual of a similar demographic as overeating (Dole, 1959). This is, perhaps in practice, a more useful definition for the study of eating behavior and its relationship with overweight and obesity, as this then allows us to use observables to determine status both with regard to weight and with regard to overeating. A third definition, and perhaps that which has become most important in both the medical and behavioral literatures, defines overeating as eating more than one wishes they had (Piccinni et al., 2015). This latter definition has been championed by those who classify food as potentially addictive, and also lands food-consumption decisions squarely outside of the purview of neoclassical economic models.

A neoclassical model of overeating relies upon the relative definition of the word. If we consider an individual who is making food-consumption decisions, we might model them as solving $\max_x U(x)$ subject to $p \cdot x \leq w$, where $p, x \in R^n_+$ represent the vector of prices and consumption for goods, some of which may be food, $w \in R$ represents wealth, and $U : R^n_+ \to R$ represents utility of consumption. This model is trivially solved (presuming no corner solutions) where where $U^i(x) = p_i$, $i = 1 \ldots n$, where the superscript i represents partial differentiation with respect to the ith good. Let $\bar{x}$ be a vector of the average consumption level for all goods. In this case, one who eats more than the average amount of food would be one for whom $U^i(\bar{x})$ is large with respect to food dimensions relative to the average. In other words, their marginal utility of food is higher than others on average. This model supposes that those who overeat simply like food more than others, and thus are willing to face the consequences of eating more than other individuals in order to have this greater joy from consuming. More generally, this model would suggest that individuals overeat foods that they enjoy more than the general population and undereat foods that they like less than the general population. This model could not say anything about regret from consuming more than one wishes, as this model supposes one has the power to execute exactly their optimal decision. Thus, this presumes that all overeating is intentional.

Behavioral models can address the notion of overeating as failing to execute one's desired consumption. For example, Ruhm (2012) models overeating as a result of a dual-process decision mechanism: one process that represents long-term cognitive objectives which wishes to eat in moderation and reap the health benefits, and one that seeks immediate pleasure from consumption. In this case, overeating is measured with respect to how much the first process desires. Similar theories have been used by psychologists to model food consumption behavior. This mirrors recent work from medical fields that examines overeating as a form of addiction (e.g., Davis and Carter, 2009; Piccinni et al., 2015). By these models, individuals will overeat foods that provide a higher utility or liking when evaluated by immediate pleasure than when evaluated by cognitive objectives.

Interestingly, the physiology and medical literatures reveal a somewhat more complicated relationship between food preferences and overeating. In experimental and survey work, obese individuals tend not to demonstrate any greater liking of foods, even when evaluating foods that are particularly calorie dense (Mela, 2001, 2006). Rather, it appears that the difference in proclivity to overeat may be due to a greater wanting to eat overall. Thus, those who are willing to put in greater effort to eat more often are more likely to be obese, rather than those who derive more pleasure from the act of eating itself. There is evidence that diminishing marginal utility from consumption is good-specific (Havermans et al., 2009). This differentiation between utility of consumption versus utility from consumption incidence is already a severe departure from even the behavioral economic models of food decision making.

But recent evidence suggests a more severe departure. Some evidence appears to suggest that preference for eating is endogenous to obesity status and may be switched on or off by status (Shin et al., 2011). Some refer to this as a restructuring or "rewiring" of the pleasure center of the brain. Such endogenous preference suggests a model something like that proposed by Becker and Murphy (1988), in which an individual's consumption alters future preferences. However, all evidence suggests that this process is not anticipated by the consumer.

Childhood food behavior

It is often argued that children should be the primary object of any obesity-related policy. This argument is generally based upon relatively agreed-upon axioms:

- Children are still in the process of forming their eating habits and thus may be more malleable in their behavior (Ventura and Worobey, 2013);
- Obesity is difficult to reverse, and somewhat easier to prevent (Summerbell et al., 2005);
- The future costs of obesity in children (due to diet-related health issues) is much larger than that of older individuals as they will live with the consequences much longer (Daniels, 2006).

When you add to this the relative convenience of addressing children as a group due to widespread school attendance, the case seems to be somewhat clear.

However, children interact with food in a much different way than their adult counterparts, which makes interventions somewhat difficult. While adults often feel a pressing need to improve their health, consequences of a poor diet are not readily apparent or salient to children. This means that convincing children to eat foods that are less appealing in the moment is relatively difficult. Indeed, consumption of fruit and vegetables among children is relatively low, with age being one of the chief determinants of accepting these foods in their diet (Rasmussen, 2006).

Between the ages of 3 and 5, children become averse to new foods and even averse to some foods they may already be familiar with (Dovey et al., 2008). This phenomenon, referred to as neophobia, is very widespread, and abates naturally as children age. There has been a significant amount of research on how to mitigate neophobia, or encourage children to try specifically fruit and vegetables. Some of this research suggests that children become more open to trying foods when they have been exposed repeatedly to the same food (Birch and Marlin, 1982), though not all types of exposure are equal in this quest (Birch et al., 1987).

Neophobia is exacerbated by a strong tendency towards reactance (Jansen et al., 2007). Reactance is defined as a behavioral rebellion or resistance to any perceived threat to one's freedom. In this case, children who are told to avoid certain foods may push back by eating more of these foods when left unchecked. In addition, children who are told they should eat certain foods may display stronger resistance to them. A long literature has found that the tone of the message (threatening versus persuasive) has an impact on the strength of reactance (Pennebaker and Sanders, 1976). Persuasive text appears to be much more effective than text that is seen as threatening or authoritarian. The same can be said of efforts to encourage children to eat healthier diets, though in this case, the literature divides such attempts by parents into three categories: authoritarian, authoritative, and permissive (Hughes et al., 2005). While authoritarian parenting is typified by strictly enforced obedience, authoritative is associated more with teaching consequences of behaviors, encouraging good behaviors while not enforcing any specific rule. Several studies find that authoritarian parenting tends towards the worst health outcomes, while authoritative parenting tends towards the best (e.g., Rhee et al., 2006).

Children are heavily influenced by social peers in food consumption. While this influence of peers is similar to adults, the way in which this influence works can be quite different. Children will often avoid foods they perceive to be socially unacceptable, and thus peer influence can be a very important motivator in trying new foods (Addessi et al., 2005). These social pressures can lead to wide changes in selection. For example, Angelucci et al. (2015) find that incentivizing kids to eat healthy snacks becomes less effective when children are able to observe who has been incentivized.

In this case, the incentive is seen as a signal that their peer would not have eaten the food in question were it not for the incentive – signaling inferiority of the good. This sensitivity to peer perceptions can also be leveraged by food marketers. Rather than engaging children by describing the sensory attributes of foods, much of food advertising to children is directed toward convincing the child of social desirability (e.g., the food is associated with excitement, fun, or freedom). While there is a tremendous amount of evidence that such tools are effective in encouraging young children to eat calorie-dense foods (Story and French, 2004), there is now only emerging evidence that such tools can be used to encourage consumption of more nutritious fare (e.g., Hanks et al., 2016).

Food preferences among low-income Americans

Food preferences and wellbeing often look different in low-income American households than among those with higher incomes and greater wealth. Low-income Americans interact with the food market in different ways, often turning to food-assistance programs to meet their needs. Approximately 47 million Americans rely on food-bank services and 42 million rely on SNAP to meet their food needs (Hunger in America, 2014; USDA Economic Research Service, 2018b). This accounts for more than one in six Americans, so when thinking about eating for pleasure it's important to consider what that looks like for this subset of the population.

This population is often the target of policy debates addressing obesity and overweight. At the onset of the secular rise in obesity in the US, rates rose primarily among lower-income individuals (Levine, 2011), with obesity rates among the lowest quintile of income rising substantially above that of other quintiles. More recently, high obesity rates are not unique to lower incomes (Ogden et al., 2006), though popular culture and even policymakers still consider this to be the case. Policymakers, public health advocates, and economists generally rely on the externality created by publicly funded medical treatment to justify interventions in the food markets to address obesity. Within the US system, only the poor, the elderly, and government employees have their medical expenses covered by public dollars. Thus, poorer populations are likely to present a larger externality from obesity than other populations. For this reason, a specific focus on the diets of poorer individuals may be of special interest.

Food prices are important to everyone, but they play a particularly important role in the food choices made by those living in poverty. There is an inverse relationship between energy density and energy cost while diets with higher nutritional value tend to have higher energy costs; simply put, nutrients are expensive and calories are cheap (Drewnowski, 2004; Lipsky et al., 2011). While there are some who attribute this to market failures or unfettered profit interests, Lipsky et al. (2011) demonstrate that this relationship is an identity and would prevail in almost any marketplace.

Many Americans living in poverty have experienced some form of poverty-associated food deprivation. Olson, Bove, and Miller (2007) found that for many of these individuals, there is a burst of excitement when food becomes available after periods of deprivation. This burst of excitement is sometimes associated with binging and hoarding. Parker and Keim (2004) interviewed low-income overweight and obese white women who reported that eating was often used for coping with stress. In terms of tastes, those in poverty show a preference for sweets and fats. As we discuss trends in American food pleasure and wellbeing, it is important to consider how income plays a role and how these trends may play out differently among low-income Americans.

Trends in American food pleasure and wellbeing

In the following section, we discuss several trends in American food behavior (Figure 3.1). This is not an exhaustive list, but rather a collection of topics that are receiving (or that we predict will receive) an increasing amount of attention in the literature. They are presented to give a variety of snapshots of how Americans are interacting with their food and how that is affecting their food pleasure and wellbeing.

Trend 1: sugar in the American diet

Americans are eating more sugar than ever before, with the average person consuming nearly 66 pounds of added sugar every year. This is over three times the maximum sugar intake recommended by the World Health Organization (WHO, 2015). While sugar consumption has grown worldwide, the US differs from other developed countries in its particular fondness for manufactured high fructose corn syrup as opposed to naturally occurring sucrose.

Sugar is undeniably a source of pleasure in many Americans' diets and has been noted by experts as being highly palatable for humans in general (Erlanson-Albertsson, 2005). While this may contribute to increased pleasure during a meal, the high palatability of sugar may be habit forming and dangerous if consumed to excess. It has been demonstrated that sugar is addictive with humans and animals exhibiting classic signs of dependence when eating sugar, including bingeing, withdrawal symptoms, and craving (Avena et al., 2008).

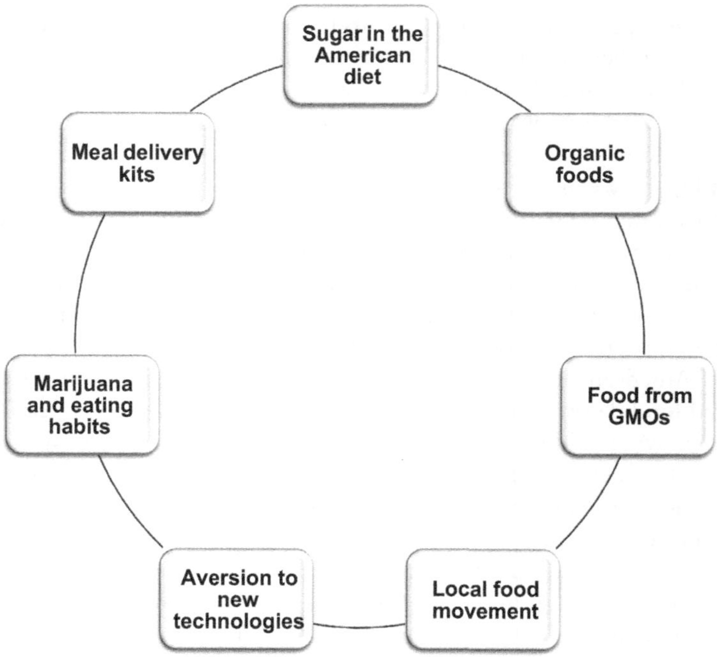

Figure 3.1 Current trends in American food pleasure and wellbeing

Some have gone as far as to compare Americans' sugar consumption habits to that of alcohol and tobacco (Lustig et al., 2012). Levine, Kotz, and Gosnell (2003) examined the neurobiology of sugar and fat preferences, finding that eating sugars and fats may alter the brain's reward systems in many of the same ways as drugs like alcohol.

Diets high in sugar are linked to many health issues including heart disease and diabetes. This has led researchers and public health officials to urge public action (Welsh et al., 2013; Lustig et al., 2012). Some have looked to policies that have successfully curbed alcohol and tobacco used as models for curbing sugar consumption (e.g., Gearhardt, et al., 2011). These include education in schools about the dangers of sugar as well as taxes on sugary items like soda. Soda taxes have been implemented in some cities, but their efficacy is still up for debate. For example, Debnam (2017) examined the Berkeley soda tax and found that while it had curbed consumption of sugar-sweetened beverages in the community, the effect was concentrated in households that already consumed very little soda; households that consumed large amounts of soda prior to implementation of the tax actually increased their consumption immediately following the policy change.

There are several striking differences between food consumption and tobacco use that may make tobacco policy a poor fit for obesity, specifically the fact that food is necessary to live and tobacco is not (Lustig et al., 2012). This includes the absolute need to consume food at all ages, as opposed to tobacco which can be entirely avoided at any age. Nonetheless, long-term evidence on individual attempts at dieting demonstrates a strikingly poor rate of long-term success (e.g., Wadden, 1993). For this reason, many have advocated for environmental interventions that make it more difficult to consume calorie-dense foods in general.

Trend 2: organic foods

Some consumers report that their pleasure in eating is tied to their relationship with the environment and their values about human interaction with nature. This has spurred several movements that seek credence foods (Wirth et al., 2011) that meet some non-verifiable objectives. The most prominent of these movements seeks products from local sources, products that are non-genetically modified (GMO), or products that are organic (in this case, organic meaning produced according to the USDA's standards for organic farming, which restricts the use of many pesticides and fertilizers).

In the US, organic food sales climbed from $28.4 billion in 2012 to $43 billion in 2016, accounting for 5.3 percent of total food sales in the US (Gelski, 2017). As this market grows, more research has been dedicated to understand why consumers want organic food and how it contributes to their overall pleasure and wellbeing. Comprehensive reviews of the literature on organic food consumption reveal a great degree of heterogeneity across what consumers think "organic" means, perceived benefits of eating organic, and motivations for choosing organic among those who regularly do so (Hughner et al., 2007). In the US, the USDA certifies organic products which then bear the USDA Organic logo, indicating to consumers that the product has met the USDA's criteria for organic. Hughner et al. (2007) summarized the literature on consumers of organic food finding that their top motivations for purchasing organic were a perception that it is healthier and it tastes better.

Fillion and Arazi (2002) conducted an experiment to test whether consumers actually prefer the taste of organic products by using blind taste tests of orange juice and milk. Using a comprehensive scoring mechanism, they had participants evaluate their beverage without being told if it was organic or conventional. Participants' evaluations of organic orange juice were significantly higher than their evaluations of conventional orange juice; however, there was no significant difference in participants' evaluations of organic and conventional milk. Health benefits of organic foods are also not uniform across products, and are difficult to document and may not exist for some goods (Smith-Spangler et al., 2012). The fact that consumers perceive these benefits even when they may not be there suggests the existence of a health halo (Peloza et al., 2015). That is, the perception of being healthy is perhaps due to consumers relying almost solely on the gist of the term organic rather than the specifics of the particular foods they may consider purchasing.

Trend 3: food from genetically modified organisms

Another trend that represents consumers' growing concern for food production and the relationship between food and the environment is the debate of GMOs, which has emerged in the past decade. While European Union consumers were relatively wary of GMOs from their first introduction on the market in the 1990s (Chern and Rickertsen, 2001), US consumers were relatively accepting of GMOs at that time. More recently, we have seen large movements to require the labeling of GMOs (Pifer, 2013) and many that associate GMOs with Mansanto – a corporation that is perceived by a growing number to have violated the public trust (e.g., Anderson, 2014). Part of the debate concerns information: Many consumers believe they have a right to know whether their food was produced using GMOs and, thus, GMO labels should be mandatory (Hu et al., 2005).

In 2016, President Obama signed into law a requirement that mass-produced food products make this information accessible, though producers do not need to provide the information on the package itself. Attitudes towards GMOs in the US remain generally more positive than in Europe and it appears that food production using this technology may be less important to Americans in their eating pleasure than it is to Europeans (Wilcock et al., 2004). An experiment with Americans found them willing to pay approximately 14 percent less for food labeled as GMO than for food with standard labels, while a similar study in the United Kingdom found consumers willing to pay anywhere between 26 and 47 percent for non-GMO food products (Burton et al., 2001; Huffman et al., 2003). Interestingly, American consumers' acceptance of GMOs is somewhat connected to their perceptions regarding their functionality. Thus, if they believe a GMO allows producers to reduce pesticide exposure, they are more willing to accept the technology (McFadden and Lusk, 2017). Such debates over food technology are likely to remain important for the foreseeable future, with new technologies such as CRSPR unlocking important possibilities for increasing productivity and addressing consumer needs.

Trend 4: the local food movement

The local food movement has also grown dramatically in America, as many consumers have developed strong preferences regarding the supply chain from farm to table. A desire to eat local, coupled with targeted rural development programs through the USDA, led to a 76 percent increase in the number of farmers' markets between 2008 and 2014 (USDA, 2014). Furthermore, demand for local food has driven agritourism and other avenues where Americans go out of their way for local food.

In terms of pleasure and wellbeing, Nie and Zepeda (2011) found that the desire to eat local was driven by a belief that local food tastes better and is better for you. Furthermore, there seem to be perceptions that local food reduces the environmental impacts by having a shorter supply chain. However, the shorter supply chain can also have some downsides. One study found that the reduction in carbon from choosing local or organic food is often offset or outweighed by emissions from driving farther to get that food (Coley et al., 2009). Another recent study suggests that farmers' markets are associated with a higher incidence of food-borne illnesses (Bellemare and Nguyen, 2018). This may be due to less oversight in the handling of food when supply chains are thinner and shorter.

Trend 5: aversion to new technologies (the case of cloned cow milk)

New technologies that increase yields, improve animal welfare, or address other challenges in agriculture can hit roadblocks when consumers grow suspicious that these productivity gains will come at the expense of consumer health or safety. While GMOs offer one example of such potential technologies, another that has received less attention in the agricultural economic literature is animal cloning. Cloning occurs when genetically identical animals are produced without sexual reproduction. The use of cloned animal products is attractive to livestock producers because it would allow them to clone their best animals, reducing some of the risks associated with traditional breeding (Britwum and Bernard, 2018). However, implementing this new technology may prove difficult given current research on consumer perceptions of cloned animal products. Brooks and Lusk (2011) reported that more Americans were unwilling to consume products from cloned animals (43 percent of those surveyed) than were willing to consume such products (31 percent). Such numbers may be mitigated by potential price differences, or perhaps after the technology becomes more widespread.

Recent research has specifically examined milk from cloned cows. The US Food and Drug Administration recently announced that milk from cloned cows is as safe to drink as milk from conventionally bred cows (FDA, 2008). However, research has demonstrated that consumers are willing to pay large premiums to ensure that their milk has not come from a cloned cow (Brooks and Lusk, 2011). Cloned cows' milk is not currently on the market, so researchers wishing to examine consumer preferences for such milk have had to rely on survey and experimental approaches. Brooks and Lusk (2011) used a method that coupled stated preferences from surveys with revealed preferences from scanner data taken from the same households. They found that consumers were willing to pay over three times more to avoid cloned cows' milk than they were to consume organic milk and that they did not differentiate between milk from a cloned cow and milk from the offspring of a cloned cow. Additionally, they found that consumers want cloned cows' milk to be labeled as such if it becomes available on the market. Given that there is no discernable difference between milk from a cloned cow and milk from a traditionally bred cow, it seems unlikely that policymakers would require such a label. It is even harder to imagine how such a requirement could be effectively enforced.

While Brooks and Lusk (2011) used a willingness-to-pay approach, Britwum and Bernard (2018) used a willingness-to-accept approach to measure the differences in consumer valuation of cloned cows' milk versus conventional milk. They argue the willingness-to-accept approach is more representative of market conditions where consumers will accept a less preferred product if they are compensated with a lower price. They completed a taste experiment with milk from cloned and non-cloned cows, asking participants to indicate how much they would need to be compensated (between $0 and $5) to switch from conventional to cloned cows' milk. Their findings align with those of Brooks and Lusk (2011); participants sought compensation for accepting milk from cloned cows. Such strong preferences essentially set a high bar for cost reduction before such innovative technologies can gain substantial consumer acceptance.

Trend 6: marijuana and eating habits

While many food consumption trends in the US have been typified by a pursuit of credence goods, changes in laws governing drug use are also beginning to change consumption patterns. The legality and use of medical marijuana in the US has grown since it was first legalized in California in 1996. Today, 30 states, the District of Columbia, Guam, and Puerto Rico have some form of legal medical marijuana. Among them, nine have legalized recreational marijuana (NCSL, 2017). There is a long history of evidence that cannabis can affect users' appetites and enjoyment of food, although the topic has not received extensive attention in the literature until recently.

Foltin, Brady, and Fischman (1986) conducted an early study of the impact of smoking marijuana on daily caloric intake, finding that small amounts had no impact but larger quantities increased daily caloric intake when compared to smoking a placebo. Other studies have aligned with these findings that marijuana increases caloric intake. However, there is more to the story when marijuana use is examined out of the lab. Sabia, Swigert, and Young (2017) examined the effects of medical marijuana laws on health outcomes, specifically body weight, physical wellness, and exercise. While the general hypothesis they pursued was that marijuana availability would increase appetite and thus body weight, this was not consistent with the observed data. They found that medical marijuana laws actually decrease the probability of obesity, a result that perhaps seems incongruous with previous results showing that marijuana increases daily caloric intake.

However, consumers do not choose marijuana in a vacuum. Rather, it appears that individuals using marijuana tend to be substituting away from alcohol (a high-calorie drug). Close to 20 percent of US residents use marijuana, but the use of several other drugs are also on the rise – particularly opioids (Case and Deaton, 2017). Americans use opioids at a higher rate than any other country (Gusovsky, 2016). Given the growing prevalence of drug use in the US, and the established ties between drug use and appetite, there is now a pressing need to more fully understand how drugs impact health through diet in addition to other more widely studied phenomena such as overdose risk, or operation of vehicles.

Trend 7: meal delivery kits

Americans are known for being pioneers of convenience. Early innovator PeaPod introduced internet grocery shopping in the US in 1996. While this concept was introduced in the US, internet grocery shopping comprises only 1.5 percent of grocery shopping done in the US and is still relatively rare compared with markets in Europe and Asia, especially South Korea, who do almost 20 percent of their grocery shopping online (Armstrong, 2017). Part of the reason for slower growth in the US is the prevalence of smaller grocery store-marketing regions with greater numbers of competitors. This increases the relative cost of delivery.

For this reason, we have recently seen an increase in modes of competition within this space. This includes larger stores providing pick-up kiosks for shoppers who pre-order online (for example, Walmart), private delivery firms that partner with local stores (for example, Instakart), and operations such as Rosie that provide an online presence for smaller grocery chains. Amazon has made significant inroads in much of this online grocery shopping space by using their network of warehousing space to ship some goods at reasonably low cost. Some firms have proposed creating such warehousing networks that could be contracted by networks of smaller grocery chains to allow them to compete with the larger competitors such as Walmart or Amazon that own their own vast networks.

While online grocery shopping is experiencing something of a revolution in the US, a related innovation has offered consumers even greater time savings. Home-delivered meal kits, originally offered by Blue Apron, send customers a box full of measured ingredients together with recipes that can be conveniently assembled in the home. The notion is that these kits will save the shopper from searching for high-quality recipes, shopping for ingredients, and still allow them to feel they have prepared a home-cooked meal. The number of such services, as well as those subscribing to them, has grown in the US. Meal kit sales grew over 40 percent in 2017 and are now a $5 billion industry (Molla, 2018). While this is only a small sector in the US food market, the trend appears to be driven by demand for convenient home-cooked meals.

Blue Apron was recently overtaken by HelloFresh as the largest meal kit provider. The meal kit industry has been typified by both horizontal and vertical mergers as competitors search for a sustainably profitable business model. In its latest expansion, HelloFresh will be selling its meal kits in Giant Food and Stop & Shop locations – perhaps signaling that home delivery is too costly to sustain (Hirsch, 2018). It is not the first meal delivery kit company to put its products in stores; Plated sells its kits in Albertsons and Blue Apron recently started selling its kits in Costco. While the literature has little to say about how consumers interact with meal kits, it is clear that they are becoming an important part of the American food economy and should be the focus of an emerging literature in home convenience-food preparation.

Conclusions

The US is a large and diverse country with a multitude of ways in which its citizens interact with their food, eating for pleasure and wellbeing. As with many industrialized nations, obesity is a major concern. American policymakers, public health officials, and community members grapple with strategies for preventing and addressing this epidemic. While there are advocates of interventions that target children, these strategies can be difficult to implement and do not fully address the American obesity epidemic. Obesity is also a special consideration in understanding food behavior among low-income Americans. Turning to the trends in American eating, we discuss seven trends that are receiving more attention. Sugar in the American diet has been a growing concern for decades and has received the attention of those who advocate for policies to curb sugar intake, like soda taxes.

Americans are also showing an increasing concern for how their food choices interact with their environmental values and connection to the entire food supply chain, opting for more organic products, demanding more information about GMOs, and seeking out local foods. The US has often been on the frontier of new technologies in agriculture and food production, although consumers are not always quick to accept products produced in ways that make them uncomfortable; a current example of this is milk from cloned cows, which American consumers appear to view as inferior to milk from conventional cows.

Another phenomenon to explore is the relationship between marijuana and eating, which is of particular interest in the US as more states legalize recreational marijuana and that industry expands. Finally, meal delivery kits have been growing in the US, following in the spirit of other American trends that have prioritized convenience in food access. While these seven trends don't represent a comprehensive overview of American eating behavior, they do provide insight into some of the key values, changes, and phenomena impacting how Americans eat today.

References

Addessi, E., Galloway, A.T., Visalberghi, E., & Birch, L.L. (2005). Specific social influences on the acceptance of novel foods in 2–5-year-old children. *Appetite*, 45(3), 264–271.

Anderson, L. (2014). Why does everyone hate Monsanto?March 4. Retrieved from: https://modernfarmer.com/2014/03/monsantos-good-bad-pr-problem/

Angelucci, M., Prina, S., Royer, H., & Samek, A. (2015). When incentives backfire: Spillover effects in food choice. *National Bureau of Economic Research*, w21481.

Armstrong, M. (2017, November 22). Where the most groceries are bought online. Retrieved from: www.statista.com/chart/11945/where-the-most-groceries-are-bought-online/

Avena, N.M., Rada, P., & Hoebel, B.G. (2008). Evidence for sugar addiction: Behavioral and neurochemical effects of intermittent, excessive sugar intake. *Neuroscience and Biobehavioral Reviews*, 32(1), 20–39.

Becker, G.S., & Murphy, K.M. (1988). A theory of rational addiction. *Journal of Political Economy*, 96(4), 675–700.

Bellemare, M.F., & Nguyen, N. (2018). Farmers markets and food-borne illness. *American Journal of Agricultural Economics*, 100(3), 676–690.

Birch, L.L., & Marlin, D.W. (1982). I don't like it; I never tried it: Effects of exposure on two-year-old childrens food preferences. *Appetite*, 3(4), 353–360.

Birch, L.L., Mcphee, L., Shoba, B.C., Pirok, E., & Steinberg, L. (1987). What kind of exposure reduces childrens food neophobia? *Appetite*, 9(3), 171–178.

Britwum, K., & Bernard, J.C. (2018). A field experiment on consumer willingness to accept milk that may have come from cloned cows. *Food Policy*, 74, 1–8.

Brooks, K.R., & Lusk, J.L. (2011). US consumers attitudes toward farm animal cloning. *Appetite*, 57(2), 483–492.

Burton, M., Rigby, D., Young, T., & James, S. (2001). Consumer attitudes to genetically modified organisms in food in the UK. *European Review of Agricultural Economics*, 28(4), 479–498.

Case, A., & Deaton, A. (2017). Mortality and morbidity in the 21st century. *Brookings Papers on Economic Activity*, 397.

Chern, W.S., & Rickertsen, K. (2001). Consumer acceptance of GMO: Survey results from Japan, Norway, Taiwan, and the United States. *Taiwanese Agricultural Economics Review*, 7(1), 1–28.

Coley, D., Howard, M., & Winter, M. (2009). Local food, food miles and carbon emissions: A comparison of farm shop and mass distribution approaches. *Food policy*, 34(2), 150–155.

Daniels, S.R. (2006). The consequences of childhood overweight and obesity. *Future of Children*, 16(1), 47–67.

Davis, C., & Carter, J.C. (2009). Compulsive overeating as an addiction disorder: A review of theory and evidence. *Appetite*, 53(1), 1–8.

Debnam, J. (2017). Selection effects and heterogeneous demand responses to the Berkeley soda tax vote. *American Journal of Agricultural Economics*, 99(5), 1172–1187.

Dole, V.P. (1959). Body fat. *Scientific American*, 201(6), 70–77.

Dovey, T.M., Staples, P.A., Gibson, E.L., & Halford, J.C. (2008). Food neophobia and "picky/fussy" eating in children: A review. *Appetite*, 50(2–3), 181–193.

Drewnowski, A., & Specter, S.E. (2004). Poverty and obesity: The role of energy density and energy costs. *American Journal of Clinical Nutrition*, 79(1), 6–16.

Erlanson-Albertsson, C. (2005). How palatable food disrupts appetite regulation. *Basic and Clinical Pharmacology and Toxicology*, 97(2), 61–73.

FDA. (2008). Animal cloning and food safety. January 15. Retrieved from: www.fda.gov/ForConsumers/ConsumerUpdates/ucm148768.htm

Fillion, L., & Arazi, S. (2002). Does organic food taste better? A claim substantiation approach. *Nutrition and Food Science*, 32(4), 153–157.

Foltin, R.W., Brady, J.V., & Fischman, M.W. (1986). Behavioral analysis of marijuana effects on food intake in humans. *Pharmacology Biochemistry and Behavior*, 25(3), 577–582.

Gearhardt, A.N., Grilo, C.M., DiLeone, R.J., Brownell, K.D., & Potenza, M.N. (2011). Can food be addictive? Public health and policy implications. *Addiction*, 106(7), 1208–1212.

Gelski, J. (2017). US organic food sales jump more than 8%. May 26. Retrieved from: www.foodbusinessnews.net/articles/9394-u-s-organic-food-sales-jump-more-than-8

Guenther, P.M., Dodd, K.W., Reedy, J., & Krebs-Smith, S.M. (2006). Most Americans eat much less than recommended amounts of fruits and vegetables. *Journal of the American Dietetic Association*, 106(9), 1371–1379.

Gusovsky, D. (2016). Americans consume vast majority of world's opioids. April 27. Retrieved from: www.cnbc.com/2016/04/27/americans-consume-almost-all-of-the-global-opioid-supply.html

Hanks, A.S., Just, D.R., & Brumberg, A. (2016). Marketing vegetables in elementary school cafeterias to increase uptake. *Pediatrics*, e20151720.

Havermans, R.C., Janssen, T., Giesen, J.C., Roefs, A., & Jansen, A. (2009). Food liking, food wanting, and sensory-specific satiety. *Appetite*, 52(1), 222–225.

Hirsch, L. (2018). HelloFresh is latest meal kit to head to the grocery store. June 3. Retrieved from: www.cnbc.com/2018/06/03/hellofresh-is-latest-meal-kit-to-head-to-the-grocery-store.html

Hu, W., Veeman, M.M., & Adamowicz, W.L. (2005). Labelling genetically modified food: Heterogeneous consumer preferences and the value of information. *Canadian Journal of Agricultural Economics/Revue canadienne d'agroeconomie*, 53(1), 83–102.

Huffman, W.E., Shogren, J.F., Rousu, M., & Tegene, A. (2003). Consumer willingness to pay for genetically modified food labels in a market with diverse information: Evidence from experimental auctions. *Journal of Agricultural and Resource Economics*, 481–502.

Hughes, S.O., Power, T.G., Fisher, J.O., Mueller, S., & Nicklas, T.A. (2005). Revisiting a neglected construct: Parenting styles in a child-feeding context. *Appetite*, 44(1), 83–92.

Hughner, R.S., McDonagh, P., Prothero, A., Shultz, C.J., & Stanton, J. (2007). Who are organic food consumers? A compilation and review of why people purchase organic food. *Journal of Consumer Behaviour*, 6(2–3), 94–110.

Hunger in America. (2014). *Hunger in America 2014: Executive Summary*. Retrieved from: http://help.feedingamerica.org/HungerInAmerica/hunger-in-america-2014-summary.pdf

Jansen, E., Mulkens, S., & Jansen, A. (2007). Do not eat the red food! Prohibition of snacks leads to their relatively higher consumption in children. *Appetite*, 49(3), 572–577.

Levine, A.S., Kotz, C.M., & Gosnell, B.A. (2003). Sugars and fats: The neurobiology of preference. *Journal of Nutrition*, 133(3), 831S–834S.

Levine, J.A. (2011). Poverty and obesity in the US. *Diabetes*, 60(11), 2667–2668.

Lipsky, L.M., Just, D.R., Nansel, T.R., & Haynie, D.L. (2011). Fundamental misunderstanding of the relation between energy density (kcal/g) and energy cost ($/kcal). *American Journal of Clinical Nutrition*, 93(4), 867–868.

Lustig, R.H., Schmidt, L.A., & Brindis, C.D. (2012). Public health: The toxic truth about sugar. *Nature*, 482(7383), 27.

McFadden, B.R., & Lusk, J.L. (2017). Effects of the national bioengineered food disclosure standard: Willingness to pay for labels that communicate the presence or absence of genetic modification. *Applied Economic Perspectives and Policy*, 40(2), 259–275.

Mela, D.J. (2001). Determinants of food choice: Relationships with obesity and weight control. *Obesity Research*, 9(S11), 249S–255S.

Mela, D.J. (2006). Eating for pleasure or just wanting to eat? Reconsidering sensory hedonic responses as a driver of obesity. *Appetite*, 47(1), 10–17.

Molla, R. (2018). HelloFresh is now bigger than Blue Apron in the US. March 26. Retrieved from: www.recode.net/2018/3/26/17165030/hellofresh-blue-apron-meal-kit-delivery-marketshare-acquisition-organic-green-chef

Nation's Restaurant News. (2017). Top 100 countdown: No. 50–No. 1. June 28. Retrieved from: www.nrn.com/top-100-restaurants/2017-top-100-countdown-no-50-no-1

NCSL. (2017). State medical marijuana laws. April 27. Retrieved from: www.ncsl.org/research/health/state-medical-marijuana-laws.aspx

Nie, C., & Zepeda, L. (2011). Lifestyle segmentation of US food shoppers to examine organic and local food consumption. *Appetite*, 57(1), 28–37.

OECD. (2017). *Obesity Update 2017*. Retrieved from: www.oecd.org/els/health-systems/Obesity-Update-2017.pdf

Ogden, C.L., Carroll, M.D., Curtin, L.R., McDowell, M.A., Tabak, C.J., & Flegal, K. M. (2006). Prevalence of overweight and obesity in the United States, 1999–2004. *Jama*, 295(13), 1549–1555.

Olson, C.M., Bove, C.F., & Miller, E.O. (2007). Growing up poor: Long-term implications for eating patterns and body weight. *Appetite*, 49(1), 198–207.

Parker, S., & Keim, K.S. (2004). Emic perspectives of body weight in overweight and obese white women with limited income. *Journal of Nutrition Education and Behavior*, 36(6), 282–289.

Peloza, J., Ye, C., & Montford, W.J. (2015). When companies do good, are their products good for you? How corporate social responsibility creates a health halo. *Journal of Public Policy and Marketing*, 34(1), 19–31.

Pennebaker, J.W., & Sanders, D.Y. (1976). American graffiti: Effects of authority and reactance arousal. *Personality and Social Psychology Bulletin*, 2(3), 264–267.

Piccinni, A., Marazziti, D., Vanelli, F., Franceschini, C., Baroni, S., Costanzo, D. … Dell'Osso, L. (2015). Food addiction spectrum: A theoretical model from normality to eating and overeating disorders. *Current Medicinal Chemistry*, 22(13), 1631–1638.

Pifer, R.H. (2013). Mandatory labeling laws: What do recent state enactments portend for the future of GMOs. *Penn State Law Review*, 118, 789.

Rasmussen, M., Krølner, R., Klepp, K.I., Lytle, L., Brug, J., Bere, E., & Due, P. (2006). Determinants of fruit and vegetable consumption among children and adolescents: A review of the literature. Part I: quantitative studies. *International Journal of Behavioral Nutrition and Physical Activity*, 3(1), 22.

Rhee, K.E., Lumeng, J.C., Appugliese, D.P., Kaciroti, N., & Bradley, R.H. (2006). Parenting styles and overweight status in first grade. *Pediatrics*, 117(6), 2047–2054.

Ruggless, R. (2017). 2017 Top 100: Top 10 fastest-growing chains. June 29. Retrieved from: www.nrn.com/node/110357/gallery?slide=1

Ruhm, C.J. (2012). Understanding overeating and obesity. *Journal of Health Economics*, 31(6), 781–796.

Sabia, J.J., Swigert, J., & Young, T. (2017). The effect of medical marijuana laws on body weight. *Health economics*, 26(1), 6–34.

Shin, A.C., Townsend, R.L., Patterson, L.M., & Berthoud, H.R. (2011). "Liking" and "wanting" of sweet and oily food stimuli as affected by high-fat diet-induced obesity, weight loss, leptin, and genetic predisposition. *American Journal of Physiology: Regulatory, Integrative and Comparative Physiology*, 301(5), R1267–R1280.

Smith-Spangler, C., Brandeau, M.L., Hunter, G.E., Bavinger, J.C., Pearson, M., Eschbach, P.J., & Olkin, I. (2012). Are organic foods safer or healthier than conventional alternatives? A systematic review. *Annals of Internal Medicine*, 157(5), 348–366.

Story, M., & French, S. (2004). Food advertising and marketing directed at children and adolescents in the US. *International Journal of Behavioral Nutrition and Physical Activity, 1*(1), 3.

Summerbell, C.D., Waters, E., Edmunds, L.D., Kelly, S.A., Brown, T.J., & Campbell, K.J. (2005). Interventions for preventing obesity in children. *Cochrane Database of Systematic Reviews*.

USDA. (2014). *New Data Reflects the Continued Demand for Farmers Markets*. August 4. Retrieved from: www.usda.gov/media/press-releases/2014/08/04/new-data-reflects-continued-demand-farmers-markets

USDA Economic Research Service. (2010). *The Impact of Food away from Home on Adult Diet Quality*. February. Retrieved from: www.ers.usda.gov/webdocs/publications/46352/8170_err90_1_.pdf

USDA Economic Research Service. (2017). *Food Availability and Consumption*. September 14. Retrieved from: www.ers.usda.gov/data-products/ag-and-food-statistics-charting-the-essentials/food-availability-and-consumption/

USDA Economic Research Service. (2018a). *Food Prices and Spending*. May 9. Retrieved from: www.ers.usda.gov/data-products/ag-and-food-statistics-charting-the-essentials/food-prices-and-spending/

USDA Economic Research Service. (2018b). *Food Security and Nutrition Assistance*. May 15. Retrieved from: www.ers.usda.gov/data-products/ag-and-food-statistics-charting-the-essentials/food-security-and-nutrition-assistance/

USDA Food and Nutrition Service. (2018). *Supplemental Nutrition Assistance Program Participation and Costs*. June 8. Retrieved from: https://fns-prod.azureedge.net/sites/default/files/pd/SNAPsummary.pdf

Ventura, A.K., & Worobey, J. (2013). Early influences on the development of food preferences. *Current Biology*, 23(9), R401–R408.

Wadden, T.A. (1993). Treatment of obesity by moderate and severe caloric restriction: Results of clinical research trials. *Annals of Internal Medicine*, 119(7), 688–693.

Welsh, J.A., Lundeen, E.A., & Stein, A.D. (2013). The sugar-sweetened beverage wars: Public health and the role of the beverage industry. *Current Opinion in Endocrinology, Diabetes, and Obesity*, 20(5), 401.

WHO. (2015). WHO calls on countries to reduce sugar intake among adults and children. March 4. Retrieved from: www.who.int/mediacentre/news/releases/2015/sugar-guideline/en/

Wilcock, A., Pun, M., Khanona, J., & Aung, M. (2004). Consumer attitudes, knowledge and behaviour: A review of food safety issues. *Trends in Food Science and Technology*, 15(2), 56–66.

Wirth, F.F., Stanton, J.L., & Wiley, J.B. (2011). The relative importance of search versus credence product attributes: Organic and locally grown. *Agricultural and Resource Economics Review*, 40(1), 48–62.

4 TV cuisine therapy through narrative cooking programs

How does culinary journalism contribute to food pleasure and wellbeing?

Julie Andrieu and Wided Batat

The field of cooking involves many actors, including the sphere of catering, such as cooks and chefs, editors of food guides, journalists and food columnists, culinary critics, culinary communication agencies, food industry, and consumers, but also more broadly, all the actors who are directly or indirectly related to the art of the table, and its gastronomic or oenological pleasures. It is understandable that the culinary realm includes many professionals, market actors that might be amateurs or not. Furthermore, nowadays, content on the theme of cooking is an integral part of the media landscape leading to the democratization and the dissemination of culinary practices amongst today's contemporary societies through popular TV shows, such as MasterChef or a more trans-media approach liking different media (e.g., TV shows, magazines, and online media, such as blogs).

The media coverage of the culinary is marked by the different historical phases that highlight the evolution of culinary TV programs, the representation of cooking activities as well as food consumption patterns amongst Western food cultures. Indeed, in the beginning culinary programs were focused on knowledge acquisition and technicality. They display the personality (most of the time a chef) on television as the holder of the know-how, who is responsible for transmitting his/her knowledge in a pedagogical way. Then, the programs integrate more and more the concept of conviviality and exchange. They gather around issues apparently closer to the concerns of viewers. The discourse becomes more entertaining and friendly than instructive. Today, culinary competition shows particularly illustrate the staging of television viewers. These shows feature a competition amongst professionals or amateurs who have multiple challenges to overcome, and thus win the competition. In the French context, which is by nature the country of gastronomy, cooking programs are not a new phenomenon. Since their appearance in the 1950s, French cooking shows have been designed in a very demonstrative format. More than four decades later the programs of the great star chef Joël Robuchon continued in the 2000s to stage the presentation of recipes in the form of lessons addressed to viewers. At the same time, however, the didactic model that had emerged as a rule of its kind has been abandoned in new programs that, under the influence of novel formats, have incorporated the practice of cooking into a narrative. In contrast to the demonstrative programs that make the performance of a recipe in front of the cameras an exercise for pedagogical purposes, the narrative programs anchor the making of a dish in a situation which links the practice of the cooking with stakes of another order. Thus, the field of representation is open to concerns that are not directly related to the goal of transmitting culinary knowledge, which results in a more or less marked dilution of the technical discourse of the recipe, and enriches the image of the cuisine that is conveyed.

Therefore, this type of program appears as one of the sources by which each individual is led to "invent" his/her own culinary universe to achieve his/her food wellbeing in a pleasurable manner where cooking appears as an activity linked to specific intentions that give meaning to the investment of those involved in the making of a dish. The questions that this chapter attempts to answer are the following: What are the different aspects of today's culinary TV programs? And how do these new narrative forms contribute to consumer wellbeing and food experiential pleasure of individuals? In this chapter, we will take a look at three successful French culinary programs led and produced by French iconic culinary journalist and food critic Julie Andrieu to show how these shows are constructed in a way to provide viewers with closeness, simplicity, and the pleasure of cooking and developing a healthy approach to food.

The manifold facets of culinary TV programs

The phenomenon of the "mediatization" of culinary and cooking activities through TV shows is not new, authors have already studied cooking TV shows as part of social phenomenon and the impact of cooking TV shows on today's individuals' food consumption behavior. Prior studies show that culinary TV shows as object of communication can be analyzed according to three main perspectives: as hyperreal communication object (e.g., Baudrillard, 1981), as object of social and cultural distinction (e.g., Bourdieu, 1979), and as a symbolic object of communication shaped by cultural meanings (e.g., Cobley and Randviir, 2009; Eco, 1976; Hodge and Kress, 1988; Parasecoli, 2011). These three perspectives are summarized in the next section.

Culinary TV shows as a hyperreal consumption realm

Culinary TV programs and food channels can also be considered from a sociological perspective as an object that is disconnected from reality, since they are paradoxical or ambiguous. The works that support this idea are grounded in what Baudrillard (1970, 1981) refers to as "simulacra," which does not reflect a representation of the culinary as it is in real life, but rather a simulation, in the sense that cooking shows produce a reality that is "without origin or reality" (Baudrillard, 1981: 10). In the postmodern era, we can refer to culinary programs as a hyperreality that is the representation of the idealistic image in communication. The universe created stands out from its referents and becomes a strategic component in marketing discourses.

For postmodernist scholars, there is no distinction between reality and fantasy. Postmodern consumers can identify with fictional individuals or experience dual reality. Regarding culinary programs, and as stated by Baudrillard, in the case of the simulation, the signs are not only without reference, but they hide that there is no real. Meister (2001), for instance, demonstrates that the happiness sought by the spectators is a lure. The Food Network's programs are based on the principle that culinary is the key and symbol for the "good life" that is a human mental and symbolic project (Meister, 2001: 171). The processes involved in food would therefore be part of the conditions for individuals of "living well." But the approach proposed by these cooking TV programs is, according to this author, inaccessible and unrealistic. Indeed, ignoring the implications of the production system, these would be far from promoting a better way of life. Furthermore, Chan (2003) states that these cooking shows distort the way individuals view food in the same way that pornography does not present a realistic and/or achievable sexuality. In fact, cooking on television, like pornography, does not replace the experience of food or sex in the "real setting." Moreover, pornography and cooking programs are, according to the author, well on the edge of fantasy, since they do not reflect real lifestyles of people.

Culinary TV shows as a distinction: Bourdieusian perspective

Researchers who define culinary TV shows and cooking programs as a cultural and social differentiator use the critical work of the French sociologist Bourdieu and his concept of distinction. In fact, Bourdieu (1979) considers that social origins determine tastes, and the notion of distinction echoes the notions of "cultivated culture" referring to elite people and upper-class consumption patterns, and "popular culture" as consumed by the masses. Following a critical sociology paradigm, food is considered as a factor of social differentiation. Several scholars in human science disciplines have highlighted how food is a social marker, whether it is related to food expenditure in a particular food culture (e.g., Darmon and Drewnowski, 2015), or to food purchasing behaviors (e.g., Jackson et al., 1985; Newman et al., 2016) and cooking practices (e.g., Meyvis and Cooke, 2007). From a Bourdieusian perspective, the study of the social structure of food consumption first of all opens up an analysis of the mechanisms of distinction as Pierre Bourdieu notably developed in his major theory of consumer taste formation, in which he defends the idea that social position in the social space determines a lifestyle and, by extension, tastes, particularly with socially marked foods (Bourdieu, 1979). Tastes being "classifying," that is to say, classifiers, are also markers of the social position in the social space. Based on Bourdieu's theory of taste formation, other authors highlight that social characteristics exert a significant influence on food consumption. Baumann and Johnston (2007) show, for example, the way in which an "ethical" diet is constructed in Canada from the observation of two distinct social groups: popular classes versus privileged classes. These authors emphasize the significant role of cultural capital, beyond social origin, in motivating consumers to buy products that are considered as "organic" or eco-friendly and healthy. However, in any case, the maintenance of social differentiations, regardless of the diffusion of new food styles on both sides of the social ladder, revives the debate on cultural "omnivorism," which refers to a consumption classification for species (including humankind) that have a digestive system allowing them to obtain chemical energy and nutrients from resources originating from plant and animal origin (e.g., Duval, 2010; Peterson, 1992; Peterson and Kern, 1996). Like any other cultural practice, nutrition follows the rules of social differentiation according to the positions of individuals and groups in the social space, particularly according to the educational level and sociocultural background of individuals.

Regarding food and cooking TV shows, the theory of taste formation and distinction is well highlighted in traditional as well as online media through different show formats, contents, and approaches. Adema (2000) was one of the first authors to examine the phenomenon of culinary TV shows. According to this author, culinary programs are breaking down social barriers as they popularize and demystify sophisticated culinary knowledge, since their approach is based on the fact that culinary know-how is part of the cultural capital (Bourdieu, 1979), and thus gives rise to a hierarchy between the elite and the middle classes. Adema states that cooking programs and food TV channels allow viewers from more popular classes to access an "elite culture." She reports, though, that the need for distinction is outweighed by the fact that these shows, frequently driven by star chefs who actively participate in the commercial image of the culinary, anchor viewers in a consumerist culture. On the other side of the spectrum, De Solier (2005) states that culinary TV shows allow individuals to legitimize their practices. The conclusions of De Solier's work underline the idea that these popular TV programs do not only convey a pedagogical dimension, but also operate implicit ideological work on gender, class, and identity.

Culinary programs massively disseminate a cultural capital of practical and aesthetic knowledge, which Bourdieu (1979) associates with the cultural capital of the "elite class." Although the author acknowledges that the middle class is more fragmented than it was before, her analysis states that there are still social strata. She focuses on the fact that television can disseminate and promote "haute cuisine," gastronomic restaurants, as well as Michelin-starred chefs amongst lower and unprivileged social classes, and thus contributes to enhance their knowledge in terms of healthy cooking habits, tips about easy and healthy food, the importance of quality of local products, and seasonality. For Ketchum (2005), the narrative conventions of these non-fiction culinary programs, by selling intimacy and pleasure, make viewers conceptualize their desires in terms of merchandise. They materialize their social connections through the acquisition and exhibition of goods related to a certain culinary lifestyle. Culinary TV shows would serve here again to distinguish themselves from the rest of society. By making haute cuisine accessible to the masses, these food TV programs would allow the most popular classes to position themselves and legitimize their culinary practices, and thus achieve their food self-confidence and their food wellbeing.

Culinary TV shows as a symbolic object shaped by cultural meanings

Culinary programs are also related to the production of meaning through content, including both discursive inputs that are technical, practical, entertaining, and economic as well as symbolic components that refer to socialization, family values, culinary identity and traditions, and so forth. Thus, in culinary TV programs, it is in terms of expression that the scope of the culinary media is understood. Indeed, the sensory cues, scenography devices, the objects used, the setting in texts, and the statutes of the characters comprise many resources and symbols to express lifestyles related to the culinary. In order to communicate intrinsic values, such as conviviality, generosity, and exchange of the culinary spirit through TV programs, and enhance the authenticity and the closeness of the program, the signs displayed in these programs can help the viewer to decode the signifiers and what they signify. The science of signs or semiotics (e.g., Cobley and Randviir, 2009; Eco, 1976; Hodge and Kress, 1988) can then help researchers to examine the symbols used in culinary TV programs and what they communicate in order to touch and create intimacy with viewers, although the culinary experience occurs within an artificial staging.

By using semiotics, we can reveal different oppositional meanings (expert versus amateur, chef versus housewife, etc.) depending on the way culinary programs are framed. For example, in competition programs like MasterChef, the roles adopted by the apprentices and the chefs demonstrate that today's society is in the throes of transmitting know-how and *savoir-vivre*. Other programs that are framed to display the culinary through socialization to enhance authenticity use other devices, symbols, storytelling, and formats to emphasize the individual and the importance of the interaction instead of chefs' expertise and know-how. From a semiotic perspective, cooking programs on television are considered as built objects. It is therefore necessary to look at how these programs work in terms of staging and speech, and then to engage in their interpretation. Semiotics, since it considers these culinary programs as constructed objects, highlights the stakes of the device as to the construction of meaning.

Therefore, to sum up, we can state that the omnipresence of cooking in today's contemporary Western societies seems difficult to escape. Further, the phenomenon gave rise not only to the proliferation of media content dedicated to cooking (e.g., websites, TV shows, magazines, literary editions, etc.), but also the creation of communities that define their world around eating practices and culinary lifestyles, such as slow food, foodies, food porn, etc., which makes cooking and the culinary amongst the most popular subjects covered in all kinds of media and through innovative formats, content, and devices in which the focus is no longer on food and cooking, but rather on wellbeing culinary narratives. This is the case of the French programs produced and led by a popular French culinary journalist Julie Andrieu, who proposed a new genre focusing more on authenticity, imperfection, closeness, and wellbeing. The next section explores three key narrative culinary TV programs created by Julie Andrieu, and shows the way they have been constructed to emphasize the wellbeing dimension related to food consumption and cooking practices.

Julie Andrieu's approach: Introspection into a culinary journalist's journey

Julie Andrieu is a French culinary journalist and TV cooking program producer. Starting her career as a photographer, Julie then decided to make her hobby her job and, therefore, turned to cooking. After publishing *Julie's Cooking* in 1999, she became a food critic at the *Lebey Guide* and then led new TV and radio culinary programs that seduced different audiences. Self-taught, Julie nevertheless quickly completed internships in the kitchens of great Michelin-starred chefs like Alain Ducasse, Michel Guérard, or Alain Passard. In the 2000s, few young people were interested in cooking activities and the doors of these gastronomic "temples" were more open to people who wanted to learn more about cooking. Knowing how to take advantage of this position, linking amateur and professional cuisine, Julie chose to bring the codes of the gastronomic cuisine as well as the cuisine of grandmothers to make cooking accessible and understandable by her audience. Since then Julie has provided her vision of cooking through television, press, publishing, and radio.

Amongst the most successful of Julie's culinary programs, in this chapter we will focus on three of Julie's culinary programs: *Julie Cuisine, Les Carnets de Julie* or *Julie's Notebooks*, and *Fourchette et sac à dos* or *Fork and Backpack*; all of them rely on very different devices to put in narrative the achievement of recipes, and give dissimilar meanings to the culinary practice. From these emblematic examples of the evolution of French cooking programs, we will try to highlight the ways in which the stories were shaped and understand their impact on the television transmission of recipes as well as how culinary programs can help individuals to achieve their food wellbeing.

Julie Cuisine *as a meaningful and a simply imperfect lifestyle*

Julie Cuisine is a short TV program that was broadcast on TF1, France's leading national television channel, in 2004 and 2005 as an advertising segment for the Whirlpool brand of home appliances. The host and producer Julie Andrieu wanted to renew the type of cooking programs offered on French screens but faced the difficulty of getting her projects accepted by national channels. Funding by Whirlpool, although required to make the program an advertising showcase intended to stage the image "modern and high end," which the brand wanted to parry its products, allowed this program to be broadcast daily around noon, in the middle of an advertising segment. Since the show was intended to stage a certain vision of cooking, the presentation of recipes is written in a fictional story that each episode develops very shortly because of its limited duration of two minutes and the inclusion of sponsors.

In contrast to the demonstrations performed in front of the cameras on a television set, *Julie Cuisine* puts forward the realistic character of situations presented as authentic – that is, not staged for television. The way in which the program is filmed gives viewers the impression that they are watching a scene that is not a performance intended for an audience, even if the presenter's words describing the steps of the recipe are directly addressed to the audience. The demonstrative discourse thus comes into tension with a taking of images that seems to be carried out by furtiveness. Imperfection, which makes the situation almost real and authentic, refers to the frequent presence of obstacles, such as curtains or utensils that clutter the image and prevent a clear vision of the actions performed by Julie Andrieu, shows the supposedly intrusive character of the presence of cameras. As a result, the viewer is placed in the position of observer of an intimate scene, as if they are watching Julie Andrieu cooking at home for herself.

The decor of the show does not appear as a television studio, but rather as an inhabited space with some disorder around to make it real. It represents a living space that does not only include a kitchen, but also an adjoining dining room and a garden visible through the windows in the background. Its layout and decoration reflect its strong personalization. The disordered arrangement of many disparate elements creates a feeling of a realistic arrangement of the set, as opposed to that of the television sets, which only show one facet of the show's host (the cook). In the case of *Julie Cuisine*, the viewer can identify with Julie Andrieu, who is seen as a close friend and portrayed as a modern and very accessible person, rather than as a cooking expert. In fact, the many books visible in the background emphasize Julie Andrieu's amateur cooking-enthusiast profile, and refer to other occupations in which the host would indulge. In this case, the culinary program is based on the representation of the intimate life of the host who is, like the viewer, learning about cooking and enjoying it in her everyday life. In spite of their limited duration, each episode illustrates the circumstances in which the preparation of the dish takes place. Thus, before going into cooking, Julie explains the reasons why she chose to make a particular dish. She prepares a macaroni gratin for a tête-à-tête dinner because, according to Julie, the dishes that we love are also the ones that she prepares for the children, in fact they are simple recipes, easy pleasures, almost regressive. Any recipe is therefore integrated into an action logic that gives it meaning, and each issue of the show ends with images depicting the consumption context of the dish. From gourmet single-course tastings to casual girlfriends, the situations in which foods are served vary and involve adjusting the recipes to the effect they must produce.

The role of Julie Andrieu is not only to perform the recipes she presents, but also to embody a true character, which distinguishes her from an expert responsible for transmitting her knowledge. Through the kitchen, the show displays various clues through which the public sees and imagines Julie's lifestyle. The multiplicity of Julie Andrieu's faces that are shown over the situations depicted during daily episodes helps to give a certain thickness to a figure whose attitude and cooking style is always adapted to the circumstances (Figure 4.1). The clothing worn by the presenter changes every episode, the apron worn for the preparation of household dishes, for example, leaving the room for an elegant outfit when it comes to receiving guests. Also, the fictitious image that is given

Figure 4.1 The *Julie Cuisine* TV cooking show

of Julie Andrieu proposes an idealized and simple way of life, according to the advertising vocation of the program, which is a perfect illustration of the Whirlpool brand's slogan for opening – namely, "cooking is a pleasure." Thus, the pleasure that the presenter derives from the culinary activity is due to the fact that she adjusts her practices to her personal tastes.

Thus, Julie Andrieu declares that she decides on the composition of her herb salad according to the varieties that she has been able to harvest in her garden, and according to a spontaneous balance established from her own preferences which also underline the fact that creativity is a central aspect within cooking activities and is the only way individuals can freely practice self-expression with the unique purpose of the pleasure provided by the preparation of a dish and its tasting. Therefore, the ability to overcome the constraints is a central element of the process, giving substance to a vision of cooking as a rewarding activity. Whoever prepares a recipe in this way does not want this time of obligatory constraints, and dreams only of freedom, of individual levity. The culinary program should emphasize an ideal culinary and domestic universe to make people dream and embrace cooking as a pleasurable mundane activity within their simply imperfect lifestyle that contributes to enhance the viewers' food wellbeing and his/her relationship to cooking and food overall.

Fourchette et sac à dos*: globetrotter foodie journey into new food cultures*

Fourchette et sac à dos or Fork and Backpack is a culinary show presented by Julie Andrieu that aims to introduce the viewer to different culinary practices around the world. The viewer can follow Julie Andrieu in her travels in the heart of diverse culinary cultures. Within this TV show, Julie combines two passions, cuisine and travel, to understand local people and their traditions through their culinary practices, and thus brings the audience on a cultural journey to discover the practices, customs, and habits and culinary traditions of each country through the travel experience of a "girl next door" that could be us. Julie offers the audience a rich culinary and cultural journey through dishes and recipes by encountering the country and its inhabitants through entering their kitchen and sharing a meal with them, where cooking language is sometimes more universal than discourse. Julie approaches strangers and new food cultures without any preparation to get a real and authentic experience. In each episode, Julie settles for a few days with a typical local family to help viewers discover the food cultures, recipes, and local know-how. In the show, Julie tastes all the local specialties: Reunion beetle, Indian chai, Peruvian swordfish ceviche, Balinese vegetable sautéed rice, etc. (Figure 4.2). Living with local families is an essential part of the show. For Julie, it is the first goal of the trip to highlight the authenticity of the cultural journey so that the viewer can easily connect with the destination and the food culture.

Julie shows empathy and interest in the local culture of people, their traditions, and their recipes. By so doing, the exchange between Julie and the local population is created more easily than if one simply came to look at how they live without being curious and involved. Viewers can learn preparation secrets and travel with Julie through her tasting discoveries, delighting viewers with anecdotes, the history of each country, and great gastronomic encounters. The show is enriched with a great website with lots of information on the countries crossed as well as detailed recipes for viewers to try the exotic cuisine.

Julie Andrieu indicates that this show generates emotions and strong memories for both the viewer and the presenter. For Julie, there are remarkable memories on every trip, such as a very beautiful crossing of the Halong Bay in Vietnam on a traditional boat, cooking what she can find on her journey, and in Peru where she had a wonderful trip in which she ended up at the top of

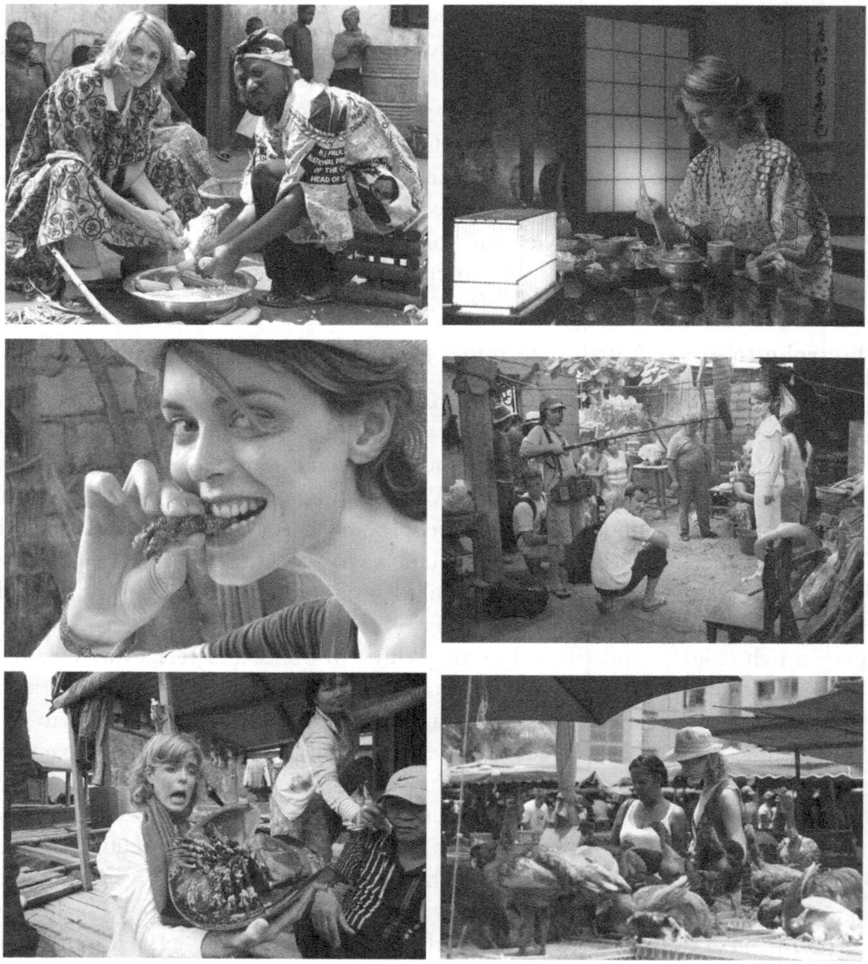

Figure 4.2 The *Fourchette et sac à dos* TV show

the Altiplano with local *campesinos* who had almost never seen a white face, or when she lived for two days in the Moroccan desert by really eating the product of the earth. The viewer can capture great moments of emotions everywhere in each episode. In this globetrotter foodie journey, Julie shows that cooking reveals much about the country's popular culture, its history, its migratory flows, and so on. For example, when she goes to Brazil, the viewer discovers that there is a large part of the cuisine that is influenced by Africa. Viewers also find out that there is an important Asian influence. In fact, every level of culinary culture is connected to a major event in the history of the country. Thanks to local products and culinary discovery, viewers understand a little better why some food products grow in one place and not another, how the culture unfolds, what the seasons are, and what the climate is (e.g., in Peru, in the Altiplano, the only thing that grew at this altitude of 4,500 meters was potatoes, there was nothing else). Through this show, the viewer can learn about new food cultures, destinations, and acquire cooking knowledge without even leaving his/her living room.

Les Carnets de Julie: *discovering local and regional culinary heritage*

Les Carnets de Julie or Julie's Notebooks is a French culinary weekly television show, presented by Julie Andrieu, broadcast since September 2012 on the national channel France 3. In each episode, Julie discovers a French terroir, meets amateur cooks, reveals gastronomic recipes that are representative of the region, and promotes elements of the local heritage. Each show ends with a banquet gathering together the people she has met. During her discoveries, region after region, Julie enters the kitchens of the French to bring up to date tastes of the terroir that have sometimes been forgotten. The concept of the show is a French culinary adventure, where viewers can watch Julie traveling in her vintage red Peugeot 304 to meet people around festive meal gatherings. In September 2016 Thierry Marx, a 2-Michelin star Parisian grand chef, and Raphaël Haumont, a chemical researcher who applies his knowledge of chemistry to the field of gastronomy, joined the show to taste and explain recipes. Each week, the show offers its viewers a theme, a region, and multiple recipes to satisfy all tastes and desires: the bar and its iodized notes, surprising jams, warming winter soups, etc. Traditions from other places in the world also have their place in the show, such as Chinese lacquered duck, Italian ravioli, or New York cheesecake.

Discovering a French region, through its history and traditional recipes to better understand its specificities and the richness of its local food culture and heritage, is the adventure that viewers will share with Julie Andrieu. As a reporter of taste and good living, Julie finds rare and uncommon places, meets warm and unique people, able to make her understand what makes the creative, gastronomic, cultural heritage, or the economic strength of a region. And since there are many ways to prepare these dishes, Julie and Thierry will prepare their own recipe sometimes inspired by the secrets and tips of unprofessional cooks. Moreover, Julie will continue to visit these amateurs everywhere in France (Figure 4.3). As for Raphaël Haumont, the culinary chemistry researcher, he will answer the various questions that these recipes raise and will deliver useful tips to succeed in all the preparations. Faithful to the tradition of the *Carnets de Julie*, it is around a convivial table that we end each episode, where Julie, Thierry, Raphael, and the guests (the amateur cooks met in different regions) share a meal for the greatest pleasure of all.

In this show, everything makes viewers want to preserve their own food heritage and local food culture by transmitting their know-how that is part of their identity through a didactic leaning. Indeed, the promise of the show is also the transmission of know-how: Everything is explained and prepared by Julie so that the viewer can reproduce the actions of the cook; the explanations are precise and detailed and the ingredients are clearly written, summarized,

Figure 4.3 Les Carnets de Julie TV show

and easily searchable. Furthermore, several times Julie reminds us that the viewer will learn throughout the show small improvements and tips for making, for example, a good apple pie thanks to the demonstration that is at the center of the process. Social values intrinsic to the culinary field are demonstrated by organizing a gathering around the dinner table at the end.

The kitchen brings people together from different worlds. Therefore, elements such as comfort, relaxation, and friends are all at the heart of the show and it is from the combination of these factors and the empathy of the presenter Julie Andrieu that we can produce a "friendly show" that makes people feel good about their food culture, identity, relationship to food, and thus find pleasure in their daily mundane cooking practices with the freedom to reproduce recipes according to their own inspiration. The freedom displayed in Julie's show, even if it is only relative, contributes to reinforcing the conviviality of the program which does not seem especially supervised, especially as Julie and the other participants seem to benefit from a great freedom of movement, and thus of speech, and in which the viewer feels that anything can happen.

Conclusions

This chapter shows that culinary programs on television can contribute to food wellbeing by leading individuals to reinvent their own culinary universe and approach cooking and food in general in a way that generates pleasure, conviviality, fun, and knowledge. Through the analysis of the shows produced by the iconic French food journalist Julie Andrieu, in this chapter we attempted to explore how TV food shows can help individuals to reconnect with cooking experiences and the kitchen sphere, and thus develop healthy eating habits. Indeed, the kitchen is the unifying element of today's TV food programs, where the pleasures of the table are identified as carrying values such as conviviality and sharing. Besides, the liberating function of the culinary programs and the gathering around a table are important factors to connect with viewers and capture their interest in cooking and food.

References

Adema, P. (2000). Vicarious consumption: Food, television and the ambiguity of modernity. *Journal of American and Comparative Cultures*, 23(3), 113–123.

Baudrillard, J. (1970). *La Société de consommation: Ses mythes, ses structures*. Paris: Folio.

Baudrillard, J. (1981). *Simulacres et simulation*. Paris: Galilée.

Baumann, S., & Johnston, J. (2007). Democracy versus distinction: A study of omnivorousness in gourmet food writing. *American Journal of Sociology*, 13(1), 165–204.

Bourdieu, P. (1979). *La distinction. Critique sociale du jugement*. Paris: Editions de Minuit.

Chan, A. (2003). La grande Bouffe: Cooking shows as pornography. *Gastronomica: Journal of Food and Culture*, 3(4), 46–53.

Cobley, P., & Randviir, A. (2009). Introduction: What is sociosemiotics? *Semiotica, 173* (1/4), 1–39.

Darmon, N., & Drewnowski, A. (2015). Contribution of food prices and diet cost to socioeconomic disparities in diet quality and health: A systematic review and analysis. *Nutrition Reviews, 73*(10), 643–660. doi:10.1093/nutrit/nuv027

De Solier, I. (2005). TV dinners: Culinary television, education and distinction. *Continuum*, 14(4), 465–481.

Duval, J. (2010). Distinction studies. *Actes de la recherche en sciences sociales*, 181–182, 146–156.

Eco, U. (1976). *A Theory of Semiotics*. Bloomington, IN: Indiana University Press.

Hodge, R., & Kress, G. (1988). *Social Semiotics*. Ithaca, NY: Cornell University Press.

Jackson, R.W., McDaniel, S.W., & Rao, C.P. (1985). Food shopping and preparation: Psychographic differences of working wives and housewives. *Journal of Consumer Research, 12*(1), 110–113. doi:10.1086/209041

Ketchum, C. (2005). The essence of cooking shows: How the Food Network constructs consumer fantasies. *Journal of Communication Inquiry*, 29(3), 217–234.

Meister, M. (2001). Cultural feeding, good life science, and the TV Food Network. *Mass Communication and Society*, 4(2), 165–182.

Meyvis, T., & Cooke, A.D. (2007). Learning from mixed feedback: anticipation of the future reduces appreciation of the present. *Journal of Consumer Research, 34*(2), 200–211. doi:10.1086/519148

Newman, C.L., Howlett, E., & Burton, S. (2016). Effects of objective and evaluative front-of-package cues on food evaluation and choice: The moderating influence of comparative and noncomparative processing contexts. *Journal of Consumer Research, 42*(5), 749–766. doi:10.1093/jcr/ucv050

Parasecoli, F. (2011). Savoring semiotics: Food in intercultural communication. *Social Semiotics, 21*(5), 645–663. doi:10.1080/10350330.2011.578803

Peterson, R.A. (1992). Understanding audience segmentation: From elite and mass to omnivore and univore. *Poetics*, 32, 169–194.

Peterson, R.A., & Kern, R.M. (1996). Changing highbrow taste: From snob to omnivore. *American Sociological Review*, 61(5), 900–907.

5 Cultural pleasures of eating and healing

Contributions to food wellbeing

Nancy N. Chen

The pleasures of food whether from production or consumption are manifold – growing, sourcing, making, eating, sharing, even playing with food facilitates concepts of taste, identity, and social status. Many cultures hold notions of the beautiful table laden with bounty or visual qualities to enhance desire, gustatory anticipation, and pleasures of eating. By contrast, medication is usually associated with bitter tastes or displeasure stemming from reductive elements of ingestion via pills, shots, or an IV drip. This chapter engages overlapping categories of food and medicine as a critical intervention and lens to address the connections rather than the divide between food and medicine as separate systems. Practices of feeding and nourishing in China are integral not only to healing practices, but also to everyday life and experiences of belonging. Chinese regional foodways, as well as other Asian cuisines, incorporate food as a significant element of health and wellbeing. Healthy foods in biomedical realms tend to be associated with scientific categories of calories, nutrition, or metabolism. Wellbeing in such contexts frequently emphasizes weight loss and food abstinence as a response to concerns about chronic diseases and metabolic disorders rather than the pleasures of eating. By considering healing from a cultural lens, it becomes possible to view how medicinal foods may form part of preventative care on a daily basis. This category and its associated practices of preparing and eating abound across diverse regional foodways from ingredients such as mushrooms or garlic to prepared meals that include soups and tonics. Knowing what to eat and how to eat inform cultural frameworks of medicinal foodways.

In what follows, I first address the pleasures of eating in recent contexts of consumption in contemporary urban China. New generations of middle-class consumers, especially Chinese youth, in cities and suburban environments experience a particular period of abundance with access to multiple forms of food amidst highly designed and curated spaces. Nonetheless, while consumption is promoted as an integral part of rising middle-class lifestyles, commensality and social engagement continues to be a crucial element of such endeavors. In the second part of this chapter, I trace the shift from ideals of longevity to contemporary notions of living. We will also explore how medicinal foods are being transformed with new products. In addition to having the world's largest population, China also has the greatest aging population with 241 million (or 17 percent of the total population) over the age of 60 in 2018. The figure is expected to continue to rise rapidly over the next three decades to comprise nearly a third of the population in 2050, according to the National Working Committee on Aging. Markets in food and medicine across the country already cater to this segment of society and emerging products will continue to be developed with this considerable projected growth in mind.

Based on ongoing ethnographic research regarding contemporary Asian foodways and health foods, this chapter will examine how pleasure through social forms of nourishment and care may offer key insights into formations of thinking, aging, and being well. For short periods over a decade of trips to mainland China, I have visited and observed shopping and consumption practices taking place in markets, pharmacies, supermarkets, restaurants, shopping malls, and home kitchens in urban settings. Such spaces in China can be viewed as diverse and immense social labs or experimental sites where consumers face new products and explore different ways of doing and being in the city. It is not uncommon for several generations of a technology or product to be available in Chinese markets before they are available elsewhere in Europe or North America. My observations as a medical anthropologist are also guided by Chinese medical and philosophical concepts which view the body with the theoretical framing of five elements (water, wood, fire, earth, metal) that systematically correspond to five viscera (kidney, liver, heart, spleen, and lung), five flavors (salty, sour, bitter, sweet, and spicy), and many more categories such as colors, sounds, emotions, directions, seasons, and even time of day. The body's internal system is influenced not only by environmental factors but also by the interactions between each entity. The principle of five flavors exists both in Chinese medicine and culinary traditions such that regional cuisines may include dishes that seek to harmonize these flavors as measures to promote taste and wellbeing.

The pleasures of eating: big tables and little eats

Across the majority of contemporary China, and in any major urban city around the world with a diasporic Chinese community, restaurants are filled with tables that may seat at minimum 10–12 people. Larger restaurants might have multiple floors each filled with salons and private banquet rooms for business meetings or numerous parties holding simultaneous banquets whether day or night. In large banquet halls, the aural landscape is filled with human social activity – hundreds of conversations, dishes being delivered, toasts being offered – the livelier the better for celebrations. Major life events, especially marriages, tend to be commemorated in such venues. Weddings may also be held at hotels with restaurants and spaces that may be booked entirely for a single party. The big table in China is an ideal which connotes status, wealth, and, above all, social obligations. Hosting such an event entails significant duties, while participating at the big table also confers certain expectations of reciprocity or gift giving. Joining the big table ultimately connotes belonging which entails obligations but also possibilities for commensality which is a significant part of social life. Eating together with others at the big table is both memorable and powerful as collective relations may be defined or reaffirmed in social and business interactions. Food idioms and metaphors abound in Mandarin and Cantonese especially around eating, character, and quality of life.

In recent years, the history of food and regional practices of cooking, eating, and sharing have become prominent in several contexts beyond the big table – in museums, on television, and via social media. The Cuisine Museum of Hangzhou in Jiangsu province is a 45 minute journey from Shanghai via high-speed train. Opened in 2012, the museum offers specific contextualization for the story of food in China. Commencing with painted depictions of Neolithic settlements claiming 10,000 years of food history, various *mise en scène* tableaus present the gradual transformation of foodways and trade along southern Chinese rivers and canals. The communities that settled in this area and the foods that they cultivated and prepared eventually led to the formation of regional foods in Hangzhou. The local dishes became a favorite of various emperors who would regularly tour the region or bring Hangzhou chefs back to the imperial court so that these dishes could be served in court meals. The main exhibits in the Professional Showroom document foods that were available or served during different dynasties, the Republic era, and the post-1949 period. In addition to displays of various cookware – pots, pans, bowls that were unearthed during archaeological excavations – a highlight of the museum includes simulated three-dimensional dishes for each period. The main designer of the museum, Professor Zhao Rongguang, took three years to make over 300 signature dish replicas using silica gel (similar to Japanese restaurant displays of plastic food models). Another major highlight is the reproduction of a typical Man-Han feast which circulates on a revolving table. The multiple dishes on three tiers illustrate the various dishes served to the emperors Kangxi and Qianlong when they toured Hangzhou. The big table in this context is a display of historical wealth with dishes that reflect not only Hangzhou specialties but also food from other regions. In addition to the exhibits and videos, there are classes for visitors to learn how to make certain dishes. Perhaps the most popular element of the museum is the restaurant which serves many of the unique dishes featured in the museum. During an initial visit to the museum in 2017, I noted that many other museum goers would head immediately towards the dining pavilion rather than the exhibits. The menu was a remarkable display itself in large format of at least 1.5 feet tall with colorful images of the voluminous dishes. As ordered foods arrived, multiple cell phones would appear around the table as friends and family members took photos of the dishes, each other, and selfie images to share later on social media. The visual presentations of signature dishes are just as celebrated as the flavor, texture, or taste of the dish.

In addition to the more familiar greeting of hello, a more customary greeting would include "Have you eaten yet?" for neighbors, family, or friends. A follow-up question to acquaintances or strangers meeting for the first time might also include "Where are you from?" to learn of one's ancestral home rather than where one lives at present. Answers to the second query usually lead to discussion of the local foods and drink or specialty dishes for which that area is known. Food in China is intensely regional with different climates that change dramatically across landscapes that include plains, deserts, plateaus, mountains, rivers, and coastline. The diversity of terrains, cultures, and dialects across the vast geographic regions is also reflected in its foodways. It is not uncommon for Chinese to define each other according to what grain they are used to consuming at home. While rice is considered the most common grain in southern China, in the northern provinces and even to the west, wheat is consumed in the form of noodles, buns, pancakes, and dumplings. In addition to the northern and southern distinctions of grains, the types of vegetables (菜 cai), spices, or cooking techniques may also give shape to distinctive notions of taste and location. The pleasure of foods engages multiple senses. Through appearance, smell, sound, texture, or flavor it may be possible to experience notions of regional cuisine and belonging as forms of pleasure.

In May 2012, Central China Television (CCTV) aired a seven-part documentary series called *Shejian shangde zhongguo* (China on the Tip of the Tongue), which translated for Western media as "Bite of China." Each episode shot in high definition follows local food makers as they cure ham, pickle vegetables, ferment bean curd or shrimp, and make other artisanal dishes. The series has drawn over 100 million viewers to pastoral scenes of faraway rural villages and artisanal foods. The screenings have been instrumental in recharging the food industry by enticing foodies with histories of regional dishes and newfound desire for culinary knowledge. Online sales of cooking tools increased during the screenings and culinary tours based on the series have also become the latest fashion. Book publishers have produced an encyclopedic compendium to the popular series. Spin-off series by other CCTV channels have also been produced. The television show has spawned a new line of restaurants in the areas where episodes have been filmed. Outside the Cuisine Museum in downtown Hangzhou there were several restaurants with the Bite of China logo which featured signature dishes of the region.

The conviviality of social eating has also become an opportunity to promote or consume foods that are uniquely linked to specific holidays, locations, or age groups with new media. While the big table connotes formal gatherings to celebrate life events or holidays, the opportunities to consume food abound considerably beyond expensive hotels or formal restaurants. Night markets, corner stores, movie theaters, trains, buses, metro stations, and street stands may sell a variety of foods that may be prepackaged snacks or foods prepared on the spot as customers arrive. Consumption of foods and snacks circulate not only in these physical spaces, but also online in virtual realms of social media, microblogs, messaging apps, and blockchain technology. The square QR (quick response) code which stores product information and online addresses is available for scanning via smartphone technology. Most restaurants, chain store outlets, entertainment centers, even street stalls feature this technology as an easy way for companies to gather information on customers and for consumers to add themselves to promotional campaigns for new products and services. WeChat is perhaps the largest and most popular platform with nearly 900 million subscribers and 10 million third-party apps that are linked to this app. The messaging app allows consumers to conduct activities on their cell phones such as online shopping, financial services, games, and the sharing of images. In addition to booking tables or movies, reserving taxis, or paying bills, new promotions for food products and restaurant deals circulate in these spaces. Foodies who post images of a dish or a brand may find promotional deals appearing on their cell phones as businesses create official accounts to keep directly in touch with individual customers.

There are many Chinese terms that translate into associated notions of pleasure (乐趣 lèqù), joy (欢乐 huānlè), fun (乐 lè), or happy (快乐 kuàilè). For China's youth, these concepts are especially intertwined with food. During the 1990s, the proliferation of fast-food chains across urban China became an immediate success because they catered to children and youth. Whether with hamburgers, French fries, fried chicken, or pizza, the new meals were often tied to promotions with plastic toys or special birthday packages for celebrations to be held at the fast-food chain. For parents and grandparents of single children, these spaces became sites of entertainment for "little emperors and empresses" (Jing 2000) in ways that restaurants could not compete with due to commercial tie-ins with children's television shows and cartoons. Shopping malls in major urban areas now cater to single-child families with recreational spaces and toys while parents shop or wait for a table at a nearby restaurant to become available. Inside a prominent mall in the center of Shanghai, an entire floor with multiple shops is devoted to infant children's clothing and accessories along with toilets scaled down to young children size. Restaurants on this floor include numerous high chairs and booster chairs so that parents and grandparents can eat out with their child.

Snacks (小吃 *xiao chi* or little eats) continue to be sold in multiple venues, however, it is less common for these to be produced by hand at a local shop. Instead, industrial food companies have come to produce more of the foods associated with in-between meals. Several decades ago, simple snacks might have consisted of watermelon or sunflower seeds and preserved plums that could be purchased in bulk. While such items are available in department stores, these are usually packaged and sold as specific units. The globalization of foodways in addition to enhanced transportation systems for food chains makes it possible for out-of-season fruits to be available at any time of the year as well as snacks produced in one region to be sold across the country. Sweets have also become ubiquitous in the form of candy, cookies, cakes, soft drinks, and other high-calorie items promoted as snack items. Boba tea drinks (iced tea beverages with chewy tapioca pearls) in addition to fruit smoothies have also become quite popular along with coffee beverages sold by global franchises. The ubiquity of fast foods and processed food products with high fat, sugar, and sodium content have contributed to the growing waistlines of youth and consumers of any age who ingest such foods on a regular, even daily basis. In recent years, state media as well as medical journals have noted that China now has the world's largest overweight population with 10.8 percent of males and 14.9 percent of females in this category which is greater than that of the United

States (Smith 2016). This rapid shift to unhealthy lifestyles and eating without regular activity has contributed to the prominence of chronic diseases such as cardiovascular disease, diabetes, and cancer among others.

In late 2016, the Healthy China 2030 campaign was announced by the Chinese Central Committee and State Council whereby health promotion would be at the forefront of school education programs and urban planning (National Health Commission 2016). In numerous speeches, President Xi Jinping has noted that health will be included in all policies, state governance, and strategic planning. This is a dramatic move as it is the first long-term strategic plan focused on health at the national level since the founding of the People's Republic in 1949. The centralized emphasis on health reflects not only the significance of citizen health as part of national wellbeing, but also how infrastructure is critical to this endeavor. In addition to the Healthy Cities initiative, another major component of the campaign includes overall reform of the health and medical system. Food, fitness, and healthy living will be promoted throughout the life spectrum from early years to aging seniors whose average life expectancy is steadily increasing to 77 years by 2020. Traditional Chinese medicine will also continue to be promoted as part of this monumental reboot of the healthcare system.

Concurrent with, and even prior to major state plans for revising healthcare in China, markets and shopping malls have already started to promote options for healthier living through products and services that highlight sustainable lifestyles and green forms of consumption that align with ideals of wellbeing. Huaihai Road in central Shanghai contains numerous flagship stores for a range of upscale global luxury brands. The 3 mile section of Middle Huaihai Road includes multiple high-rise buildings, shopping malls, and department stores. At street level, glittering window displays feature the latest designs and fashions. In addition to giant billboards alongside sidewalks and pedestrian walkways, huge wall-size LED screens play advertisements for items that feature the good life. In 2013, the K11 Art Mall of Shanghai opened in this major shopping area as a venue for the "union of art and retail." The company brand promotes the space as a key site "where culture, entertainment, shopping and living revolve around art. It is where ideas, trends and lifestyles collide to form new ideas and new inspirations" (K11, 2018). During a sultry summer exploration in 2017, the blend of art and lifestyle was on full display. In addition to multiple sculptures, an "art village," and exhibit spaces, each level included cafes with third-wave coffee hand brewed with micro-roasted beans globally sourced from bags that featured the faces of individual growers and coffee pickers. Visitors could also participate in the K11 Kulture Academy which featured the themes of art, design, food, and wellness. Flagship restaurants of the most well-known chefs in Asia and Europe as well as boutiques selling accessories and clothes blended in this luxury landscape. The highest retail floor featured several rows of marble-enclosed indoor urban gardens with a hipster chalkboard in English listing the herbs and vegetables being grown under high-intensity lamps. Nearby a wall-sized enclosed refrigerated room with sliding glass doors under the label "The Grass Room" included eight rows of containers of different consumable greens to highlight the focus on sustainability. The lower floors also included cooking schools with special courses on cake decoration and sandwich making. While this mall showcases aspirational luxury, as Abélès notes in his recent ethnography of luxury brands, such spaces feature what may be unobtainable for most as a paradoxical means of shaping the present through priceless items of value and lifestyle (2018). While other shopping malls and department stores may include hypermarkets for everyday goods and desires, the food halls at ground level or in the basement of major department stores contain incongruous mixtures of abundance and promotional wellness.

In the second part of this chapter, we turn to notions of wellbeing and how this ideal has shifted from longevity to practices of everyday life, especially consumption.

The pleasures of wellbeing: from longevity to living

In early Han Chinese culture (206 BC–220 AD), the notion of longevity (*shou* 寿) was considered to be a blessing together with prosperity and happiness. The written character can be found in multiple contexts and objects such as paintings, architecture, furniture, textiles, jewelry, or ceramics. While the notion of longevity continues to be held as an iconic ideal of the good life, contemporary notions of life worth and wellbeing are more often animated by the notion of life itself or living (*shenghuo* 生活) which connotes everyday life or existence. Furthermore, by viewing spaces whereby ordinary persons – students, white-collar workers, factory workers, migrant workers, or elderly – negotiate daily living, it is possible to consider conditions that give texture to meanings of quality of life.

Chinese medicinal foodways and Daoist notions of food as energetic relationships between people and environment offer longstanding awareness of the continuum between bodies, diet, and wellbeing. The preservation of health and extension of life, particularly for elites, was a common goal of many practitioners for their clientele. Healing foods, foods that can be eaten raw or cooked in combination with other items, were a critical component of maintaining wellbeing. In this sense, the "doctoring" of foods whether with spices or herbs was a basic form of preventative medicine that all traditional systems of healing shared. The preparation of medicinal dishes may involve a process of cooking or distilling to attain the healing properties of the herbs or spices. Food therapy, known as *shi liao* in Mandarin, has a long history in Chinese medicine. Eating each meal and specific food items with an intent to maintain health, promote vitality, or alleviate illness is the central principle of food therapy and can be an integral part of daily life. The practice is based on an extensive classification of foods in specific food groups, tastes, and characteristics. Following these categories, food therapy also entails the preparation of foods with medicinal herbs or spices that become medicinal dishes. The practice offers a way to conceptualize food and medicine as a continuum rather than as separate entities. This knowledge continues most extensively in contemporary Cantonese foodways which many Chinese scholars, medical practitioners, and consumers note for their adherence to the balance of flavors, tastes, and medicinal healing principles that extend back to the *Huangdi Neijing Suwen* (Yellow Emperor's Canon of Internal Medicine). The consumption of nourishing soups and rice porridge or congee (*jook* in Cantonese) is a prime example of Chinese food therapy that continues in the Cantonese tradition.

The concept of bu (补) in Chinese medicine refers to the ability of substances to replenish and tonify the body. The *Suwen* corpus includes this method, as part of eight total strategies, to address any deficiencies in the qi, blood, yin, yang, or organs. Herbal prescriptions and supplements may be formulated depending upon the needs of the patient. Foods are also categorized according to yin and yang properties as well as the ability to allow bodily functions to recover and strengthen the body overall. Perhaps the most famous formulary for the aid of tonifying the middle and raising one's qi or energy is *Bu Zhong Yi Qi Tang*, a prescription developed in 1247 by a famous physician Li Dongyuan in his treatise *Nei Wai Shang Bian Huo Lun* (Clarifying Doubts about Injury from Internal and External Causes). Today this herbal remedy continues to be prescribed and is readily available in most pharmacies as over-the-counter medicine as well as sold online.

The transformation of patients and citizens into consumers which was prevalent during the early 20th century (Cochran, 1999, 2006) resumed during the late 20th century when Big Pharma began to infuse local markets and transform daily life. The 1990s in mainland China has been deemed by many participants in the pharmaceutical industry, or Big Pharma, as the gold rush era. With the opening of the China market to multinational firms as well as local pharmaceutical firms, new meanings of the good life were promoted through consumption of medicinal products and beauty aids. The growth of this industry was facilitated with ubiquitous street pharmacies that made over-the-counter drugs readily available. The promotion of wellbeing and use of medical technologies animated much of everyday consumption in China's public spaces. Airports, rail stations, subway stations, street pharmacies, hospitals, hotel lobbies, department stores, supermarkets, and small vendors all sold medicinal and health goods often with posters and elaborate displays.

Prior to meeting with long-term colleagues during summer 2017, I strolled into a well-known hotel and former bank in the center of Shanghai along Nanjing Road. Once the tallest building in the city during the 1930s, the art deco building looked onto what used to be a race course and what is now People's Park. While waiting I toured the Chinese medicinal store inside the hotel lobby. The quiet museum-like space had special stage lighting, customized stands, and window cases which displayed numerous forms of expensive Chinese medicines. Rare forms of ginseng resembling anthropomorphic figures were encased on red velvet and framed on the wall while large porcelain bowls containing caterpillar fungus and other materia medica were placed in standalone pedestals.

Care for family members, especially for elderly parents, often entails offering a range of special foods, medicines, and supplements. Mrs Yang was a widow in her 80s when I regularly visited her family in Shanghai during the 1990s. While most of her adult children had moved into their own homes, one continued to live with her so that she wasn't alone. Multiple visitors including friends, neighbors, and grandchildren came to visit on a regular basis. Though bed-ridden, she would arrange to sit at a small table by the window for meals and nap in a lounge chair nearby. In her room was a dresser table with a surface that was completely covered with bottles of prescription drugs for her diabetes and heart condition along with vitamin supplements, tinctures, lotions, tubes, and other medications that were not marked. During one evening visit, she pointed to the table and remarked, "That's my show case you see. My children bring me the latest vitamins or medicinal goods whenever they come visit once a week." When I followed up with a query of what strategies her children and family members used to ensure the authenticity of medicines she quickly replied, "You have to verify where your medicine comes from. My children purchase my medication only from the hospital pharmacy. You carefully look at the packaging, label, and seal to make sure the drug is authentic." Mrs Yang's thoughtful remarks were echoed by many other seniors whom I had come to know over the years. Chinese consumers have emerged in the 21st century as citizens concerned with ethics, care, and governance. Familial and social practices of consumption shape contemporary notions of care and the valuation of everyday life.

Conclusion

Practices of dietary therapy and medicinal foodways continue in 21st-century China even as new forms of medicines and supplements have become widely available. While it may be easy to take a vitamin or other supplements, the pleasures of eating one's medicine offer many possibilities for selective practices of daily care and preventative medicine. Consumers may choose to eat local foods in season, have special dishes prepared with ingredients that are restorative, or take tonics in soup form. Perhaps a more significant element of these practices is that eating one's medicine retains social forms of intergenerational engagements and care. While the cultural ideal of longevity is quickly becoming a lived reality and norm for the growing senior population in China, the pleasures of daily life such as food facilitate forms of wellbeing that may not be available in a pill bottle or hospital care.

References

Abélès, M. 2018. *Un Ethnologue au pays du luxe*. Paris: Odile Jacob.

Cochran, S. 1999. *Inventing Nanjing Road: Commercial Culture in Shanghai, 1900–1945*. Ithaca, NY: Cornell University Press.

Cochran, S. 2006. *Chinese Medicine Men: Consumer Culture in China and Southeast Asia*. Cambridge, MA: Harvard University Press.

Jing, J. ed. 2000. *Feeding China's Little Emporers*. Stanford, CA: Stanford University Press.
K11. (2018). *Brand Story*. Retrieved from: www.k11.com/corp/brand-story/
National Health Commission. (2016). *Healthy China 2030*. Retrieved from: http://en.nhfpc.gov.cn/HealthChina2030.html.
Smith, G.D. 2016. A fatter, healthier but more unequal world. *Lancet*, 387: 1348–1350.

6 The coffee-drinking experience

Contributions to pleasure, wellbeing, and consumer engagement

Danielle L. Eiseman

Climate change has become one of humanity's most pressing issues (Santos and Feygina, 2017; Stevenson and Peterson, 2015). The world will experience increasing temperatures, droughts, and extreme weather events such as hurricanes and flooding (IPCC, 2014). These changes in the global climate are predicted to lead to social unrest, increased poverty, economic shocks, and disruption of the global food supply (Santos and Feygina, 2017). Despite the mounting evidence of climate change and its impacts, a 2015 survey of the American public indicates that although 70 percent of Americans believe climate change is happening, only 52 percent think human activities cause climate change and only 38 percent think they will personally be harmed by the impacts of climate change (Howe et al., 2015). Thus, there is a significant disconnect between public perceptions about climate change and its current impacts.

There is a significant body of work on engaging the public with climate change, such as frames (Nisbet, 2010; Scannell and Gifford, 2013); attitudes (Carrington et al., 2010); beliefs and values (Stern, 2000); and identity (Cherrier, 2007); as well as promoting behavior change to reduce the impacts of human activities on the climate through normative messaging (Goldstein et al., 2008; Schultz et al., 2007); status motives (Griskevicius et al., 2010); informational campaigns (Peattie and Peattie, 2009); and identity projects (Cherrier, 2007). The extant literature indicates that among these approaches informational campaigns do not work (Peattie and Peattie, 2009); normative messaging does lead to some changes in behavior (White and Simpson, 2013); yet, social and cultural ideologies strongly connected to an individual's identity will hinder a person's attitudes toward accepting scientific information about climate change (Dunlap et al., 2016). Thus, there is a need for novel approaches to shifting public attitudes on the threats of climate change.

In this chapter, we seek to address the need for novel approaches to public engagement on climate change by examining the coffee-drinking experience as a potential marketing tool for increasing awareness. The chapter is a conceptual exploration of the experiential marketing approach to the coffee-drinking experience and wellbeing within the context of climate change. The chapter first defines the coffee-drinking experience. Next, the notion of third place is discussed, followed by perceptions of wellbeing in the American mind. Lastly, we discuss a conceptualization of applying experiential approaches to marketing pro-social behaviors to connect consumers with societal problems such as climate change.

The rise of the coffee-drinking experience

The coffee-drinking experience is considered to be either hedonic or utilitarian and is associated with both stimulation and sensory enjoyment (Labbe et al., 2015). It is further described as a "source of satisfaction through smell and taste" and elicits a variety of emotions (Labbe et al., 2015). We can link this experience to the act of savoring, which Bryant and Veroff (2007: 7) define as a "deliberate, conscious awareness of the pleasures of taste". This awareness of the pleasurable experience of savoring further includes touch, smell, vision, and hearing, all components that enhance and contribute to the pleasurable experience of consuming coffee. Therefore, the coffee experience may be defined as a conscious, multisensory, and emotive activity that invokes an overall feeling of satisfaction and wellbeing.

From coffee bean to third place

For those who drink coffee, the ritual of consuming coffee is described as forging "an emotional bridge" that reconnects them with fond memories (Richelieu and Korai, 2014). The coffee-consumption experience is a reflection of the consumer's core identity, who is often unable to imagine life without it (Quintão et al., 2017; Richelieu and Korai, 2014). Highlighting the future risks to this multisensory, emotional beverage could therefore threaten a person's identity. It could also break through the existing barriers to encourage people to take action on climate change, as it is a significant threat to future coffee production.

The majority of the global coffee supply is grown across 36 countries near the Equator (Bunn et al., 2015). The coffee plants take seven to ten years to reach their full production potential and are highly sensitive to changes in both temperature and rainfall (Bunn et al., 2015). This region along the Equator has already begun to feel the impacts of climate change, experiencing extremes in heat, precipitation, and drought, as well as an increase in pests and crop diseases (Jaramillo et al., 2011). These impacts, which are predicted to intensify in the next few decades, already threaten current coffee production, so much so that farmers are turning to other crops, such as cocoa, to maintain their livelihoods. It is predicted that within the next 30 years global coffee production will decrease by half, should the global climate continue to change (Bunn et al., 2015). This decrease in coffee production will lead to lower quantities, higher prices, and significantly threaten the emotional bond many people have with coffee and their identity. Given this threat, we question whether or not experiential marketing techniques could be used to increase climate change awareness, concern, and action among individuals when applied to the coffee-drinking experience. The coffee-drinking experience is chock-full of symbolic cultural meanings, as well as encompassing the aspect of third place.

Although coffee can be consumed alone, historically the coffee experience has primarily engendered symbolic social meanings. Considering the history of coffee and coffee consumption, the coffee experience – particularly in coffeehouses – has symbolized democratic debate. Coffeehouses enhanced the coffee experience by further activating a sense of engagement. They were known as a neutral ground for political debate, social change, and egalitarian ideals. This led to the eventual conceptualization of the coffeehouse as a third place.

The emergence of Seattle and the coffee culture built in-place attachments with coffee consumption (Lyons, 2005). Coffee culture, although rooted in the century-old practice of coffeehouses through the Middle East and then Europe, in itself became a commodity through the spread of the "Seattle coffeehouse experience." Howard Schultz, the former CEO of Starbucks, sought to bring the urban, premium coffeehouse experience to the masses (Lyons, 2005). The inviting décor and unique position of the brand allowed consumers to enjoy "landscapes of leisure" (Smith, 1996: 508), whereby consumers could see and be seen while enjoying a premium beverage.

The coffeehouse was first identified as a "third place" in 1997 by Ray Oldenburg. It is defined as a space between work and home and is thought to be a space where people can connect with each other, share ideas, and build friendships (Broadway et al., 2018). Third place is characterized by its neutral ground, in that it is not controlled by one or more hosts, and these spaces are inclusive to all people (Broadway et al., 2018). In the late 1600s, coffeehouses in the American colonies became a critical space for political, literary, and informational discourse. However, the coffeehouse as a third place has been slightly shifted due to the emergence of smartphones, laptops, and free wi-fi. Broadway et al. (2018) observe coffeehouse consumer behavior, indicating the space of the coffeehouse has transitioned into a space for people to be alone together. That said, the space of the coffeehouse has the potential to re-emerge as a space for the exchange of ideas through several points of contact. This includes messaging on coffee cups, art on the walls, and the presence of reading materials available for free use. It is further argued that social engagement could return to the coffeehouse upon the removal of wi-fi and the banning of laptops. Broadway et al. (2018) report that many coffeehouses are eliminating free wi-fi to promote conversation and engagement among customers.

From a branding perspective, a coffeehouse chain such as Starbucks creates a cultural space where consumers are encouraged to create a social identity, experience, and meaning through consumption (Bookman, 2014), provided the retail space is congruent with the patron's self-image (Sirgy et al., 2000). For example, a small, independent coffeeshop that promotes discussion of social issues may not appeal to the standard Starbucks consumer. Thus, approaching the coffee-drinking experience as an engagement tool for polarized topics such as climate change must consider potential conflicts of patron self-image and the retail environment. If coffeehouses maintain the historical roots as a neutral territory, there may be more significant potential to use that space combined with the coffee experience as an engagement tool for discussion and debate on complex or politicized topics. It is from this perspective that the coffeehouse has the potential to challenge political ideologies, such as those surrounding the debate on climate change, its causes, and need for individual action. The place between home and work is where different identities are activated and others are downplayed. It could also mean political identity is not activated in this space.

The symbolic consumption of coffee and pleasure

In its earliest days of consumption, coffee served as a stimulant, enabling hunters to survive for days, unleashing untapped energy and alleviating hunger (Topik, 2009). The stimulating bean further functioned as a pleasurable gift to be served to the god Waqa (Topik, 2009). Over time and through the spread of the international spice trade in the 14th and 15th centuries, coffee served as a valuable commodity to trade – it offered income and livelihood. As it spread from Africa to the Middle East, it led to the creation of the coffeehouse, where consumers would sip the energizing liquid and discuss politics and other forbidden topics. (For a full review of the history of coffee consumption, see Lyons (2005) and Topik (2009)). As coffee made its way to Europe through trade, war, and diplomatic endeavors, consumption of coffee symbolized luxury, prestige, and exotic pursuits, as Dutch traders brought it over from Turkey (Lyons, 2005; Topik, 2009). The production side has a much more nefarious symbolism, tied to neocolonialism, slavery, and wholesale conglomerates (Lyons, 2005).

Modern-day coffee consumption takes on a symbolic meaning centered around stimulation, sensation, and socialization. Coffee, once perceived as an essential piece of United States national security for the wartime effort, is functionally stimulating for specific groups. Labbe et al. (2015) examined the levels of emotion, pleasantness, and perceptions of two different types of coffee drinkers: those who drink it for the stimulating effects and those who drink it for a pleasurable experience. They found that even people who drink coffee purely for its functionality still experienced high levels of arousal and enjoyment from drinking coffee, even though they stated they are motivated purely by the functionality of coffee. These findings indicate that coffee, although it may be perceived as a functional good, still gives people positive emotions and perceptions about the coffee-drinking experience.

The positive emotions associated with the coffee-drinking experience extend to overall wellbeing. The relationship we have with coffee is consistent with the relationship described by Block et al. (2011) regarding food and wellbeing. Thus, the pleasurable, emotive, and social components of drinking coffee extend to an individual's overall sense of wellbeing. The framework proposed by Block et al. (2011) on food and wellbeing de-emphasizes the relationship between food and nutrients or calories. The coffee experience is approached in the same manner: there is less emphasis on health benefits with coffee, except for the potential impacts of caffeine, and greater focus on the symbolic, multisensory experience of coffee. Beyond the aspects of wellbeing, coffee consumption taken to higher levels symbolizes identity, but also the type of coffee an individual chooses to consume exemplifies a certain level of taste, aspiration, and social class (McDonnell, 2016).

Taken to the extreme, in their exploration of coffee connoisseurs, Quintão et al. (2017) introduce the taste transformation ritual, by which consumers are transformed into connoisseurs through consumption ritual. It is through rituals associated with consumption that culture and the symbolic meanings associated with consumption are understood. Coffee consumption is ubiquitous with starting the day. The ritual ranges from a simple instant cup, the slow process of a French press or stovetop percolator, the morning stop at Starbucks, or the high-tech offerings of Keurig or Nespresso machines that convert tiny sealed pods into variations of desirable coffee drinks at the push of a button. Coffee is a necessity for most and an exotic hobby for some (Labbe et al., 2015; Quintão et al., 2017).

The American "coffee break" evokes a sense of leisure, relaxation, and the increasingly important concept of self-care. This aspect of wellbeing extends to the digital realm, where individuals share stylized images of coffee drinks on social media, such as Instagram. Thus, the multisensory coffee-drinking experience extends to the digital self, where an individual can share his or her moment of wellbeing with millions of strangers, further enhancing the desire to consume (Kozinets et al., 2016). As individuals increasingly connect through images on social media sites, so can a sense of wellbeing increase, provided a person's image receives a significant amount of "likes." Visiting unique and local coffeehouses around the world is a way to further feed into the subjective sense of wellbeing, where individuals compare themselves to peers.

Fantasies, feelings, fun, and coffee

Although food and water are necessary for survival, the relationship people have with food is more than purely functional. The preparation and consumption of food are symbolic, emotional, full of fantasy, and enhance our overall wellbeing. Belk et al. (1989) identify eating as a sacred experience, well beyond the simple function of restoring energy and nutrients the body needs. Meals are symbolic of family, holidays, tradition, and culture, as well as nostalgia. Wallendorf and Arnould (1991: 13) extend this work by examining the rituals around Thanksgiving in the United States. Consumption of food, in their analysis, is "an active force in the construction of culture." Construction of culture in this manner is further enhanced with the rituals around presenting and displaying food and food experiences on social media, extending perceptions of wellbeing and consumption experiences to the digital realm.

Digital transformations of pleasurable food experiences

This emotional attachment to food, as demonstrated through the internet, is akin to a star athlete on steroids. Our love of food is exemplified among millions of images on Instagram. Consumers search for the most Instagrammable foods, and producers oblige with colorful foods such as rainbow bagels, unicorn frappuccinos, and smoothie bowls. These conspicuous displays of exotic, colorful, or healthful foods further enhance the American perception of wellbeing, which is connected to one's ability to afford to consume (De Choudhury et al., 2016; Destin et al., 2012; Guven and Sørensen, 2011). Consuming food, or at least posting images of food, allows people to boast about their taste, social standing, health, and overall wellbeing.

Food, whether served to friends or shared on social media, is often representative of an individual's social positioning or aspiration of a higher social position. Kozinets et al. (2017) delve into the digital fantasies of consumption, including those that elevate images of food to porn-star status. Technology and social media facilitate the desire to consume. McDonnell (2016) emphasizes this rich relationship in her exploration of food porn. Images of food evoke a sense of voyeurism and fantasy. These works, however, exemplify extreme cases of our relationship with food, suggestive of the intense emotional ties we have with food and the experience of eating. Schmitt (1999) describes consumer experiences to be filled with sensory, emotional, cognitive, behavioral, and relational values, which he argues replace functional values.

American perceptions of wellbeing

The relaxing, nostalgic, and pleasurable aspects of drinking coffee are thought to enhance an individual's sense of wellbeing. The characteristics of the experience are consistent with the holistic framework for food and wellbeing as defined by Block et al. (2011), which includes health. The extant literature defines wellbeing as a multidimensional assessment of people's lives, typically associated with success, health, and happiness (Ares et al., 2014). Notions of wellbeing, and thus happiness, from the economic perspective are derived from activities such as consumption that result in feelings of satisfaction (Guven and Sørensen, 2011). In their exploration of wellbeing in the United States, Guven and Sørensen (2011) find the American perception of wellbeing has less to do with overall health and happiness and is linked to subjective social status, or overall life satisfaction relative to peers.

Americans derive feelings of happiness from their ability to consume. However, it hinges upon their ability to consume more than their neighbor (Guven and Sørensen, 2011). Goods that increase the perception of status have a higher utility compared to other goods because status is more valuable to individuals than other types of utility and therefore leads to greater feelings of happiness (Heffetz, 2011). This sense of wellbeing, in the American context, is highly complex. For example, Destin et al. (2012) found high school students that perceived themselves to be of higher status among their peers had a much more positive sense of wellbeing (Destin et al., 2012). An individual's sense of subjective social status affects mood, perceived ability, and motivation to undertake specific actions, such as pursuing a healthier lifestyle.

Recent work, however, has explored the connection between food, positive emotions, and subjective wellbeing (Ares et al., 2014). Although this work was carried out in Uruguay, the study found emotions were strongly linked to subjective wellbeing, and food wellbeing was strongly associated with health and quality of life (Ares et al., 2014). Later work by Ares et al. (2015) reinforces this perception across five countries – Brazil, France, Portugal, Spain, and Uruguay – however, they did find some differences in overall perceptions of wellbeing. Block et al. (2011: 5) provide the argument and framework for "food as wellbeing." This conceptualization on the relationship between food and overall wellbeing consists of the emotional, social, psychological, and physical relationship individuals and societies have with food, or in the case of this chapter, coffee.

Food wellbeing overall is at risk due to changes in the global climate. These changes include increasing temperatures, drought, intensive rainfall events, and invasive pests or weeds (Myers et al., 2017). Climate change is not only resulting in reduced crop yields both in the United States and abroad, but food prices are expected to rise anywhere between 3 and 84 percent by 2050 (Goldenberg, 2014). Furthermore, staple food items most individuals are familiar with and have significant emotive bonds with may no longer be available or may be too costly for the average consumer to purchase. Lastly, recent evidence has shown that due to a high concentration of carbon dioxide in the air, the nutritional value of staple crops such as rice and wheat is decreasing (Ebi and Ziska, 2018). Moreover, for those individuals that rely on their morning cup of coffee, global production is expected to decrease by 50 percent in the next 30 years. As most Americans struggle with understanding or accepting the causes of climate change, even more fail to understand when and how it will impact them (Leiserowitz et al., 2015). Tim Gore, the head of food policy and climate change for Oxfam, stated: "The main way that most people will experience climate change is through the impact on food: the food they eat, the price they pay for it, and the availability and choice that they have" (Goldenberg, 2014). Thus, there is a critical need to engage consumers on the causes and risks associated with climate change in a way that connects with them beyond traditional means.

Experiential and social marketing in the food sector

Experiential marketing engenders a multisensory approach to communications and has had a significant role in enhancing retail environments and building brand loyalty. Starbucks has become a global leader in developing the American coffee market and has transformed gourmet coffee into a typical consumer good. By developing their stores around the consumer experience, Starbucks has commodified the "third place" by providing a servicescape for consumers that facilitates hedonic experiences and social interactions (Thompson and Arsel, 2004). Starbucks continues to push the envelope forward on the coffee experience by developing higher-end coffee experiences as a way of attracting coffee connoisseurs who have previously rejected Starbucks for unique coffee experiences (Rostan, 2017; Sears, 2016).

According to Thompson and Arsel (2004), critical qualities a coffeeshop must possess are to not only deliver a quality coffee-drinking experience but also exude the essence of third place. Coffeehouses that facilitate pleasurable experiences, social interaction, and identity transformations:

> include prominent displays of visual art; background music that can be classified as either sophisticated (in the high culture sense), hip, or in some way countercultural, but certainly not Top 40 mainstream; and a hedonically rich menu featuring oversized gourmet muffins, oversized cookies, focaccias, bagels, and epicurean sandwiches. The interior decor should convey a sense of warmth coupled with a distinctive aesthetic flair.
>
> (Thompson and Arsel, 2004: 633)

The pleasurable coffee-drinking experience in this instance relies on more than just the company one keeps; it is contingent upon an atmosphere that facilitates cultural exchanges that engage with multiple senses, such as thinking, feeling, touching, seeing, and smelling. Consumption activities, especially those driven by hedonic motivations, enhance the sense of self, build confidence, and thus contribute to an overall sense of wellbeing (Richelieu and Korai, 2014; Sirgy et al., 2000). This perspective, however, has had very little application to social marketing practices, which are typically used to encourage pro-social activities that enhance individual and societal wellbeing (Zainuddin, 2013).

Social marketing applies traditional marketing methods to pro-social behaviors, or behaviors thought to have positive effects on the health and safety of a population (Andreasen, 1995). This type of marketing is often used to encourage pro-social behaviors such as vaccinations, wearing seatbelts, and regular doctor visits, as well as discourage antisocial behaviors such as smoking, driving while intoxicated, or littering. In the arena of climate change, social marketing has been used to encourage a variety of pro-environmental behaviors, or behaviors that minimize the negative impact we have on the global environment. Peattie and Peattie (2009) argue that since marketing is long steeped in the tradition of encouraging consumption, promoting reduced consumption in favor of protecting the environment would require an alternative approach, such as techniques based in social marketing.

Peattie and Peattie (2009) rework the traditional 4Ps (promotion, place, price, and product) principles of marketing to establish a framework for marketing-reduced consumption in the name of sustainability. In place of products, the social marketer supplies a proposition or behaviors to be adopted and maintained over time. The behavior, in the context of pro-environmental behavior, could range from reducing energy consumption, buying ethically produced clothing, or recycling. Next, Peattie and Peattie (2009) substitute accessibility for place, citing the example of the TravelSmart campaign in Victoria, Australia. The desired behavior was to encourage more people to cycle to work in place of driving. To effectively encourage this, individuals who had expressed interest in cycling received information on routes, maintenance, and bike parking. The framework replaces price with the cost of involvement in adopting the behavior, such as time, and social communication substitutes promotion. Although Peattie and Peattie (2009) provide examples of successful social marketing campaigns in the context of reduced consumption, the complexity associated with climate change, particularly in the United States where it has become highly politicized, could benefit from the methods employed in experiential marketing.

Experiential marketing enhances the connection a consumer has with a brand through emotions and pleasurable experiences. Consumer satisfaction during these experiences is determined by consumer return on investment, escapism, service excellence, and aesthetics (Lee et al., 2017). Applying these elements to social marketing, particularly in the context of the coffee-drinking experience, could enhance connections consumers have not only to overall wellbeing but the environment and climate change. Zainuddin (2013) examines the application of experiential techniques in the social marketing of preventative health behaviors and finds that individuals gain better value and satisfaction and therefore are more likely to maintain the behavior. Zainuddin further argues that adopting an experiential approach enables marketers to understand the value derived from socially desirable behaviors more fully. In the instance of health screenings examined by Zainuddin, the value of the experience is established both functionally and emotionally. The service provides a functional value of early detection of life-threatening diseases, and emotional value is derived from the peace of mind due to screening for early detection of cancer. The experiential approach to social marketing has yet to be explored within the context of pro-environmental behavior change with food as the tool or approach for messaging.

Given the strong emotive, multisensory aspect of the coffee-drinking experience, there is significant potential to apply climate change information and encourage climate action among Americans. The pleasure, satisfaction, and sense of wellbeing throughout the experience could enhance a person's openness to accepting information he or she may typically be opposed to accepting in other contexts. This is especially pertinent to the coffeehouse, which creates a sense of third place and neutral ground for discussing ideas.

Contribution to consumer wellbeing and food literature

The coffee-drinking experience has yet to be examined in the wellbeing and food marketing literature. This chapter explores the coffee-drinking experience within the context of consumer wellbeing and food as a potential method for engaging consumers on climate change. Climate change poses a threat to food security and wellbeing, thereby threatening future opportunities for pleasurable experiences, such as drinking coffee. Americans do not perceive themselves to be at risk to climate change; however, by engaging them through the coffee-drinking experience, there is potential to change these perceptions, more so than through traditional social marketing methods.

The coffee-drinking experience enhances consumer wellbeing as a result of the multisensory, emotional, pleasurable, and social aspects of consuming coffee. As consumers, our taste in foods, brands, or uniqueness of coffees further enhances our sense of wellbeing by maintaining our core identity and signaling to others our place in society (Quintão et al., 2017; Tucker, 2011). The ability to choose specific food items or to achieve the level of coffee connoisseur increases life satisfaction and sense of wellbeing. The demonstration of taste is particularly relevant to the American context, where subjective wellbeing and life satisfaction are often derived from the ability to consume. Despite the focus in the United States on the ability to consume, the literature on subjective wellbeing has yet to examine the American coffee-drinking experience within the framework of food wellbeing.

There is also the physical process of tasting and drinking coffee, which enhances the emotional connection consumers have to coffee, as well as enhancing feelings of wellbeing. Bryant and Veroff (2007) discuss savoring as a conscious, pleasurable activity resulting in positive emotions. The positive emotions derived from such a pleasurable activity enhance a person's sense of wellbeing with an overall good feeling about life. Coffee has been shown to be a pleasurable experience and should be examined further in the wellbeing and food marketing literature (Bhumiratana et al., 2014; Labbe et al., 2015).

Within the food marketing literature, there has been an emphasis on nutritional value and food labeling (Van Loo et al., 2015). The consumer research literature has examined the sacred experiences associated with preparing and sharing food (Wallendorf and Arnould, 1991). The emotional connection to food further enhances feelings of wellbeing and our quality of life (Ares et al., 2014). The nutritional value of coffee is often debated in the medical literature, with little to no conclusion on how consumption impacts overall health (Tucker, 2011). Coffee has a complex composition, which changes through the process of roasting and brewing, making it difficult to ascertain the specific impacts it has on the body. Despite the uncertainty with regard to health, however, the coffee experience enhances consumer wellbeing through the pleasure of consuming the beverage, the social interactions associated with it, and the emotional response it induces.

Conclusions

People use consumption to reconcile identity conflicts (Ahuvia, 2005), develop a collective identity (Cherrier, 2007), and create and transmit culture (McCracken, 1986). Coffee, although commoditized and widely consumed, encompasses this unique cornerstone of consumer culture, whereby the multisensory experience elicits emotive responses. Although experiential marketing has only recently been examined as a social marketing tool, it has yet to be explored as a tool for engagement on the complex issue of climate change. This chapter introduced the notion that the coffee-drinking experience could be an effective method for engaging consumers with the impacts and potential actions to mitigate climate change. The multisensory experience of coffee drinking is a pleasant one that evokes enjoyment. Furthermore, the coffeehouse is a neutral third place with a rich history of encouraging social engagement and thought-provoking discussions. It is because of these characteristics that the coffee-drinking experience may break down barriers to raising awareness, concern, and action among the politically divided American public on the issue of climate change.

While food, in general, provides the perfect example of consumer experience, coffee, in particular, provides a unique example for experiential marketers, especially within the context of climate change. Coffee and our love for it may connect the consumer with broader social issues, typically promoted through social marketing techniques. Messaging around climate change impacts and action combined with the coffee-drinking experience – whether the messaging is in the store, on the bag, or on the cup – may increase awareness. No matter how a person takes his or her coffee – black, with foamed milk, sweet, or strong – coffee has a significant place in the heart of consumers all over the world. This multisensory experience incorporates aroma, touch, sound, and taste, activating memories, waking the mind, and engaging the consumer in multiple ways.

References

Ahuvia, A.C. (2005). Beyond the extended self: Loved objects and consumers' identity narratives. *Journal of Consumer Research*, 32(1), 171–184. Retrieved from: www.journals.uchicago.edu/doi/abs/10.1086/429607

Andreasen, A.R. (1995). *Marketing Social Change: Changing Behavior to Promote Health, Social Development, and the Environment.* San Francisco, CA: Josey-Bass.

Ares, G., De Saldamando, L., Giménez, A., & Deliza, R. (2014). Food and wellbeing: Towards a consumer-based approach. *Appetite*, 74, 61–69.

Ares, G., De Saldamando, L., Giménez, A., Claret, A., Cunha, L.M., Guerrero, L. … Deliza, R. (2015). Consumers' associations with wellbeing in a food-related context: A cross-cultural study. *Food Quality and Preference*, 40, 304–315. Retrieved from: http://dx.doi.org/10.1016/j.foodqual.2014.06.001

Belk, R., Wallendorf, M., & Sherry, J.F. (1989). The sacred and the profane in consumer behavior: Theodicy on the Odyssey. *Journal of Consumer Research*, 16(1), 1–38. Retrieved from: www.journals.uchicago.edu/doi/abs/10.1086/209191

Bhumiratana, N., Adhikari, K., & Chambers, Edgar, IV. (2014). The development of an emotion lexicon for the coffee drinking experience. *Food Research International*, 61, 83–92.

Block, L.G., Grier, S.A., Childers, T.L., Davis, B., Ebert, J., Kumanyika, S. … van Ginkel Bieshaar, M. (2011). From nutrients to nurturance: A conceptual introduction to food wellbeing. *Journal of Public Policy and Marketing*, 30(1), 5–13. Retrieved from: http://journals.ama.org/doi/abs/10.1509/jppm.30.1.5

Bookman, S. (2014). Brand and urban life: Specialty coffee, consumers and co-creation of urban café sociality. *Space and Culture*, 17(1), 85–99.

Broadway, M., Legg, R., & Broadway, J. (2018). Coffeehouses and the art of social engagement: An analysis of Portland coffeehouses. *Geographical Review*, 108(3), 433–456. https://doi.org/10.1111/gere.12253

Bryant, F.B., & Veroff, J. (2007). *Savoring: A New Model of Positive Experience*. Mahwah, NJ: Lawrence Erlbaum Associates.

Bunn, C., Läderach, P., Ovalle Rivera, O., & Kirschke, D. (2015). A bitter cup: Climate change profile of global production of Arabica and Robusta coffee. *Climatic Change*, 129(1–2), 89–101. Retrieved from: https://doi.org/10.1007/s10584-014-1306-x

Carrington, M.J., Neville, B.A., & Whitwell, G.J. (2010). Why ethical consumers don't walk their talk: Towards a framework for understanding the gap between the ethical purchase intentions and actual buying behaviour of ethically minded consumers. *Journal of Business Ethics*, 97(1), 139–158. Retrieved from: https://doi.org/10.1007/s10551-010-0501-6

Cherrier, H. (2007). Ethical consumption practices: Co-production of self-expression and social recognition. *Journal of Consumer Behaviour*, 12(6), 321–335. Retrieved from: https://doi.org/10.1002/cb

De Choudhury, M., Sharma, S., & Kiciman, E. (2016). Characterizing dietary choices, nutrition, and language in food deserts via social media. *Proceedings of the 19th ACM Conference on Computer-Supported Cooperative Work and Social Computing: CSCW '16*, 1155–1168. Retrieved from: http://dl.acm.org/citation.cfm?doid=2818048.2819956

Destin, M., Richman, S., Varner, F., & Mandara, J. (2012). "Feeling" hierarchy: The pathway from subjective social status to achievement. *Journal of Adolescence*, 35(6), 1571–1579. Retrieved from: www.ncbi.nlm.nih.gov/pubmed/22796063

Dunlap, R.E., McCright, A.M., & Yarosh, J.H. (2016). The political divide on climate change: Partisan polarization widens in the US environment. *Science and Policy for Sustainable Development*, 58(5), 4–23. Retrieved from: https://doi.org/10.1080/00139157.2016.1208995

Ebi, K.L., & Ziska, L.H. (2018). Increases in atmospheric carbon dioxide: Anticipated negative effects on food quality. *PLOS Medicine*, 15(7), p.e1002600. Retrieved from: http://dx.plos.org/10.1371/journal.pmed.1002600

Goldenberg, S. (2014). Climate change "already affecting food supply" – UN. *Guardian*, March 30. Retrieved from: www.theguardian.com/environment/2014/mar/31/climate-change-food-supply-un

Goldstein, N.J., Cialdini, R.B., & Griskevicius, V. (2008). A room with a viewpoint: Using social norms to motivate environmental conservation in hotels. *Journal of Consumer Research*, 35(3), 472–482. Retrieved from: https://doi.org/10.1086/586910

Griskevicius, V., Tybur, J.M., & Van den Bergh, B. (2010). Going green to be seen: Status, reputation, and conspicuous conservation. *Journal of Personality and Social Psychology*, 98(3), 392–404. Retrieved from: https://doi.org/10.1037/a0017346

Guven, C., & Sørensen, B.E. (2011). Subjective wellbeing: Keeping up with the perception of the Joneses. *Social Indicators Research*, 109(3), 439–469. Retrieved from: www.springerlink.com/index/10.1007/s11205-011-9910-x

Heffetz, O. (2011). A test of conspicuous consumption: Visibility and income elasticities. *Review of Economics and Statistics*, 93(4), 1101–1117.

Howe, P.D., Mildenberger, M., Marlon, J.R., & Leiserowitz, A. (2015). Geographic variation in opinions on climate change at state and local scales in the USA. *Nature Climate Change*. Retrieved from: https://doi.org/10.1038/nclimate2583

IPCC. (2014). Climate change 2014: Synthesis report. Contribution of working groups I, II and III to the Fifth Assessment Report of the Intergovernmental Panel on Climate Change. Geneva: IPCC.

Jaramillo, J., Muchugu, E., Vega, F.E., Davis, A., Borgemeister, C., & Chabi-Olaye, A. (2011). Some like it hot: The influence and implications of climate change on coffee berry borer (Hypothenemus hampei) and coffee production in East Africa. *PLOS ONE* 6(9): e24528. doi:10.1371/journal.pone.0024528

Kozinets, R.V., Patterson, A., & Ashman, R. (2016). Networks of desire: How technology increases our passion to consume. *Journal of Consumer Research*, 43, 1–54. Retrieved from: https://doi.org/10.5061/dryad.7r153

Labbe, D., Ferrage, A., Rytz, A., Pace, J., & Martin, N. (2015). Pleasantness, emotions and perceptions induced by coffee beverage experience depend on the consumption motivation (hedonic or utilitarian). *Food Quality and Preference*, 44, 56–61. Retrieved from: https://doi.org/10.1016/j.foodqual.2015.03.017

Lee, W., Sung, H.K., Suh, E., & Zhao, J. (2017). The effects of festival attendees' experiential values and satisfaction on re-visit intention to the destination: The case of a food and wine festival. *International Journal of Contemporary Hospitality Management*, 29(3), 1005–1027.

Leiserowitz, A., Maibach, E., Roser-Renouf, C., Feinberg, G., & Rosenthal, S. (2015). *Climate Change in the American Mind: October 2015 (Yale Program on Climate Change Communication).* New Haven, CT: Yale University and George Mason University. Retrieved from: http://environment.yale.edu/climate-communication-OFF/files/Climate-Change-American-Mind-October-2015.pdf

Lyons, J. (2005). "Think Seattle, act globally": Specialty coffee, commodity biographies and the promotion of place. *Cultural Studies*, 19(1), 14–34.

McCracken, G. (1986). Culture and consumption: A theoretical account of the structure and movement of the cultural meaning of consumer goods. *Journal of Consumer Research*, 13(June), 71–85.

McDonnell, E.M. (2016). Food porn: The conspicuous consumption of food in the age of digital reproduction. *Food, Media and Contemporary Culture: The Edible Image.* Retrieved from: https://doi.org/10.1057/9781137463234_14

Myers, S.S., Smith, M.R., Guth, S., Golden, C.D., Vaitla, B., Mueller, N.D. … Huybers, P. (2017). Climate change and global food systems: Potential impacts on food security and undernutrition. *Annual Review of Public Health*, 38, 259–277.

Nisbet, M.C. (2010). Civic education about climate change: Opinion-leaders, communication infrastructure, and participatory culture. In *Climate Change Education Roundtable.* Washington, DC: National Academies.

Peattie, K., & Peattie, S. (2009). Social marketing: A pathway to consumption reduction? *Journal of Business Research*, 62(2), 260–268. Retrieved from: https://doi.org/10.1016/j.jbusres.2008.01.033

Quintão, R.T., Brito, E.P.Z., & Belk, R.W. (2017). The taste transformation ritual in the specialty coffee market. *Revista de Administração de Empresas*, 57(5), 483–494. Retrieved from: https://doi.org/10.1590/s0034-759020170506

Richelieu, A., & Korai, B. (2014). The consumption experience of Tim Hortons' coffee fans. *Qualitative Market Research: An International Journal*, 17(3), 192–208. Retrieved from: https://doi.org/10.1108/QMR-06-2012-0032

Rostan, T. (2017). Willy Wonka inspired Howard Schultz to put the world's biggest Starbucks in Chicago. *MarketWatch.* Retrieved from: www.marketwatch.com/story/willy-wonka-inspired-howard-schultz-to-put-worlds-biggest-starbucks-in-chicago-2017-04-26

Santos, J.M., & Feygina, I. (2017). Responding to climate change skepticism and the ideological divide. *Michigan Journal of Sustainability*, 5(1). Retrieved from: http://dx.doi.org/10.3998/mjs.12333712.0005.102

Scannell, L., & Gifford, R. (2013). Personally relevant climate change: The role of place attachment and local versus global message framing in engagement. *Environment and Behavior*, 45(1), 60–85. Retrieved from: https://doi.org/10.1177/0013916511421196

Schmitt, B. (1999). Experiential marketing. *Journal of Marketing Management, 15*(1–3), 53–67. Retrieved from: https://doi.org/10.1362/026725799784870496

Schultz, P.W., Nolan, J.M., Cialdini, R.B., Goldstein, N.J., & Griskevicius, V. (2007). The constructive, destructive, and reconstructive power of social norms. *Psychological Science*, 18(5), 429–434. Retrieved from: https://doi.org/10.1111/j.1467-9280.2007.01917.x

Sears, S.M. (2016). Taking a shot on Starbucks shares. *Barron's*. Retrieved from: www.barrons.com/articles/taking-a-shot-on-starbucks-shares-1481350220?link=mktw

Sirgy, M.J., Grewal, D., & Mangleburg, T. (2000). Retail environment, self-congruity, and retail patronage: An integrative model and a research agenda. *Journal of Business Research*, 49(2), 127–138.

Smith, M.D. (1996). The empire filters back: Consumption, production, and the politics of Starbucks Coffee. *Urban Geography*, 17(6), 502–524.

Stern, P. (2000). Toward a coherent theory of environmentally significant behavior. *Journal of Social Issues*, 56(3), 407–424.

Stevenson, K., & Peterson, N. (2015). Motivating action through fostering climate change: Hope and concern and avoiding despair among adolescents. *Sustainability*, 8(1), 6. Retrieved from: https://doi.org/10.3390/su8010006

Thompson, C.J., & Arsel, Z. (2004). The Starbucks brandscape and consumers' (anti-corporate) experiences of glocalization. *Journal of Consumer Research*, 31(3), 631–642. Retrieved from: https://doi.org/10.1086/425098

Topik, S. (2009). Coffee as a social drug. *Cultural Critique*, 71(1), 81–106. Retrieved from: https://doi.org/10.1353/cul.0.0027

Tucker, C. (2011). *Coffee Culture: Local Experiences, Global Connections*. New York: Routledge.

Van Loo, E.J., Caputo, V., Nayga, R.M., Seo, H.-S., Zhang, B., & Verbeke, W. (2015). Sustainability labels on coffee: Consumer preferences, willingness-to-pay and visual attention to attributes. *Ecological Economics*, 118, 215–225. Retrieved from: https://doi.org/10.1016/j.ecolecon.2015.07.011

Wallendorf, M., & Arnould, E. (1991). "We gather together": Consumption rituals of Thanksgiving day. *Journal of Consumer Research*, 18(June), 13–31.

White, K., & Simpson, B. (2013). When do (and don't) normative appeals influence sustainable consumer behaviours? *Journal of Marketing*, 77(March), 78–95.

Zainuddin, N. (2013). Examining the impact of experience on value in social marketing. *Journal of Social Marketing*, 3(3), 257–274. Retrieved from: https://doi.org/10.1108/JSOCM-04-2013-0024

7 The method of creative ethnography

Exploring food consumption and pleasurable experiences

Zafeirenia Brokalaki and Jeff B. Murray

Bhutan is one of the most beautiful places on earth, shrouded in mystery and magic. This last great Himalayan kingdom sits at the feet of the mighty mountains of Nepal. Kiba is a typical teenager from Bhutan, and she is slowly learning how to cook the traditional meals of her homeland. Today, she is hard at work over an open flame in a traditional Bhutan kitchen, stirring the chili and cheese, which will eventually become her favorite *ema datshi*, the national dish of Bhutan. Interestingly, no two *ema datshi* are the same; every cook has their own version, some being lighter or more watery, and others being richer and thicker – sticky with cheese. *Ema datshi* is a simple stew made from a variety of chilies and a special cheese from the yak called *datshi*. The chilies used in the *ema datshi* are really spicy, and this dish is served over a bed of red rice, another staple of the Bhutanese. Kiba struggles to read the yellowed pages from her great grandmother's recipe book. She yells to her mom on the porch, "Mom, how much *datshi*?" Her mother yells back, "Well, that depends. Do you want to make your great grandmother's, or your grandmother's, or my ema datshi?" Kiba, a little confused, yells, "My grandmother's!" (She loved her grandma.) "Okay then," her mother replies. "Lots of cheese! And add tomato and garlic!" Kiba continues with her task until dinner is ready.

As researchers, how can we begin to understand this interesting context? Nestled in the folds of the Himalayan mountain range, and landlocked between India and China, Bhutan has been isolated for centuries. Its cuisine is uninfluenced by cultural diffusion. The strongest roots come from Tibetan cuisine, which was gradually adapted according to local tastes and agriculture. But there is so much more here: an ancient recipe book passed down from generation to generation, a relationship between a daughter and her mother, love for her grandmother, and enculturation. How can the researcher bring the richness of this world to life? How can the smell of fresh chili peppers, the taste of cheese, a cherished book, and the love of family be described so that it becomes a sensory experience? If you are a consumer scholar, a marketing practitioner, or a social researcher interested in pleasurable consumption experiences, you might have already asked yourself the same questions in the past. How can we foster a creative approach to seeking and producing knowledge about social phenomena that trigger our curiosity? How can we use the multisensoriality of our experiences to deepen our knowledge about real social contexts? How can our imagination help us understand better consumers and their behavior?

In this chapter, we take a creative approach to research, and we explore ethnography as a method to interact, sense, perform, imagine, and live with others. Ethnography is one of the few interpretive methods that have been used so broadly in academia as well as in industry and popular culture. Its story is dramatic, involving a world war, the skyscrapers of our modern cities, the creative industries in London, and local wet markets. So let's start this adventure together. Welcome to *Ethnography in Three Acts*; the curtain is beginning to move, the lights are dimming …

Act 1: the rise of ethnography

The curtain opens and there is a single standing microphone in the center of the stage. A rather ruffled anthropologist wearing a wrinkled corduroy sports coat, loosened tie, jeans, unshaven with long messy hair emerges from the side. He walks slowly to the microphone, "Good evening ladies and gentlemen. I will be your narrator this evening. Let's begin with a story of how we might walk in the shoes of another … the story of ethnography." He continues, "Ethnography is the research, study, and writing about humans. The etymology of the term, which follows its Greek origin, indicates the practice of writing (graphy) about a nation/race/folk (ethnos), and, by extension, the writing about a foreign culture, or the 'other'" (Vidich and Lyman, 1994). The aim of ethnography, as a research method, is to study the inhabitants of a particular culture and depict local people's lives. The final outcome of an ethnographic experience is typically a detailed written description, analysis, and interpretation of an unfamiliar contemporary culture.

To conduct an ethnographic study, ethnographers – researchers who employ this method – work, eat, converse, play, sleep, listen to music, travel, laugh, pray, dance, share stories, drink, dream, or in other words, live together with those who want to understand. Clifford Geertz (1998), the renowned anthropologist, vibrantly claims that ethnographers engage in "deep hanging out" with people so as to seek knowledge about human life, action, and behavior. In contrast to a scientist in a laboratory, who examines human behavior in an isolated manner conducting experiments, a scholar in a library, who studies people through archives and books, or a researcher in an office, who investigates human responses through questionnaires from an exogenic standpoint, an ethnographer, as an interpretive researcher, becomes an active participant in the social milieu.

Ethnographers aim at capturing the human lived experience from the inside, immersed within the real social context. As a consequence, ethnography requires intensive, rigorous, and high-level involvement fieldwork, and is conceptualized as the method of data collection, analysis, interpretation, and presentation achieved through intimate familiarity with the lived experiences, viewpoints, and practices of individuals in natural settings (Clifford, 1988; Schwartzman, 1993).

The beginning of classical ethnography

How it all started? Ethnography originates, as a research method, from anthropology and, more specifically, cultural anthropology, a discipline based upon culture as an organizing concept. The fundamental commitment of ethnography is the search for prediscursive understandings, shared meanings, and patterns of behavior that are shaped through intersubjective relations, dynamic cultural systems, and processes of socialization (Schutz, 1964). Ethnography moves beyond the exploration of individual, conscious, and verbally expressed experiences to examine folkways: the hidden norms, the informal rules, the customs, values, and conventions of daily human life that guide cultural practice (Sumner, 2007 [1906]). This is why, instead of an artificial study environment, ethnographers choose to immerse themselves into ordinary settings and engage with participants' everyday contexts, interactions, and practices. Hence, ethnography can be found under numerous terms, including field research, naturalistic inquiry, interactionist research, Chicago School research, participant observation, participation, and observation study or physical research amongst other definitions (Prus, 1996).

Rosalie Wax's (1971) historical overview of ethnography implies that a detailed descriptive reporting of non-familiar cultures and people's lifestyles is as old as recorded human history. If we consider all those people who traveled to foreign, "exotic" lands to observe and study "the natives," such as the Greeks of the 5th century BC, the Romans of the 1st century, the Chinese of the 5th century, Catholic missionaries, European traders of the 13th century, as well as the 15th-century European colonization travelers, we can easily demonstrate that the essence of ethnography neither originates nor is limited to anthropological ventures (Prus, 1996; Vidich and Lyman, 1994). However, it was not before Lewis Henry Morgan (1818–81) explored the American Indian cultures that ethnography was first conducted as a research inquiry (Morgan, 1959; Prus, 1996). Thus, we can argue that ethnography, as a method, grew out of the curiosity of early explorers and administrators, who wished to understand the internally shared meanings of the colonized cultures of the "new" world (Asad, 1973; Prasad, 2005; Vidich and Lyman, 1994).

Undoubtedly, the most celebrated ethnographer is the Polish-born anthropologist Bronisław Kasper Malinowski (1884–1942). Malinowski was a researcher in the London School of Economics in the 1910s, using ethnographic documents and literature data to study Aboriginal Australia. This work earned him respect within the anthropological circles of the time and allowed him to continue his research conducting fieldwork. His dream was to travel to New Guinea, spend some time on the island, and achieve an intimate closeness with the local people. In 1914, Malinowski receives permission to travel to the new land and live with the Mailu, the people on the south coast of New Guinea. However, some months after his arrival in New Guinea, World War I breaks out, and Malinowski, who holds Austrian citizenship, is viewed now as an enemy of the British Commonwealth, and he is not allowed to return to

England. Desperate to return to his life and school in London, he asks for help from the Australian government, which decides to provide him with the permission and funds to continue his fieldwork in their territories instead. Malinowski embraces this opportunity and decides to stay in Australia and continue his research until the war ends. In the following years, he travels to the Trobriand Islands in Melanesia, where he learns how to live in a tent among the locals, speak their language, and cook from local recipes. He travels with the Trobriand Islanders, interacts with them, and becomes their friend (Malinowski, 1985, 1989 [1967]). Because of the unfortunate historical event of World War I, Malinowski is the first ethnographer who conducts ethnographic fieldwork for a prolonged period of time and maintains a sustained contact with an indigenous culture. This adventure changes him, inspires him to publish novel anthropological work, and establishes him as one of the most important anthropologists in Europe. Upon returning to England, he becomes a distinguished professor and is viewed as the founding father of social anthropology to this day. Since Malinowski, who has been lionized as the first ethnographer, more legendary anthropologists, such as A. R. Radcliffe-Brown, Franz Boas, Marcel Griaule, Claude Levi-Strauss, and Margaret Mead, have similarly sallied forth to faraway places, lived among the natives, partook of their wisdom, and returned the hero.

Malinowski's adventure, and these early explorations of pioneer ethnographers, have established the foundations of classical ethnography and have forged the key ideas of ethnographic research. First, the primary concern of ethnographers is to deepen our understanding about local sociocultural expectations of how others act and behave. As Geertz (1973) suggests, ethnography is based on the concept of *the webs of significance*. Meaning is the central principle of human life and culture is the web forming human meanings. Everyday experiences are constituted by layers of meanings, which are woven together in complex symbolic ways. Going back to the story of Kiba, what does it mean for her to add more cheese to the dish she is making? How does this action change her experience, her dish, and her relation to her family and community? Human action and meaning is shaped by the symbolisms attached to everyday routines, practices, and interactions of the local members of the community.

Second, meaning is shaped within particular cultural contexts. Everyday actions, events, and interactions are shaped by the context within which they unfold. Thus, ethnography is committed to understanding the context in which daily experiences take place and the wider social, cultural, political, economic spheres of life that influence cultural practices, interactions, and social actions (Bate, 1997; Wolcott, 1995).

A third significant dimension of ethnography is the need for deep cultural familiarity. As previously discussed, much of culture is prediscursive; thus, ethnography aspires to explore the prediscursive aspects of a particular culture through participation in social experiences, intense immersion in the cultural context, involvement in the flow of activity, and engagement with local practices (Grindstaff, 2002). In other words, ethnographers are expected to spend a significant amount of time with the subjects under study and develop strong familiarity, interacting and learning about their meanings, values, attitudes, beliefs, and practices. According to Malinowski (2014 [1922]: 25), doing ethnography means to "grasp the native's point of view, his relation to life, to realize his vision of the world," and to convey this experiential familiarity to readers. It is important to note here that the main advantage of ethnography is the researcher's ability of "being there" for an extended period of time (Bate, 1997). By immersing themselves in local cultural practices, rituals, and customs, and by developing and cultivating intimate relationships with the locals for a sustained period of time, researchers can understand, interpret, and convey meanings of the inhabitants in an authentic fashion (Golden-Biddle and Locke, 1993).

Most importantly, ethnography enables the researcher to develop an empathetic understanding of situated meanings that can be expressed to the reader. Ethnography is all about finding empathy; empathy is key to understanding the other, empathy fosters sensitivity to differences, empathy encourages depth of thinking about an unknown culture. Empathy makes us walk in the shoes of another and see through their eyes; it allows us to feel another's pain and pleasure, it supports compassion and cultivates care for the fellow man. Empathy makes us human (Howe, 2012; Watts, 2008). Also, ethnography is about thick description (Geertz, 1973). A good ethnographer offers an insightful descriptive narrative of the fieldwork, which incorporates observations, sensual analyses, reflections, and interactions in a comprehensive way for the reader. Thick descriptions can help the researcher to disentangle constellations of meaning, reveal layers of interest and unveil their interrelations.

Finally, the last key characteristic is the narrative dimension of ethnography (Geertz, 1973). Ethnographers are expected to collect, analyze, and present the data collected in an insightful, convincing, nuanced, and understandable manner. Through an ethnographic study, the researcher can bring the culture under examination to life for readers. By turning their lived experiences into written narratives, ethnographers can convey their familiarity with the locals' lives in a vivid and detailed textual way, and they can share their interpretations about the wider context in a coherent, truthful, and articulate fashion (Bate, 1997; Van Maanen, 1987).

How does ethnography work?

How do ethnographers work? What are their methodological procedures and what techniques do they employ to collect data? As Goffman (1958: 125) beautifully explains, ethnography means participating in people's daily lives and "subjecting yourself, your own body and your own personality, and your own social situation, to the set of contingencies that play upon a set of individuals, so that you can physically and ecologically penetrate their circle of response to their social situation, or their work situation, or their ethnic situation." The most popular fieldwork techniques for conducting classical ethnography are participation, observation, interviewing, photography, and archival study. These techniques enable the researcher to collect, reflect upon, interpret, and share informants' meaning-making processes, experiences, activities, emotions, practices, beliefs, and behaviors as well as social norms, cultural values, and community customs. The final ethnographic corpus of data usually comprises written and recorded field notes, photographs, transcribed interviews and interactions, analysis of socioeconomic, cultural, political, and physical contexts, archival and textual material.

The first step before you start an ethnographic exploration is to define the research problem, to familiarize yourself with the phenomenon under study, and to select the appropriate context for its investigation. Once you feel confident with your research objective, and you have specified your phenomenon and context, you may start the actual research. Usually, ethnography neither follows a logically sequential research process nor is conducted in distinct stages (Seale, 2004). On the contrary, ethnographic fieldwork is a constant process of living, interacting, and acting with people. However, different routes to ethnographic research may involve diverse forms of passive, or active, investigation. Passive investigation can occur before entering the field with the goal to collect secondary data. This can include the study of archival material, literature on the subject, media products such as feature stories, press interviews, articles and press releases, audio-visual records, online conversations, etc. It may also include some initial observations. Passive investigation can work as a second step to help the researcher refine the research questions, develop a conceptual orientation to the phenomenon, understand the broader sociocultural, economic, and political context of the study, formulate some sort of structure on which the research may progressively focus over its course, and identify some preliminary themes to be empirically examined later (Seale, 2004; Sherry, 2006).

As a third step, the researcher enters the field. Active investigation can be achieved through extensive fieldwork, deep immersion, participation, and engagement with locals' lived experiences. Active investigation can help the researcher to gain new, rich, and focused empirical and conceptual insights, become sensitive to local concerns, develop the preliminary themes already identified, seek theoretical relevance in mundane practices, and develop an emergent research design. Active investigation enables the researcher to come closer to the lived experiences of locals, participate in people's daily routines, witness how phenomena are experienced and constructed by individuals, listen to what informants say, watch how they interact with others, and take part in the performance of their everyday practices (Hammersley and Atkinson, 2007). Active investigation can also help the ethnographer identify people's patterns of behavior and those attributes, processes, operations, and procedures that shape human experiences, ideologies, attitudes, and aspects of their realities. Additionally, it enables researchers to interact with locals in a dynamic, verbal, and embodied way, it allows them to cultivate trust with different stakeholders, and it encourages them to establish ongoing and intimate relations with gatekeepers in order to gain access to key informants. The first active encounters and experiences in the field also help the researcher to identify a set of foreshadowed problems and gain a further understanding of the sociocultural, economic, and political life in the context being studied.

Different ethnographic processes might take place on a full-time or a part-time basis, covertly or overtly, depending on the researcher's intentions, goals, and strategies. Covert ethnography means that the researcher does not reveal their status and intentions as an ethnographer in the field, since this is not always feasible or productive. Overt fieldwork means that the researcher publicly proclaims their research commitments, and asks permission to interact in the field, turn their experiences and observations into research data, and write about events on site; the informants are aware of the presence, role, and objectives of the researcher (Hammersley and Atkinson, 1995).

There are also different levels of involvement ranging from complete participation to participant observation, to observant participation, and finally, to complete observation (Junker, 1960). Complete participation refers to processes when the researcher is fully immersed in the unknown culture. The ethnographer acts as a covert participant deeply involved in all different activities and experiences of the people under study, aiming at gaining insights and perspectives from locals in a naturally curious way. This is a stage when the ethnographer adopts a fully experiential style of fieldwork and participates constantly and intensively in the ongoing processes and events. Participant observation allows the ethnographer to participate in some events, observe, interact, and interview different stakeholders and community members in an explicit way. Observant participation refers to processes when the researcher's participation in the social activity is limited; the researcher maintains some distance from the informants and focuses mainly on observations. Complete observation entails no participation or interaction with the people under study but only observation of informants' experiences, practices, and relations. These different levels of involvement can work in a complementary fashion for the collection of primary data. The dynamic and often evolutionary course of ethnography can help the researcher gather new information, identify new problems, and look for new lines of enquiry (Schouten and McAlexander, 1995; Seale, 2004).

The fourth step is all about participating, observing, and taking notes. Once the researcher has entered the field and established a basic understanding, the focus is placed on participating, observing, documenting, and reflecting upon the shared experiences, events, and activities. Hence, this phase of data collection follows a more detailed and reflective writing-oriented mode. During this phase, the first encounters in the field can be further developed and enriched with a constant circulation of new engagements taking place through intense immersion in the daily rhythms and ordinary activities of the locals. This helps the ethnographer to facilitate familiarization and bonding with the subjects under study. Being an active participant, and positioning yourself consciously in the unfolding events, enables you to examine intuitively the unfamiliar culture and keep notes. Through close and long-term observation and participation in social events, the ethnographer can capture, document, and preserve insights, understandings, and interpretations about the human group life on site.

This participating-in-order-to-write fieldwork phase can take advantage of the interconnections between writing, participating, and observing. The researcher's aim is to inscribe detailed, context-sensitive, locally informed field notes with empathetic and intuitive reflections on the participants' stories (Emerson et al., 1995). Based on the supposition that no field researcher can be completely neutral, detached, and independent from contextual processes, you can embrace your involvement in the lives of the locals and get exposed to varying points of view while retaining a balanced, scholarly perspective to avoid overinvolvement or the "going native" phenomena (Tedlock, 1991; Vidich and Lyman, 1994). In this way, ongoing relations, fluid processes, and multiple perspectives of the social life examined can be revealed.

Field notes can take the form of personal, idiosyncratic diaries, describing encounters, experiences, observations, recollections, emotions, thoughts, and records of others' reactions. By using jottings, the researcher can take down details such as senses, tastes, smell, sounds, characteristics of the physical environment, impressions, key events and incidents, the flow of ongoing activity, feelings, verbal and non-verbal interactions, voice tones, people's physical characteristics, etc. In this way, private thoughts, backstage experiences, messy notes, comments, memories, quotes, photographs, videos and interview interactions, processes, reflections, interpretations, and emergent meanings produced through prolonged social interactions in the field can be documented and used to create a world on the page (Emerson et al., 1995). Notes can be taken overtly in real time, while social events are taking place, or privately after the events have taken place, to keep interactions uninterrupted. The first strategy allows the researcher to memorize, record, and write down expressions, subtle movements, and key content produced during the interaction. The second strategy enables the researcher to gain important information about sensitive matters that the informants might feel hesitant, afraid, or embarrassed to talk about when recorded (Emerson et al., 1995). Key words, phrases, and sentences about to-be-remembered observations can help the researcher interpret and analyze the data later. Also, photographs, videos, and sound memos with the use of notes can be very useful to recreate and bring the experiences to life (Hill, 1991). In other words, field notes and audio-visual material enable the researcher to revive the witnessed events, lived experiences, and natural occurring speech into extended entries and, ultimately, words on paper.

The fifth, and final, step would involve conducting ethnographic interviews. The objective of the ethnographic interview is to uncover and depict a variety of experiences in the field by letting locals speak in their own voices. Through interviews, informants can share opinions, beliefs, and feelings about local practices, behaviors, and ideologies that may lead to deeper insights into participants' life situations. Discussions in the field can expose the researcher to meanings, actions, interpretations, and lived experiences of the participants that might not be captured through observation and participation. They can also shape the researchers' initial thoughts, ideas, and questions, or intensify their curiosity about participants' lifeworlds.

Ethnographic interviews can range from impromptu, informal, and episodic discussions to strategic, formal, and prolonged conversations. Verbal encounters in the field may occur spontaneously, through casual, brief, opportunistic interactions with a range of participant types, or purposefully engaging key stakeholders and informants in deep and repeated-over-time conversations (Berry, 1989). Also, ethnographic interviews may take place in the form of structured, semi-structured, or unstructured meaning-cantered discussions. To select the appropriate interview participants, a range of sampling techniques can be used, such as random, snowball, or purposeful sampling including maximum variation, typical case, extreme case, critical case, expert or homogeneous sampling, and theory-based sampling amongst others (Miles and Huberman, 1984).

Ethnographic interviews can add depth and richness to the insights about participants' meaning-making processes, emotions, values, beliefs, and actions. However, ethnographers need to be careful before engaging in discussions with participants. The data produced through verbal interactions with informants can only be used if the researcher designs, distributes, and receives a signed, written consent form stating that the interviewees' responses can be employed for research purposes. Also, issues of confidentiality and anonymity need to be taken into consideration.

To conclude, classical ethnography is dedicated to pursuing local meanings of unfamiliar cultures through participation, observation, and interaction. To understand how participants create, shape, and express meanings, the ethnographer needs to pay attention to the participants' descriptions, stories, questions and answers, terms, greetings, typologies, senses, movements, and theories (Emerson et al., 1995). These interactions may reveal the participants' relationships, forms of expression, ways of understanding of events, activities, concerns, personal views, feelings, perceptions, behaviors, values, significant and special situations, evaluations, and social conditions. Embodied encounters and interviews can also help the investigator to identify and classify experiences through naturally occurring verbal and non-verbal interactions. Pursuing local meanings can help us explore multiple stories that may contribute to the comprehension of wider institutional and societal contexts.

These five steps can help you navigate through your ethnographic explorations. Although ethnographic research does not compartmentalize into distinct stages, the active work in the field can be realized in a processual fashion, as the one suggested above, giving a funnel structure to the ethnographic experience (Seale, 2004). How will you know when to end your primary research? Certain tasks, such as cultivating trust with gatekeepers, interacting with key informants, collecting data, interpreting stories from the field, and triangulating findings can be iterative and persistent throughout the ethnographic period with a constant movement between the library, the desk, and the field.

However, when you feel that you have been engaged with the locals for a prolonged period of time through tenacious participation, you might experience evidence of repetition in your observations and interactions. In other words, data collection can be concluded when you reach empirical redundancy and theoretical saturation (Glaser and Strauss, 1967). The narrator concludes, "Okay, now that you know what classical ethnography is, are you ready for some acting?" There is shuffling behind the narrator standing at the microphone; moving of furniture and a backdrop of the London skyline emerges from the ceiling. The narrator announces, "Ladies and gentlemen, I take you to the Royal Society of Arts, a lecture in London …"

Act 2: ethnography enters corporate food culture

Scene 1

A young scholar is finishing up a lecture at the Royal Society of Arts in London. The Royal Society for the Encouragement of Arts, Manufactures and Commerce is the perfect place for a lecture on contemporary ethnography given its commitment to finding practical solutions to social challenges and contributing to human progression and wellbeing. The event's host thanks the young woman for the lecture and asks the audience for questions, hoping to generate an engaging discussion. The first question comes from a rather skeptical-looking audience member in the back: "Professor, can you summarize for us again why ethnography as a method needs to change in a corporate context? Why not just use classical ethnography?" The speaker pauses for effect and begins to pace the front of the room, "Yes, of course, this is something I tried to emphasize during my lecture. As you recall, classical ethnography is based on the 1:1:1 ratio – one person, one culture, one year. But think about it, the challenges companies face need fast, creative solutions. We don't have a whole year, we have maybe six weeks." The speaker continues, "In addition, Malinowski did not have access to a whole team of ethnographers working with innovative technology, such as digital cameras, video, and visual data techniques to represent culture. This technology can be used to bring segments of consumers to life for decision makers."

Another audience member stands suddenly and blurts out, "But then how can you say that this is ethnography?" The speaker moves to the podium to focus, "Okay, let me ask you a question!" The audience begins to whisper reacting to the confrontation. The speaker waits for silence, "What is the definition of ethnography?" The person from the audience, now sitting, responds. "Well, you mentioned earlier that it is participation and observation." The speaker quickly responds, "Well, is there participation in corporate ethnography?" The questioner quietly knows where she is going, "Yes." "And is there observation?" "Yes." The speaker asks an additional question, "And what is the goal of ethnography?" The person from the audience answers, "Empathetic understanding." The speaker again asks, "Well, is there empathetic understanding?" The questioner from the audience is thinking, "Maybe, but it might be different, really. How do you know that you have achieved empathetic understanding?" The speaker could see the host beginning to walk to the front of the room. The lecture is about over, and she decides to conclude the discussion. "Think about it this way: When the early ethnographers were exploring new exotic lands and cultures around the world, they needed time – just learning the language itself took months, not to mention new rituals, customs, values, economic and symbolic systems, kinship networks, and so on. The tribes of consumers we study in the corporate world are familiar, they are not that different from you and I, and we have a whole team of experienced ethnographers working with innovative technology. This makes a difference. Finally, empathetic understanding is an ideal – not something one achieves. It is something that we strive for, something that is approximated. At the end of the day, this method helps us reach deep into culture. It helps us understand people, food experiences, and places. For classical ethnography, the goal is the understanding itself; and for contemporary ethnography the goal is problem solving in a practical context – but either way, it is a method designed to step into the role of the other, to walk in the shoes of someone different from ourselves." The host now walks to the front of the room, "I would like to thank the speaker, RSA for the lovely invitation, and all of you for the engaging discussion!" (Applause.)

Scene 2

A corporate boardroom high above the teeming energy of the streets of Shanghai. Wang Wei, a famous Chinese food retailer, is frustrated. He is making a passionate speech to his board of directors, clearly disturbed by recent events. The name Wang Wei means "great," and as a recent graduate of Harvard's MBA program, he is not used to failure. Wang Wei continues, "I am telling you! China is once again in the midst of an invasion, this time from the West! Maybe not with guns and tanks, but with something far more dangerous to our way of life, threatening our company, food culture, and economy!" The slow march of globalization has resulted in a set of circumstances where Wang Wei's company is losing financial standing to the powerful food retailers of the West. These retailers include Tesco from the United Kingdom, Carrefour from France, Germany's Metro Group, and Walmart from the United States. These food retailers are dialed in to the Asian market; they embrace sophisticated technology, big data, customer insights, and shopper marketing research. They have deep pockets, learn from mistakes, and embrace continual improvement – they don't compete, they dominate – and Wang Wei senses the peril. Just as it appears that Wang Wei is going to have a heart attack, his colleague and friend, an older gentleman with a grey beard of wisdom, begins to pacify the mood in the room, "Wang Wei, calm down, all is not lost. Let me ask you, what do we have that the other retailers don't?" Wang Wei responds, "I don't know, a bleak future?" (Laughter.) The colleague smiles, "No, not at all. Think about it. We are the only big food retailer in the group that is Chinese. What if we could integrate the Chinese character, the new emerging Chinese identity, and the Chinese food culture throughout our stores? Weave it into everything we do: our corporate identity, marketing and advertising, product development, store layout, category assortment, service offerings, community outreach, associate training, everything!" Wang Wei lights up, "Wow, yes, this just might work, but there is one problem. What is the new emerging Chinese character? This global Asian identity that is evolving with the new generation of consumers? How do we find it?" The wise colleague acknowledges the problem, "Yes, we need help. I know a small ethnographic marketing research firm in Australia called Ethno-Insights. Let me contact them to see if they can help." Wang Wei's demeanor begins to calm down. He walks to the window, scans the sea of skyscrapers below, and there is a glint of hope in his eyes.

Scene 3

A small pub in Sydney, Australia. The Ethno-Insights team is in fast discussion around their favorite wooden table and the beer is flowing. Ethan, the team leader, is struggling to get the attention of the group, "Everyone! Listen up! We have six weeks to complete a new food retail study in three phases. We need to get organized!" Amelia, the team videographer, notes with a smile, "We haven't been organized since you had us all do that stupid food study in New Zealand for the Kiwi Corner Dairy." (Laughter.) Ethan can't help but laugh, "Okay, fine, not the best project, but seriously gang, this study is important." The group begins to focus and Ethan explains, "These guys are good food retailers, really good. I visited them last week and they have some creative ideas. What they need from us is a description, visual presentation, and some short videos explaining the new emerging Chinese character. We have done these types of studies before and, folks, the money is good." (Now he has the team's attention.) Ethan begins, "Okay, I am open to ideas ..." Noah responds first, "How about we begin with something visual, maybe some storytelling?" Amelia adds. "Then maybe enter the field? Do some participation?" Olivia contributes, "How about giving the informants the cameras, and then we auto drive them through the pictures later?" Ethan looks encouraged, "Fantastic ideas! Let's meet early tomorrow morning in the office and finalize the project." Amelia again smiles, "Ethan-early or normal-person-early?" (Laughter.) Ethan returns, "See everyone around noon." After a couple of days of working out the details, the team travels to Shanghai to make their presentation. Ethan and Amelia present together: "Good afternoon, we would like to propose a contemporary ethnography with three distinct phases.

The first phase is called projective interviews. Here we will ask informants to create a photo diary capturing what it means to be Chinese and what Chinese food means to them. Then we will ask informants to select three pictures and write a short story about each picture. Finally, we will auto-drive consumers through the photographs, asking for interpretations and additional storytelling. The second phase involves fieldwork. First, we will arrange in-home interviews to better understand informants' food consumption. Second, we will accompany informants shopping food, participating, and making observations. Then third, we will make additional observations and conduct interviews in the food retail environment. The third phase involves creative videos. Here, we will give informants video cameras and ask them to capture contemporary versus traditional Chinese symbols and food experiences. Then we will view the videos with informants interviewing them for further interpretation. We will then combine the results of the three studies, develop themes, and use the themes to build a presentation and a video to help all of you better understand how the emerging Chinese character can be integrated throughout your corporate identity, company, and food products." For the first time since he returned to China, Wang Wei smiles.

Act 3: igniting the creative imagination for food research

The stage is quiet and empty. There is a long pause and the audience is wondering, "What will happen next?" The lights are on. Four executives from America walk onto the stage. We are still in Shanghai. The executives work for a large American food retailer in China. They seem confused. One of the four executives asks, "Why are consumers not buying seafood in our markets? What are we doing wrong?" His colleague responds, "Everything has been organized and arranged with the utmost care. The seafood has been carefully packaged, arranged on beds of ice, the smell of fish has been removed, and the floor has been sanitized." The third person comments, "I don't understand, in America this works, everything is in place, but no one is interested!" The fourth member of the group replies, "Maybe we should do some research? Let's visit popular local wet markets and take a look?" So the four colleagues take a trip to the culinary backstreets of one of the largest cities in the world.

Arriving at the wet market, the executives are enthralled – stocked with fresh seafood and live fish flopping on the beds of ice, knocking ice to the floor, which eventually melts giving the name "wet market." The freshest fish and fowl to be had, cut and cleaned right before you eyes – you won't find shrink-wrapped plastic, branded packaging, or expiration dates here. Not only is there fresh fish, they are shoulder to shoulder, jostling crowds of families, bikes, fish scales flying, and the noise of old-fashioned marketing. Here, the sounds and smells of the market, the pushing crowds, and passion for bartering create a feeling of freshness and health. As the executives continue to immerse themselves deeper in the culture of this food experience, they slowly discover, and begin to appreciate, a rare charm and authenticity that is completely lacking in their stores. One of the executives turns to his colleagues, "This is amazing, there is so much more here than the food itself; there is history, community, local neighborhoods, family, laughter, and spectacle." As they glide through the streets of Shanghai on their way home, they are busily taking notes in their journals. One of them turns to the others to conclude their experience, "Everything needs to be changed."

A young woman with purple hair begins to wander onto the stage, wearing large white earphones. She removes her earphones, walks towards the edge of the stage, and turns to you, the audience: "Our bodies, senses, and corporeal lived experiences can be a fascinating object of study as well as a valuable means to understand human experience. Although a significant corpus of interpretive research in social sciences explores, analyzes, and represents language, text, and verbal interaction, body-centered, sensual, and extra-discursive methods of inquiry can help us 'embody' our epistemologies about consumers' lived experiences. How do we experience a moment in space and time with all our senses? How can we use our body to reach a deeper understanding about a consumption experience? How can we communicate an embodied experience that is inexpressible in language?

Emergent creative ethnographic practices, whose significance has been emphasized in the last two decades, focuses on imaginative, sensory, and experimental ethnographic image and sound making, filmmaking, storytelling, moving, and performing. My aim is to offer some ideas about how the practice of ethnography could be experienced in a more creative, imaginative, and multisensory fashion, integrating observations, experiences, and stories of smells, tastes and touches, acoustics, sounds and music, colors, textures and sights, visuals, graphics and new media, spatial appreciations, movement and performances, cinematography, exhibitions and installations as expressive, relational, and communication forms.

Based on the premise that aesthesis, creativity, and imagination are human capabilities that can be found in every individual, characterizing our everyday lived experiences, our social relations, and our cultural formations, ethnography can be considered an appropriate terrain to exercise embodied, affective, sensorial, and performative practices for seeking and producing knowledge (Green and Hopwood, 2015; Katzman, 2015; Madison, 2005; Westmoreland, 2011). Humans share the universality of sensory capabilities; they are embodied, multisensory, emplaced beings, who make sense of the world around them through sensing, feeling, and bodily experiencing others and their environments (Pink, 2015; Porcello et al., 2010). Recent discussions on epistemology have raised questions about the privileged position of language, cognition, and textual representation of knowledge. The opposing argument challenges conventional ethnographic methods supporting that careful observation, verbal interactions, thorough descriptions, and cognitive linguistic processes can be extended, enriched, and strengthened through polysensory, experiential, and imaginative processes in the field. In other words, creative, embodied, and arts-based practices can help us study sonic and visual stimuli, voices, noises and silences, rhythms, movements and immobilities, haptics, tastes, and smells, which can be a precious source of knowledge. 'Something happens differently when your body must move and adjust to the rhythms, structures, rules, dangers, joys and secrets of a unique location. Ethnography is as much, or more, about bodily attention – performing in and against a circumscribed space – as it is about what is told to you in an interview' (Madison, 2006: 401). Additionally, embodied imaginations can expand the sensed, felt, and experienced by highlighting our dreams, expectations, memories, fears, desires, and fantasies and by recovering the unspoken, the absent, the invisible, the hidden, the forgotten, the taken for granted, the lost (Culhane, 2017; Mittermaier, 2011). Consequently, embodiment, creativity, and imagination can become the epistemological focus of research generating insights, feelings, emotions, and affects about the human experience contributing to empathetic understanding, self-awareness, and intersubjective knowledge.

Furthermore, embodied, creative, and imaginative ethnographic practices encourage participation, pluralism, and knowledge co-creation; the researcher and the participants can develop strong affective relationships, dialogue, and work together in the field to conceptualize, design, conduct, and disseminate knowledge that is produced collaboratively. Our suggestion is that aspiring ethnographers can build upon the foundations of classical ethnography, and possibly the modern implications of corporate ethnography, to use creative methods that may help them extend, enrich, and deepen their understandings about how humans experience, challenge, resist, experiment, transform, reimagine, reassemble, and reconstruct consumption practices, relations, contexts, and systems.

One creative way to enrich ethnographic observations and field notes is by using visual resources such as photographic collections, short videos, graphics, drawings, animation, collages, sketches, and paintings (Barry, 2008; Bateson and Mead, 1942; Causey, 2016; Hendrickson, 2008; Ingold, 2011; Sousanis, 2015; Taussig, 2011). These techniques can be used by the researcher to convey their own sensual experiences in the field, or by the participants to share their stories and future wishes in a more emotional, sensual, and subconscious way. Also, ethnographers and participants can work together to develop creative visual representations of local meanings and experiences. These techniques enable the researcher to represent local stories in a more imaginative way through visual novels, installations, and exhibitions. Visual representations may entail criticism, irony, sarcasm, satire, and humor; elements that stimulate a sensorial, affective, and empathetic awareness about the people under study from the side of the researcher and the reader. Also, recording of sounds and images, filmmaking, and editing of audio-visual material can provide a novel approach to cinematic ethnographic narratives. Through the curation of images and sounds, multimedia installations, and experimental filmmaking techniques, we can achieve a multisensory knowledge that is rich in personal and intimate feelings, memories, and imaginations. Digital recording, montage, and creative presentation of audio-visual data can trigger sensorial impressions that may connect and engage researchers, participants, and audiences with the cultural context under study. Symbolic images, metaphorical scenes, movement, voices, and noises from the field can contribute to a creative storyline that may help us become more sensitive to the social, sensual, and spatial surroundings of the unfamiliar culture (Feld and Brenneis, 2004).

A second creative ethnographic technique includes the employment and study of the 'peripheral' sensorial stimuli produced through sounds, smells, tastes, and touches. The prevailing epistemological orientation presents a sensitivity to sight, textual, and visual representations of knowledge. Sight, and sometimes sound, are viewed as the higher senses, whereas smells, tastes, and haptics are considered to be the lower senses (Pink, 2015). However, ethnography, as an embodied practice allows us to explore how multisensory, bodily, corporeal lived experiences may enhance our epistemologies (Conquergood, 1991; Magnat, 2011). Our bodies, feelings, senses, and imaginations are trained through processes of socialization and cultural practice. Pink (2015), in her celebrated work *Doing Sensory Ethnography*, argues that the experiencing, sensuous, knowing body is vital to ethnography. The way people see, listen, smell, taste and touch shape human sensory processes of knowing, feeling and communicating with others (Robben, 2008; Stoller, 1989).

Although this sensorial type of knowledge is hard to be expressed verbally, sensory ethnography enables us to empirically explore the relationships between our sensory experiences, the interconnectedness of different senses, and our sensory knowledge about others' experiences, expanding dominant ways of cognitive knowing. Being sensitive and paying attention to how somatic experiences, bodily sensations, embodied affective codes, and corporeal sensory orders are culturally shaped and how they shape our knowledge about ourselves, our fellow men, unknown cultures, and the social world around us can help us develop another type of 'felt,' 'affective,' or imaginative theory (Csordas, 1993; Million, 2013). Sensory observation (Nugent, 2018), memory work (Gillies et al., 2004; Stevenson, 2014), body-anchored interviewing (Harris and Guillemin, 2012), sensory elicitation interviewing (Pink, 2015), performance ethnography (Denzin, 2003; Madison, 2006; Oberg, 2008), and embodied reflexivity (Burns, 2006; Rice, 2009; Sandelowski, 2002) are some of the techniques that can be used to explore the sensual, the felt, and the embodied. Sounds, tastes, touching, gestures, facial expressions, scents, movements, textures can be explored through performative sensory activities such as eating, walking, drinking, doing sports and trying hobbies, dressing, learning, cooking together, as well as sensory-focused discussions.

Creative writing is a third imaginative approach to ethnography. When descriptive field notes are inadequate to capture the complex emotional, sensorial, and unexpected experiences of everyday life, creative forms of writing, such as ethnographic poetry, ethnographic narratives, non-fiction stories, novels, memoirs, fiction, narrative pose, satire, digital (micro) writing (i.e., Twitter or WhatsApp interactions), experimental writing, collaborative writing, and auto-ethnographic narratives can help us delve into consumers' cultural experiences, mundane practices, and extraordinary events in a sensitive, honest, and lyrical way (Elliott, 2017; Johnson, 2011; Sherry and Schouten, 2002). Creative storytelling has the power to tell different affective stories about people, social relations, power dynamics, inequalities and contradictions, cultures, collective memories, and places, conveying emotions, reflections, concerns, dreams, and desires artfully. Ethnographers can experiment with the content, style, and format of their writing, and they can also invite informants to produce their own powerful stories through simple creative-writing practices. Such process-based writing techniques may help us engage with consumers in imaginative ways free of academic jargon, encouraging participants to share their own stories and aid us to theorize the world in an inspiring, artistic, and expressive fashion (Cvetkovich, 2012; Elliott, 2017).

The study, employment, and representation of movement, kinesis, and performance can also be valuable when conducting ethnographic research. Participating in people's lives means occupying a physical space and moving amongst humans and non-humans, in spaces, through spaces, and between spaces. Spatial kinesis can reveal significant information about the social, cultural, and political processes, contexts, and relations. Human movement in space stimulates embodied encounters, fuels bodily conversations, and generates corporeal experiences, stories, and performances. Moving in space means participating in social life and in place making (Moretti, 2017). Our everyday movements in the house or the workplace, our journeys, our commutes, our walks, our dances, our gestures, our momentary, temporal, or more permanent positions can all impact social interactions, connections, inclusions, and exclusions. In other words, movement shapes and is shaped by public life. By inhabiting a space and moving ourselves, we shape our experiences, images, sounds, memories, understandings, and identities. We form and perform, we comment on, question, and change our shared reality. Capturing, reflecting upon, analyzing, and representing movement of others helps us learn untold experiences, remember places, people, and stories of the past, but also imagine future common narratives (Ingold and Vergunst, 2008). Changing physical positions, or researching in motion with others, allows us to discover hidden spaces, lost sights, unusual realities, and marginal spatial positions. In this sense, moving in space is a practice of experiencing, learning, and navigating through possible routes of the past, the present, and the future (Gordon, 1997). The embodied, dynamic, improvisational character of movement encourages us to appreciate spatial sensual stimuli, expands the ways in which we reach new knowledge, and contributes to how we theorize about our world.

An alternative way to seek, produce, and represent knowledge about embodied lived experiences of an unfamiliar culture is through performance. Performance-cantered ethnography mainly refers to the development of performance as an ethnographic research process, the staging of a performance as a product of ethnographic research, or the combination of both (Kazubowski-Houston, 2010). Different performance ethnography techniques include instructional theatre (Schechner, 1985; Turner and Turner, 1982), ethnographic street performance (Conquergood, 1988), performative ethnography (Fabian, 1990), ethnodrama (Mienczakowski, 2000; Saldana, 2005), performative community ethnography (Papa and Lassiter, 2003), ethnotheater (Saldana, 2016), ethnographic theatre (Lucas, 2006), ethnographic performance activism (Madison, 2010), improvisation ethnography (Culhane, 2011), and ethnography as performative ceremony (Magnat, 2012).

Such performance-based ethnographic techniques can potentially lead to a rich, experiential, kinetic and imaginative knowing, representation and dissemination of insights about people (Saldana 2003; Denzin, 2003). First, performance making can be participatory and collaborative. Engaging locals as storytellers, dramaturgists, directors, playwrights, performers, and actors allows for an accountable, honest, and reflective representation of the cultural life under study (Kazubowski-Houston, 2017). Second, performance development and staging processes can stimulate, express, and portray participants' thoughts, feelings, affects, embodied senses, moods, and discussions in an emotional, affective, and dramatic way, triggering audiences' imagination about the unknown, new, and different social world. By transforming local tales, folk stories, and participants' narratives into dramatic action on stage, a compelling, embodied, and empathetic understanding of the unfamiliar culture can be encouraged for academic and non-academic audiences (Conquergood, 1988; Foster, 2012; Madison, 2005; Zipes, 2012). Third, the improvisation techniques, the embodied metaphors, the gestures, the symbols, and the rituals of performance making have the power to move us beyond cognitive learning processes to experiential, practicing, and subconscious learning, which may motivate feelings, attitudes, and actions for the participants and the spectators (Jackson, 1992; Peters, 2009). In this sense, the performative turn in ethnography has the potential to lead to social transformation triggered by emotional learning experiences."

The young lady concludes, "New creative approaches to ethnographic study can expand our sensuous, experiential, and imaginative adventures, allowing us to take risks, experiment, and look beyond visual observations, verbal interactions, and reason-based interpretations. Creative ethnographies motivate an embodied sensorial participation that can enhance our perception, our empathetic understanding, and our knowledge about food experience." She bows, puts her earphones on, and leaves the stage.

Discussion and conclusions

As the curtain falls and the lights fade, what are your thoughts and feelings about the drama of ethnography? Are you excited to become a creative ethnographer yourself? How could you use this method resourcefully, creatively, and imaginatively to explore, learn, and discuss human life, pleasurable sensory experience, and food consumption? Through our *Ethnography in Three Acts*, we propose that the possibilities of ethnography are endless. A curious, inventive, and respectful researcher can select amongst, and across, a range of ethnographic approaches to delve deeper into human feelings, thoughts, senses, perceptions, and food practices. Participation, observation, verbal and non-verbal interaction are all techniques that can help us become active participants – performing actors – ready to open ourselves to the situation of others and share aspects of their worlds and our common experiences.

Ethnography is a method that allows us to get immersed into people's lifeworlds and soak up the nuances of their culture. By examining day-to-day activities, experiences, interactions, senses, practices, and processes, ethnography encourages a detailed analysis of particular settings and facilitates a holistic conceptualization of human reality. Instead of looking for external, or internal, forces and variables that determine human group life, ethnography enjoys the privilege of presence, which allows us to live and envision human life as an ongoing process of communication, multisensory experience, and action, shaped by active, living, thinking, sensing, feeling beings in physical and verbal interaction. As a consequence, using ethnography in academia can help us develop theorizations, concepts, and abstract knowledge that interpret food experiences, consumer behavior, and marketplace interactions. Using ethnography in industry can help us bring to life food perceptions, emotions, senses, preferences, and lifestyles of segments of the population that are still unexplored, uncharted, and obscure.

Although ethnography enables us to approach, access, and collect human experiences, behaviors, and actions like no other method, positivist scientists find ground for criticism arguing that ethnographic approaches are subjective and unscientific because they overemphasize individual meanings and local experience attached to human behavior. They also argue that these meanings are not scientifically observed, counted, processed, and operationalized (Antaki, et al., 2002; Labuschagne, 2003). As a result, ethnography is seen as not efficient in producing objective measurements of causes and effects that can be generally and universally employed. Also, conducting ethnography can be a very time-consuming, demanding, and labor-intensive undertaking, which requires from the researcher, not only the passion to understand the "other," but also the extensive patience, the financial resources, and the time to explore nuanced, multilayered, and complex local lifeworlds.

How can we evaluate the ethnographic outcome? The criteria of reflexivity, viability, and transferability can help us assess whether our interpretations of others' worlds are accurate, respectful, well justified, and transferable to other contexts (Atkinson, 1990; Clifford and Marcus, 1986; Czarniawska, 1998; Denzin, 1984; Denzin and Lincoln, 1984; Hudson and Ozanne, 1988; Van Maanen, 1987). Triangulation, comparative, and member-checking techniques can also help us add accuracy. Combining different techniques, texts, and samples, getting feedback from participants, and receiving comments from academic colleagues about our interpretations can contribute to a more honest attempt to share participants' lived experiences and to a more precise effort to convey local everyday stories (Glaser and Strauss, 1967; McCracken, 1988; Miles and Huberman, 1984). Taking into consideration time, resource, and methodological limitations as well as ideological, theoretical, and cultural influences, the ultimate goal of an ethnographer is to craft a story that could portray slices of the participants' lives vividly, honestly, and comprehensively. The final outcome of an ethnographic experience cannot be anything more than a respectful filtered, highly selective, and partial version of reality (Emerson et al., 1995).

Pleasurable consumption experiences, especially food, cooking, and gastronomy experiences, are constituted, understood, lived, and evaluated through our sensing bodies, our corporeal processes, and our physical interactions with people, objects in our environments, and our historical, political, and sociocultural contexts. Ethnography does not only offer access to consumers' thoughts and prediscursive meanings; the sensing body can become the center of our research focus engaging, analyzing, presenting, and communicating a wide pallet of tastes, aromas, smells, images, sounds, touches, and movements. A creative path to research that builds upon the principles of classical ethnography and its corporate extensions can inspire a new generation of imaginative academics and industry professionals to attune their bodies, minds, and senses to the lives of others and learn alongside consumers how people remember, live, perceive, and imagine through experiential, embodied, performative, aesthetic, affective, collaborative, and practicing ways. Creative ethnography has the power to offer a full-bodied sensory understanding of consumer food experience and its interconnection to culture, power, and society.

Returning to the story of Kiba, we would like you to reflect on how an aspiring ethnographer, like yourself, would try to grasp the multisensoriality of her food experience. How would you, as a creative conductor or an imaginative choreographer, improvise to orchestrate in harmony the bodies in the field, the scholarly voices, and your own lived experiences? Are you ready to take creative risks, experiment, and open yourself to a new unexplored world? If the answer is yes, close your eyes, draw a deep breath, and take the plunge. Your ethnographic adventure awaits …

References

Antaki, C., Edwards, B.M., & Potter, J. (2002). Discourse analysis means doing analysis: A critique of six analytic shortcomings. *Discourse Analysis Online*, 1(1).

Asad, T. (1973). *Anthropology and the Colonial Encounter*. London: Ithaca Press.

Atkinson, P. (1990). *Understanding Ethnographic Texts*. London: Sage.

Barry, L. (2008). *What It Is*. Vancouver: Raincoast Books.

Bate, S.P. (1997). Whatever happened to organizational anthropology? A review of the field of organizational ethnography and anthropological studies. *Human Relations*, 50(9), 1147–1175.

Bateson, G., & Mead, M. (1942). *Balinese Character: A Photographic Analysis*. New York: New York Academy of Sciences.

Berry, J.W. (1989). Imposed etics-emics-derived etics: The operationalization of a compelling idea. *International Journal of Psychology*, 24(6), 721–735.

Burns, M. (2006). Bodies that speak: Examining the dialogues in research interactions. *Qualitative Research in Psychology*, *3*(1), 3–18.

Causey, A. (2016). *Drawing to See: Drawing as an Ethnographic Method*. Toronto: University of Toronto Press.

Clifford, J. (1988). *The Predicament of Culture: Twentieth-Century Ethnography, Literature and Art*. Cambridge, MA: Harvard University Press.

Clifford, J., & Marcus, G.E. (1986). *Writing Culture: The Poetics and Politics of Ethnography*. Berkeley, CA: University of California Press.

Conquergood, D. (1988). Health theatre in a Hmog refugee camp: Performance, communication and culture. *Drama Review: Journal of Performance Studies*, 32(3), 174–208.

Conquergood, D. (1991). Rethinking ethnography: Towards a critical cultural politics. *Communication Monographs*, 58(2), 179–194.

Csordas, T. (1993). Somatic modes of attention: Interview with Thomas Csordas. *Cultural Anthropology*, 8(2), 135–156.

Culhane, D. (2011). Stories and plays: Ethnography, performance and ethical engagements. *Anthropologica*, 53(2), 257–274.

Culhane, D. (2017). Imagining: An introduction. In D. Elliott & D. Culhane, *A Different Ethnography*. New York: University of Toronto Press, pp. 1–21.

Cvetkovich, A. (2012). *Depression: A Public Feeling*. Durham, NC: Duke University.

Czarniawska, B. (1998). *A Narrative Approach to Organisation Studies*. Thousand Oaks, CA: Sage.

Denzin, N.K. (1984). *On Understanding Emotion*. San Francisco, CA: Jossey-Bass.

Denzin, N.K. (2003). *Performance Ethnography*. Thousand Oaks, CA: Sage.

Denzin, N.K., & Lincoln, Y.S. (1984). *Handbook of Qualitative Research*. London: Sage.

Elliott, D. (2017). Writing. In D. Elliott, & D. Culhane, *A Different Ethnography*. New York: University of Toronto Press, pp. 23–44.

Emerson, R.M., Fretz, R.I., & Shaw, L.L. (1995). *Writing Ethnographic Fieldnotes*. Chicago, IL: University of Chicago Press.

Fabian, J. (1990). *Power and Performance*. Madison, WI: University of Wisconsin Press.

Feld, S., & Brenneis, D. (2004). Doing anthropology in sound. *American Ethnologist*, 31 (4), 461–474.

Foster, V.A. (2012). *Dramatic Revisions of Myths, Fairy Tales and Legends*. Jefferson, NC: McFarland & Company.

Geertz, C. (1973). *The Interpretation of Cultures*. New York: Basic Books.

Geertz, C. (1998). Deep hanging out. *New York Review of Books*, 45(16), 69–72.

Gillies, V., Harden, A., Johnson, K., Reavy, P., Strange, V., & Willig, S. (2004). Women's collective constructions of embodied practices through memory work: Cartesian dualism in memories of sweat and pain. *British Journal of Social Psychology*, 43(1), 99–112.

Glaser, B.G., & Strauss, A.L. (1967). *The Discovery of Grounded Research: Strategies for Qualitative Research*. London: Adline Transaction.

Goffman, C. (1958). *The Presentation of Self in Everyday Life*. New York: Doubleday Anchor.

Golden-Biddle, K., & Locke, K. (1993). Appealing work: An investigation of how ethnographic texts convince. *Organization Science*, 4(4), 595–616.

Gordon, A. (1997). *Ghostly Matters: Haunting and the Sociological Imagination*. Minneapolis, MN: University of Minnesota Press.

Green, B., & Hopwood, N. (2015). Introduction: Body/practice? In B. Green & N. Hopwood (Eds), *The Body in Professional Practice*. Cham, Switzerland: Springer International, pp. 3–27.

Grindstaff, L. (2002). *The Money Shot: Trash, Class, and the Making of TV Talk Shows*. Chicago, IL: University of Chicago Press.

Hammersley, M., & Atkinson, P. (1995). *Ethnography: Principles in Practice* (2nd ed.). London: Routledge.

Hammersley, M., & Atkinson, P. (2007). *Ethnography: Principles in Practice*. London: Routledge.

Harris, A., & Guillemin, M. (2012). Developing sensory awareness in qualitative interviewing. *Qualitative Health Research*, 22(5), 689–699.

Hendrickson, C. (2008). Visual field notes: Drawing insights in the Yucatan. *Visual Anthropology Review*, 24(4), 117–132.

Hill, R.P. (1991). Homeless women, special possessions, and the meaning of "home": An ethnographic case study. *Journal of Consumer Research*, 18(3), 289–310.

Howe, D. (2012). *Empathy: What It Is and Why It Matters*. New York: Palgrave Macmillan International.

Hudson, L.A., & Ozanne, J.L. (1988). Alternative ways of seeking knowledge in consumer research. *Journal of Consumer Research*, 14(4), 508–521.

Ingold, T. (2011). *Redrawing Anthropology: Materials, Movements, Lines*. Farnham: Ashgate.

Ingold, T., & Vergunst, J.L. (2008). *Ways of Walking: Ethnography and Practice on Foot*. Aldershot: Ashgate.

Jackson, A. (1992). Translator's introduction. In A. Boal (Ed.), *Games for Actors and Non-Actors*. New York: Routledge, pp. xxii–xxvii.

Johnson, C. (2011). *Microstyle: The Art of Writing Little*. New York: Norton.

Junker, B.H. (1960). *Field Work: An Introduction to the Social Sciences*. Chicago, IL: University of Chicago Press.

Katzman, E.R. (2015). Embodied reflexivity: Knowledge and the body in professional practice. In B. Green, & N. Hopwood, *The Body in Professional Practice, Learning and Education* (Vol. 2). Cham, Switzerland: Springer, pp. 157–172.

Kazubowski-Houston, M. (2010). *Staging Life: Lessons from Performing Ethnography with Polish Roma Women*. Montreal: McGill-Queen's University Press.

Kazubowski-Houston, M. (2017). Performing. In D. Elliott & D. Culhane (Eds), *A Different Kind of Ethnography*. New York: University of Toronto Press, pp. 113–132.

Labuschagne, A. (2003). Qualitative research-airy fairy or fundamental? *Qualitative Report*, 8(1), 100–103.

Lucas, A.E. (2006). *Performing the Unimagined Nation*. San Diego, CA: University of California.

Madison, D.S. (2005). *Critical Ethnography: Method, Ethics, and Performance*. Thousand Oaks, CA: Sage.

Madison, D.S. (2006). Staging fieldwork/performing human rights. In D.S. Madison & J. Hamera (Eds), *Handbook of Performance Studies*. London: Sage, pp. 397–419.

Madison, D.S. (2010). *Acts of Activism*. Cambridge: Cambridge University Press.

Magnat, V. (2011). Conducting embodied research at the intersection of performance studies: Experimental ethnography and indigenous methodologies. *Anthropologica*, 53(2), 213–227.

Magnat, V. (2012). Can research become ceremony? Performance ethnography and indigenous epistemologies. *Canadian Theatre Review*, 151, 30–36.

Malinowski, B. (1985). *Crime and Custom in Savage Society*. Totowa, NJ: Rowman & Littlefield.

Malinowski, B. (1989 [1967]). *A Diary in the Strict Sense of the Term*. Stanford, CA: Stanford University Press.

Malinowski, B. (2014 [1922]). *Argonauts of the Western Pacific*. New York: Routledge.

McCracken, G. (1988). *The Nature and Types of Sociological Theory*. London: Sage.

Mienczakowski, J. (2000). Ethnography in the form of theatre with emancipatory intentions. In C. Truman, D.M. Merters, & B. Humphries (Eds), *Research and Inequality*. London: UCL Press, pp. 126–142.

Miles, M.B., & Huberman, A.M. (1984). *Qualitative Data Analysis: An Expanded Sourcebook*. Beverly Hills, CA: Sage.

Million, D. (2013). *Therapeutic Nations: Healing in an Age of Indigenous Human Rights*. Tucson, AZ: University of Arizona Press.

Mittermaier, A. (2011). *Dreams that Matter: Egyptian Landscapes of the Imagination*. Berkeley, CA: University of California Press.

Moretti, C. (2017). Walking. In D. Elliott & D. Culhane (Eds), *A Different Kind of Ethnography*. New York: University of Toronto Press, pp. 91–111.

Morgan, L.H. (1959). *The Indian Journals 1859–1862*. Ann Arbor, MI: University of Michigan Press.

Nugent, C.L. (2018). Sensory-ethnographic observation at three nature kindergarten. *International Journal of Research and Method in Education*, 41(4): 468–479.

Oberg, C.M. (2008). Performance ethnography: Scholarly inquiry in the here and now. *Transformative Dialogues: Teaching and Learning Journal*, 2(1).

Papa, L., & Lassiter, E. (2003). The Muncie Race Riots of 1967: Representing community memory through public performance, and collaborative ethnography between faculty, students, and the local community. *Journal of Contemporary Ethnography*, 32(2), 147–166.

Peters, G. (2009). *The Philosophy of Improvisation*. Chicago, IL: University of Chicago Press.

Pink, S. (2015). *Doing Sensory Ethnography*. London: Palgrave.
Porcello, T., Meintjes, L., Ochoa, A., & Samuels, D.W. (2010). The reorganization of the sensory world. *Annual Review of Anthropology*, 39(1), 51–66.
Prasad, P. (2005). *Crafting Qualitative Research: Working in the Postpositivist Traditions*. London: M.E. Sharpe.
Prus, R.C. (1996). *Symbolic Interaction and Ethnographic Research: Intersubjectivity and the Study of Human Lived Experience*. New York: State University of New York Press.
Rice, C. (2009). Imagining the other? Ethical challenges of researching and writing women's embodied lives. *Feminism and Psychology*, 19(2), 245–266.
Robben, A. (2008). Introduction: Sensorial fieldwork. In A. Robben & J.A. Sluka (Eds), *Ethnographic Fieldwork: An Anthropological Reader*. Oxford: Blackwell, pp. 385–388.
Saldana, J. (2003). Dramatizing data: A primer. *Qualitative Inquiry*, 9(2), 218–236.
Saldana, J. (2005). *Ethnodrama*. Oxford: AltaMira.
Saldana, J. (2016). *Ethnotheatre*. New York: Routledge.
Sandelowski, M. (2002). Reembodying qualitative inquiry. *Qualitative Health Research*, 12(1), 104–115.
Schechner, R. (1985). *Between Theatre and Anthropology*. Philadelphia, PA: University Pennsylvania Press.
Schouten, J.W., & McAlexander, J.H. (1995). Subcultures of consumption: An ethnography of the new bikers. *Journal of Consumer Research*, 22(61), 43–61.
Schutz, A. (1964). *Collected Papers II: Studies in Social Theory*. The Hague: Martinus Nijhoff.
Schwartzman, H.F. (1993). *Ethnography in Organizations*. London: Sage.
Seale, C. (2004). *Researching Society and Culture*. London: Sage.
Sherry, J.F. (2006). Fielding ethnographic teams: Strategy, implementation and strategy. In R.W. Belk (Ed.), *Handbook of Qualitative Research Methods in Marketing*. Cheltenham: Elgar, pp. 268–276.
Sherry, J.F., & Schouten, J. (2002). A role for poetry in consumer research. *Journal of Consumer Research*, 29, 218–234.
Sousanis, N. (2015). *Unflattening*. Cambridge, MA: Harvard University Press.
Stevenson, L. (2014). *Life beside Itself: Imagining Care in the Canadian Arctic*. Berkeley, CA: University of California Press.
Stoller, P. (1989). *The Taste of Ethnographic Things: The Senses in Anthropology*. Philadelphia, PA: University of Pennsylvania Press.
Sumner, W.G. (2007[1906]). *Folkways: A Study of Mores, Manners, Customs and Morals*. New York: Cosimo.
Taussig, M. (2011). *I Swear I Saw This: Drawings in Fieldwork Notebooks, Namely My Own*. Chicago, IL: University of Chicago Press.
Tedlock, B. (1991). From participant observation to the observation of participation: The emergence of narrative ethnography. *Journal of Anthropological Research*, 47(1), 69–94.
Turner, V., & Turner, E. (1982). Performing ethnography. *Drama Review: Journal of Performance Studies*, 26(2), 33–50.
Van Maanen, J. (1987). *Tales of the Field: On Writing Ethnography*. Chicago, IL: University of Chicago Press.
Vidich, A.J., & Lyman, S.M. (1994). Qualitative methods: Their history in sociology and anthropology. In N.K. Denzin & Y. Lincoln (Eds), *Handbook of Qualitative Research*. Thousand Oaks, CA: Sage, pp. 23–59.
Watts, J.H. (2008). Emotion, empathy and exit: Reflections on doing ethnographic qualitative research on sensitive topics. *Medical Sociology*, 3(2), 3–14.
Wax, R. (1971). *Doing Fieldwork*. Chicago, IL: Chicago University Press.

Westmoreland, M. (2011). Ethnography + art: Convergence or collision? *IBRAAZ*.

Wolcott, H.F. (1995). Making a case study more ethnographic. In J.V. Maanen (Ed.), *Representations in Ethnography*. Thousands Oaks, CA: Sage, pp. 79–111.

Zipes, J. (2012). *The Irresistible Fairy Tale: The Social and Cultural History of a Genre*. Princeton, NJ: Princeton University Press.

8 Cooking, food experiential learning, and connectedness

Food wellbeing construction from Lebanese villages

Ghina Chammas and Nadine A. Yehya

The Mediterranean diet is a living evolutionary result of the millennial history of the Mediterranean, transmitted from one generation to the next, and continuously recreated by communities influenced by environmental and historical changes (Berry et al., 2011). It constitutes "a set of skills, knowledge, practices and traditions ranging from the landscape to the table, including the crops, harvesting, fishing, conservation, processing, preparation and, particularly, consumption of food" (UNESCO, 2010: 21). Despite its increasing popularity worldwide, the Mediterranean diet is currently endangered in all Mediterranean countries with the abandonment of traditional healthy habits and the emergence of new lifestyles associated with socioeconomic changes (Dernini, 2011).

Changes in intergenerational and gender relationships, interrelationships with the rest of the world (migrations and tourism), and the role of women in society have created significant implications for Mediterranean lifestyles. In addition, the Westernization of food consumption patterns in the Mediterranean area poses important threats to the preservation and transmission of the Mediterranean diet to future generations. These changes are also influenced by urbanization, organization of working time, growing participation of women in economic life, fewer household members, fewer generations living together, desocialization, and the collective environment (Berry and De Geest, 2012; Padilla, 2008).

Factors such as the standardization of lifestyles, the loss of appreciation and awareness, particularly amongst younger generations, about their own cultural food heritage have successfully diminished the pattern of the Mediterranean diet (Dernini, 2011). The new fast-paced lifestyles and modernity's invasion of cooking experiences have resulted in a silent cultural erosion, affecting the diversity of the Mediterranean food cultures and its traceability to local territories and traditions. This erosion is directly sabotaging the special link between millions of people's identities and traditions and their food culture (Dernini, 2011).

Lebanon, a small Mediterranean country in the Middle East, has an established reputation for its gastronomy and traditional healthy Mediterranean diet. The Lebanese diet, known for its favorable sensory properties, is highly popular on the international scene as well as among the local population (Hwalla and El Khoury, 2008). In fact, Lebanon has repeatedly been placed on top food destination lists. In addition, Beirut, the capital of Lebanon, was recently voted as the best international city for food by *Travel + Leisure* magazine (Lieberman, 2016). The Lebanese traditional diet constitutes an intangible cultural heritage and is well known for its variety. The diet is based on an abundance of fruits, cereals, vegetables, and nuts, and consists of recipes which use lemon, garlic, and olive oil, resulting in a collection of minimally processed vegetarian meals and a diverse set of traditional Lebanese dishes.

Food in Lebanon, like in many Mediterranean countries, plays a central role in the social and cultural life. Although the present Lebanese dietary habit has retained many of its Mediterranean characteristics, it has exhibited a rising tension between the modern Western diet and traditional healthy Mediterranean cooking, which has been accentuated by globalization and modernization (Hwalla and El Khoury, 2008). The new food habits created from this "culinary transition" have actually caused a "deskilling" of citizens, resulting in many people no longer possessing the necessary skills to prepare meals from whole-food ingredients, furthering their reliance on pre-prepared items (e.g., Caraher, 2012; Caraher and Lang, 1999; Deer et al., 2014; Jabs et al., 2007; Jaffe and Gertler, 2006; Lang and Caraher, 2001). The concept of cooking seems to have become outdated as there is an increased tendency to prepare a "home-cooked meal" by combining processed foods and heating them up together (Engler-Stringer, 2010).

In this chapter, we will examine Lebanese cooking experiences as an example of a Mediterranean diet by looking at how Lebanese women define cooking practices, learn how to cook, and adapt to changing palettes by adopting new modern recipes while still preserving the old. Anchored in the food wellbeing (FWB) approach and inspired by the food socialization and experiential learning theory as a theoretical framework, we seek to understand the learning and practicing of cooking skills for Lebanese women living in rural areas. We specifically seek to answer: How do Lebanese women get socialized into cooking for their families? And what food socialization practices do Lebanese mothers experience and enact to preserve a traditional Lebanese diet?

A transformative consumer approach of food experiences

In 2005, the Transformative Consumer Research (TCR), a movement within the field of consumer research, formed to deliberate key issues related to consumer welfare, including chronic social problems affecting consumers worldwide (e.g., Bublitz et al., 2013; Mick, 2006). One central TCR research stream explores how food decision making influences health and wellbeing by advocating for research and consumer programs that foster a positive relationship with food (Block et al., 2011; Bublitz et al., 2011). TCR helped craft a vision for the FWB paradigm, emphasizing the holistic understanding of the role of food in wellbeing (Block et al., 2011; Bublitz et al., 2013). Defined as "a positive psychological, physical, emotional, and social relationship with food at both individual and societal levels" (Block et al., 2011: 6), the FWB paradigm promotes a healthy relationship with food by adopting a positive approach (Block et al., 2011). Block et al. (2011)

proposed five primary domains of FWB: food socialization, food literacy, food marketing, food availability, and food policy. In this chapter, we will focus on food literacy as a main component of FWB, as we examine the food literacy of Lebanese rural women when describing their journey learning how to cook and practicing cooking in the traditional Mediterranean approach.

Food literacy and cooking skills

Cooking skills have been associated with various health benefits and better-quality diets (Carter, 2010; Engler-Stringer, 2010; Foley et al., 2011; Woodruff and Hanning, 2009; Worsley et al., 2014). There has been a rising interest in interventions that promote the learning of cooking skills as a way to improve people's diet and the population's general health (Beets et al., 2007; Bukhari et al., 2011; Clifford et al., 2009; Fisher et al., 2011; Gatenby et al., 2011; Worsley et al., 2014). Being food literate became a vital aspect to living well, beyond individual physical health (García-González et al., 2018).

The concept of "food literacy" emerges from frameworks developed for health literacy (e.g., Ratzan, 2001) and is being studied as a new approach to food that has the ability to enable healthier food relationships (Block et al., 2011). By acquiring knowledge about food and nutrition, consumers seem to improve the quality of their food choices (Worsley, 2002). Food literacy extends beyond knowledge to also include one's willingness to apply nutrition information to food choices (Block et al., 2011; Nutbeam, 2008). Food literacy entails both the cognitive and the behavioral aspects in the promotion of nutrition goals and FWB. It adds to the nutritional recommendations and cooking lessons a connection between food, people, health, and the environment (García-González et al., 2018). The development of food literacy involves "the ability, opportunity, and motivation to identify, understand, interpret, communicate, and use information about food in various contexts" (Block et al., 2011: 8).

Food literacy is connected to food socialization. The way people come to learn about food and how to practice it is shaped by their food socialization experiences. Food and its cultural links are learned through a socialization process (Moschis, 1985). Block et al. (2011: 7) define "food socialization" as the "processes consumers use to learn about food, its role, and FWB in a person's cultural realm." Food socialization is a dynamic process that begins in childhood (Birch, 1998), a formative period in shaping food consumption practices (Janz et al., 2005; Mikkilä et al., 2005) but continues throughout one's life (Block et al., 2011). Learning cooking skills at a younger age has a positive effect on many cooking-related behaviors and practices, boosting skill retention, confidence, cooking attitude, and diet quality (Deer et al., 2014). According to Berger and Luckmann (1989), primary socialization takes place almost exclusively within the family, in the child's direct exchange with the parents. Families are perceived to have the greatest socializing effect, broadly shaping the paths their children will take (Block et al., 2011; Judd et al., 2014; Moschis and Moore, 1979).

According to Judd et al. (2014), familial food socialization practices are categorized into three possible feeding styles, namely, *authoritarian, permissive,* and *authoritative* (Birch and Fisher, 1995). An *authoritarian* feeding style prioritizes the parents' need to control the eating practices of their children over the child's food preferences (Blissett and Haycraft, 2008; Hubbs-Tait et al., 2008; Patrick et al., 2005). The style involves forcing certain forms of food onto the child while eliminating others. A *permissive* feeding style allows for a much more relaxed approach to what a child may or may not eat, as they are provided with the agency to choose what they can eat and in what quantity (Patrick et al., 2005), allowing for experiences of pleasure, happiness, and nutrition to co-exist in one meal. The parents' memories with regards to their own food socialization practices and particularly strict rules on how and what they ate may influence them to become more permissive. This style is typically linked to a set diet, as meals were approved by the children (Judd et al., 2014). An *authoritative* feeding style finds cohesiveness between the parents' concern for the nutritional quality of their child's diet and the child's food preferences (Hubbs-Tait et al., 2008). The style encourages children to consume healthy meals while also making room for their own eating choices (Blissett, 2011; Judd et al., 2014; Patrick et al., 2005). In all cases, parents' feeding styles were molded not only by the children's behaviors but also by the parents' own childhood experiences (Judd et al., 2014).

Food experiential learning

A basic principle of socialization theory is the understanding that people do not only learn by being attentive and observant of the actions of others and their consequent result (social cognitive learning), but also through their own experiences (experiential learning) (Bandura, 1977). López Torres (2016) defines two phases in the culinary learning process: the "transmission phase" and the "learning phase." In the transmission phase, the learners unconsciously and passively acquire knowledge and skills, by socialization, observing, assisting, and talking with cooks around them. In the learning phase, the learners actively search for information, asking, reading, practicing, and learning by trial and error (García-González et al., 2018; López Torres, 2016).

According to García-González et al. (2018), people tend to learn to cook from their family (42.2 percent) and through self-experience (43.3 percent). The Experiential Learning Theory defines learning as "the process whereby knowledge is created through the transformation of experience" (Kolb, 1984: 41). Experiential learning pools together four different learning modes – experiencing, reflecting, thinking, and acting – to create a more complete manner of constructing knowledge (Kolb and Kolb, 2012). The experiential learning cycle starts when a concrete experience is enriched by reflection, given meaning by thinking, and transformed by action, resulting in a richer, broader, and deeper new experience. It is actually a learning spiral whereby all learning is relearning (Kolb and Kolb, 2012).

According to Trubek and Belliveau (2009), the kitchen is an ideal place to start multisensory experiential learning and to hone these senses. Cooking instinctively engages an individual's five senses as well as his or her mind.

Drawing from the FWB literature, we approach rural Lebanese women to understand their food socialization practices and the experiential learning process to negotiate the tensions between the traditional Lebanese diet and modernization's influence.

Exploring food experiential learning within the Lebanese food culture

Fieldwork, methodology, and data collection

Among the different research approaches, qualitative research is highly suitable "when the focus of attention is the process by which household members negotiate everyday life" (Gregory, 1995: 32). As this approach gained popularity in consumer research, methods from the fields of anthropology and sociology were introduced to it (Pettigrew, 2000). Particularly, ethnography was advocated as an effective tool to employ in consumer behavior (Johnson, 1990). Using ethnography, we explore experiential food learning and food socialization for Lebanese women.

This study is part of a larger project driven toward the improvement of mindful production, consumption, and waste generation in six villages in Mount Lebanon. After approval from the Institutional Review Board, we commenced fieldwork using the ethnographic method as the study's framework. The richest data this technique captures are obtained from the informal talks between the researcher and the participants (Geertz, 1973). Interviewing took place in various contexts, while drinking coffee, having breakfast or lunch, watching television, or working with the participants on a shared task (setting the table for lunch). All interviews were held at the participants' homes (living room or kitchen), except for three cases, where they occurred at the participants' workplaces (family-owned business). It was important to ensure the privacy of the participants and foster trusting relationships to be able to understand their daily food preparation and socialization (Slocum, 2008).

We employed both observational and interviewing methods as part of our ethnographic design. Our data set consisted of recorded interviews with participants, photos, field notes, and diaries. These activities included tours of the kitchen and kitchen cupboards; they were useful in getting a more rounded description of family consumption choices, preferences, and food-storage practices. Special attention was also placed on recording the social encounter as soon as possible afterwards to fully contextualize the event. We attentively documented any activity carried out by the participants as they were being interviewed, the emotions they felt and expressed, their guest reception and treatment, the physical setting, and the kind of home artifacts which included home photographs and decorations.

The data collection was done over a two month period, between November 2017 and January 2018, with subsequent data analysis based on constant comparison and emerging themes. In-depth interviews were conducted until no new themes or interpretations emerged from our conversations. Theoretical saturation was reached after ten interviews in each village, leading to a total of 60 Lebanese women participants. We recruited the participants using local community gatekeepers and snowballing sampling techniques (Biernacki and Waldorf, 1981) through direct and indirect social ties. Members from the citizen committees established as part of the larger project referred us to most of the participants, who also suggested additional informants from among their acquaintances. Within each community, we sought to recruit a sample of households with various upbringings, lifestyles, age groups, and economic status. The inclusion criteria included that the participant be a female resident of the village, 18 years old or above, head of her household, and able and willing to participate in a conversation about grocery shopping, cooking practices, and food-exchange habits. We chose to limit the study to women simply because they are normally more involved in the cooking compared to men in the Lebanese society. According to Dixey (1996), no other household task seems to be as strongly gendered as food preparation.

These villages are mostly inhabited by the Druze community, with only 8 percent of Christians residing in the villages on a permanent basis. The communities have impoverished economic circumstances and are not incorporated in the industrial sector (Yehya and Dutta, 2010). Although the area is of agrarian development, planting is modestly practiced among the interviewees, as less than half of our participants grow fruits and vegetables in their backyards. The majority of the participants are married and have kids, seven are widowed, and two are divorced. On average, each family consists of five members; the number of household members varies depending on a handful of factors ranging from the accommodation of family relatives to the presence of unmarried children and household helpers. Only 17 out of the 60 interviewed participants are employed, and work in food service, retail, beauty, and education sectors. The interviewed participants' ages ranged from 22 to 87 with an average age of 53. In multigenerational households, the experience was even richer, as we were able to examine intergenerational similarities and differences in food preparation and consumption practices.

As a first step, the participants were informed about the study and its voluntary nature, and were assured of their information's confidentiality. Their consent was verbally obtained to audio-record the interview. Four of the participants expressed their unwillingness to be audio-recorded, preferring that we take extensive notes of the interview. The interviews were conducted in Arabic, specifically in the Lebanese colloquial (the mother tongue of the participants and the research team). The audio-recorded interviews were translated and transcribed from Arabic to English. The translations were conducted by expert translators well conversed in English and Arabic and checked for accuracy by the researchers who are proficient in both languages.

The interviews lasted 60 minutes on average, with the longer taking up to 90 minutes. They were semi-structured; the participants usually took part in in-depth discussions based on a set of open-ended questions grouped around key themes, such as learning how to cook, shopping and cooking practices, and mindfulness in consumption. The transcription of the recorded interviews produced approximately 526 single-spaced pages of translated text, including small talk and verbal exchanges unrelated to the main topic. The interview quotes were well documented and unchanged except for some cases, where names of locations and participants were changed for confidentiality purposes.

Data analysis

There is a high degree of compatibility between ethnography and grounded theory, as according to Glaser and Strauss (1967), ethnographic studies provide the thick description useful for grounded theory analysis. Grounded theory techniques can formalize and enlarge the limited theoretical component of ethnographic research (Pettigrew, 2000). We discussed and analyzed the data on multiple occasions by conducting constant comparison of data during the readings to highlight commonalities and divergences. We analyzed the data based on grounded theory techniques using thematic analysis. Going line by line through the interview transcripts, we first simultaneously engaged in open coding and note taking to break down the data, identify, and sort the concepts that belong to the same phenomenon. This resulted in a preliminary set of broad codes which we were able to put together into categories and subcategories.

As a second step and engaging in a more focused process, we formulated connections within and between categories. When categories became redundant, we refined them into one or two core categories and collapsed them into themes. After organizing, analyzing, and summarizing the data, we coupled it with information from our field notes and journal entries to enhance the theoretical sensitivity of our analysis and generate the findings of our study. This chapter focuses on two main themes, namely, the dynamic experiential learning of mothers and their food socialization.

Food wellbeing through experiential learning within the Lebanese food culture

A woman's cooking is thought of as an extension of her care towards others. Moreover, the process of preparing proper meals was understood as an essential part of creating a home and family (Bugge and Almås, 2006). Consequently, all women were expected to learn and practice cooking as soon as they became heads of their households. All interviewed mothers assume the role of their families' main food providers and view themselves as nutritional gatekeepers of their children's diet.

They consider cooking as a paramount obligation they have towards their children's wellbeing and feel a need to provide their family with healthy food. Ghada (53), [1] like many participants, linked cooking to "being entrusted with the health of the kids." Marriage, cooking, and motherhood are a package deal for some of the participants. Women are expected to take up cooking and depend on themselves to harness their cooking skills. In the traditional rural Lebanese context, women are socially expected to learn how to prepare healthy food for their families. Our participants discussed different sources and ways to learn how to cook.

Learning how to cook

The participants reflected on their learning experience, as they had to learn cooking when they got married and especially after they became mothers. Cooking was acquired with time and practice through an experiential learning process. In the Lebanese rural community, they describe women who cannot cook by saying "she cannot fry an egg or prepare coffee!" Yet, this lack of cooking experience became more accepted with time and was even expected among the younger generation. Maha (52) reasoned why young single women do not learn cooking. She said, "There is no time. As children, they come home from school, have homework, then they need to sleep early. I prefer them to focus on their studies rather than learning how to cook. Cooking is easy to learn, you can take it up when you most need it."

When it comes to food literacy, mothers were identified as the primary transmitters of cooking skills (Caraher et al., 1999; Lavelle et al., 2016). Similar to the literature, our participants reported that their mothers were the major source for learning basic cooking skills (Caraher et al., 1999). Scholars conceptually describe how food practices are transferred from mothers to daughters, who are also mothers, through "solidarity and separation processes" (Bugge and Almås, 2006; Johnston et al., 2010). The mother–daughter relationship is characterized both by the daughter's desire to reproduce and mirror her mother's routine and rituals and her wish to set herself apart from her mother, by choosing a food pattern that fits her lifestyle as a modern woman. In their study, Bugge and Almås (2006) showed how a mother becomes an important figure in a woman's life when she becomes a mother herself.

Lebanese women start the learning process by observing their mothers and helping out in basic kitchen tasks. Leila (70) used to assist her mother in the kitchen as her community "likes girls to learn and become independent before getting married." On the other hand, Soraya (57) got married at the age of 16 and "did not know how to fry an egg." She said, "Life teaches you, and cooking books came in handy for any recipe." Rima (57) also taught herself and now claims to be a great cook. However, for Diala (76), cooking is a God-given gift rather than a talent that took time to master.

The interviewed mothers show openness in trying out new recipes along with traditional Lebanese dishes. Their willingness to try is made easier with their access to TV cooking shows and online recipes, and sometimes pressure to cook fast-food meals from their children. Diana (54) relies on watching, reading, writing, and repeating recipes in order to improve her cooking skills. She acquired some common knowledge about cooking from her mother but constantly seeks to develop her skills from various sources. She said, "After my children go to school, I would have time to prepare their meals and take notes while watching Chef Oussama's show. However, the internet now opened many doors for me, I am able to learn recipes I had no idea existed online."

This exposure to various sources to learn cooking allowed for the integration of modern recipes into the repertoire of traditional Lebanese cuisine. The younger generation has taken a liking to fast-food meals and international cuisine, which forces mothers and sometimes grandmothers to cater to their children's food preferences. As Lynn (42) said, "I usually keep up with all upcoming cooking trends, and I try them all at home such as Kentucky chicken mix. I enjoy preparing new recipes for my family, even French, or Italian food; variety is always welcome in our household."

Jamale (58) laments how families moved away from traditional vegetable-based meals to more meat-based dishes influenced by American cuisine. She said, "Grains and vegetables were a main part of everyday traditional meals, but look at what we have become, meat in every dish." Stews, vegetables, and grains are disappearing from children's diet, not because of their lack of nutritious wholesomeness, but rather, the child's unwillingness to consume such meals.

There is an apparent shift in children's food preferences as accommodated by mothers. Traditional meals such as stuffed intestines and stomachs, sheep heads or hooves, are now confined to the memories of mothers, grandmothers, and great grandmothers. In some cases, mothers resist preparing modern international recipes and insist on raising their children to consume traditional Lebanese recipes. In rare cases, the children were the ones holding on to the wholesome Mediterranean cuisine, asking their mothers to refrain from trying and learning new recipes.

Constructions of cooking experiences

The learning process was also influenced by the mothers' constructions of cooking and its role in the family's wellbeing. All the Lebanese women interviewed refused to consider cooking as a burden; they agreed that it is a mother's duty to cook. Predominantly, the participants constructed cooking as their "responsibility" and "the most important thing for a mother." Diala (76) even took this responsibility further and said, "If a mother does not prepare food for her family, it is as if she did nothing." The participants were very proud of themselves when talking about their cooking and their roles as the responsible individuals for food preparation in their households.

Mothers do not see food preparation as a burden, but rather, as an activity they enjoy doing. Mona (56) considers cooking "a game" that she enjoys participating in as she prepares difficult and time-consuming meals such as "shish barak". Joumana (57) finds cooking entertaining, insisting on "enjoying the moment" while cooking for the food to be delicious. The mothers believe that a meal hastily prepared will not be delicious, even if it contains the same ingredients. Noha (51) would not cook if she was angry as negative emotions ruin meals. She said, "When anger enters the process, you start cooking just to get it over with, it becomes a duty. It is all about the vibes you bring to cooking, if you are relaxed and comfortable, cooking is going to come from the heart and the food is going to be delicious."

Food is cooked with love as mothers see their affection as a necessary ingredient for cooking tasty meals. The mothers always said that they cooked from their hearts. Rima (57) sees cooking as a genuine emotional investment of love that makes food taste better, transforming a simple nutritious meal into a reservoir of love. Cooking with love becomes like a charm translating into positive vibes. Lina (50) believes that, for a mother, cooking is an immersive state that is woven with emotions and the aspiration to create a warm and welcoming sensation to the house through a single dish. For Lina, a home with no prepared meals is a cold home. She said,

> I think that a house without delicious aromas has no life. The smell of food gives out a positive atmosphere in the house; although it may be annoying sometimes, but, like warmth during winter, we need it. This is what I believe. A woman's house with no food is so cold. The tenderness, the love, the family, these are the things I have always loved.

Mindfulness is a crucial part of the cooking process, as expressed by Lina who said, "With the ingredients I have, I cook with so much love because I want to. While I am cooking, I am thinking of how I am going to arrange the table. Nothing is random. I like to decorate food as what you see comes before what you taste."

While mindfulness and love in cooking are mentally rewarding for mothers giving them a feeling of purpose and self-worth, for some mothers, deciding what to cook is a source of anxiety. Although cooking itself is not a burden, it is still a toll on some to decide what to cook for that day or the next. Roula (46) expressed this never-ending decision-making process as a worry that she and other mothers have to face every day. She said, "Let us assume you cooked food for today, you start thinking about what you will prepare tomorrow." In extreme cases such as Mona's (56), a mother is absorbed by the idea of food preparation for her loved ones to an extent that she dreams of what to cook for the next day. Similarly, Ghiwa (41) will not sleep before deciding what to cook the next day and would worry that her girls would come home to find that the food is not ready. In Ghiwa's words, "I would be going nuts until I finish preparing food for them." This anxiety of what to prepare for the family is subsided when the food is ready. Mirna (49) feels relieved when she prepares food, knowing that whoever comes home would find a ready home-cooked meal.

Despite this love, there was a clear reluctance among the mothers in having someone in the kitchen while they do their magic. Most of the participants do not like the presence of others in their kitchens while preparing food. In fact, many of them reject outside help or an extra set of hands as that "spoils the food." This might impede the younger generation's learning process. The younger generation rarely had the chance to observe their mothers cook and thus missed out on getting socialized into the cooking process. Kitchens were constructed as places which make "mothers feel at home"; any outsider who enters in the hope of helping would definitely disturb the peace and the performance of cooking. For example, Hiyam (45) hates any help when it comes to cooking because she likes to be in control of the whole process as she "is already used to it and knows where everything is placed." Having someone in the kitchen during food preparation opens the door to chaos. The insistence of these mothers on having their own space while cooking with no interference reflects on their obsession with controlling the process to guarantee a positive result. Rima (57) said that while cooking, entering the kitchen is forbidden for all other family members, as she hates someone watching her or touching the food during its preparation. In rare cases, when the mother needs some support in food preparation, she might ask the helper (many Lebanese housewives have home helpers) to squeeze lemons or crush garlic cloves, but assembling the food and the cooking process itself is under her sole authority. Cooking is perceived as a divine mission that should not be desecrated by other hands. A possible interpretation could be that mothers possibly derive some sort of control over their households and a sense of self-worth from being responsible for cooking and having their own space at home, as explained by Dixey (1996).

Food socialization influencing cooking experiences and ordering behaviors

The attachment to cooking and the entangled relationship of mothers with this practice is a function of their culture and upbringing. Ghorra (60) said, "I cannot tell them [her kids] to buy a sandwich or order food. We were brought up on that principle, and during our time, there was no such thing as delivery food." To Ghorra, it was a matter of principle and upbringing. Consequently, most of the interviewed were very hostile to the "new trend" of ordering food or "eating out." This was more expressed by the older participants who were brought up eating home-cooked meals only. Despite the enmity towards fast-food meals and restaurants, the community is witnessing a burgeoning food business based on delivery services of fast food as well as traditional, authentic Lebanese dishes.

Yet, and consistent with the literature, it was clear that all interviewed mothers believe that home-cooked meals were cleaner and healthier than ready-made and vendor-based meals (Mills et al., 2017). They also prefer their food over any ready-made meals or snacks, food products sold in markets, and meals offered from their neighbors. They took pride in their cooking and more so in preparing what is locally referred to as "Moune," traditional Lebanese preserved foods. They were generally confident in their cooking skills and, as Soraya (57) bragged, "In all honesty, no one cooks food that is tastier than mine." With such commitment to and identification with cooking, when do these mothers order food or eat out?

Participants resorted to ordering food or eating out only in specific circumstances, such as special occasions or when it is impossible for the mother to cook. Ghorra (60), who is against fast food, said, "I only buy food when it is impossible for me to cook. I worry about eating in restaurants." It is this impossibility of fulfilling her role that she would feel obliged to order from restaurants. There is an issue of trust in the quality of food ordered and how it pales in comparison to the meals prepared by the mothers.

On rare occasions, mothers like Mounia (51) might order food when they do not feel like cooking. Although Mounia strongly believes that her food is better than anything being sold in the market, she would still order, "Sometimes, just because people are in the mood for non-Lebanese food." Still, the main reason to eat out or order food is celebrating special occasions like weddings and anniversaries. Maya (57) and her family only eat out when celebrating very special occasions; these outings are seen as a chance for children to eat out and for mothers to take a break from the kitchen. This means that Maya eats out four to five times a year as she prefers to gather the family at home and make them have what she prepared. But, for her comfort, they go out. Wardeh (45) and her family eat out only when invited to a wedding or to a restaurant by a close relative or friend. She thinks of it as "only eating out when we have to."

Food socialization: the good old days

The older participants lamented the good old days and drew a very pessimistic view of the younger families. The older women accused young mothers of being lazy and cutting corners, forsaking the health of their families. Lynn (42), for example, said,

> The new generation [24–25 years old] buys a hefty amount of canned food and even relies on ready-made products for their kids to spare themselves any additional work. Why not offer my child better-quality food if it only requires a little extra effort from my side? Why get them ready-made meals if there are a lot of things a mother can prepare at home?

Diana (54) believes children nowadays rarely hear the word "no" and are overaccommodated in their whims by their parents. Like Diana, Soraya (57) cannot accept the permissive style of parents these days. She said,

> My children did not have a choice but to eat what I prepared, otherwise they would get spanked. They had two options: either eat or go to bed hungry. But if my 9 year old grandson wants a pizza at 11 pm, he will get a pizza. At 11 pm, my grandson, who is thin and does not eat much, told

> his dad "I crave Nifa (lamb head)"; his dad then drove all the way to Bourj Hamoud and got him three lamb heads. If I were him, I would never do that! Let the morning come and then I would make him some.

The mothers discussed the need for kids to learn to respect food and eat leftovers, because food is a blessing. Hanan (45) emphasizes this by saying "It is a matter of principle. Food is supposed to be eaten. Leftover or not, it is still food. Food on the table is always a blessing." The older generation took respect for food very seriously as they experienced the blessing of having food in times of scarcity. Zehri (36) said, "I was brought up to respect food and finish any meal that was prepared. The old generation placed sacred value on everything, including food."

Yet, children are becoming more vocal about their food choices. Most mothers cook while catering to their children's food preferences. They consult with their children ahead of time, and try to avoid preparing meals they do not like. While the older generation grew up eating whatever they were offered and rarely challenged their parents with their food choices, the younger generation seems to be more open to preparing food their kids like, thus avoiding unnecessary clashes and situations of force feeding. Many mothers share the view of Nada (30) when she said,

> You know, there are people who apply this rule: "you have to eat this meal, or you will not eat anything else." No, I do not really apply this, because I feel that the kids are like adults, they do not like eating everything. I usually pick meals that everyone loves.

Mothers use techniques such as consulting with their children on preferred dishes and accommodating their food requests, to avoid clashes over food. They sometimes find themselves adjusting and adapting their cooking regimes and household routines to satisfy their children's demands. Some of them described how they tend to pair leftovers with a side dish, or keep the leftover meals for the next day in order to cater to their children's daily appetite for "something different." Other mothers exhibit great versatility when faced with conflicting demands from family members. Zehri (36) designates a meal day for each of her children, where each one of them gets to eat whatever he or she wants. Lynn (42) does not fully cater to her children's food preferences as she believes cooking two to three meals is absurd and downright "forbidden."

According to Nada, who has adopted a permissive feeding style when introducing her children to food, there are some meals she cannot force her children to eat since she cannot oblige herself either. Similarly, Lina (50) believes that if kids find a particular ingredient unpalatable, then they do not have to eat it. She said, "I do not force my son; I let him choose, or I approach the matter nicely. He makes his own decisions and has the freedom of choice." Some mothers often go to greater lengths and cook separate meals for their children and themselves. When Joumana (57) or Diana (54) cook meals their children do not eat, they prepare something kids like on the side. In a few cases, a mother gives up and opens canned food or orders in. In Salwa's case (52), her children are now men who usually order in when they do not like the food she has prepared, or they eat fries, salads, or canned tuna.

Some mothers tend to take an authoritative approach with regards to their children's eating habits. They force their children to eat what is available by threatening them with punishment. Ghiwa (41) always finds success when convincing her children to eat meals she has cooked under the pretext of "not having money to eat the next day." Other mothers negotiate food with their kids by striking special deals which involve rewards. For instance, Lamia (44) would promise to prepare something else like French fries with ketchup for her children, and Zalfa (33) would bribe her daughter to eat by offering her a chocolate bar. Some mothers tend to juggle their children's demands with healthy eating. Youmna (50), for example, forces her children to eat "makhlouta," "hrisseh," "berghol," and lentil-based meals because they are "healthy" dishes; but sometimes, she has to prepare meals that would "please them."

Feeding a fast-paced lifestyle

When making food choices, some mothers take into consideration time and effort, and attach great importance to convenience. As such, they might decide to go for easier and quicker alternatives like ready-to-eat meals, pre-packed products, and delivered food. The reductionist trend in food preparation is influencing the Lebanese food culture, thus changing traditional food practices. Mothers attribute this shift to the rise of working mothers, fast-paced lifestyles, and smaller family sizes. Souad (48) would not prepare a time-consuming traditional meal if there was no one around to share it with. She said, "Why go through the hassle of preparing Hrisseh when my husband and I are alone. It is more convenient to order than to preparing it myself."

Many mothers believe times have changed, with women pursuing careers and no time to prepare three meals a day. Back in the day, homemakers grew their own vegetables, and prepared and stored food in their food pantries to use over the winter. People also raised cattle and used the fresh milk to make butter, yoghurt, or cheese. Maya (57) described the traditional rural lifestyle with an Arabic proverb, "A sufficed farmer is a hidden Sultan."

According to Linda (44), "The sheer amount of products available on supermarket shelves nowadays is confusing." The desserts like "maamoul," "kaak," and "rice pudding" were homemade using local ingredients, instead of the processed sweets of jello, custard, cake, and crème caramel. As everything became readily available, food preparation and preservation became pointless to some. Compared to traditional dishes, modern Western dishes take less time to prepare. Ghorra (60) explains,

> New modern meals are easier, and there are ready-made things that one can buy like hamburgers and nuggets; it is much easier. In contrast, the Lebanese

meals need at least one to two hours to prepare, no matter how much you rush the process. Traditional cooking still exists, but to a lesser extent.

Food is a love letter

Food plays a vital role in bringing family members together. Feeding the family with hearty home-cooked meals strengthens family ties and is perceived as a special social activity with loved ones, where emotions and experiences are shared around the table. For Wardeh (45), talking about their day with her children is a perfect way of staying connected. She said, "It is all about getting together at 3 o'clock and having lunch together. It is less about the food and more about catching up." Yet, families rarely find the time to get together and share a meal. Many mothers describe how family members no longer sit around the table during dinnertime; instead, they tend to have light meals or snacks in a hurry. Mounia (51) said, "Gathering around food was something special. We were raised on certain traditions and principles; these traditions are on the brink of extinction."

The fast-paced lifestyle leaves families with little time to prepare nutritious wholesome meals. Mothers routinely send over food to their married children to make sure they are eating healthily. Some mothers take it to the extreme and alter their diets in order to cater to their children's food preferences. Ghorra (60) even travels to see her working daughter in Dubai to prepare and store her favorite meals in the freezer for whenever she is feeling under the weather or tired. Haniyeh (85), who is elderly now, still prepares traditional dishes for her adult children because of their hectic schedule, and drops off the food for them in their residences.

Not all mothers received food from their parents, but for most of them, they still believe food sharing (sending and receiving) in the family was very common, transcending geographic limitations and age. Food can be thought of as a love letter from a mother to her child no matter how old she or he is. Even when the children no longer reside with their parents, mothers still feel the need to provide for them the same way she does for their other siblings.

Mothers tend to take food sharing to a whole new level as they sometimes end up with no food at all but still come out satisfied knowing their children are well fed and happy. Guilt about enjoying food urges some mothers to continue sending meals to their children. Haniyeh (85) said, "If I eat a meal my children enjoy, I start to feel bad and think about them because they might not be having this meal." While children moving out of the family house for work or marriage is normal, parents worry that their children are not well fed. Hanadi (66) still cooks and sends her sons their favorite meals. Leila (70) cannot eat anything without sharing her food with her children; she said, "When I cook a meal, I want everyone to eat and enjoy themselves. I come out of all that having eaten nothing but still satiated from the joy of seeing everyone happy." Mothers who cannot share the food with their children feel sad; Jinan (78) laments the experience of eating without her children, "I am aware of the fact that my children are independent grown-ups, but I cannot eat a meal without them, I just cannot. Swallowing every bite seems like a hard-fought battle." These findings are consistent with those of Barakat (1993), who states that some Arab parents, and particularly mothers, prioritize their children's happiness over their own in a very extreme manner; their children's happiness is the foundation of theirs.

On the receiving end, Wassima (33) considers her mother's food-sharing practice as a blessing; "They put their heart and sweat into everything they cook; you are eating healthy food that has no chemicals." Children see their parents' food as an extension of their love and commitment to take care of them and their wellbeing. Sentiment is always attached to food in the Lebanese culture. Zehri (36) and Souad (48) both agree that they can never prepare food that tastes as good as their mothers', "it will always be different". Children perceive their mothers as great cooks with the ability to add a unique flavor to food with a single touch. Lina (50) believes that a "mother's touch" can make or break a perfect meal. The participants reflected on their mothers' food-sharing practices as an uncut umbilical cord to home and the good old times. They idolized their mothers so much that Diala (76) said, "Even if a mother cooks a bag of stones, they will taste delicious."

Mothers who could cook traditional time-consuming meals strive to maintain the authenticity of Lebanese cuisine in their communities, not just on the family level. The villages are known to be tightly knit communities with strong social ties. When Jinan (78) bakes, her happiness lies in watching her family and friends enjoy her delicious pastries. Her happiness and wellbeing come from making others happy through food preparation and sharing. Salwa (52) concurs with "the more, the merrier" attitude. We experienced this generosity and hospitality during our house visits, capturing it in one of the journal entries:

> The coffee table would always be filled with finger food (fresh and dried fruits, and homemade sweets), and I was never allowed to leave without bags filled with local produce (soap, tea leaves, mouneh, and manakich). Their pride was also evident whenever something they had made or grown was handed over.

Food cooking experience and its contribution to wellbeing and food marketing

Consumers hold different types of food-related goals which influence FWB, namely *functional, hedonic,* or *symbolic* (Bublitz et al., 2013). Consumers with functional goals examine their food consumption to improve health or reduce health risks by eating healthily (Vallis et al., 2003). The hedonic goals revolve around enjoying the savory sensation of food. Consumers with symbolic goals strengthen social bonds through eating and strive to express their identity through food-related activities (Motley & Perry, 2009).

The FWB concept defines a positive relationship with food by balancing and satisfying the aforementioned goals. In this study, mothers integrate the three types of goals into their cooking to ensure their own and families' wellbeing. With regards to the functional goal, mothers think of themselves as the nutritional gatekeepers of their children's diets, be it through their weekly food schedule, their authoritative approach to making their children eat healthy food, or the deals they strike with their children. Mothers also achieve the functional goal by using known ingredients to prepare wholesome home-cooked meals in place of consuming ready-made meals or fast food, or going out for a family meal. This goal is also reached by the mother's willingness to share healthy home-cooked meals with her grown children in today's fast-paced world. Research has shown that home cooking is associated with a range of benefits, such as consuming smaller portions, fewer calories, more fruits and vegetables (Chu et al., 2014), and has advantages in terms of food literacy and skills, confidence, and attitudes (Mills et al., 2017).

The hedonic goal is reached through enjoying every moment of the cooking process, from getting the ingredients, to transforming those ingredients to home-cooked meals, and savoring the food itself. The study sheds light on this point when discussing the constructions of cooking, specifically when mothers view the cooking process as an entertaining activity that should not be trivialized. With regards to eating, mothers work towards the hedonic goal by involving their families in the decision-making process of meal choices, permissively catering to their happiness through preparing meals they will definitely enjoy. In turn, their happiness becomes hers as well. Moreover, the hedonic goal is further expressed via children's impression of their mothers' food. Whenever they eat a home-cooked meal, they will show gratitude and happiness, and express how their mothers' food is different and always a blessing. The pleasure associated with food is likely intertwined with memories that connect some foods with positive experiences such as social occasions or family. Mothers tend to balance the hedonic and functional goals to both satisfy their own and children's needs. They are inclined to give in to their children's food demands; however, their duty is to always oversee their children's health and wellbeing.

Mothers integrate the symbolic goal into their cooking by constructing a social get-together around food; it is no longer about socializing their children to good nutritional habits but the social benefits it is accompanied by. Family ties are usually reinforced with food and eating home-cooked meals together. Mothers gain a sense of fulfillment, a confidence booster, and a sense of self-worth and purpose whenever they prepare and send over home-cooked meals, as it will make their families and loved ones happy. They use cooking to explore themselves further and achieve a higher level of individual and societal wellbeing, consistent with the FWB framework (Block et al., 2011).

The current Lebanese market and mothers usually stand on opposite sides of the spectrum. The food market's mission does not appeal to Lebanese mothers, as they tend to favor home-cooked meals over ready-made meals, fast food, and eating out. The older generation considers current food marketing methods to be a negative impact on the younger generation's food and eating habits.

As such, they are not an eligible target audience even if mothers are central to home cooking and food marketing in general. Ready-made meals and fast food are staple parts of today's food marketing campaigns, and the younger generation is constantly bombarded with food ads from several fast-food chains, supermarkets, and restaurants and through a plethora of mediums. However, it is the mothers' responsibility to advocate traditional Lebanese cuisine in their own homes and properly socialize their children to consuming home-cooked meals. With that in mind, the market has also shown signs of accommodating the mindset of Lebanese mothers by filling supermarket shelves with Lebanese food products, and traditional preserved food, and including families in advertisements and food campaigns to foster the construction of family mealtime. It is up to the market to downsize its focus on convenient meals and shift it towards reinforcing cooking healthy traditional home-cooked meals. Food marketing can do well to glorify the hardships and complex processes of cooking in an attempt to get mothers and children inside the kitchen.

Conclusions

This ethnographic study explored the ways rural Lebanese women get socialized into cooking and the kind of food practices they pass on to their children. It situates cooking as a contested process where modernity and traditions get negotiated. The study also reflects the constructions of mothers as they contrast the older generations' food practices compared to the younger, more Westernized generations. It furthers our understanding of the central role cooking, especially traditional Lebanese cuisine, plays in the Lebanese mothers' lives and their families' wellbeing. By doing that, the study contextualizes the experiential food learning process of Mediterranean cuisine by mothers in a rural setting.

The study found that mothers not only conceptualize cooking as an ordinary necessary daily routine task but also a social connector and food socializer for their families. Through their cooking practices, mothers socialize their children to good nutritional habits. Cooking wholesome meals from the Lebanese repertoire of recipes allows mothers to care for their families' overall psychological, physical, emotional, and social wellbeing. This is in line with previous studies where mothers viewed food as a social lubricant to reinforce ties with their family members (Judd et al., 2014).

Home food preparation was portrayed as a complex activity, with heterogeneous practices, experiences, and perceptions over different life stages for every mother, according to shifting priorities and circumstances with social role change.

For most of the participants, their role as mothers proved to be a personal motivation to cook, and was recognized as part of their identities. They saw it as part of their duty as homemakers to provide wholesome meals for their households. This finding was also reported by Tapper and Zubeida (2000) who noted that an important component of Arab women's definition of self is attributed to their role as the main meal providers for their families.

Through their cooking practices, mothers might aspire to meet some of the sociocultural expectations from their societies and themselves. This finding corroborates the arguments brought forward by Bugge and Almås (2006: 210) that it is socially safe to be portrayed as a "good mother" and that mothers who rarely cook or do not cook at all are generally looked down upon. According to Mills et al. (2017), social desirability and behavioral norms drive mothers to provide home-cooked meals for their children, as serving meals straight out of a packet without adding a personal touch was often embarrassing. In our case, it is evident that women who "make sandwiches," "order food delivered to their doorsteps," or "rely on frozen or canned products" are examples of people mothers do not want to be associated with or even compared to. Preparing traditional healthy meals could have been driven by the fulfilment of self-identity as competent cooks. Our study also indicated that mothers have ideals that they try to live or look up to in their food practices, which are, in most cases, their own mothers. This further supports the idea that there is a strong bond between mothers and daughters mediated by food and cooking, where adopting elements of childhood patterns is an important component of the social reproduction of a family identity across generations (Bowen and Devine, 2011).

As with any research, this work has a set of limitations. First, the qualitative research approach adopted for the study limits the generalizability of the findings to broader Lebanon. However, our findings are in line with those of previous studies on mothers' constructions of home food preparation and their learning experiences, which suggests that the main themes identified are likely to be transferable. Second, the interview context might have inclined some of the participants to provide us with socially desirable responses, particularly when they were asked about their family food consumption practices, which could have biased some of their answers. With an effort to reduce this possibility, we employed a reflexive interviewing approach that involved providing adequate time for the participants to consider their responses, reminding them that honesty was better than any perceived correct answer, and making sure all questions were well understood by rephrasing as we saw fit.

Acknowledgments

This research was supported by a grant from the United States Agency for International Development (USAID). The content is the sole responsibility of the authors and does not necessarily reflect the official views of USAID or the United States government.

We thank the interview participants for generously giving their time to participate in this research; the research team who assisted with the transcription and translation processes, Elie Marj and Elie Kanaan; and the Nature Conservation Center (NCC) for making this effort possible. In this context, we acknowledge the fine work done by NCC's copy-editor for this chapter, Ahmad Ayoub. Finally, we would like to thank the editor for her comments on earlier drafts.

Note

1 All participants' names were changed for confidentiality purposes. The number in the brackets after each participant's name is her age.

References

Bandura, A. (1977). *Social Learning Theory*. Englewood Cliffs, NJ: Holt, Rinehart, and Winston.

Barakat, H. (1993). *The Arab World: Society, Culture, and State*. Berkeley, CA: University of California Press.

Beets, M.W., Swanger, K., Wilcox, D.R., & Cardinal, B.J. (2007). Using hands-on demonstrations to promote cooking behaviors with young adolescents: The culinary camp summer cooking program. *Journal of Nutrition Education and Behavior*, 39(5), 288–289.

Berger, P.L., & Luckmann, T. (1989). *Die gesellschaftliche Konstruktion der Wirklichkeit: eine Theorie der Wissenssoziologie (The social construction of reality: A theory of the science of knowledge)*. Frankfurt: Fischer.

Berry, E.M., & De Geest, S. (2012). Tell me what you eat and I will tell you your sociotype: Coping with diabesity. *Rambam Maimonides Medical Journal*, 3(2).

Berry, E.M., Arnoni, Y., & Aviram, M. (2011). The Middle Eastern and biblical origins of the Mediterranean diet. *Public Health Nutrition*, 14(12A), 2288–2295.

Biernacki, P., & Waldorf, D. (1981). Snowball sampling: Problems and techniques of chain referral sampling. *Sociological Methods and Research*, 10(2), 141–163.

Birch, L.L. (1998). Development of food acceptance patterns in the first years of life. *Proceedings of the Nutrition Society*, 57(4), 617–624.

Birch, L.L., & Fisher, J.A. (1995). Appetite and eating behavior in children. *Pediatric Clinics*, 42(4), 931–953.

Blissett, J. (2011). Relationships between parenting style, feeding style and feeding practices and fruit and vegetable consumption in early childhood. *Appetite*, 57(3), 826–831.

Blissett, J., & Haycraft, E. (2008). Are parenting style and controlling feeding practices related? *Appetite*, 50(2–3), 477–485.

Block, L.G., Grier, S.A., Childers, T.L., Davis, B., Ebert, J.E., Kumanyika, S. … Pettigrew, S. (2011). From nutrients to nurturance: A conceptual introduction to food wellbeing. *Journal of Public Policy and Marketing*, 30(1), 5–13.

Bowen, R.L., & Devine, C.M. (2011). "Watching a person who knows how to cook, you'll learn a lot": Linked lives, cultural transmission, and the food choices of Puerto Rican girls. *Appetite*, 56(2), 290–298.

Bublitz, M.G., Peracchio, L.A., Andreasen, A.R., Kees, J., Kidwell, B., Miller, E.G. … Vallen, B. (2011). The quest for eating right: Advancing food wellbeing. *Journal of Research for Consumers*, 19, 1.

Bublitz, M.G., Peracchio, L.A., Andreasen, A.R., Kees, J., Kidwell, B., Miller, E.G. … Vallen, B. (2013). Promoting positive change: Advancing the food wellbeing paradigm. *Journal of Business Research*, 66(8), 1211–1218.

Bugge, A.B., & Almås, R. (2006). Domestic dinner: Representations and practices of a proper meal among young suburban mothers. *Journal of Consumer Culture*, 6(2), 203–228.

Bukhari, A., Fredericks, L., & Wylie-Rosett, J. (2011). Strategies to promote high school students' healthful food choices. *Journal of Nutrition Education and Behavior*, 43(5), 414–418.

Caraher, M. (2012). *Cooking in Crisis: Lessons from the UK*. London: Centre for Food Policy.

Caraher, M., & Lang, T. (1999). Can't cook, won't cook: A review of cooking skills and their relevance to health promotion. *International Journal of Health Promotion and Education*, 37(3), 89–100.

Caraher, M., Dixon, P., Lang, T., & Carr-Hill, R. (1999). The state of cooking in England: The relationship of cooking skills to food choice. *British Food Journal*, 101(8), 590–609.

Carter, W. (2010). Cooking your way to good health. *Perspectives in Public Health*, 130(4), 161–162.

Chu, Y.L., Storey, K.E., & Veugelers, P.J. (2014). Involvement in meal preparation at home is associated with better diet quality among Canadian children. *Journal of Nutrition Education and Behavior*, 46(4), 304–308.

Clifford, D., Anderson, J., Auld, G., & Champ, J. (2009). Good Grubbin': impact of a TV cooking show for college students living off campus. *Journal of Nutrition Education and Behavior*, 41(3), 194–200.

Deer, F., Falkenberg, T., McMillan, B., & Sims, L. (2014). Sustainable wellbeing: Concepts, issues, and educational practices. Retrieved from: www.cityuniversity.ca/wp-content/uploads/2015/02/Sustainable-wellbeing-2014.pdf

Dernini, S. (2011). The erosion and the renaissance of the Mediterranean diet: A sustainable cultural resource. *Quaderns de la Mediterrania, IEMED, Barcelona*, 16, 75–82.

Dixey, R. (1996). Gender perspectives on food and cooking skills. *British Food Journal*, 98(10), 35–41.

Engler-Stringer, R. (2010). Food, cooking skills, and health: A literature review. *Canadian Journal of Dietetic Practice and Research*, 71(3), 141–145.

Fisher, C., Nicholas, P., & Marshall, W. (2011). Cooking in schools: Rewarding teachers for inspiring adolescents to make healthy choices. *Nutrition Bulletin*, 36(1), 120–123.

Foley, W., Spurr, S., Lenoy, L., De Jong, M., & Fichera, R. (2011). Cooking skills are important competencies for promoting healthy eating in an urban Indigenous health service. *Nutrition and Dietetics*, 68(4), 291–296.

García-González, Á., Achón, M., Alonso-Aperte, E., & Varela-Moreiras, G. (2018). Identifying factors related to food agency: Cooking habits in the Spanish adult population – a cross-sectional study. *Nutrients*, 10(2), 217.

Gatenby, L.A., Donnelly, J., & Connell, R. (2011). Cooking communities: Using multicultural after-school cooking clubs to enhance community cohesion. *Nutrition Bulletin*, 36(1), 108–112.

Geertz, C. (1973). 1993. *The Interpretation of Cultures: Selected Essays*. New York: Basic Books.

Glaser, B.G., & Strauss, A.L. (1967). *The Discovery of Grounded Theory: Strategies for Qualitative Theory*. New Brunswick, NJ: Aldine Transaction.

Gregory, S. (1995). Using qualitative research for the sociology of food. *British Food Journal*, 97(7), 32–35.

Hubbs-Tait, L., Kennedy, T.S., Page, M.C., Topham, G.L., & Harrist, A.W. (2008). Parental feeding practices predict authoritative, authoritarian, and permissive parenting styles. *Journal of the American Dietetic Association*, 108(7), 1154–1161.

Hwalla, N., & El Khoury, D.T.D. (2008). Lebanese traditional diets and health effects In *Wild-Type Food in Health Promotion and Disease Prevention*. New York: Humana Press, pp. 493–498.

Jabs, J., Devine, C.M., Bisogni, C.A., Farrell, T.J., Jastran, M., & Wethington, E. (2007). Trying to find the quickest way: Employed mothers' constructions of time for food. *Journal of Nutrition Education and Behavior*, 39(1), 18–25.

Jaffe, J., & Gertler, M. (2006). Victual vicissitudes: Consumer deskilling and the (gendered) transformation of food systems. *Agriculture and Human Values*, 23(2), 143–162.

Janz, K.F., Burns, T.L., & Levy, S.M. (2005). Tracking of activity and sedentary behaviors in childhood: The Iowa Bone Development Study. *American Journal of Preventive Medicine, 29*(3), 171–178.

Johnson, J.C. (Ed.). (1990). *Selecting Ethnographic Informants* (Vol. 22). New York: Sage.

Judd, S.M., Newton, J.D., Newton, F.J., & Ewing, M.T. (2014). When nutritional guidelines and life collide: Family fruit and vegetable socialisation practices in low socioeconomic communities. *Journal of Marketing Management*, 30(15–16), 1625–1653.

Kolb, D. (1984). *Experiential Learning as the Science of Learning and Development*. Englewood Cliffs, NJ: Prentice Hall.

Kolb, A.Y., & Kolb, D.A. (2012). Experiential learning theory. In *Encyclopedia of the Sciences of Learning*. Boston, MA: Springer, pp. 1215–1219.

Lang, T., & Caraher, M. (2001). Is there a culinary skills transition? Data and debate from the UK about changes in cooking culture. *Journal of the HEIA*, 8(2), 2–14.

Lavelle, F., Spence, M., Hollywood, L., McGowan, L., Surgenor, D., McCloat, A. ... Dean, M. (2016). Learning cooking skills at different ages: A cross-sectional study. *International Journal of Behavioral Nutrition and Physical Activity, 13*(1), 119.

Lieberman, M. (2016). Beirut awarded best city for food. *Travel + Leisure – Food and Drink*, August 12. Retrieved from www.travelandleisure.com/food-drink/worlds-best-cities-for-food#beirut-lebanon-market-food

López Torres, L.P. (2016). *Para mí, lo nutritivo es lo hecho en casa. Desde la cocina hacia la alimentación y la salud: habilidades culinarias y decisiones alimentarias*. Barcelona: Universitat de Barcelona.

Mick, D.G. (2006). Meaning and mattering through transformative consumer research. *Advances in Consumer Research*, 33(1), 1–4.

Mikkilä, V., Räsänen, L., Raitakari, O.T., Pietinen, P., & Viikari, J. (2005). Consistent dietary patterns identified from childhood to adulthood: The cardiovascular risk in young Finns study. *British Journal of Nutrition*, 93(6), 923–931.

Mills, S., White, M., Wrieden, W., Brown, H., Stead, M., & Adams, J. (2017). Home food preparation practices, experiences and perceptions: A qualitative interview study with photo-elicitation. *PloS one*, 12(8), e0182842.

Moschis, G.P. (1985). The role of family communication in consumer socialization of children and adolescents. *Journal of Consumer Research*, 11(4), 898–913.

Moschis, G.P., & Moore, R.L. (1979). Decision making among the young: A socialization perspective. *Journal of Consumer Research*, 6(2), 101–112.

Motley, C.M., & Perry, V.G. (2009). Home for dinner: Exploring family food traditions. In *Enriching Theoretical and Practical Understanding of Marketing, Proceedings of the 2009 Annual Association for Marketing Theory and Practice Conference* (Vol. 18). Statesboro, GA: Georgia Southern University, p. 125.

Nutbeam, D. (2008). The evolving concept of health literacy. *Social Science and Medicine*, 67(12), 2072–2078.

Padilla, M. (2008). Dietary patterns and trends in consumption. *Mediterra*, 149–170.

Patrick, H., Nicklas, T.A., Hughes, S.O., & Morales, M. (2005). The benefits of authoritative feeding style: Caregiver feeding styles and children's food consumption patterns. *Appetite*, 44(2), 243–249.

Pettigrew, S.F. (2000). Ethnography and grounded theory: A happy marriage? *ACR North American Advances*.

Ratzan, S.C. (2001). Health literacy: Communication for the public good. *Health Promotion International*, 16(2), 207–214.

Slocum, R. (2008). Thinking race through corporeal feminist theory: Divisions and intimacies at the Minneapolis farmers' market. *Social and Cultural Geography*, 9(8), 849–869.

Tapper, R., & Zubaida, S. (Eds). (2000). *A Taste of Thyme: Culinary Cultures of the Middle East.* New York: Tauris Parke.

Trubek, A.B., & Belliveau, C. (2009). Cooking as pedagogy: Engaging the senses through experiential learning. *Anthropology News*, 50(4), 16–16.

UNESCO. (2010). *Representative List of the Intangible Cultural Heritage of Humanity.* Retrieved from: https://ich.unesco.org/doc/src/17331-EN.pdf

Vallis, M., Ruggiero, L., Greene, G., Jones, H., Zinman, B., Rossi, S. ... Prochaska, J.O. (2003). Stages of change for healthy eating in diabetes: Relation to demographic, eating-related, health care utilization, and psychosocial factors. *Diabetes Care*, 26(5), 1468–1474.

Woodruff, S.J., & Hanning, R.M. (2009). Effect of meal environment on diet quality rating. *Canadian Journal of Dietetic Practice and Research*, 70(3), 118–124.

Worsley, A. (2002). Nutrition knowledge and food consumption: Can nutrition knowledge change food behaviour? *Asia Pacific Journal of Clinical Nutrition*, 11, S579–S585.

Worsley, A., Wang, W., Ismail, S., & Ridley, S. (2014). Consumers' interest in learning about cooking: The influence of age, gender and education. *International Journal of Consumer Studies*, 38(3), 258–264.

Yehya, N.A., & Dutta, M.J. (2010). Health, religion, and meaning: A culture-centered study of Druze women. *Qualitative Health Research*, 20(6), 845–858.

9 Exploring bicultural (Japanese and American) food experiences

Food aesthetic, pleasure, and wellbeing

Emily M. Moscato

Food both unites us and differentiates us. Taste preferences, shared meals, and ritualized consumption provide opportunities to savor food and reinforce our interpersonal, communal, and cultural belonging every day. Through these means, we can derive pleasurable rewards and enhance meaningful fulfillment through food and positively contribute to our wellbeing and that of others (Ryan and Deci, 2001). A culture's orientation towards food – established through activities and shared understandings that are perpetuated through traditions, media, and other cultural institutions – has significant consequences as to how food is interpreted by those in the culture and how it impacts their wellbeing. This chapter explores two food cultural orientations and how cultivating pleasurable experiences with food may increase wellbeing and health outcomes (Cornil and Chandon, 2016a; Rozin et al., 1999). It examines the food practices and the lived experiences of a bicultural Japanese and American family to investigate how everyday actions, norms, materials, and institutions of culture influence the pleasure derived from food.

Food cultural orientations can be conceptualized as a spectrum anchored by anxiety on one end and pleasure on the other (Rozin, 2005). The common exemplars for these two different orientations are the United States and France. The American orientation towards food consumption is based on a health focus and personal responsibility (Rozin et al., 1999). Food is perceived to be a source of contention, where individuals need to exercise restraint and take personal responsibility for their failings (Rozin, 1989). Ironically, these feelings of worry and guilt about food reduce perceived behavioral control and are counter-productive to weight management (de Witt et al., 2013; Kuijer and Boyce, 2014). This American health and avoidance orientation contrasts with the pleasure-based orientation of the French, which upholds that food is appreciated for its experiential pleasure and should be savored. The French generally consume a richer diet, yet they have lower rates of cardiovascular disease than Americans (Rozin et al., 1999).

The Japanese orientation is recognized as a balance between pleasure and health approaches, sharing similarities with both the American and French orientations (Rozin et al., 1999). Compared to these heavier meat-based Western diets, the Japanese diet is typically lower in fat and higher in fruits and vegetables

(Kudo et al., 2000; Satia-Abouta et al., 2002). In terms of health outcomes, Japanese have a longer life expectancy than the French and Americans (ranked 2, 17, and 43, respectively; CIA World Factbook, 2017). Moreover, there is growing evidence that dietary acculturation – the adoption of food choices and eating patterns of a host country, such as the United States, reduces positive health outcomes for Japanese-Americans and other immigrant groups (Satia-Abouta et al., 2002). This concern is further compounded by nutritional transition, which finds that as developing countries become more prosperous, they move from traditional diets to more Western diets (Satia, 2009).

Through comparing routine behaviors and individual experiences in Japanese and American food cultures, I sought to explore the following two questions: What food practices can increase experiences of pleasure? How do the elements of these practices enhance wellbeing? Three areas emerged in which pleasure-enhancing practices impact wellbeing: aesthetics, appreciation, and engagement. The discussion extends this exploration to pose a third question: Are there elements of Japanese practices that could be incorporated into the American culture to promote a more pleasurable relationship to food and promote wellbeing?

Worldwide over the last half century, our relationship with food has come under a spotlight, scrutinized because of the rapid increase in non-communicable (chronic) diseases (e.g., cardiovascular disease, cancer, respiratory disease, and diabetes) concurrent with excessive calorie consumption and lower exercise rates, both of which are associated with diet and lifestyle changes (World Health Organization (WHO), 2017). The United States and Mexico have two of the highest rates of overweight and obese populations in the world. In contrast, Japan has some of the lowest rates (WHO, 2016). Threatening to wellbeing are the comorbidities of excessive weight with other non-communicable diseases and mental health issues (Prince et al., 2007; Van Lente et al., 2012). These are complicated issues with many environmental, social, economic, and biological factors. There is not one single solution, but there are multiple areas for investigation and improvement. The connection between food, pleasure, and wellbeing is one such area for investigation. Interestingly, consumers define food pleasure and healthy eating quite differently. Food pleasure is associated with sensory qualities and psychosocial context, while healthy eating is related to nutrition and regulation of consumption (Landry et al., 2018). Taken in a positive light, this reveals opportunities to create stronger associations with healthier food choices and pleasure.

The dynamic construct of wellbeing is explored through the perspectives of hedonic wellbeing and eudaimonic wellbeing (Ryan and Deci, 2001). These viewpoints have select overlapping antecedents, mechanisms, and outcomes, but they take on two different positions on what constitutes wellbeing. The hedonic viewpoint focuses on increasing pleasure while minimizing punishment to promote happiness. The eudaimonic viewpoint focuses on meaning and self-realization, what it means to be a fully functional person, and how to actualize this goal (Ryan and Deci, 2000). Both viewpoints are valuable in supporting positive outcomes, such as increased life satisfaction. Food practices have the ability to promote both types of wellbeing. The focus here is on the promotion of pleasurable rewards associated with hedonic wellbeing, and the relatedness of affiliation and supportive relationships and competency associated with eudaimonic wellbeing (Ryan and Deci, 2001).

First, I set the stage by discussing practice theory, its relationship to the aesthetics of taste regimes, and contextualize both food practice and aesthetics in Japanese and American cultures. I then turn my investigation to the lived experiences of a bicultural family by first establishing my approach. Then I discuss the main participant (Yuki) in order to further situate her experiences within the two cultures and her positioning towards food. From this foundation, I explore embodied practices and the mechanisms by which they foster pleasure and wellbeing. I end with a reflection on the value of these practices and how the investigation of practices can assist in finding ways to incorporate more pleasure into the American routines.

Food practices, taste regimes, and aesthetics

The focus on food practices allows for greater understanding of how pleasure can be infused into the everyday experience with food. Through these seemingly mundane routines and rituals, we establish our orientation towards or away from the experiential pleasure of food. *Food practices* is used here as an encompassing term for production, purchasing, preparation, consumption, and disposal activities (Warde, 2016). As compound practices, food practices are made up of integrated activities and performances (Southerton and Yates, 2015; Warde, 2016). Practice theory holds that social life is constructed from ongoing routinized and recurring processes, which form habits and normalize performances (Nicolini, 2012). Examining practices and their connection to each other sheds light on pragmatic and meaning behind ways of doing as they develop, persist, shift, and fade to form social structures (Shove et al., 2012). Practices are formulated from a combination of three elements: materials – objects and technologies; competencies – techniques, ability, and skills; and meaning – symbolism, ideas, and desires (Shove et al., 2012). Investigating food through the unit of practices allows for a new perspective on how cultural beliefs and norms can influence our food relationship.

Contextualizing food practices within culture

The histories, philosophies, geographies, and demographics of Japan and the United States highlight distinctions that influence their food orientations, practices, and aesthetics. Japan has a multimillennial and unbroken cultural history whereas the United States is a combination of borrowed and newly formed cultures. Religion and spirituality play roles in shaping both cultures. Distinctions of the two philosophical orientations can be observed through numerous means, including the food rituals connected to paying homage and celebrations.

Japan's population (126.5 million) is roughly two fifths (38.7 percent) of the United States population (326.6 million). Yet Japan's landmass is 25 times smaller than the United States, allowing for approximately 1,000 people per 3 sq km compared to 1,000 people per 28 sq km in the United States (CIA World Factbook, 2017). This population density has an influence on the cultural ecology of the two countries. The wider spaces in the United States allow for larger kitchens, including larger appliances, pantries, and more living space within the kitchen while Japanese kitchens remain relatively small. This also has an influence on purchasing habits. Americans generally have more room to stockpile packaged foods and they shop less frequently. These factors also influence package size, access, and salience of food within the household (Wansink and Chandon, 2014).

The geographical and cultural orientations of the two diets create certain prototypical material differences even as globalization and localization create porous boundaries that reduce the opportunity to definitively define these cuisines (Cwiertka, 2006). For example, chicken stock, generally associated with a salty taste, is common in American cooking and flavoring while a marker in Japanese cuisine is *dashi* (made from *kombu* (edible kelp) and *katsuobushi* (preserved skipjack tuna)) broth, generally associated with *umami* or savory taste. In an illustration of globalization, *umami* has been adopted into the Western lexicon during the last century to express perceptions and appreciation for the depth of savory in foods (Ninomiya, 2015). Table 9.1 outlines some of these material differences, which have significant influence on how individuals develop tastes and competencies within their culture. Such materials, uses, and their meanings are reinforced through taste regimes.

Taste regimes and contextualizing aesthetics

Practices are culturally situated and aesthetically curated through taste regimes, which form shared understandings of materials that permeate consumer messaging and products in the marketplace (Arsel and Bean, 2012). It is through taste regimes that we acquire objects (such as a set of white eating bowls), connect objects to behavior (serving home-made squash soup), and meaning (color,

Table 9.1 Prototypical materials in Japanese and American food practices

	Eating tool	*Eating medium*	*Cooking instrument (methods)*	*Cuisine focus*
Japan	Chopsticks	Multiple small dishes	Stove top (steaming, simmering, grilling)	Fish, rice, miso, vegetables
United States	Fork	Single plate	Oven (roasting, baking)	Red meat, bread (wheat products), potatoes

warmth, and care). Taste regimes provide the structure by which objects are problematized and evaluated on how they fit within the meanings prescribed to aesthetically pleasing norms of a culture or subculture (Arsel and Bean, 2012). Satisfaction increases when practices align with taste regimes. Thus, as practices and their elements link to taste regimes, taste regimes link to the aesthetics orientation of the culture.

Aesthetics – the philosophy of defining beauty and what is beautiful – plays an important role in Japanese culture, including its food (Cwiertka, 2006; Richie, 2007). After all, "No food is 'just' food in Japan" (Allison, 1991: 196). At the same time, Japanese aesthetics cannot be easily defined (Richie, 2007) although many of its qualities have become familiar to Westerners, such as *wabi* (sober restraint, meagerness) and *sabi* (evidence of age and experience, slightly bleak). There is a strong influence of an "elegance of simplicity," which commands attentiveness to nature and discipline in art creation and consumption (Richie, 2007). Unlike Western modes of thinking, there is less focus on dichotomies (e.g., body/mind, self/group) and self-expression, which translates to Japanese aesthetics being "more concerned with the process than with the product, with the actual construction of the self than with self-expression" (Richie, 2007: 15). This orientation is reflected in Japanese food aesthetics with a focus on the processes of selection, preparation, and composition of ingredients in dishes presented – with attention paid to simplicity and curated naturalness. Aesthetics in food practices take on different material forms to highlight the meaning infused in taste regimes. With the establishment of these food practices and aesthetics – and a glimpse into their bidirectional influence on culture, I shift now to the investigation of pleasure-enhancing practices found in everyday activities and their explicit or implicit connections to wellbeing.

Investigation approach: the food experiences of a bicultural family

The research context here for exploring pleasure-enhancing practices was the lived experiences of one bicultural family. The family in question consists of my near relations: my brother, Sam (age 45); my sister-in-law, Yuki (age 42); and my two nieces, Hana and Sakura (ages 9 and 6). The primary informant was Yuki, who is Japanese and the family's nutritional gatekeeper. Yuki has lived primarily in Japan, except for spending two years with her family in the American Midwest near Chicago (2013–15) and living for several weeks on the Oregon coast with an exchange program during university. The family's experiences in the Midwest provide a valuable perspective for exploring food practices because comparison to the less familiar, the more novel, or the less comfortable is easier than reflecting on our situated, enculturated experiences as they are "too close" and go unnoticed (Hill et al., 2014).

This investigation employed a modified ethnography case study approach, complemented by an interpretative phenomenological perspective to gain further richness and accounting for my outsider position (Smith and Osborn, 2004). Data collection culminated in a six-day trip to Tokyo in March 2018 and combined previous correspondence, participant observations, a semi-structured interview, and personal introspection. The analysis focused on understanding food practices and their relationships to pleasure and wellbeing. Practices were examined through a combined exploration of their sociocultural-situated practicality and their meaning from the perspective of the participants (Hill et al., 2014). This endeavor involved paying attention to the practical and symbolic aspects of practices. Specifically, it attended to objects and embodied activities performed habitually, without contemplation, and the influences of personal history and the broader culture in the participants' life-world. Analysis moved in dynamic, iterative cycles to derive constructions of practices and situated experiences of the participants.

As a postmodern exploration of food, culture, and practices, this investigation required attention to the positioning of the participants, to my positioning, and to intersubjectivity (Gould, 2012). It was with the upmost respect that I compared these two cultures: one I was born into and the other I have experienced only as a visitor through my family connections. I felt a great weight in constructing this discussion because of the magnitude of comparing Japanese and American cultures and the respect I wished to convey to both my main informant (my sister-in-law) and a culture that was not my own. I became more comfortable in my positioning after revisiting Woermann's article on methodological situationalism (2017). Woermann argued that attention needs to be paid to lived, everyday experience in order to represent practices because "society and culture manifest in concrete, local situations" (2017: 149). I was conscious that I am decoding from an American orientation the experiences of my Japanese sister-in-law and those of my nieces. It was impossible to separate out my orientation, but I strove to present and explore findings consciously. I am also mindful that my experience as a white, non-Latinx American is different from many in the United States. Similarly, I did not want to characterize my sister-in-law as representative of all Japanese. I endeavored to take care in using an appropriate interpretivist lens to situate, analyze, and construct this exploration. As part of this process, Yuki read through this manuscript before the final submission. She made minor requests (removing a brand name from a photograph) and expanded on the meaning of *itadakimasu* and *gochisonsama* (see Appreciation section).

The art of doing food with pleasure

Situating Yuki's food practices

In their flat in the Roppongi district of Tokyo, on a quiet evening in March 2018, my sister-in-law and I sat across from each other at the dining room table. I asked Yuki about her views on food and pleasure. It was clear she has a strong interest in the subject; Yuki had taken the initiative to schedule the time for the interview. In regards to her acculturation experience, the transition to Midwest America was not easy for Yuki for many reasons, including the limited options and availability of certain fresh ingredients, especially seafood and organics. In actions indicative of her proactive nature, Yuki emailed a request to Trader Joe's to open a location in her town. She also spoke to the manager of her local supermarket requesting that they stock coffee from a favorite, small coffee roaster located on the Oregon Coast. Neither request was granted.

About an hour after our semi-structured interview, Yuki emailed me the following: "'Pleasure food' reminds me of Brillat-Savarin. I like his quote. 'The discovery of a new dish confers more happiness on humanity than the discovery of a new star.'" Yuki is passionate about food; she has taken classes in French and Japanese cuisine in order to learn "from their professional skills." To directly quote my field notes, Yuki has "mad knife skills." She cuts with precision, her knuckles perfectly placed to guide the knife and protect herself. She has a pension for quality – she seeks out and selects the best-quality proteins and fresh ingredients. When asked what foods give her pleasure, Yuki replied enthusiastically, "Consommé. It's just amazing. Wow. It's rich but not oily. Just gorgeous, golden … At the same time, not only do I remember the dish, old memories come back: fun and happy memories." In evoking both sensory pleasure and nostalgia, Yuki also illustrates how her tastes are reflective of the globalized food system.

Yuki's personal food practices demonstrate the integration of the bicultural positioning of her family (Figure 9.1). Yuki's dinner table offers a mix of Japanese and American materials used for serving and eating. The types of dishes demonstrate the global influence on her cooking. The presentation and multitude of dishes is indicative of the Japanese orientation – aesthetics that will be examined next. The remainder of the findings are structured around the three orientations to food routines and rituals summarized in Table 9.2.

Aesthetics

The aesthetics of food presentation in Japan is immediately apparent in the sizes and types of tableware and the portions of food presented at meals and for snacks. An epicurean eating perspective suggests that wellbeing can be increased by focusing on a pleasurable multisensory food aestheticism (Cornil and Chandon, 2016a). In the United States, it is common to have one main protein and "sides" (such as starches or cooked vegetables) served on a single plate with the foods coming into contact with each other and covering most of the plate. In Japan, food is typically presented in multiple small dishes to be sampled or combined by the eater. An example of this style of food presentation was offered on my flight to Japan on the Japanese-based airline ANA. Within one of the four food containers on the tray, pickled radish was placed inside a separate translucent, iridescent pink cellophane mini-cup. The container reinforced the food's distinctiveness among the other foods, and the difference in colors and textures provided a sense of variety.

Figure 9.1 Mix of influences. Japanese and Western-style serving and eating materials. Foods include (left to right): boiled *gyoza* (dumplings), Chinese-influenced; *Nabe* (hot pot), traditional Japanese meal for colder times of the year; and spring rolls with dipping sauce, Vietnamese-influenced. Credited to the author

Table 9.2 Examined Japanese food practices

Orientation	*Routines and rituals*	*Associations*	*Implications for wellbeing*
Aesthetics	Multiple, small dishes Attention to presentation	Variety Quality Admiration	Pleasure Satisfaction Mindfulness
Appreciation	*Itadakimasu* (gratitude before eating) *Gochisonsama* (after eating) Clean your plate	Value Recognition Reverence	Self-regulation Mindfulness Competency
Engagement	*Okuizome* (first meal ceremony) *Osechi* (New Year's meal) Preparing *gyoza* (dumplings)	Tradition Togetherness Sharing	Camaraderie Competency Nostalgia

The importance of aesthetics in Japanese cuisine is highlighted in the inclusion of *washoku* (a Japanese meal) in Japan's registration with the United Nations Educational, Scientific, and Cultural Organization (UNESCO) under the Representative List of the Intangible Cultural Heritage of Humanity. In the description and support for including *washoku*, UNESCO (2016) stated, "It is associated with an essential spirit of respect for nature … beautifully decorated dishes using fresh ingredients, each of which has a symbolic meaning." While the authenticity of *washoku* and its UNESCO definition has come under critical examination for its generalizations and inaccurate emic understanding (Kohsaka, 2017), certain practices that are standard in *washoku* are widely observed in Japanese meals such as visual, textural, and taste variety (Freedman, 2016). For example, food is sliced, portioned, and presented in such a way as to be easily handled by chopsticks, hands, or in limited cases, such as with *chawanmushi* (steamed egg custard), a wooden spoon. The aesthetic ideals of simplicity and the beauty found in nature are embedded in the materials and competencies of Japanese food presentation taste regimes (Figure 9.2). The food presentations emphasize separation and fragmentation; contrast and balance of oppositions in colors, shapes, and textures; and construction of the natural ideal in the food's taste and appearance (Allison, 1991; Pilcher, 2006). These qualities manifest in the Japanese food culture in multiple ways that connect aesthetics and pleasure to desirable attributes of variety and quality.

Figure 9.2 Presentation at a Tokyo fine-dining restaurant: appetizer plate (front) and *chawanmushi* (steamed egg custard; back). Credited to the author

"Not only one dish, five or six dishes"

Variety at mealtimes was a noticeable difference for Yuki between Japan and the United States. For example, Yuki was surprised by the lack of variety in the school lunches given to children in the United States: "Sometimes, I would ask about school lunch menus – 'what do you eat?' Pasta, hot dog, chicken nuggets ... every day, just the same thing." She continued,

> In Japan, there is more variety. You know, over here we have rice and miso soup – fish and meat. But with the fish, for example, we have different ways of cooking it: raw fish, fried fish, sautéed fish. Chinese, French, Italian styles ... Also of course, we have not only one dish, five or six dishes.

Variety in dishes that contain a diversity of sensory qualities fuels perceptions of distinctive experiences with consumption (Raynor, 2012). This tends to increase consumption – for both healthy and unhealthy foods (Kahn and Wansink, 2004; Raynor, 2012) and can also lead to increased pleasure (Parizel et al., 2017; Raynor and Wing, 2006).

Since variety can lead to overconsumption, portion size plays a significant role in minimizing this potential. Portion sizes in Japan are observably smaller in the majority of foodservice and grocery items. For example, in a four-pack yogurt cup, the Japanese individual serving size is typically 80 g (2.8 oz) whereas in the United States, a small four-pack cup serving size is 113 g (4 oz). These larger portion sizes have consequences in the amount of food consumed (Zlatevska et al., 2014). Individuals operate with a unit bias: "at home or in a restaurant, there is a strong tendency to finish what is served, as that is the effective unit" (Geier et al., 2006, 521). The perception of what is an adequate portion is determined by what is served, making the amount feel appropriate and optimal. Taking the visual focus away from the quantity of the food on a single plate and placing attention onto the variety and sensory qualities of the food presentation can not only increase pleasure but also reduce risks of overconsumption.

Presentation and mindfulness

Gaining pleasure from aesthetics requires attention and reflection in the moment; it connects to mindful embodiment – being conscious of our bodily states (Petit et al., 2016). Imagining the sensory stimuli – the sight, taste, smell, sound, and feel – of a food item has the ability to increase savoring and satiate with less actual consumption (Cornil and Chandon, 2016b; Morewedge et al., 2010). The aesthetic orientation of Japan is evident in the inconsistency between the prevalence of sweets and the country's comparably low level of confectionary consumption (Holtzman, 2016). Research suggests that sweets are valued highly for their attractive aesthetics and satisfaction can be gained from visual admiration of these qualities (Holtzman, 2016). From my outsider's positioning, the care placed in appearance, wrapping, and packaging aesthetics in Japan is fascinating because of the novelty and beauty. Although the reasons for these packaging norms have many origins, two aspects of culture likely have a significant impact: Japan's gift-giving customs and attentiveness to preventing the spread of germs. The latter is arguably reflected in the abundance of single-serving packaging for snacks and sweets. This can have the additional benefit of providing individuals with a cue as to when to stop eating and prevent excessive mindless eating (Stroebele et al., 2009). Gift giving when visiting someone at home or returning from holidays are common and train stations are filled with available items – mainly consumable goods that highlight regional and seasonal selections. Wrapping these items is done with a level of care and aesthetics that surpasses what is seen in the United States. Whether it is for a gift or a simple purchase, by associating the content with gift-giving rituals (Belk, 1996), the attention to presentation elevates the value of the items and the pleasure derived from them.

Appreciation

The act of appreciation has the ability to facilitate pleasure through mindful attention. Mindfulness in turn promotes self-regulation, leading to greater enjoyment and wellbeing (Petit et al., 2016; Ryan and Deci, 2001). This mindfulness is reflected in Japanese practices that honor the efforts of food production and preparation, the value of the food provided, and the act of consumption.

"Itadakimasu *means you should appreciate*"

Certain activities done in preparation for eating are reinforced in children starting with nursery school and are common across the two cultures, including washing their hands and sitting down before starting to eat. In Japan, more attention is often given to having children focus on the activity of consumption itself. Children are taught "how you should eat. They are taught manners. It's simple, but they are taught to sit down, to be quiet, and don't make a mess" (Yuki, interview). Through these means, there are fewer distractions and more attention is paid to the activity, thus, reinforcing the engagement of the five senses in the eating practice.

Before eating, children are taught to say "*itadakimasu*," which is accompanied by bringing hands together in a prayer gesture with extended fingers and a momentary slight bowing of the head towards the food. This activity continues to be practiced by adults to various degrees, sometimes said in a whisper with a slight head bow. It is not unusual to see an individual perform the ritual before eating at a restaurant. As Yuki explains, "*Itadakimasu* means you should appreciate the parent, the cook, of course, the farmer – everyone, because this food comes from someone." Yuki feels there is a lack of emphasis placed on teaching children to appreciate and respect food during its consumption. "In America, a kid's meal is *just* kid's meal"; there is little relating the food to its meaning or attention paid to understanding the process of creating the food or connecting it to its nutritional value.

In reviewing this manuscript, Yuki wanted to emphasize a missing component to *itadakimasu* – "it's appreciation for life; the life of what you ate" (July 2018). She was sure it had religious origins and wanted to provide more information on its meaning. She followed up with an email containing a quote from a website that stated it was based on Buddhist beliefs that objects contain spirits: "By taking spirits from their origins and using them to replenish yourself, you are giving honor and gratitude to the organisms that originally housed those spirits … Even if you made the meal yourself, you are still giving respect to the lives used in its creation" (nihongoshark.com/itadakimasu-meaning/). In addition, Yuki wanted to add that *gochisosama* is commonly said after the meals, with different etiquette for eating at home and away from home. She quoted another website, "There are a lot of work and effort of many people behind each meal we eat … If you had a feeling of gratitude, you wouldn't be able to throw the food so easily and could say, *Gochisosama* to all the lives and effort you received" (iromegane.com/japan/culture/the-real-meaning-of-gochisosama/). Heightening the spiritual appreciation of the food itself and those involved in its creation promotes mindfulness during the meal consumption and to the amount of food consumed. In honoring the labor and the intangible energies of the food, it is considered appropriate to "clean your plate."

Cleaning your plate

The practice of "clean your plate" is fraught with social judgments in American society. It is still a widely established norm in the United States (Loth et al., 2013), yet it is a food rule associated with an authoritarian parenting style and has been shown to encourage overeating, which can lead to adverse consequences in adulthood (Bourcier et al., 2003). The practice has the advantage of requiring children to stay at the dinner table longer, in turn giving more time together as a family and delaying the need to direct attention to other activities such as cleaning up. In addition, the tangible form of food and its consumption has the potential to act as a daily measure of nurturing, demonstrating care for the child, similar to the "good provider" motivation found in the overpurchasing and overpreparation of food (Graham-Rowe et al., 2014). It is different from other actions that are less visible or easy to monitor; food acts as a continual demonstration that the parent is satisfying needs of his or her child (Belkin, 2013). The concern with this practice is its correlation with abundance in American food presentations marked by large portion sizes; there is a danger of overeating when enforcing the clean-your-plate norm.

It was surprising to discover that this norm is also a common practice in Japan. Hana (age 9) related that on one of the first days she attended school in the United States, she astonished her principle by not having any food left on her lunch tray to throw away in the garbage bin. She was accustomed to eating everything that was given to her: "Otherwise, why is it on there?" she asked. Another time, Hana had tried to refuse a food item being added to her tray in the lunch line, and she was told, "Just take it. You don't have to eat it." These stories were retold in the family and appeared to symbolize an American orientation towards food as a simple utilitarian commodity, creating a connection between food and wastefulness. For Yuki, it provided the rationale for smaller portions. "The reason for small dishes is because you should eat everything. Usually, you should eat everything in Japan." Yuki points to a disservice she sees in minimizing the value in food, especially in socializing children,

> It's "oh, you should just eat and go play" … It becomes just about *feeding*. If you do that for kids, how do they know you should respect what is on your plate? Who made it? That food came from someone … If you select the food, you should eat it. For some adults, food is just energy. So they don't respect it.

Without respect for what is on the plate, the practice of eating is reduced to the functional action of "feeding," void of reflection and meaning, which can increase the likelihood of mindless eating and decrease the opportunity for pleasurable consumption experiences. Moreover, the discrepancies between the practices of cleaning the plate at home and throwing away food at school may cause inconsistencies with how certain healthy and unhealthy foods are perceived.

Engagement

Rituals are established through an "expressive, symbolic activity constructed of multiple behaviors that occur in a fixed, episodic sequence, and that tend to be repeated over time" (Rook, 1985: 252). Through social and shared rituals, practices encourage interpersonal relationships and increase competencies. Everyday practices are accentuated with traditions and celebrations that connect particular foods to meaningful, shared experiences. For example, in Japan, a ritual that occurs around the 100th day of life is *okuizome* or the first meal ceremony. This primarily symbolic meal can take various forms, but generally it is celebrated by presenting the infant with tastes of traditional foods such as rice, fish, soup, and pickled plum. The ceremony can also include *hagatame-ishi* which is rubbing a smooth stone on the gums of the child to ensure strong teeth. For Hana, my older niece, Yuki conducted this ceremony at a family dinner while visiting the United States. It was a modified performance surrounded by Americans unacquainted with the ritual. Yuki had selected a small smooth river stone from the garden which she washed before the meal. Hana had been gifted with a small set of red chopsticks for the occasion, which were set before her at the table. The stone was gently touched to Hana's gums, and she received a small taste of food as she sat on her mom's lap. Seeing this ceremony stands out in my mind because it was new to me and because of the materials – the prepared sampling of food, the child-size chopsticks, the stone – and the meaning of this cultural ritual – a transition to joining the communal meal, a wish for a healthy and long life. *Okuizome* can be interpreted as a welcoming into a capacious tradition of ritualized and social food practices in Japan. After all, eating together is viewed across most, if not all, cultures as critical to affiliation and enculturation (Ochs and Shohet, 2006).

Japan has a number of food traditions connected to holidays and social celebrations, such as *hishi mochi* (a tricolor sweet) associated with the ancient holiday of *Hinamatsuri* (Girl's Day); chocolate associated with the modern marketplace holidays of Valentine's Day (February 14 when gifts are given to men) and White Day (March 14 when men reciprocate to women); and *osechi* dishes for New Year's. With these foods, aesthetics plays a significant role in providing visual and ritualistic meaning to promote pleasure (Holtzman, 2016). In addition, these social food traditions focus on relationship-enhancing activities that strengthen bonds and promote affiliations (Ryan and Deci, 2001).

"It should be fun. It should come with good memories"

It is clear that Yuki finds value in having foods associated with holiday and traditions, especially homemade meals. "In [Midwest town] for Easter, on the day before the holiday, I noticed they put out hams. So wow, they have nice traditional American food. It's funny because in Japan, for us, America doesn't have many traditional homemade meals." While the Japanese and American perspectives on traditional foods may not align, both cultures appear to associate homemade food with demonstrations of caring and concern for the wellbeing of others (Moisio et al., 2004).

When asked what makes a food experience pleasurable, Yuki associates it both with consumption and preparation: "It should be fun. It should come with good memories." Interestingly, in elaborating her meaning by discussing the practice of preparing *osechi* (the New Year's meal), her explanation aligns more with the efforts of eudaimonic wellbeing than the instant reward of hedonic pleasure.

> It takes a long time to do. It takes two, three days because we use many dried foods, like dried beans, dried mushrooms – you know, shiitake mushrooms – so it takes time. So we can show, "Oh today, on the schedule, we should do this" … As a kid I didn't think it was fun, because I didn't like the taste. I didn't find it delicious. But it's important to continue the tradition, talk while making it, and build memories. So now I understand, that's why I want to demonstrate it and get the kids involved.

Yuki described how she assists in building competencies for her children through preparing *osechi* and the value she perceives in creating positive memories. Indeed, nostalgia can provide numerous benefits towards greater pleasure including generating positive affect, increasing positive self-regard, and bolstering social bonds (Wildschut et al., 2006). Additionally, research finds participation in food preparation increases the liking of healthy foods and the willingness to try novel foods (Allirot et al., 2016; Dohle et al., 2016).

"Everyone can be involved"

Connecting food with making memories and participating in preparations were also benefits Yuki highlighted in everyday food preparation. On the last night of our March visit to Tokyo, we had *temaki* (hand-rolled) sushi (see Figure 9.3). It was beautifully presented: Each type of fish came with a small delicate stem of flowers inside their wrapped trays, which were placed on the fish after they were transferred to a serving plate. The sticky rice was steamed and cooled through the use of a wide wooden bowl and a hand fan. Hana and Sakura assisted with the cooling process, transferring the rice and taking turns fanning it (see Figure 9.4). Yuki explained,

> In Japan, we can buy sushi that is cheaper. But next time we have *temaki* sushi, you know, Hana and Sakura will be like [mimics excited voice] 'last time I had *temaki* sushi was with Emily and James. Ah, James likes that type of fish and Emily liked this on hers!' So yeah, it makes it special.

Figure 9.3 Temaki sushi dinner. Credited to the author

Figure 9.4 Helping to cool sushi rice. Credited to the author

Similarly, Yuki discussed the practice of making *gyoza* as less about the competencies or materials and more about the experience for those involved: "So everyone is chatting – someone is cutting the veggies and someone is sautéing the meat and, you know, mixing it in a bowl and everyone can be involved. Hana and Sakura love to make gyoza. 'I want to do that. I want to do that.'" When asked if she thought there was a comparable tradition in the United States, Yuki responded, "You know, that's why I asked [their American grandma] to show them how to make chocolate chip cookies or oatmeal cookies." It is interesting that traditional foods, which are individually portioned and prepared together, such as gyoza or pierogis, are savory foods that make up part of a meal and are consumed together. On the other hand, in the United States, such participatory foods are generally desserts or sweets. Nonetheless, in Yuki's estimation, the time spent together in the performance of the practice matters more than the product. The communal nature of the food preparation allows family members to spend time together and create memories, and they are rewarded with the pleasure of consuming their creations.

The bicultural food experience and its contributions

The bicultural experience provides a unique lens for exploring food practices and wellbeing. It offers a window into the mundane routines that typically go unnoticed and the practical understandings that are enacted with minimal consideration (Warde, 2016). An individual's attention is heightened as products and materials are structured differently in the environment of each culture – be it in the boundaries of an individual household or in a country – leading to more interpretations of sensory information and more reflection on its meaning as individuals switch between cultures. With increasing migration, growing cultural-minority populations, and more multiethnic and multiracial households in the United States and many other countries (Livingston, 2017), investigations into food practices provide value for how the marketplace and policy can help preserve healthy routines and prevent negative dietary acculturation (Satia, 2009).

In this investigation, the bicultural family provides one perspective on food practices and has its limitations. First, the investigator is not situated between these two cultures. Second, the focus was on the family's nutritional gatekeeper and is thus less representative of other perspectives in the family. Third, the family in question has high economic status and corporate employee benefits, giving them access to a higher level of resources than the majority of new immigrants.

At the same time, the investigation provides a contextualization to the examination of practices and experiences of enculturation and acculturation. The vignettes highlight the complex relationship that exists in managing multiple cultures and the relevance of situated experiences to discovering aspects of pleasure and associated wellbeing.

Finding pleasure with food: promoting wellbeing in the marketplace

Food creates and signifies a vastly greater range of meaning, emotions, and behaviors than its core utilitarian value would suggest. Indicative of culture and interpersonal affiliations, our personal relationship with food is reinforced through daily practices and the aggregated marketing system. The positive/pleasure or negative/anxiety orientation of this relationship has bearing on wellbeing. It is argued that in the United States our relationship to food has become dysfunctional – centering on regulations of "good" foods and rejection of "bad" foods in order to maintain health and longevity (Bublitz et al., 2010; Rozin, 1989). Health outcomes have not improved under this system; moreover, these food dichotomies create compromises on pleasure that have an impact on overall wellbeing.

With a balance between pleasure and health in its food orientation, Japan offers a benchmark for the United States in modifying its course towards valuing the experiential pleasure of food. This discussion explored the connections between several Japanese food practices and pleasure. There are clear differences in the cultures, institutions, and marketplaces that sustain these differences in food practices. That said, are there elements (materials, competences, or meanings) of Japanese practices that could be incorporated into American culture to promote a more pleasurable relationship to food and better wellbeing? This poses an interesting line for further inquiry – for which I will provide an abridged commentary.

Socialization is an important factor in creating routines. The Japanese have found power in reinforcing food practices through a formal education program, *shokuiku* (Miyoshi et al., 2012). In this program, school children learn about nutrition, food preparation, and manners. The program was created to uphold Japanese traditions involving food and promote family mealtime. This program is similar to the French *l'éducation sensorielle* (and *classes du goût*) in which cultural norms and values are reinforced in children. Such taste education programs have been developed to a degree in the United States but not on a national policy level (Amin et al., 2018). A marker of this education is pride in the cultural heritage. Within the United States, this can be difficult to navigate because of the vast number of cultural heritages that make up the country. Then again, food can provide an advantageous vehicle for opening up discussion and exploring similarities and differences, multiple identities, problematic histories, and issues of othering – while celebrating the vast variety of food heritages.

Some of the practices found in Japan, such as *itadakimasu*, are embedded ritualized religious or spiritual practices and traditions. In America, prayer before a meal is common, but the prayer is typically focused on thanking the Divine for the food instead of directing gratitude to the people in the food-production process (a distinction between abstract and concrete references). This may be indicative of more deeply engrained cultural values and religious inclinations. Yet because of growing desires for more transparency in our food system and for teaching children about food production (Moscato and Machin, 2018), it is beneficial to examine how these embedded rituals, such as prayer before meals, align or misalign with societal goals of wellbeing.

Establishing new norms across a culture is a difficult process but certainly possible. We only need to look at social initiatives such as wearing a seat belt or recycling and the history of the American Thanksgiving holiday to see the possibilities. The latter falls under the category of "invented traditions" (Hobsbawm, 2012). These curated ritualized events convey a sense of long history, but in reality they are more recent creations that leverage historical trappings to increase feelings of authenticity and instill certain values and norms. Examining invented traditions can offer means to create new, meaningful pleasure-enhancing food rituals that support wellbeing.

Food marketing continues to present opportunities to represent diversity and promote food practices that improve wellbeing. In these terms, the importance of taste regimes in helping normalize behaviors and perpetuate practices through materials and competencies in the marketplace should not be overlooked. For example, through the study of taste regimes, more can be discovered on how to integrate materials into food practices that may help curb overconsumption, such as the use of small plates and dishes for serving. Taste regimes can also benefit exploration of compound food practices such as grocery shopping. Because of the limited space in households in Japan, food shopping occurs more frequently. This reduces stockpiling of food and offers opportunities to buy more fresh items. Access to fresh foods is also influenced by population density and infrastructure.

For example, most people in the major cities use public transport and the *eki biru* (station building) typically has a store, grocery store, or convenience store attached; providing an easy way to buy fresh what is need that evening. Current aesthetics in the United States promote taste regimes which demonstrate the complexity of practices but also opportunities for change. Although social structures appear enduring, a practice approach contends that under all "durable features of our world" are activities and performances created by individuals (Nicolini, 2012: 3).

Conclusions

A tremendous number of food practices are routinely exercised by individuals, many with the possibility of providing pleasure. Aesthetics, appreciation, and engagement practices have ripple effects on how pleasure is infused into our cultural orientation of food. The continued exploration of food practices has value in determining how wellbeing is both promoted and undermined in our daily routines. Through a greater understanding of taste regimes and evaluation of materials, competencies, and meanings associated with such practices, we are presented with opportunities to enhance the marketplace in support of culturally relevant and beneficial food routines and rituals.

References

Allirot, X., da Quinta, N., Chokupermal, K., & Urdaneta, E. (2016). Involving children in cooking activities: A potential strategy for directing food choices toward novel foods containing vegetables. *Appetite*, 103, 275–285.

Allison, A. (1991). Japanese mothers and obentōs: The lunch-box as ideological state apparatus. *Anthropological Quarterly*, 195–208.

Amin, S.A., Panzarella, C., Lehnerd, M., Cash, S.B., Economos, C.D., & Sacheck, J.M. (2018). Identifying food literacy educational opportunities for youth. *Health Education and Behavior*, 1–8.

Arsel, Z., & Bean, J. (2012). Taste regimes and market-mediated practice. *Journal of Consumer Research*, 39(5), 899–917.

Belk, R. (1996). The perfect gift. In C. Otnes & R.F. Beltramini (Eds). *Gift-Giving: A Research Anthology*. Bowling Green, OH: Bowling Green University Popular Press, pp. 59–84.

Belkin, L. (2013). Why do parents still urge children to "clean your plate"? *Huffington Post*, April 23. Retrieved from: www.huffingtonpost.com/2013/04/23/clean-your-plate-parents_n_3141473.html

Bourcier, E., Bowen, D.J., Meischke, H., & Moinpour, C. (2003). Evaluation of strategies used by family food preparers to influence healthy eating. *Appetite*, 41(3), 265–272.

Bublitz, M.G., Peracchio, L.A., & Block, L.G. (2010). Why did I eat that? Perspectives on food decision making and dietary restraint. *Journal of Consumer Psychology*, 20(3), 239–258.

CIA World Factbook. (2017). Country comparison: Life expectancy at birth. Retrieved from: www.cia.gov/library/publications/the-world-factbook/rankorder/2102rank.html

Cornil, Y., & Chandon, P. (2016a). Pleasure as an ally of healthy eating? Contrasting visceral and epicurean eating pleasures and their association with portion size preferences and wellbeing. *Appetite*, 104, 52–59.

Cornil, Y., & Chandon, P. (2016b). Pleasure as a substitute for size: How multisensory imagery can make people happier with smaller food portions. *Journal of Marketing Research*, 53(5), 847–864.

Cwiertka, K.J. (2006). *Modern Japanese Cuisine: Food, Power and National Identity*. London: Reaktion.

de Witt Huberts, J.C., Evers, C., & de Ridder, D.T. (2013). Double trouble: Restrained eaters do not eat less and feel worse. *Psychology and Health*, 28(6), 686–700.

Dohle, S., Rall, S., & Siegrist, M. (2016). Does self-prepared food taste better? Effects of food preparation on liking. *Health Psychology*, 35(5), 500.

Freedman, I. (2016). Cultural specificity in food choice: The case of ethnography in Japan. *Appetite*, 96, 138–146.

Geier, A.B., Rozin, P., & Doros, G. (2006). Unit bias: A new heuristic that helps explain the effect of portion size on food intake. *Psychological Science*, 17(6), 521–525.

Gould, S.J. (2012). The emergence of consumer introspection theory (CIT): Introduction to a JBR special issue. *Journal of Business Research*, 65(4), 453–460.

Graham-Rowe, E., Jessop, D.C., & Sparks, P. (2014). Identifying motivations and barriers to minimizing household food waste. *Resources, Conservation and Recycling*, 84, 15–23.

Hill, T., Canniford, R., & Mol, J. (2014). Non-representational marketing theory. *Marketing Theory*, 14(4), 377–394.

Hobsbawm, E. (2012). Introduction: Inventing traditions. In E. Hobsbawm & T. Ranger. (Eds), *The Invention of Tradition*. New York: Cambridge University Press, pp. 1–14.

Holtzman, J. (2016). To love sugar one does not have to eat it. *Gastronomica: Journal of Critical Food Studies*, 16(3), 44–55.

Kahn, B.E., & Wansink, B. (2004). The influence of assortment structure on perceived variety and consumption quantities. *Journal of Consumer Research*, 30(4), 519–533.

Kohsaka, R. (2017). The myth of washoku: A twisted discourse on the "uniqueness" of national food heritages. *Journal of Ethnic Foods*, 4(2), 66–71.

Kudo, Y., Falciglia, G.A., & Couch, S.C. (2000). Evolution of meal patterns and food choices of Japanese-American females born in the United States. *European Journal of Clinical Nutrition*, 54(8), 665.

Landry, M., Lemieux, S., Lapointe, A., Bédard, A., Bélanger-Gravel, A., Bégin, C. … Desroches, S. (2018). Is eating pleasure compatible with healthy eating? A qualitative study on Quebecers' perceptions. *Appetite*, 125, 537–547.

Livingston, G. (2017). The rise of multiracial and multiethnic babies in the US. Pew Research Center, June 6. Retrieved from: www.pewresearch.org/fact-tank/2017/06/06/the-rise-of-multiracial-and-multiethnic-babies-in-the-u-s/

Loth, K.A., MacLehose, R.F., Fulkerson, J.A., Crow, S., & Neumark-Sztainer, D. (2013). Food-related parenting practices and adolescent weight status: A population-based study. *Pediatrics*, 131(5), 1443–1450.

Miyoshi, M., Tsuboyama-Kasaoka, N., & Nishi, N. (2012). School-based "Shokuiku" program in Japan: Application to nutrition education in Asian countries. *Asia Pacific Journal of Clinical Nutrition*, 21(1), 159–162.

Moisio, R., Arnould, E.J., & Price, L.L. (2004). Between mothers and markets: Constructing family identity through homemade food. *Journal of Consumer Culture*, 4(3), 361–384.

Morewedge, C.K., Huh, Y.E., & Vosgerau, J. (2010). Thought for food: Imagined consumption reduces actual consumption. *Science*, 330(6010), 1530–1533.

Moscato, E.M., & Machin, J.E. (2018). Mother natural: Motivations and associations for consuming natural foods. *Appetite*, 121, 18–28.

Nicolini, D. (2012). *Practice Theory, Work, and Organization: An Introduction*. Oxford: Oxford University Press.

Ninomiya, K. (2015). Science of umami taste: Adaptation to gastronomic culture. *Flavour*, 4(1), 13.

Parizel, O., Labouré, H., Marsset-Baglieri, A., Fromentin, G., & Sulmont-Rossé, C. (2017). Providing choice and/or variety during a meal: Impact on vegetable liking and intake. *Appetite*, 108, 391–398.

Petit, O., Basso, F., Merunka, D., Spence, C., Cheok, A.D., & Oullier, O. (2016). Pleasure and the control of food intake: An embodied cognition approach to consumer self-regulation. *Psychology and Marketing*, 33(8), 608–619.

Pilcher, J.M. (2006). *Food in World History*. New York: Routledge.

Prince, M., Patel, V., Saxena, S., Maj, M., Maselko, J., Phillips, M.R., & Rahman, A. (2007). No health without mental health. *Lancet*, 370(9590), 859–877.

Ochs, E., & Shohet, M. (2006). The cultural structuring of mealtime socialization. *New Directions for Child and Adolescent Development*, 111, 35–49.

Raynor, H.A. (2012). Can limiting dietary variety assist with reducing energy intake and weight loss? *Physiology and Behavior*, 106(3), 356–361.

Raynor, H.A., & Wing, R.R. (2006). Effect of limiting snack food variety across days on hedonics and consumption. *Appetite*, 46(2), 168–176.

Richie, D. (2007). *A Tractate on Japanese Aesthetics*. Berkley, CA: Stone Bridge Press.

Rook, D.W. (1985). The ritual dimension of consumer behavior. *Journal of Consumer Research*, 12(3), 251–264.

Rozin, P. (1989). Disorders of food selection: The compromise of pleasure. *Annals of the New York Academy of Sciences*, 575(1), 376–386.

Rozin, P. (2005). The meaning of food in our lives: A cross-cultural perspective on eating and wellbeing. *Journal of Nutrition Education and Behavior*, 37, S107–S112.

Rozin, P., Fischler, C., Imada, S., Sarubin, A., & Wrzesniewski, A. (1999). Attitudes to food and the role of food in life in the USA, Japan, Flemish Belgium, and France: Possible implications for the diet–health debate. *Appetite*, 33(2), 163–180.

Ryan, R.M., & Deci, E.L. (2000). Self-determination theory and the facilitation of intrinsic motivation, social development, and wellbeing. *American Psychologist*, 55(1), 68.

Ryan, R.M., & Deci, E.L. (2001). On happiness and human potentials: A review of research on hedonic and eudaimonic health. *Annual Review Psychology*, 52, 141–166.

Satia, J.A. (2009). Diet-related disparities: Understanding the problem and accelerating solutions. *Journal of the American Dietetic Association*, 109(4), 610.

Satia-Abouta, J., Patterson, R.E., Neuhouser, M.L., & Elder, J. (2002). Dietary acculturation: Applications to nutrition research and dietetics. *Journal of the American Dietetic Association*, 102(8), 1105–1118.

Shove, E., Pantzar, M., & Watson, M. (2012). *The Dynamics of Social Practice: Everyday Life and How It Changes*. London: Sage.

Smith, J.A., & Osborn, M. (2004). Interpretative phenomenological analysis. In G.M. Breakwell (Ed.), *Doing Social Psychology Research*. Malden, MA: BPS Blackwell, pp. 229–254.

Southerton, D., & Yates, L. (2015). Exploring food waste through the lens of social practice theories: Some reflections on eating as a compound practice. In K.M. Ekström (Ed.), *Waste Management and Sustainable Consumption*. London: Routledge, pp. 133–149.

Stroebele, N., Ogden, L.G., & Hill, J.O. (2009). Do calorie-controlled portion sizes of snacks reduce energy intake? *Appetite*, 52(3), 793–796.

UNESCO. (2016). Washoku, traditional dietary cultures of the Japanese, notably for the celebration of New Year. Retrieved from: https://ich.unesco.org/en/RL/washoku-traditional-dietary-cultures-of-the-japanese-notably-for-the-celebration-of-new-year-00869

Van Lente, E., Barry, M.M., Molcho, M., Morgan, K., Watson, D., Harrington, J., & McGee, H. (2012). Measuring population mental health and social wellbeing. *International Journal of Public Health*, 57(2), 421–430.

Wansink, B., & Chandon, P. (2014). Slim by design: Redirecting the accidental drivers of mindless overeating. *Journal of Consumer Psychology*, 24(3), 413–431.

Warde, A. (2016). *The Practice of Eating*. Malden, MA: Polity Press.

Wildschut, T., Sedikides, C., Arndt, J., & Routledge, C. (2006). Nostalgia: Content, triggers, functions. *Journal of Personality and Social Psychology*, 91(5), 975–993.

Woermann, N. (2017). Back to the roots! Methodological situationalism and the postmodern lesson for studying tribes, practices, and assemblages. *Marketing Theory*, 17(2), 149–163.

World Health Organization. (2016). Global Health Observatory (GHO) data: Overweight and obesity. Retrieved from: www.who.int/gho/ncd/risk_factors/overweight/en/

World Health Organization. (2017). Noncommunicable diseases progress monitor 2017. Retrieved from: www.who.int/nmh/publications/ncd-progress-monitor-2017/en/

Zlatevska, N., Dubelaar, C., & Holden, S.S. (2014). Sizing up the effect of portion size on consumption: A meta-analytic review. *Journal of Marketing*, 78(3), 140–154.

10 Food storytelling, pleasure, and wellbeing

Narratives from food cultural experiences

Adrienne F. Muldrow and Jamie L. Grigsby

Storytelling is an important part of individuals' lives. Telling stories about food is a normative part of US culture. The chapter begins with a discussion about the origins of storytelling and narrative structures. In the next part of the chapter, an in-depth discussion about the importance of telling stories and current storytelling research in the marketing discipline are discussed, including the benefit of narrative transportation and the use of brand biographies. The next section explores the many ways that food stories can be told and by whom. The latter section is followed by a discussion on how food consumers can use stories to improve the wellbeing of those around us. Finally, a conclusion of chapter information is given.

Box 10.1 A remembrance food story

My first indication that food was something other than a substance one stuffed in one's face when hungry—like filling up at a gas station—came after fourth grade in elementary school. It was on a family vacation to Europe, on the *Queen Mary*, in the cabin-class dining room. There's a picture somewhere: my mother in her Jackie O sunglasses, my younger brother and I in our painfully cute cruisewear, boarding the big Cunard ocean liner, all of us excited about our first transatlantic voyage, our first trip to my father's ancestral homeland, France.

It was the soup.

It was *cold*.

This was something of a discovery for a curious fourth grader whose entire experience of soup to this point had consisted of Campbell's cream of tomato and chicken noodle. I'd eaten in restaurants before, sure, but this was the first food I really noticed. It was the first food I enjoyed and, more important, remembered enjoying. I asked our patient British waiter what this delightfully cool, tasty liquid was.

"Vichyssoise," came the reply, a word that to this day - even though it's now a tired old warhorse of a menu selection and one I've prepared thousands of times - still has a magical ring to it. I remember everything about the experience: the way our waiter ladled it from a silver tureen into my bowl; the crunch of tiny chopped chives he spooned on as garnish; the rich, creamy taste of leek and potato; the pleasurable shock, the surprise that it was cold.

© Anthony Bourdain, 2007, "Kitchen Confidential: Adventures in the Culinary Underbelly," Bloomsbury Publishing

Introduction

Consumers tell stories about food. We talk to our friends about our experiences at restaurants and on exotic vacations. We talk about food to our co-workers as we decide to go out to eat. We talk about foods we like to eat, who helped prepare the food, how we go about finding our favorite foods, where we like to eat them, what brands of food we like to purchase, what foods we are allergic to, what foods we tried on vacation, and how we go about disposing of our discarded food items. We talk to our kids about food. We describe food from our heritages and why certain food items were appropriate to the region and thus important to our families. We tell stories about why it is important to maintain and keep secret Maria's tomato sauce recipe from Sicily. We tell stories about food when we pass down recipes.

With all this talk about food, it is hard for food stories not to abound in the marketplace. Food bloggers tell stories about various facets of food from the sourcing of hard-to-find ingredients to the proper techniques on food composting. Food critics allow us to be a fly on the window as they tell their stories of their experience at restaurants and with food from grocers. Restaurants selling food pack their websites with customers who tell stories about their experiences with customer reviews. Everyone talks about food. Let's be honest. Everyone talks about food in terms of the good, the bad, and the ugly.

Like consumers, marketers tell millions of stories about food. Marketers sell food for restaurants, for manufacturers, for vending machines, for food distributors, and for consumers. Marketers tell stories in writing, in pictorials, by sales people, in traditional advertisements, on menus, online, in person, on social media, when responding to food reviews, and for anyone who will pay attention.

Just telling a story does not mean that it carries an effective message. We all tell stories, but we are not always conscious about what happens after a story is told. Often, consumers as individuals tell food stories by announcing whatever is on their mind when delivering a story face to face. However, some stories may move consumers to pursue more beneficial outcomes. At present, a dearth of research exists regarding how consumers can learn how to tell stories for the greater wellbeing of others.

There is a lot of research and discussion out there about stories and storytelling. The purpose of this chapter is to condense all that information and develop a better understanding of the ways in which consumers tell stories about food and how marketers can tell better food stories. Overall the chapter reveals a number of take-aways. The first take-away is what makes a story a good one. Other take-aways include how marketers develop stories that consumers want to hear and the importance of co-created stories. A final take-away is how individuals can learn to be more cautious about how to tell worthwhile stories about their food experiences.

What is storytelling, and why is it important to tell stories?

A story is defined as an account of event(s) as told by a storyteller with four required elements: (1) a plot (i.e., a beginning, middle, and end); (2) characters; (3) a climax (i.e., drama or conflict); which leads to (4) the outcome or conclusion of the story (Ardelet et al., 2015; Green and Brock, 2000; van Laer et al., 2014). Storytelling, then, is the sharing of the story by the storyteller with story receivers, whether through text (Argo et al., 2008; Hamby et al., 2015; van Laer and de Ruyter, 2010; Wentzel et al., 2010), television ads (Deighton et al., 1989; Escalas et al., 2004; McFerran et al., 2010), sales people (Gilliam and Zablah, 2013), or other media, such as online viral videos (e.g., Chen and Lee, 2014).

All cultures practice some form of storytelling (Brown, 1991). The ability to discern narrative forms of storytelling begins before the age of 3 (Mancuso, 1986).[1] Despite the premise that stories, and thus the underlying narratives, seem simple and understandable, complex forms of reasoning occur when narratives are told, including cause-and-effect and spatial reasoning (Sugiyama, 2001). Essential traditional story elements leading to reasoning include a plot (that should be understood from beginning to end), characters, meaning in wording, and a type of conflict and/or contemplation that needs solving (Fergusson, 1961). Stories are not only beneficial to individuals because stories are memorable and pleasurable, but also because they expand one's base of accumulated knowledge; they are a way of acquiring vicarious knowledge, and they have the ability to make individuals see things more clearly and have the chance of changing their opinion (Sugiyama, 2001; Woodside, 2010).

In marketing, early research in storytelling examined the format of existing ads; in other words, brands began using stories in ads before researchers explored the extent to which storytelling was a persuasive method of communication. Preliminary research (e.g., Deighton et al., 1989; Wells, 1989) classified existing television ads onto a continuous scale in which the end points were argument and drama ads. Argument ads did not have characters or plot and tended to provide facts and tell the audience what they should think or believe about the product (Deighton et al., 1989). Conversely, a drama ad had characters and a plot. Events unfolded in the ad without explanation. An ad could fall near one of the end points on the continuum or be a hybrid of the two. Deighton et al. (1989) showed that a persuasive drama produced less counterarguing by the viewer as compared to a persuasive argument; however, the two ad formats were not significantly different in terms of their ability to influence beliefs about the product being advertised.

The authors argued that the reduced level of counterarguing associated with drama ads is due to drama ads being processed empathetically while argument ads were processed more analytically (Deighton et al., 1989). The research by Deighton and colleagues was one of the first to suggest that ads that take a drama format and tell a story are processed differently than those that are argument-based, hence laying the foundation for a growing stream of research related to the effectiveness of storytelling in marketing. Research continued to explore the persuasive capacity of stories and to build an understanding of the process through which stories persuaded their audience. It became apparent that story processing involves an emotional response, such as empathy and sympathy with the story characters (Escalas and Stern, 2003; Escalas et al., 2004; Argo et al., 2008). Empathy and imagination emerged as two key antecedents to a process called narrative transportation (van Laer et al., 2014).

The role of narrative transportation in storytelling

Narrative transportation is the process of becoming lost and immersed in the story world. It is associated with less awareness of the real world and heightened awareness and attention to the world presented in the story (Green and Brock, 2000). Narrative transportation was particularly interesting to marketing researchers because it does not involve much critical thought, yet it has a consistently positive influence on brand and ad attitudes (e.g., Bhatnagar and Wan, 2011; Escalas 2004a; Escalas 2004b; Escalas et al., 2004; van Laer and de Ruyter, 2010). As a persuasive process, narrative transportation does not fit into dual-processing models like the Elaboration Likelihood Model (ELM) (van Laer et al., 2014). Evidence suggests that narrative transportation is cognitively effortful (Chang, 2009; Nielsen and Escalas, 2010; Wentzel et al., 2010), which according to an ELM framework should predict higher levels of counterarguing and require strong arguments for persuasion to occur. However, narrative persuasion is not sensitive to argument strength (Escalas, 2007; Lien and Chen, 2013). Researchers reached the conclusion that narrative persuasion is a unique path to persuasion (Escalas, 2007; van Laer et al., 2014). Taken together, narrative transportation is the element in storytelling that allows the consumer to become immersed in the story.

Elements of an effective story

Researchers then branched out into several areas of additional exploration: the influence of story elements, including the similarity or dissimilarity of characters in the story, the influence of individual consumer characteristics, instances in which consumers create their own stories (i.e., restaurant reviews), and stories that are developed over time, such as brand biographies. These various research streams will each be described briefly.

- **When characters are similar to the audience**. Research that explored the elements of the story often emphasized the influence of story characters. Self-character similarity, or the extent to which the audience is similar to the lead character in the story, emerged as a variable of interest. In some instances, a high level of self-character similarity has positive outcomes; consumers look for people they can relate to and identify with when they consume media (Mandel et al., 2006), and brands can benefit by producing ads that include a diverse population so that the range of people that relate to the brand is enhanced (Russell et al., 2013). However, narrative transportation is a cognitively effortful process, and research has found that increased cognitive effort in processing increases the narrative transportation experience; hence increasing favorable evaluations of the brand and ad (Addis and Holbrook, 2010; Bhatnagar and Wan, 2011).
- **When characters are dissimilar to the audience**. When a character in a story is dissimilar to the audience (as in Addis and Holbrook, 2010; Bhatnagar and Wan, 2011) or when the story setting is unfamiliar (as in Addis and Holbrook, 2010), more cognitive effort is required to process the story, hence increasing narrative transportation. As a result, evaluations of the brand and story were higher than when similarity and familiarity were higher (Addis and Holbrook, 2010; Bhatnagar and Wan, 2011).
- **Non-character aspects and stories**. While research exploring how non-character aspects of a story ad can be used to increase narrative transportation is a smaller body of literature, research does suggest that in picture-based ads, the use of grotesque imagery in fashion ads can generate more narrative transportation (Phillips and McQuarrie, 2010). In a face-to-face sales situation, salespeople that share product stories from a business point of view were also effective at generating narrative transportation and positively influencing purchase intentions (Gilliam and Zablah, 2013).
- **Individual characteristics and storytelling**. The audience is also influenced by individual characteristics. For example, if the viewer holds a belief that is central to the story, such as the belief in good luck, they are more likely to experience narrative transportation (McFerran et al., 2010). When consumers that believed in good luck viewed a television ad for the lottery that used a story format, they experienced narrative transportation and, as a consequence, paid more attention to the possible outcomes of winning the lottery and less attention to the likelihood that they would actually win. Absorption, a trait tendency to be immersed in experiences in general, is also positively associated with narrative transportation (Sestir and Green, 2010). People that are high empathizers also tend to experience higher levels of narrative transportation (Argo et al., 2008). Those populations that tend to read more, such as women and the more highly educated, also tend to experience more narrative transportation (van Laer et al., 2014). See Table 10.1 for how to use the 4 Cs for good storytelling.

Table 10.1 How to tell a story effectively: 4 Cs for good storytelling

4 Cs for Good Storytelling
Construction
Avoid explanation or facts; let events unfold naturally
Have a beginning, middle, and end (a plot)
Encourage the audience to use their imagination
Characters
Stimulate empathy with the characters
Create characters that seem familiar
But keep the characters unique to maintain interest
Climax
Introduce a problem-solving dilemma or conflict for the characters
Make the problem or conflict relatable to your audience
Encourage the audience to wonder what will happen next
Conclusion
Encourage the audience to connect their personal experiences to the story
Have a message that connects to what your audience cares about
Motivate the audience to continue the story or create their own

Consumers, food experience, and storytelling

Food research can be enhanced by known research on storytelling itself. Marketing research has explored situations in which consumers create their own stories. Early research suggested that when consumers are prompted to write their own stories about experiences, elaboration about the experience is increased (West et al., 2004). For example, West and colleagues state that when consumers wrote their own stories about viewing a painting in a museum, elaboration about the painting is increased along with the consumer's liking of the painting. Research also suggests that prompted stories are influenced greatly by the consumer's individual experience and the home culture of the consumer (Kim et al., 2016). Even without prompting, consumers may create their own product-relevant story while shopping (as in Ardelet et al., 2015). These stories are more likely for brands that have a strong brand story or heritage. The story produced by the consumer seems to increase preference for the product (Ardelet et al., 2015).

Stories are told through a variety of mediums (Table 10.2). Consumers also create stories about experiences that they share with others through word of mouth, blog posts, or product reviews. Research has found that as stories are passed through an online community, marketing messages about the product can be influenced, shaped, and modified (Kozinets et al., 2010). Story reviews also positively influence purchase intent when the review is positive (Hamby et al., 2015). Find the many ways that consumers, marketers, and brand managers can use storytelling effectively.

The manner in which stories are told can elevate narrative transportation. Further, the way in which the story is told can influence the storyteller as a consequence; when a storyteller shares a story, they also experience narrative transportation (Moore, 2012). One caution is that following the storytelling and narrative transportation experience, the storyteller tends to experience a less extreme evaluation of hedonic products and a more extreme evaluation of utilitarian products (Moore, 2012).

Food brand stories or biographies that are developed over time, either throughout the lifetime of the brand or in a campaign that serves to develop the story, have also been explored. In an attempt to convey trustworthiness and authenticity on which to base such relationships, brands have turned to storytelling (Athey, 2016; Udell, 2016). In practice, brand biographies have become especially important in recent years (Athey, 2016). In developing food brand stories, researchers have found that authenticity, conciseness, reversal, and humor are all

Table 10.2 The art of telling food stories by medium

Medium	*Consumers*	*Marketers*	*Brands*
Word-of-mouth	To friends, family, co-workers, strangers.	Consumer reviews-both to consumers and to business-to-business clients.	Use quotes about quality, taste, ingredients, and ambiance from consumers.
Online	Consumer food reviews, personal food blogs, show pictures and experiences in social media.	-Create and select stories to be used on food websites and on menus. -Maintain food blogs, Facebook content, Twitter content, product videos for YouTube.	-Use brand website to tell stories about the brand, tell stories about who might use certain food products, and they re-tell the good stories from actual consumers. -Showcase brand biographies.
Retail food environments	-Speak directly with people at your table or retail establishment about prior experiences and recommendation for product selections. -Fill out a consumer survey in narrative form while at the retail food environment or shortly after the visit.	-Narrative signage on the product directly. -Narrative signage in the retail environment. -Narratives through satellite radio. -Automatic audio signage that tells a narrative story.	-Narrative descriptions on many forms of branded products. -Narratives about the start and essence of the owner of the restaurant on audio/visuals around the restaurant. -Brand biography of the restaurant on the menu.

valuable tools in telling a story that aligns a brand and product (Chiu et al., 2012). Other research has found that relying on nostalgia and developing a strong brand heritage can build greater brand attachment (Merchant and Rose, 2012). See a traditional storytelling brand approach in Figure 10.1.

Importantly, brand stories can become a co-created dialogue or a multilogue between the consumer and the brand (Berthon et al., 2007). Nevertheless, unlike traditional stories, brand stories lack an element of conflict or flaws (Beverland and Farrelly, 2010).

Sometimes food brand stories share congruent features of traditional storytelling. As with other forms of stories, when the brand serves as a character in its own brand biography and when self-character similarity is high, the brand biography will be particularly successful (Paharia et al., 2010). For example, Paharia and colleagues found that underdog food brand biographies were especially successful when the consumer saw themselves as an underdog. The effect was further enhanced when the consumer was also from a culture which included the underdog as part of the national identity (Paharia et al., 2010). Through stories, food brands can become part of a larger cultural narrative, as they are cultural narrators, a concept known as sociocultural branding (Cayla and Arnould, 2008; Hirschman, 1986; Woodside, 2010). Food brands that have been able to effectively tell a broader cultural narrative have become cultural icons. Iconic brands that have been able to tell efficacious stories around food or how we relate to food include McDonald's (Ritzer 1983) and Weight Watchers (Moisio and Beruchashvili, 2010). Sometimes brands can learn how to find the true essence of their brand and are thus given a chance to retell their brand story. See the example in Figure 10.2 about a company that reinvented itself by telling a story that focused upon its core food initiates.

The art of telling food stories and consumer wellbeing

Telling an effective story about food can differ from telling a story in general. For example, Fenger et al. (2015) found that shorter descriptions of localized food products could be an effective marketing tactic for some product types. In the author's study, they describe redcurrants and lingonberries as "redcurrants and lingonberries from the summer fields of Funen Island – harvested just before they are completely ripe, when the anti-oxidant content is at its highest" (Fenger et al., 2015: 240). The authors were able to demonstrate that storytelling helped increase preference for the new product meat variant (i.e., cubed, herbal ham) among consumers who were the most skeptical. Overall, the authors suggest that having short, descriptive stories may help the reticent consumer overcome doubts with a new variety.

Using food for wellbeing is an important marketing topic (e.g., Block et al., 2011; Bublitz et al., 2013). Besides food, storytelling is important to the marketing discipline (Woodside, 2010). Therefore, storytelling about food could be a path to creating better wellbeing. One such storytelling case study is described below. Food represents wellbeing. Food is intertwined with various forms of wellbeing, including mental, physical, and spiritual health. For indigenous people food is interconnected with religion, lifestyle, traditions, and the physical

Figure 10.1 Bush Brothers & Company, 2018 (https://www.bushbeans.com/en_US/history-heritage). 2018 by © Bush Brothers & Company. Reprinted with permission.

Figure 10.1 (Cont.)

environment (Egeland et al., 2009). Importantly, traditional foods of indigenous people are often more healthy than food from outside of their native environments, especially more highly marketed modern foods that are often higher in sugar, fats, and sodium with the consequence of a concomitant increase in obesity-related health problems. Hence, elder storytelling might be helpful as such storytelling gives the younger people awareness regarding the procurement of traditional food, the preparation of traditional food, and the importance of eating a traditional diet while sharing their culture heritage (e.g., Egeland et al., 2012).

In the case study of the Inuit people, a mixed-methods survey was created with the goal of producing a DVD series on the stories of five elders to investigate a storytelling intervention to improve the eating habits of the young people. First, during May 2006, 75 youth completed a food frequency survey indicating that annually, 80 percent of Inuit youth only consumed five traditional foods (i.e.,

Figure 10.2 "Chipotle—A farewell to GMOs," by Chipotle Mexican Grill, 2018 (https://www.chipotle.com/gmo). 2018 by © Chipotle Mexican Grill. Reprinted with permission.

Caribou, blueberries, ringed seal) in additional to non-traditional foods, such as chips, fruit juice, and carbonated beverages. As of the time of write-up of the mixed-method case study, the post-intervention quantitative results were not available (Egeland et al., 2012). Nevertheless, the storytelling intervention represents a methodology used by researchers to improve the wellbeing of the youth in the community by representing their cultural heritage and social cohesion.

Food storytelling and its contribution to food wellbeing and food marketing

Food wellbeing is "a positive psychological, physical, emotional, and social relationship with food at both the individual and societal levels" (Block et al., 2011: 6). Furthermore, Block and colleagues (2011) suggest that wellbeing is not simply a functional approach to health, based on restraint and biomedical health markers (i.e., body mass index), but rather a more multifaceted approach that includes more holistic approaches to viewing food in a positive, consumer-oriented manner. According to the authors, food wellbeing includes elements that could be used in storytelling, such as having a positive relationship with food, culture, community, and pleasure. In conclusion, food wellbeing is a more expansive concept than the negativity felt when individuals struggle to eat unappetizing food for short-term health goals towards a more rewarding transition where marketers and academics seek to find ways that consumers may embrace more positive aspects of food to accomplish long-term health goals (Bublitz et al., 2013). Basically, food wellbeing is part of the positive marketing philosophy that seeks to improve the lives of individuals for the betterment of society (Mittelstaedt et al., 2015).

One way of accomplishing food wellbeing is to have consumers and marketers promote healthy eating by encouraging consumers to embrace more pleasurable food experiences instead of focusing on restraint (Batat et al., forthcoming). Thus, food wellbeing can be accomplished by using food marketing. Food marketing is an important factor of the food wellbeing concept in addition to food socialization, food literacy, food policy, and food availability (Block et al., 2011). Specifically, on the societal level, food marketing represents marketing elements of targeting, positioning, the correct marketing mix (4 Ps), and appropriate segmentation. On the individual level, food marketing represents consumers' emotions and consumption decisions (Block et al., 2011).

Marketers and consumers may use concrete initiatives to further positive food wellbeing. For example, in a multicultural study by Rozin and colleagues (1999), the authors found that Americans tend to worry the most about food and the least likely to associate food with pleasure were the ones who were the least likely to classify themselves as healthy eaters, whereas the French tend not to worry about food and the most likely to associate food with pleasure were the most likely to classify themselves as healthy eaters. In other words, something about the pleasure of food is ironically driving more healthful eating.

At the present time, not much is known about how food storytelling directly relates to food wellbeing outcomes. Prior marketing studies have used storytelling but as an independent predictor of wellbeing (e.g., Wallendorf and Arnould, 1991), or the studies may have used elements of storytelling without relating it to storytelling directly (e.g., Cornil and Chandon, 2016). For example, Cornil and Chandon (2016) show that in comparison to individuals who had a health-based intervention, hungry and non-dieting individuals who were able to imagine themselves indulging in multisensory experiences – something individuals would be encouraged to do in an effective story – were the individuals who decided to take smaller portions of unhealthy foods, enjoy these smaller portions more, and be willing to pay more for the smaller portion. Hence, individuals who were able to take advantage of a multisensory narrative transport in storytelling were able to reduce the consumption of unhealthy food products.

Conclusion

Storytelling is persuasive. Storytelling is an effective way of conveying food information. Although traditional storytelling has elements of characterization and plot, food storytelling in the marketing discipline can be reduced to less elements without sacrificing efficaciousness. Furthermore, storytelling is of the upmost importance for brands and brand managers who need to achieve a sense of trustworthiness and authenticity. Nostalgic elements of stories enhance brand attachment. Conciseness and humor are valued aspects of storytelling. Overall, food storytelling is one way that allows consumers to possess and maintain fuzzy feelings about the brand without thinking about more concrete aspects of the brand. Moreover, telling stories may encourage previously disinterested consumers to try another food product or a different variation of a food product. Importantly, the essential element in any story is narrative transport. Lastly, a great opportunity regarding research about how food storytelling enhances or can augment elements of food wellbeing exists for marketing scholars and practitioners.

Note

1 In this chapter, we use the terms stories and narratives interchangeably.

Appendix: Methodological additions to food storytelling within the marketing literature

- What is the delineation line between a quick, but descriptive food description and a food "story"? In other words, are there limitations to narrative transportation within a food story context where concrete elements of the story might transport the consumer back to thinking about unfavorable memories? For example, do I want to know that a food tastes like bark, but I will be better off eating it in the long run?
- Use psychophysiological approaches with storytellers to evaluate which elements of the stories told are the most engaging and impactful. Psychophysiological approaches are able to detect small changes in heart rate or physiological skin changes that researchers can use to tell a consumer's physiological involvement with different storytelling elements.
- Is there greater synergy combining food information to drive later nutritional decisions (Keller et al., 1997) and does this food storytelling synergy extend beyond more health-conscious individuals? For example, is an individual who hears a story about someone who is gluten free being in better health before seeing a gluten-free food item more likely to choose the item, pay more for the item, or only choose gluten-free brands within the product category?
- Use more longitudinal studies to trace the history of consumers who regularly engage in multisensory storytelling (Cornil and Chandon, 2016) at their dinner tables to track the actual buying patterns of these family members. Also, diaries/semi-structured interviews may bring insights.
- Continue to find ways that significant others tell stories about more beneficial changes in diet that could help improve the long-term wellbeing of all family members (e.g., Block et al., 2011). For example, marketers can try to engage in more interdisciplinary research to find out about how structural and economic barriers work in conjunction with family storytelling about food to

influence individual food choices. Using longitudinal, semi-structured interviews with a panel of participants with demographic information collected each year may bring more marketing insight about family stories.

- Researchers should find out ways that food pictures/smells/sounds (e.g., Kahn and Wansink, 2004; Krishna and Morrin, 2007; Lwin et al., 2010) might interact with food stories to produce more synergistic stories for brands. For example, how much more are consumers willing to pay for stories about food with pictures and does the amount willing to be paid vary by the type of food item (i.e., steak versus a salad)? This is a within-subjects experimental design with different food items, both with and without stories.
- Can one food story influence willingness to pay for an entire range of food products? For example, does presenting a brand biography at the beginning of a menu influence the price consumers will be willing to pay for all food products? An experimental, counterbalanced design with some participants reading the biography and other participants who have not before presenting food products would be beneficial.
- Do highly favorable and "flawless" brand stories bring about positive judgments about the brand for all consumers or do more honest "return back to the brand" stories have more relevance and for which consumers?
- Researchers should continue to investigate if individual consumer differences exist and which consumers might be more attracted to which brand and consumer stories (Baumgartner, 2002).
- Researchers should continue to explore the boundaries of co-created consumer stories with those of the brand (Moore and Homer, 2008) in ways that benefit the consumer and the brand (Prahalad and Ramaswamy, 2004).
- How can food stories better influence servicescapes (Bitner, 1992)? How does storytelling fit in with research on abstract and concrete construal (White et al., 2011)? Are there boundary conditions on messages that may benefit more from having consumers look at a concrete message construal?

References

Addis, M., & Holbrook, M.B. (2010). Consumers' identification and beyond: Attraction, reverence, and escapism in the evaluation of films. *Psychology and Marketing*, 27(9), 821–845.

Ardelet, C., BarbaraS., & de Kerviler, G. (2015). Self-referencing narratives to predict consumers' preferences in the luxury industry: A longitudinal study. *Journal of Business Research*, 68, 2037–2044.

Argo, J.J., Zhu, R., Dahl, D.W. (2008). Fact or fiction: An investigation of empathy differences in response to emotional melodramatic entertainment. *Journal of Consumer Research*, 34(5), 614–623.

Athey, J. (2016). Storytelling: Out of the campfire and into your marketing campaign. *Marketing Profs*, April 13. Retrieved from: www.marketingprofs.com/articles/2016/29729/storytelling-out-of-the-campfire-and-into-your-marketing-campaign

Batat, W., Peters, P., Chan, S., Moscato, E., Chugani, S., Castro, I., & Muldrow, A. (Forthcoming). A conceptual introduction to experiential pleasure of food (EPF) and wellbeing.

Baumgartner, H. (2002). Toward a personology of the consumer. *Journal of Consumer Research*, 29(2), 286–292.

Berthon, P., Holbrook, M.B., Hulbert, J.M., & Pitt, L.F. (2007). Viewing brands in multiple dimensions. *MIT Sloan Management Review*, 48(2), 37–43.

Beverland, M.B., & Farrelly, F.J. (2010). The quest for authenticity in consumption: Consumers' purposive choice of authentic cues to shape experienced outcomes. *Journal of Consumer Research*, 36(5), 838–856.

Bhatnagar, N. & Wan, F. (2011). Is self-character similarity always beneficial? The moderating role of immersion in product placement effects. *Journal of Advertising*, 40(2), 39–50.

Bitner, M.J. (1992). Servicescapes: The impact of physical surroundings on customers and employees. *Journal of Marketing*, 56(2), 57–71.

Block, L.G., Grier, S.A., Childers, T.L., Davis, B., Ebert, J.E., Kumanyika, S. … Pettigrew, S. (2011). From nutrients to nurturance: A conceptual introduction to food wellbeing. *Journal of Public Policy and Marketing*, 30(1), 5–13.

Brown, D.E. (1991). *Human Universals*. New York: McGraw-Hill.

Bublitz, M.G., Peracchio, L.A., Andreasen, A.R., Kees, J., Kidwell, B., Miller, E.G. … Vallen, B. (2013). Promoting positive change: Advancing the food wellbeing paradigm. *Journal of Business Research*, 66(8), 1211–1218.

Cayla, J., & Arnould, E.J. (2008). A cultural approach to branding in the global marketplace. *Journal of International Marketing*, 16(4), 86–112.

Chang, C. (2009). "Being hooked" by editorial content: The implications for processing narrative advertising. *Journal of Advertising*, 38(1), 21–33.

Chen, T., & Lee, H.-M. (2014). Why do we share? The impact of viral videos dramatized to sell. *Journal of Advertising Research*, 54(3), 292–303.

Chiu, H.-C., Hsieh, Y.-C., & Kuo, Y.-C. (2012). How to align your brand stories with your products. *Journal of Retailing*, 88(2), 262–275.

Cornil, Y. & Chandon, P. (2016). Pleasure as a substitute for size: How multisensory imagery can make people happier with smaller food portions. *Journal of Marketing Research*, 53(5), 847–864.

Deighton, J., Romer, D., & McQueen, J. (1989). Using drama to persuade. *Journal of Consumer Research*, 16(3), 335–343.

Egeland, G.M., Charbonneau-Roberts, G., Kuluguqtuq, J., Kilabuk, J., Okalik, L., Soueida, R., & Kuhnlein, H.V. (2009). Back to the future: Using traditional food and knowledge to promote a healthy future among Inuit. In H.V. Kuhnlein, B. Erasmus, & D. Spigelski (Eds), *Indigenous Peoples' Food Systems: The Many Dimensions of Culture, Diversity and Environment for Nutrition and Health*. Rome: FAO, pp. 9–22.

Egeland, G.M., Yohannes, S., Okalik, L., Kilabuk, J., Racicot, C., Wilcke, M., Kuluguqtuq, J., & Kisa, S. (2012). The value of Inuit elders' storytelling to health promotion during times of rapid climate change and uncertain food security. In H.V. Kuhnlein, B. Erasmus, & D. Spigelski (Eds), *Indigenous Peoples' Food Systems and wellbeing: Interventions and Policies for Healthy Communities*. Rome: FAO, pp. 141–150.

Escalas, J.E. (2004a). Imagine yourself in the product: Mental simulation, narrative transportation, and persuasion. *Journal of Consumer Research*, 33(2), 37–48.

Escalas, J.E. (2004b). Narrative processing: Building consumer connections to brands. *Journal of Consumer Psychology*, 14(1–2), 168–180.

Escalas, J.E. (2007). Self-referencing and persuasion: Narrative transportation versus analytical elaboration. *Journal of Consumer Research*, 33(4), 421–429.

Escalas, J.E., Stern, B.B. (2003). Sympathy and empathy: Emotional responses to advertising dramas. *Journal of Consumer Research*, 29(4), 566–578.

Escalas, J.E., Moore, M.C., & Britton, J.E. (2004). Fishing for feelings? Hooking viewers helps! *Journal of Consumer Psychology*, 14(1–2), 105–114.

Fenger, M., Aschemann-Witzel, J., Hansen, F., & Grunert, K. (2015). Delicious words: Assessing the impact of short storytelling messages on consumer preferences for variations of a new processed meat product. *Food Quality and Preference*, 41, 237–244.

Fergusson, F. (1961). *Aristotle's Poetics*, trans. S.H. Butcher. New York: Hill and Wang.

Gilliam, D.A., & Zablah, A.R. (2013). Storytelling during retail service encounters. *Journal of Retailing and Consumer Services*, 20(5), 488–494.

Green, M.C., & Brock, T.C. (2000). The role of transportation in the persuasiveness of public narratives. *Journal of Personality and Social Psychology*, 79(5), 701–721.

Hamby, A., Daniloski, K., & Brinberg, D. (2015). How consumer reviews persuade through narratives. *Journal of Business Research*, 68(6), 1242–1250.

Hirschman, E.C. (1986). Humanistic inquiry in marketing research: Philosophy, method, and criteria. *Journal of Marketing Research*, 23(3), 236–249.

Kahn, B.E., & Wansink, B. (2004). The influence of assortment structure on perceived variety and consumption quantities. *Journal of Consumer Research*, 30(4), 519–533.

Keller, S.B., Landry, M., Olson, J., Velliquette, A.M., Burton, S., & Andrews, J.C. (1997). The effects of nutrition package claims, nutrition facts panels, and motivation to process nutrition information on consumer product evaluations. *Journal of Public Policy and Marketing*, 16(2), 256–269.

Kim, J.-E., Lloyd, S., & Cervellon, M.-C. (2016). Narrative-transportation storylines in luxury brand advertising: Motivating consumer engagement. *Journal of Business Research*, 69(1), 304–313.

Kozinets, R.V., De Valck, K., Wojnicki, A.C., & Wilner, S.J. (2010). Networked narratives: Understanding word-of-mouth marketing in online communities. *Journal of Marketing*, 74(2), 71–89.

Krishna, A., & Morrin, M. (2007). Does touch affect taste? The perceptual transfer of product container haptic cues. *Journal of Consumer Research*, 34(6), 807–818.

Lien, N.H., & Chen, Y.L. (2013). Narrative ads: The effect of argument strength and story format. *Journal of Business Research*, 66(4), 516–522.

Lwin, M.O., Morrin, M., & Krishna, A. (2010). Exploring the superadditive effects of scent and pictures on verbal recall: An extension of dual coding theory. *Journal of Consumer Psychology*, 20(3), 317–326.

Mancuso, J.C. (1986). The acquisition and use of narrative grammar structure. In T.R. Sarbin (Ed.), *Narrative Psychology: The Storied Nature of Human Conduct*. New York: Praeger, pp. 91–110.

Mandel, N., Petrova, P.K., & Cialdini, R.B. (2006). Images of success and the preference for luxury brands. *Journal of Consumer Psychology*, 16(1), 57–69.

McFerran, B., Dahl, D.W., Gorn, G.J., & Honea, H. (2010). Motivational determinants of transportation into marketing narratives. *Journal of Consumer Psychology*, 20 (3), 306–316.

Merchant, A., & Rose, G.M. (2012). Effects of advertising-evoked vicarious nostalgia on brand heritage. *Journal of Business Research*, 66(12), 2619–2625.

Mittelstaedt, J.D., Kilbourne, W.E., & Shultz, II, C.J. (2015). Macromarketing approaches to thought development in positive marketing: Two perspectives on a research agenda for positive marketing scholars. *Journal of Business Research*, 68(12), 2513–2516.

Moisio, R., & Beruchashvili, M. (2010). Questioning for wellbeing at weight watchers: The role of the spiritual-therapeutic model in a support group. *Journal of Consumer Research*, 36(5), 857–875.

Moore, D.J., & Homer, P.M. (2008). Self-brand connections: The role of attitude strength and autobiographical memory primes. *Journal of Business Research*, 61(7), 707–714.
Moore, S.G. (2012). Some things are better left unsaid: How word of mouth influences the storyteller. *Journal of Consumer Research*, 38(6), 1140–1154.
Nielsen, J.H., & Escalas, J.E. (2010). Easier is not always better: The moderating role of processing type on preference fluency. *Journal of Consumer Psychology*, 20(3), 295–305.
Paharia, N., Keinan, A., Avery, J., & Schor, J.B. (2010). The underdog effect: The marketing of disadvantage and determination through brand biography. *Journal of Consumer Research*, 37(5), 775–790.
Phillips, B.J., & McQuarrie, E.F. (2010). Narrative and persuasion in fashion advertising. *Journal of Consumer Research*, 37(3), 368–392.
Prahalad, C.K., & Ramaswamy, V. (2004). Co-creation experiences: The next practice in value creation. *Journal of Interactive Marketing*, 18(3), 5–14.
Ritzer, G. (1983). The McDonaldization of society. *Journal of American Culture*, 6(1), 100–107.
Rozin, P., Fischler, C., Imada, S., Sarubin, A., & Wrzesniewski, A. (1999). Attitudes to food and the role of food in life in the USA, Japan, Flemish Belgium and France: Possible implications for the diet–health debate. *Appetite*, 33(2), 163–180.
Russell, C.A., Schau, H.J., & Crockett, D. (2013). Cultural diversity in television narratives: Homophilization, appropriation, and implications for media advocacy. *Journal of Public Policy and Marketing*, 32(special issue), 119–130.
Sestir, M. & Green, M.C. (2010). You are who you watch: Identification and transportation effects on temporary self-concept. *Social Influence*, 5(4), 272–288.
Sugiyama, M.S. (2001). Food, foragers, and folklore: The role of narrative in human subsistence. *Evolution and Human Behavior*, 22, 221–240.
Udell, M. (2016). AWXII: How to build a better brand narrative. *AMA Marketing News*, Retrieved from: www.ama.org/publications/eNewsletters/Marketing-News-Weekly/Pages/awxii-brand-narrative.aspx?utm_content=buffer8f959&utm_medium=social&utm_source=facebook.c om&utm_campaign=buffer
van Laer, T., & de Ruyter, K. (2010). In stories we trust: How narrative apologies provide cover for competitive vulnerability after integrity-violating blog posts. *International Journal of Research in Marketing*, 27(2), 164–174.
van Laer, T., de Ruyter, K., Visconti, L.M., & Wetzels, M. (2014). The extended transportation-imagery model: A meta-analysis of the antecedents and consequences of consumers' narrative transportation. *Journal of Consumer Research*, 40(5), 797–817.
Wallendorf, M. & Arnould, E.J. (1991). We gather together: Consumption rituals of Thanksgiving day. *Journal of Consumer Research*, 18(1), 13–31.
Wells, W.D. (1989). Lectures and dramas. In P. Cafferata & A.M. Tybout (Eds), *Cognitive and Affective Responses to Advertising*. Lexington, MA: Lexington Books, pp. 13–20.
Wentzel, D., Tomczak, T., & Herrmann, A. (2010). The moderating effect of manipulative intent and cognitive resources on the evaluation of narrative ads. *Psychology and Marketing*, 27(5), 510–530.
West, P.M., Huber, J., & Min, K.S. (2004). Altering experienced utility: The impact of story writing and self-referencing on preferences. *Journal of Consumer Research*, 31(3), 623–630.
White, K., MacDonnell, R., & Dahl, D.W. (2011). It's the mind-set that matters: The role of construal level and message framing in influencing consumer efficacy and conservation behaviors. *Journal of Marketing Research*, 48(3), 472–485.
Woodside, A.G. (2010). Brand-consumer storytelling theory and research: Introduction to a Psychology and Marketing special issue. *Psychology and Marketing*, 27(6), 531–540.

11 Fusing East with West

How Asian epicurean experience evolves and embraces wellbeing

Steven Chan

Many food memories are formed during childhood (Wilson and Lee, 2016). I grew up in California as a Chinese-American, often going to Chinese restaurants to eat with my family. On a typical trip to a local Chinese restaurant, New Canton, the waitress seats my family at a large circular table and then hands a single menu to my parents or uncle to order for our whole family. Then come large dishes of food: a pot of seafood and tofu soup, a whole steamed fish, a plate of bok choy stir-fried with garlic, a plate of crispy roasted pork, a whole poached chicken with ginger scallion sauce, and a large pot of white rice. My aunt would ladle bowls of soup and scoop bowls of rice for my sisters and I to pass to everyone around the table. The dinner feast begins as we share in the family-style dishes. All the dishes are placed in the center of the table on a circular rotating tray. As the youngest, I wait my turn to locate my favorite roast pork.

For me, this anecdote typifies an Asian meal, but only in contrast to my childhood memories of an American eating experience. While my palette now enjoys Asian cuisine as much as American or other global cuisines, growing up, the choice of where to eat when bestowed by my parents always gravitated against Asian and for American cuisine. Whereas my Asian eating experience consisted of eating the food ordered collectively for my whole family, my American eating experience opened up the individual freedom to choose what I wanted. I remember the first time my parents took me to TGI Friday's, the quintessential American family restaurant, at least for my family. In contrast to my Chinese restaurant memories, at this American eatery, the waiter seats us and then hands each of us a menu to order individual entrées. I relished in this individual freedom as a child. I could pick my own entrée and not feel obligated to share with my older sisters. I would typically order a cheeseburger at TGI Friday's. The choice of cheese, condiments, and type of fries, all decisions I made on my own accord.

Comparing my memories of a Chinese versus an American eating experience, I observe the surface-level distinctions. A Chinese meal is a collective family experience centered on sharing plates of food; conversely, the American meal allows individual choice in ordering individual plates of food (Zili, 2017). I now reflect on my childhood and adult memories of eating meals of both Asian and Western varieties: I enjoy both sets of experiences, but the sentiment and manner of enjoyment are fundamentally different in meaning and expression. These childhood anecdotes of mine motivate and act as the starting point for this chapter on the experience of Asian food culture. Does the Asian eating experience warrant distinct examination? I aim to reveal how prior research, my ongoing experiments in cultural psychology and consumer behavior, and recent frameworks on examining gastronomy, work together to provide a distinct perspective on the expression, meaning, and enjoyment of food in Asian cultures.

For the 2017 Transformative Consumer Research conference, my co-authors and I developed the construct Experiential Pleasure of Food (EPF). We formed EPF as a new lens and set of tools to understand the consumption and enjoyment of food. We ultimately defined EPF as "the cognitive and emotional value that a consumer perceives from the multisensory, symbolic and sociocultural aspects of food activities," with multiple domains that encompass "food aestheticism, food socialization, food sharing, food storytelling, food symbolism, food memory and nostalgia, and food taste and sensory factors" (Batat et al., 2018). Like many constructs that inform our human experience in the social sciences, EPF generalizes and applies to peoples of all shapes, sizes, and cultures across the globe. In this chapter I would like to tease apart whether and how the experience and enjoyment of food should assume a differential analysis across cultures. Specifically I focus on the experience of East Asian populations, which cultural psychology has long singled out as the subject of cross-cultural differences (Peng and Nisbett, 1999; Spencer-Rodgers et al., 2009). Each researcher makes a strong attempt to eliminate bias when examining a topic and yet absolute objectivity stands as a goal to strive for, but never fully actualized. After all, as an Asian American, I will bring the passion of my cultural heritage to enrich and bring to life the examples that showcase how the cultural make-up of peoples across cultures warrants isolated examination. At the same time, having spent more than a decade striving to apply the techniques of cultural psychology to understand consumer behavior, scientific rigor will ensure that culture as a variable here does not act like a stereotype to reduce observed differences to mere surface-level explanations.

Since EPF focuses on the cognitive and emotional aspects of how people perceive and ultimately enjoy food, psychology becomes an important field to apply to this analysis. Psychology, whether the subfields of cognition or emotion, has long tried to understand human populations as a single universal group, where cognitive processes remain stable across cultures (Nisbett et al., 2001; Triandis, 1995).

After explaining psychology research findings as introduced here, this chapter will apply those findings to show how they manifest across cultures and through various domains of the epicurean experience, including food aesthetics and food nostalgia. Because cross-cultural comparisons can be controversial, I also discuss the complexities, limitations, and benefits of this novel view on the Asian epicurean experience. Finally, the Asian epicurean experience will be revealed to embrace a different form of epicurean wellbeing, one that is shaped by a more collectivistic and interdependent self-identity.

Cultural psychology as a foundation to interpret food culture

In more recent decades, foundational research has brought a shift towards a cultural psychology perspective, which views socialization and one's culture as having an important role in the development and expression of cognitive processes. The dichotomy of individualism and collectivism gave rise to the individualism-collectivism scale, which measures the extent an individual sees the self as part of a collective group or as fully autonomous (Triandis, 1995; Triandis and Gelfand, 1998). Measures of individualism-collectivism have broadly acknowledged differences across cultures, with populations representing Western European cultures scoring higher on individualism, while East Asian cultures score higher on collectivism (Hofstede, 1984; Leung and Bond, 1984). In Hofstede's country analysis, individualism represents the extent to which people in a particular country prefer to act as individual beings versus as members of a group. Conversely, for people in countries defined by collectivism, children learn to see themselves as part of a collective in-group with shared identity and goals that is separate from all other people, the out-group (Hofstede, 1984).

Parallel to the individualism-collectivism paradigm, the theory of independent and interdependent self-construal developed by Markus and Kitayama (1991) delves into another dimension of the psyche. The notion of independent self-construal sees the individual as behaving and understanding the world through one's own thoughts and feelings; the interdependent self-construal embodies a psyche that sees the self as bound to close others, behaving and understanding the world in connection with the thoughts and feelings of close others (Markus and Kitayama, 1991).

Together, the more individualistic and more independent self characterizes Western societies more than non-Western cultures (Markus and Kitayama, 1991; Nisbett et al., 2001; Spencer-Rodgers et al., 2009). Anecdotally, cultural examples highlight this Western divide. In Maslow's hierarchy of needs, a pillar of Western psychology and philosophy, the highest level of achieving one's full potential is self-actualization, which focuses on mastery of individual achievements in life (1943). It is no coincidence that Maslow focused on icons of Western society such as Albert Einstein and Frederick Douglass to construct his paradigm of the self (Mittelman, 1991). While many non-Western societies can be classified as collectivist and interdependent, East Asian cultures have been a key focus of collectivism and interdependent self-construal research (Markus and Kitayama, 1991; Nisbett et al., 2001; Spencer-Rodgers et al., 2009). Consider the example from Markus and Kitayama (1991), where *jibun*, the Japanese word for self, is defined not in absolute individualistic terms, rather the self is a space defined in a context shared with others (Esyun et al., 1985). Therefore, the individual self has a place in collectivist cultures, not separate from, but part of a group identity.

While examples provide a more illustrative view of these self theories, scale measurements quantify the cultural populations more accurately. For the individualism-collectivism paradigm, East Asian countries including China, Japan,

South Korea, and Southeast Asian countries score higher on collectivism and lower on individualism, while Western cultures including those in North America and Western Europe score the opposite, higher on individualism and lower on collectivism (Hofstede, 1984, 1993; Hofstede and Bond, 1988). Applying the independent-interdependent self-construal scale measures, multiple cross-cultural studies have directly compared and confirmed the general thesis that Western societies (including but not limited to the United States, Canada, Western Europe, and Australia), as compared with East and Southeast Asian societies (including but not limited to Japan, China, South Korea, India, Philippines, and Malaysia), score higher on independent self-construal and lower on interdependent self-construal (Markus and Kitayama, 1994; Miramontes, 2011; Singelis, 1994; Vignoles et al., 2016).

The implications for theories that challenge a universal view of the human psyche can be far reaching. Individualism-collectivism research has led to findings of cultural differences in family structures (Fiske, 1993), emotions (Wang, 2001), and personality (Triandis and Suh, 2002), to name just a few. The list of findings that stem from independent versus interdependent self-construals also runs long with examples including decision making (Mandel, 2003), emotions (Dean and Fles, 2016), and wellbeing (Kitayama et al., 2010). With this foundation of tools to examine cross-cultural differences, I would like to circle back to the premise of this chapter, that the experience and enjoyment of food also differs across cultures in systematic ways.

Contrasting Chinese and American food cultures

As a starting point, let us reconsider the examples from my own childhood: Starting with the American family restaurant, notice that even before the food arrives, the ordering of the food assumes a more individualistic and independent quality. Even though this American eating experience stands as a social activity of a group meal, each dinner guest at the table receives an individual menu and independently chooses his or her own meal preferences. At the traditional Chinese restaurant, the head of the household receives the only menu and has the responsibility to order for the entire group. If the social occasion involves a special guest, that guest may be bestowed the honor of ordering for all. As the youngest child in my family, I must respect the choices made for the entire group. This ordering practice has all the qualities of a collectivistic and interdependent frame.

Next, the presentation of the food holds consistent with the cultural qualities of this discussion. At the American restaurant, when I receive my individual order of food, the entrée arrives on a plate designed for one person to consume. The individually portioned food is not meant for sharing. That is not to say Western dining precludes any shared social interactions with respect to food: Appetizers and side dishes are often ordered specifically for group sharing. However, the individual entrée as the main focal point of a Western meal reveals the more individualistic quality of the dining experience as compared to the Asian meal. Interestingly, even the word entrée, which is commonly used to refer to the main dish in North America, comes from the French word for the entry appetizer course. However, over time the usage of the term has come to represent the main course in North American usage (Jurafsky, 2015). Even with shifts in meaning, the Western European origin of our food terminology still hints at the roots of these Western practices.

The traditional Chinese restaurant will not typically adopt categories like entrées on the menu. Many traditional Chinese restaurants will offer family meal sets, which often include a large pot of soup, cold first-course dishes, and an assortment of main dishes for the whole family or group. These group meal sets facilitate the more hierarchical ordering by the head of the table, who may also choose to order unbundled dishes as part of the group meal. All of the dishes arrive in communal style portions, which highlight a collective eating experience. Meal guests often praise the choice and quality of the food, to show respect for the head of the table. Since all guests enjoy the same set of dishes at the table, the conversations related to the food show greater interdependence. Younger guests will often scoop food for older guests, such as grandparents, as a sign of respect for the more elder generation. At the same time, older guests often plate portions of food for younger guests to show parental care or affection.

The family-style dishes, the circular table, and the placement of the dishes in the center, all facilitate these eating practices for the Chinese meal. The pouring of tea during a Chinese meal takes on specific cultural significance. As a child, my elders taught me that pouring tea for myself first represents an inconsiderate gesture. The proper etiquette requires you to first pour tea for the guests sitting beside you, preferably pouring for elder guests before younger guests. Even if the tea cups are near full, the gesture asks you to pour even a ceremonially small amount of tea for your neighboring guests first, before you pour any tea for your own cup (Parkinson, 2009). These eating customs express the implicit values and hierarchy of a social order for relationships in a Chinese eating context.

Unpacking these food memories from my American and Asian eating experiences does not suggest that Western epicurean experiences are not social by nature. Myriad research showcases the social experience of eating in Western societies (Miller et al., 1998; Ochs and Shohet, 2006). The crux of my comparison shows the level of collectivistic and interdependent values manifest in Asian eating practices as compared to Western ones. These cultural dichotomies, when taken to polarizing extremes, exaggerate cultural differentiation into reductive stereotypes. I have a contrary goal, to instead show appreciation of the nuances in the continuum of cultural differences. In this way, the nuances of thought-to-be universal theories of epicurean experience and wellbeing can be understood in the context of cultural and situational factors.

Balancing epicurean aesthetics from West to East

The plating of food and pouring of tea represent characteristics at the aesthetics level of an epicurean experience. The positioning of food on a plate represents another epicurean aesthetic quality assumed consistent across cultures. Prior research has shown that patrons would pay more for food placed in the center of a plate versus off-center (Spence, 2017). However, these studies predominantly measured diners from Western European ethnic backgrounds. This finding converges with research showing a Western preference for objects in the foreground versus background of one's focal attention: When compared to an American sample (of Western European background), Japanese participants preferred photos of a smaller foreground subject in a larger background context (Masuda et al., 2008). East Asian preferences in multiple domains, including visual objects, lean towards achieving a harmonious and holistic balance (Peng and Nisbett, 1999). Balancing or applying greater attention to background versus foreground objects in visual attention reduces preference for central or focal objects (Masuda et al., 2008). That would predict East Asians would not prefer nor pay materially more for food plated in the center versus off-center on a plate.

Interestingly, Spence (2017) considered the center-plated food condition as the "balanced" and the off-centered plate condition as "unbalanced." Assessing these semantics reveals that the meaning of "balance" rests in the interpretation of the beholder. While Western thought prefers a more linear and stable order, East Asian beliefs more holistically accept the changing ebb and flow of nature as harmonious (Peng and Nisbett, 1999). In the Western view, a linear order for aesthetics would adopt a more formal order, where centered objects in a fixed position rank highest in value. The more holistic East Asian aesthetic embraces a less formally ordered world. Therefore, balance in the Western sense values precise visual positioning while the Asian aesthetic values the changing "disorder" of natural equilibrium.

The Japanese aesthetic provides illuminating clues for the origin of the cultural differences at hand. For the Japanese to value off-center plating in food and other contexts converges with the notion of *Wabi Sabi*, a Zen Buddhist philosophy on impermanence that defines the Japanese aesthetic (Koren, 1994). *Fukinsei*, a key tenant of *Wabi Sabi*, means asymmetry or irregularity, and values the "balance" found in the existence of the natural world (Juniper, 2003). Beyond Japan, many East Asian philosophical traditions including other sects of Buddhism and Confucianism adopt similar appreciation of a harmonious natural world full of asymmetry and find balance in the irregularity (Peng and Nisbett, 1999; Spencer-Rodgers et al., 2009). In contrast, Western aesthetics traditionally values symmetry as defined by classicism and Renaissance art in Western Europe (Larsen, 1978). So while contemporary and postmodern art has shifted away from the symmetry of realism, the Western preference for centered food plating likely draws from the longer history of symmetry aesthetics found in Renaissance art.

Complexity in comparing cultural cuisines

Thus far I have presented to you epicurean examples from my own Chinese heritage that contrast with my American food experiences. The research literature has often precisely compared cultural differences in perception and behavior. And yet, what does this provide us in terms of an Asian epicurean understanding versus a non-Asian one? This question has no easy answers. I address the issue openly because examining cultural differences can augment theoretical understanding. Still, the goal in doing so must prevent reducing human differences to simplistic cultural group explanations without robust evidence.

Scholars have criticized research that uses binary Western and Eastern categories to understand cultural differences, instead calling for greater precision and discovery of underlying explanations for the differences (Oyserman et al., 2002; Vignoles et al., 2016). I concur with this call to action for greater depth in understanding human behavior. However, do not forget that universal theories that study one cultural group as representative of all people can be just as misleading. Therefore, research should balance the extremes of ignoring culture as a variable on one end and collapsing cultures into black boxes like "Asian" on the other end. In using such terms as Asian or Western here, the admitted caveat remains that research has yet to explain underlying geographic and cultural processes at work. But this is true in the strictest scrutiny even if we were to focus on examining two specific ethnic cultures. For example, Masuda et al. (2008) compared American students in Michigan and Japanese students in Japan for their visual attention research, but that does not mean each of those groups provides a valid representation of all American or Japanese populations.

Outside of academic theory, our lay use of cultural terms to categorize food can be said to oversimplify regional cuisines: for example, American food, Asian food, Latin food, European food, and African food. All those terms at a glance help us recall knowledge and memory of our food experiences. If a European citizen visits the United States and samples American food, this culinary adventure could start on the West Coast with a Cobb salad originating from Los Angeles and end with a bowl of shrimp and grits from the southern state of Georgia. The two dishes come from vastly different regions in the United States with different values and customs, but a single national history.

The same is true for my experience with Chinese food. Growing up in a Cantonese family, we predominantly enjoyed dishes native to Hong Kong and Guangzhou province. I would characterize the flavors as mostly savory and sweet, but never spicy. In contrast, vibrant red chili peppers and pungent numbing spices dominate Chinese dishes from Sichuan province. The premise of a cultural or a regional cuisine has both value and yet misrepresentation in our epicurean memories. To deny our psychological tendencies to oversimply information into categories inaccurately portrays our human experience. But at the same time, the limitations of these categories should be recognized, and that recognition allows us to appreciate new perspectives and further refine the supporting evidence. A tourist in China can use the term Chinese food to understand the similarities of Sichuan and Cantonese epicurean experiences as both collectivistic in the family-style meals and consumption of rice as the primary starch to accompany dishes: Those characteristics are shared by an ethnic culture linking the two regional populations. But the vastly differing flavor profiles already alluded to showcase the diversity of regional differences as well. The epicurean experience should appreciate both the comparisons and the contrasts to fully understand the essence and diversity of Chinese food. That holds true not just for Chinese food but all types of food across the globe.

The role of memory and nostalgia for epicurean experiences

The representation of food experiences in memory opens another unexplored avenue of cultural difference in the epicurean experience: food nostalgia. In developing the EPF paradigm, we highlighted the crucial role of memory and nostalgia for the experience of food (Batat et al., 2018). Our direct experience of food and our recollection of food experiences do not correspond one to one. Therefore, how we store and process information about food in memory impacts the effect of food nostalgia. For EPF, food nostalgia represents a longing for past food memories, especially those from childhood. A food experience more recently stored in memory should be more easily recalled given a recency bias that focuses attention on events closer to the present (Jones and Goethals, 1987). The strong associative meaning of a childhood food memory can cultivate longing for the food object and combat the decay of the memory over time. However, this classic view of memory and nostalgia can be challenged by more recent evidence of cultural differences. Studies show East Asians exhibit a more holistic view of past and present (Peng and Nisbett, 1999). For example, Ji and colleagues (2009) found that in making judgments, Chinese as compared to Canadian participants recruited past information with greater weight and detail, while subjectively judging the past as feeling closer to the present. This temporal difference across cultures suggests a more holistic view of time frames for East Asian cultures as compared to Western cultures. That further suggests a different pattern of memory.

For the concept of food nostalgia, I theorize that the Asian mindset likely balances past and present by default, so there is less need for the longing and grasping for the past as called for with nostalgia. In this way, food nostalgia would have less impact for the Asian consumer as compared to consumers in North American or Western Europe. The traditional view of food nostalgia posits a linear view of time, where the distant past grows further away from the present; where the foods one eats as a child are categorized as distinctly further in time from foods one eats as an adult. These conditions, more prominent in a Western than Eastern consumer culture, create greater distance and potential for food nostalgia. An American child might eat a children's cereal and order chicken nuggets from a children's menu at an American restaurant while growing up. The American child, even from a young age, has been provided a more individualistic and independent food experience crafted for the child. Conversely, children in Asian cultures have a more collectivistic and interdependent food upbringing: Foods may be simplified and cooked more to aid digestion for a child, but traditional meals do not typically segment dishes by age group. You will not see a children's menu at the traditional Asian restaurant. Shared family-style meals best serve the interdependent values of the Asian collectivist context.

In this way, both time perception and food segmentation can influence food nostalgia behavior. I contend East Asian cultures experience food nostalgia in less pronounced ways. Perceiving the past more holistically in time perception yields a less biased focus on the present and enhances memory for the past (Ji et al., 2009; Lam et al., 2005). Furthermore, food segments are less defined by age and time in the Asian context. For example, if my family prepared dumplings to celebrate the Lunar Chinese New Year in my youth, the degree of nostalgic longing for that epicurean experience could be proportional to the time elapsed since last participating in that family tradition. Maybe I only have time to participate every few years given a busy work schedule as an adult. That may stand in contrast to my nostalgia for American foods, like making Rice Krispy treats with my sisters as a toddler. This American treat, segmented for children, creates greater psychological and temporal distance as a category for the adult to long for with nostalgia. The nostalgia in this case functions not just proportional to time, but heightens given a categorical boundary of child and adult. Future research should directly test the temporal and categorical variables named here with empirical data to confirm their application in the food domain.

How food categorization affects epicurean experiences across cultures

The way we categorize food changes our epicurean experiences in multiple ways. In my work on consumption of counterfeit products across cultures, my co-author and I empirically demonstrate how consumers of East Asian ethnicity, when compared to Caucasian consumers, are more accepting of the ways a counterfeit product deviates from an authentic product (Chan and Amaral, 2015). This finding transfers into the food domain if we treat authentic cuisine as a genuine product and deviations from that genuine form as a "counterfeit" product. Western European philosophy follows a more linear thinking, such as syllogistic logic: For example, if all men drink water, and Plato is a man, then Plato drinks water (Peng and Nisbett, 1999). This linear logic creates a process of categorization with more rigid, "black or white" attributions. For instance, an authentic Neapolitan pizza must use San Marzano tomatoes, grown in Naples. Deviating from the fixed ingredients results in categorizing the pizza a "fake" or inauthentic.

East Asian philosophy follows a more evolving and holistic view of the world (Nisbett et al., 2001; Spencer-Rodgers et al., 2009). Consider the principle of yin and yang, where everything in the universe exists as unified and yet contradictory opposites; dark and light, while opposing forces, exist as one in a harmonious relationship. Applied to an epicurean example, consider the origin of the dish "chop suey." In the authentic form, it comes from the Chinese village town of Toisan and means stir-fried animal intestines (Anderson, 1988). But the original form of this dish did not inhibit Chinese immigrants in San Francisco, in the 1890s, from modifying it to include chopped meat, vegetables, and stir-fried egg. The evolved chop suey won over not only American palettes, but also Chinese guests, including an esteemed Chinese premier, Li Hongzhang (Liu, 2009). While anecdotal, this example highlights the greater acceptance of change over time, a more holistic view of how original dishes adapt over time. Contrast the evolution of the Asian dish chop suey with the Western Neapolitan pizza: In 1984, the Associazione Vera Pizza Napoletana formed in Italy with the mission to protect the "true Neapolitan pizza" with strict guidelines and certification. Compared to Western European culture, East Asian culture embraces a greater amount of change in seeing the world, which results in a wider acceptance of what counts for the authenticity of a given food experience. Greater acceptance translates into higher enjoyment of foods that stray further from a recipe's origin in the Asian context. Conversely, in the Western context, diminished authenticity would reduce enjoyment: For example, using roma tomatoes instead of the San Marzano ones on Neapolitan pizza would equate to inauthentic and reduce epicurean enjoyment.

The acceptance of change and greater tolerance for deviating from traditional or authentic recipes may have provided a ripe environment for an abundance of fusion foods linked to Asian cuisines. While the fusing of different culinary traditions has a long history, the modern fusion food movement is often traced back to the 1980s when Wolfgang Puck opened Chinois, a mix of French and Chinese cuisines (Dickerman, 2012). On the food review site Yelp.com, Asian fusion represents a cuisine of its own, the only such fusion category listed. While anecdotal, the category of Asian fusion leads the current food trends environment. Surveying the variety of fusion foods in recent decades, the movement of Asian-inspired fusions appears most dominant: California sushi rolls, Korean taco trucks, Indo-Chinese, Vietnamese-French bahn mi sandwiches. Asian food as the focal point of a fusion food movement fits with the East Asian perspective of an interdependent self.

With self-identity understood as part of a collective group identity in the East Asian context, the case of bicultural integration remains an interesting one: How do Asians adapt growing up in or moving to a Western culture? In the United States, one quarter of the immigration since 1965 has come from Asian countries; the American-Asian population has grown 72 percent since 2000 with the latest census totaling 20.4 million in 2015 (López et al., 2017). Researchers have examined the process of acculturation, where individuals and groups must adapt to a new culture after immigration. Benet-Martinez and Morris (Benet-Martínez et al., 2002) developed the theory of cultural frame switching, whereby East Asian immigrants shift between two culturally based perspectives. In general, these immigrants switch between behaviors consistent with the Asian interdependent self-view and the Western independent self-view based on environmental cues that trigger the cultural frame (Hong et al., 2001). In the present context, this cultural frame switching for Asian immigrants contributes to the view of Asian fusion food. Asian fusion food focuses on being able to switch cultural viewpoints in blending two cultures for culinary creation.

The ability to malleably switch between cultural lenses, while true of all people, is particularly suitable for the Asian psyche. Consistent with the theories discussed earlier, the self-concept holds a more interdependent origin with greater acceptance for change and contradictions. The influence of Western consumerism, with the emphasis of individualism, inevitably shifts Asian assimilation towards adopting more individualistic values. Over the last several decades, brands advertising in China have shifted from appealing to a wholly collectivistic self to appealing to a Chinese consumer that recognizes more individualistic values (Doctoroff, 2012). Just as the notion of authentic Asian food can comfortably shift over time, so can the authentic self-concept for the Asian immigrant or Asian-American. The authentic self does not stay fixed in one dominant culture by principle. Consistent with the East Asian philosophical traditions of holism and change over time, the Asian self-identity can flexibly evolve around multiple cultures.

On the wellbeing of epicurean experiences

What is the outcome we care about in EPF? It is the experience of pleasure in the moment and the extended wellbeing that results from the domain of food. This domain of judging our experiences with food matters most because if the final result does not reward the eater with enjoyment, then what else is it for? Pleasure represents a hedonic affective response to stimuli. Food as that stimuli surely elicits an in-the-moment pleasurable response that each of us recognizes. Food also serves a nutritional benefit in our lives, which encompasses a more long-term measure of wellbeing. Therefore, food presents two avenues of benefits, one for short-term pleasure, and the second for long-term wellbeing.

First, the avenue of pleasure considers how we savor a morsel of our favorite food at the moment our brain processes the signals from our taste buds. That momentary experience mirrors how happy we might feel the moment we step onto a sunny beach during a vacation. Both are momentary feelings with subjective valuation. Do we isolate that momentary experience and elevate it above all of the other more mundane moments in our life? Or do we more holistically average that great moment in the context of our entire day or life? Cross-cultural theories consistently show that East Asians take the later approach with multiple forces at work. The greater consideration of past memories in the context of judging the present suggests that the present stands out less (Ji et al., 2009). The more balanced weighting of information in the past and present reduces focal bias on the present (Lam et al., 2005). This results in lower ratings of pleasure and happiness for East Asians as compared with Western samples. It may be difficult to conceptualize what this difference means. What does rating the pleasure you feel when eating your favorite food a 6 out of 7 versus a 5 out of 7 mean? The difference represents more than a matter of rating, it represents a different process by which cultures interpret experience, a different way of being.

Chinese scholars have highlighted that the word happiness does not even historically exist in the Chinese language, only added in more contemporary additions to the language (Lu et al., 2001). *Fu-qi* is the closest word linked to happiness in Mandarin Chinese, but the meaning, when elaborated, links more closely to the following values: longevity, prosperity, health, peace, and virtue (Wu, 1991). Even today, Chinese custom calls for greeting family and friends with these "five fu's" during the spring festival (Lu, 2001). So the individual happiness so common to our Western understanding does not traditionally hold the same meaning in the East Asian context. For the interdependent collective self in the East Asian context, good fortune and harmony are appreciated most readily. That intuitively makes sense for a philosophical system that views balance in a changing natural world as the state of being. This is not to say that East Asians cannot experience happiness as understood in the Western view. Human experience is not necessarily limited to the words in our language, but our language does influence our subjective experience (Boroditsky, 2001). And so the explication of the Chinese words for happiness reveal key evidence for the culturally different experience of happiness. Epicurean pleasures, as understood in Western individualistic terms, should be reinterpreted. Such eating pleasure while present in the Asian experience are dampened by a holistic view of time and being. The East Asian interdependent self enjoys experience in the context of an in-group. For example, even if I did not order my favorite shrimp dish at the family banquet, my experience of enjoyment hinges more on the harmony of the family experience in being able to order and enjoy the ceremonial roast duck for the occasion.

As for the longer-term benefits of the epicurean pleasure of food, we examine our extended wellbeing in relation to food. Recent work in defining a "food wellbeing" has even created categories of subdomains for food that impact our lives over time: food socialization, food literacy, food marketing, food availability, and food policy (Block et al., 2011). While those subdomains are justifiably relevant to our society with regard to food, they are still embedded in a Western context, because what is good and valued within each subdomain depends on a value system of a culture. For instance, food socialization encompasses the parenting styles of a culture and how food restrictions might be imposed on children (Block et al., 2011). For an individualistic society, individual freedom and freedom of choice in food are highly valued. But a collectivist society values harmonious family relations higher than individual freedoms, limiting individual freedom of choice. Consider the example of religious belief systems, which forbid consumption of certain meats. Those religious communities act as collectivist in-groups, where food restrictions maintain interdependent group relations. An individual in that group, who exercises individual freedom to eat the restricted food, would ultimately harm social wellbeing. In this way, cultural group values shape wellbeing.

Traditional Western psychology measures life satisfaction, positive affect and negative affect as components of subjective wellbeing (Andrews and Withey, 1976). Given our extended discussion of cultural differences, we should not be surprised that East Asian psychology shows important differences. For example, influenced by Taoist philosophy, wellbeing in the Chinese context centers on equilibrium with nature, society, and the individual (Lu et al., 2001). We return to the underlying theme of an individualistic Western viewpoint contrasted with a collectivistic East Asian perspective. I interpret these differences in the context of food wellbeing. Where individual wellbeing can enjoy epicurean pleasures without conflict to the harmonious relations of family and nature, the Asian epicurean wellbeing mirrors the Western view. However, where there is conflict with in-group goals, the East Asian epicurean experience will defer to group wellbeing. Once again, the starting point for epicurean wellbeing in this Asian context begins with the group identity. Once the sense of group wellbeing satisfices, then the individual's wellbeing can be freed to express the individual will. For example, circling back to the Chinese dinner of my youth, the family orders food as a group and the meal is served to the group, that is akin to serving the group's wellbeing. However, once the family-style dishes are brought to the table and the group's will is served, I am free to choose my own food and enjoy the epicurean experience of my own accord.

Exploring cultural comparisons and their contribution to food marketing and wellbeing

This chapter concludes with a look at how the exploration of the Asian epicurean experience contributes to our understanding of food marketing and wellbeing. As discussed earlier, cultural comparisons are complex and messy to the extent that the underlying processes of a finding may not be fully understood, at least not just yet. Further research needs to refine surface-level findings concerning cultural comparisons. However, along the way, we should not pretend that findings studying one cultural group are universal. Therefore, prior general understandings of the epicurean experience that do not take into account cultural differences are limited in their perspective. Applying cultural psychology in this chapter has contributed a new approach to understanding the epicurean experience. I hope the reader has gained a new appreciation of how food aesthetics, nostalgia, and more, can vary across cultures based on different knowledge structures and processes with which humans understand the world. These findings benefit our understanding of consumer behavior in the domain of food.

Different cultures and ethnicities represent different segments in the marketplace. Understanding each segment in more detailed ways allows the practitioner in the marketplace to more effectively serve the needs of the consumers, whether Asian or American. By recognizing and addressing each cultural group's differentiated approach and experience in the domain of food, the individual consumer can be better served and satisfied. Food marketing strives towards this higher satisfaction and the approach in this chapter elevates that possibility.

Inspired by the work in food wellbeing (Block et al., 2011) I recognize that the practitioners in the marketplace do not simply represent corporations and firms that produce and distribute food. The key stakeholders in food wellbeing are the everyday people, food consumers, whose psychological and social needs in relation to food are just as important as the physical attributes of food. Therefore, food wellbeing defined as a broader more encompassing term than just food as nutrition, requires a full understanding of the person. I contend that culture is quite important in understanding people. In unpacking the Asian epicurean experience, the ability to understand the collective interdependent self-identity of the Asian food consumer has increased. Attempts to enhance Asian food wellbeing must account for the tension between individual and collective goals. As globalization evolves, so do cultures and the Asian epicurean experience. The influence of globalization fuses elements across cultures as I have detailed in this chapter. By continuing the approach here, of addressing the evolution of cultural differences versus seeing cultures as fixed, we will continue to elevate and improve how we eat and live.

References

Anderson, E.N. (1988). *The Food of China*. New Haven, CT: Yale University Press.

Andrews, F.M., & Withey, S.B. (1976). *Social Indicators of wellbeing: Americans' Perceptions of Life Quality*. New York: Plenum Press.

Batat, W., Peter, P., Moscato, E.M., Castro, I.A., Chan, S., Chugani, S.K., & Muldrow, A.F. (2018). The experiential pleasure of food: A savoring journey to food wellbeing. *Journal of Business Research*. Advance online publication. doi: 10.1016/j.jbusres.2018.12.024

Benet-Martínez, V., Leu, J., Lee, F., & Morris, M.W. (2002). Negotiating biculturalism: Cultural frame switching in biculturals with oppositional versus compatible cultural identities. *Journal of Cross-Cultural Psychology*, 33(5), 492–516.

Block, L.G., Grier, S.A., Childers, T.L., Davis, B., Ebert, J.E.J., Kumanyika, S. … van Ginkel Bieshaar, M.N.G. (2011). From nutrients to nurturance: A conceptual introduction to food wellbeing. *Journal of Public Policy and Marketing*, 30(1), 5–13.

Boroditsky, L. (2001). Does language shape thought? Mandarin and English speakers' conceptions of time. *Cognitive Psychology*, 43(1), 1–22.

Chan, S., & Amaral, N. (2015). Not all fakes are created equal: Cultural differences in consuming counterfeits. In B. Schimitt & L. Lee (Eds), *The Psychology of the Asian Consumer*. New York: Routledge, pp. 55–58.

Dean, K.K., & Fles, E.H. (2016). The effects of independent and interdependent self-construals on reactions to transgressions: Distinguishing between guilt and shame. *Self and Identity*, 15(1), 90–106.

Dickerman, S. (2012). Fusion reaction: How America fell in love, and then out of love, and then in love all over again, with Asian-influenced cuisine. *Slate Magazine*.

Doctoroff, T. (2012). *What Chinese Want: Culture, Communism and the Modern Chinese Consumer*. New York: St. Martin's Press.

Esyun, H., Shumpei, K., & Creighton, M.R. (1985). A contextual model of the Japanese: Toward a methodological innovation in Japan studies. *Journal of Japanese Studies*, 11(2), 289–321.

Fiske, A.P. (1993). *Structures of Social Life: The Four Elementary Forms of Human Relations: Communal Sharing, Authority Ranking, Equality Matching, Market Pricing*. New York: Free Press.

Hofstede, G. (1984). *Culture's Consequences: International Differences in Work-Related Values*. Beverly Hills, CA: Sage.

Hofstede, G. (1993). Cultural constraints in management theories. *Academy of Management Perspectives*, 7(1), 81–94.

Hofstede, G., & Bond, M.H. (1988). The Confucius connection: From cultural roots to economic growth. *Organizational Dynamics*, 16(4), 5–21.

Hong, Y., Ip, G., Chiu, C., Morris, M.W., & Menon, T. (2001). Cultural identity and dynamic construction of the self: Collective duties and individual rights in Chinese and American cultures. *Social Cognition*, 19(3), 251–268.

Ji, L.-J., Guo, T., Zhang, Z., & Messervey, D. (2009). Looking into the past: Cultural differences in perception and representation of past information. *Journal of Personality and Social Psychology*, 96(4), 761–769.

Jones, E.E., & Goethals, G.R. (1987). Order effects in impression formation: Attribution context and the nature of the entity. In E.E. Jones, D.E. Kanhouse, H.H. Kelley, R. E. Nisbett, S. Valins, & B. Weiner (Eds), *Attribution: Perceiving the Causes of Behavior*. Hillsdale, NJ: Lawrence Erlbaum Associates, pp. 27–46.

Juniper, A. (2003). *Wabi Sabi: The Japanese Art of Impermanence*. Boston, MA: Tuttle Publishing.

Jurafsky, D. (2015). *The Language of Food: A linguist Reads the Menu*. New York: W.W. Norton.

Kitayama, S., Karasawa, M., Curhan, K., Ryff, C.D., & Rose Markus, H. (2010). Independence and interdependence predict health and wellbeing: Divergent patterns in the United states and Japan. *Frontiers in Psychology*, 1, 163.

Koren, L. (1994). *Wabi-Sabi for Artists, Designers, Poets and Philosophers*. Berkeley, CA: Stone Bridge Press.

Lam, K.C.H., Buehler, R., McFarland, C., Ross, M., & Cheung, I. (2005). Cultural differences in affective forecasting: The role of focalism. *Personality and Social Psychology Bulletin*, 31(9), 1296–1309.

Larsen, M. (1978). Italian renaissance painting by John Hale. *Journal of the Royal Society of Arts*, 126(5260), 243–244.

Leung, K., & Bond, M.H. (1984). The impact of cultural collectivism on reward allocation. *Journal of Personality and Social Psychology*, 47(4), 793–804.

Liu, H. (2009). Chop suey as imagined authentic Chinese food: The culinary identity of Chinese restaurants in the United States. *Journal of Transnational American Studies*, 1(1).

López, G., Ruiz, N.G., & Patten, E. (2017). Key facts about Asian Americans, a diverse and growing population. *Pew Research*, September 8.

Lu, L. (2001). Understanding happiness: A look into the Chinese folk psychology. *Journal of Happiness Studies*, 2(4), 407–432.

Lu, L., Gilmour, R., & Kao, S. (2001). Cultural values and happiness: An East–West dialogue. *Journal of Social Psychology*, 141(4), 477–493.

Mandel, N. (2003). Shifting selves and decision making: The effects of self-construal priming on consumer risk-taking. *Journal of Consumer Research*, 30, 30–40.

Markus, H.R., & Kitayama, S. (1991). Culture and the self: Implications for cognition, emotion, and motivation. *Psychological Review*, 98(2), 224–253.

Markus, H.R., & Kitayama, S. (1994). A collective fear of the collective: Implications for selves and theories of selves. *Personality and Social Psychology Bulletin*, 20(5), 568–579.

Maslow, A.H. (1943). A theory of human motivation. *Psychological Review*, 50(4), 370–396.

Masuda, T., Gonzalez, R., Kwan, L., & Nisbett, R.E. (2008). Culture and aesthetic preference: Comparing the attention to context of East Asians and Americans. *Personality and Social Psychology Bulletin*, 34(9), 1260–1275.

Miller, L., Rozin, P., & Fiske, A.P. (1998). Food sharing and feeding another person suggest intimacy: Two studies of American college students. *European Journal of Social Psychology*, 28(3), 423–436.

Miramontes, L.G. (2011). *The Structure and Measurement of Self-Construals: A Cross-Cultural Study of the Self-Construal Scale*. Seattle, WA: Washington State University.

Mittelman, W. (1991). Maslow's study of self-actualization a reinterpretation. *Journal of Humanistic Psychology*, 31(1), 114–135.

Nisbett, R.E., Peng, K.P., Choi, I., & Norenzayan, A. (2001). Culture and systems of thought: Holistic versus analytic cognition. *Psychological Review*, 108(2), 291–310.

Ochs, E., & Shohet, M. (2006). The cultural structuring of mealtime socialization. *New Directions for Child and Adolescent Development*, 11, 35–49.

Oyserman, D., Coon, H.M., & Kemmelmeier, M. (2002). Rethinking individualism and collectivism: Evaluation of theoretical assumptions and meta-analyses. *Psychological Bulletin*, 128(1), 3–72.

Parkinson, R.L. (2009). *The Everything Chinese Cookbook: From Wonton Soup to Sweet and Sour Chicken: 300 Succulent Recipes from the Far East*. Cincinnati, OH: F+W Media.

Peng, K.P., & Nisbett, R.E. (1999). Culture, dialectics, and reasoning about contradiction. *American Psychologist*, 54(9), 741–754.

Singelis, T.M. (1994). The measurement of independent and interdependent self-construals. *Personality and Social Psychology Bulletin*, 20(5), 580–591.

Spence, C. (2017). *Gastrophysics: The New Science of Eating*. London: Penguin.

Spencer-Rodgers, J., Boucher, H.C., Mori, S.C., Wang, L., & Peng, K.P. (2009). The dialectical self-concept: Contradiction, change, and holism in East Asian cultures. *Personality and Social Psychology Bulletin*, 35(1), 29–44.

Triandis, H. (1995). *Individualism and Collectivism*. Boulder, CO: Westview Press.

Triandis, H.C., & Gelfand, M.J. (1998). Converging measurement of horizontal and vertical individualism and collectivism. *Journal of Personality and Social Psychology*, 74(1).

Triandis, H.C., & Suh, E. (2002). Cultural influences on personality. *Annual Review of Psychology*, 53, 133–160.

Vignoles, V.L., Owe, E., Smith, P.B., Easterbrook, M.J., Brown, R., Becker, M. … Bond, M.H. (2016). Beyond the "East-West" dichotomy: Global variation in cultural models of selfhood. *Journal of Experimental Psychology: General*, 145(8), 966–1000.

Wang, Q. (2001). "Did you have fun?" American and Chinese mother–child conversations about shared emotional experiences. *Cognitive Development*, 16(2): 693–715.

Wilson, B., & Lee, A. (2016). *First Bite: How We Learn to Eat*. New York: Basic Books.

Wu, Y. (1991). *The New Transcription of "Shang Shu"* Taipei: Shan Min Books.

Zili, X. (2017). The differences of Chinese and Western food cultures. *Chinese Language, Literature and Culture*, 2(1), 6–9.

12 The food gastronomy experience

A French perspective on food wellbeing

Gwarlann De Kerviler

The present study provides in-depth understanding of the features of French gastronomy and the unique association that French consumers attach to food and wellbeing. The study identifies the specificities as well as considers the explanatory factors for the French consumers' approach to cuisine and wellbeing. Therefore, the first section reviews the history of French gastronomy and its institutionalization as a specific field. The second section investigates the unique approach of French consumers to food and wellbeing as well as the social and cultural dimensions associated with gastronomy. For a comprehensive understanding of French gastronomy and wellbeing, the study explored vast literature on gastronomy. The study also included interviews with renowned French chefs with three Michelin star restaurants (Christian Le Squer – chef at Le Cinq Restaurant: Four Seasons Hotel George V Paris; Guy Savoy – chef at Le restaurant gastronomique Guy Savoy la Monnaie de Paris; Eric Frachon – chef at Epicure Le Bristol Paris), famous chef patissier Pierre Hermé and food experts (Elizabeth Picciotino, Marie Eve Laporte, and Elsa Ammal).

Food gastronomy: development of French culinary art

Delving into the history of French cuisine would reveal fine details of gastronomy and its evolution in France. The study presents the development of the gastronomic field in France in three major phases: emergence during the era of Louis XIV's Versailles, consolidation following the French Revolution, and dominance in early 20th-century Parisian restaurants. Louis XIV, known as the Roi Soleil (Sun King), was the monarch who reigned from 1643 to 1715. During his reign, the classic French haute cuisine (literally "high cuisine") became well known and renowned cooks became important members of the Royal Court. Subsequently, the French Revolution (1789–99) abolished the dominance of the nobility and chefs left royal and noble families to serve the bourgeois gourmets. Economic growth, marked by urbanization and industrialization, heralded a new era, with chefs departing from the privileged homes of the affluent aristocratic families to cater to diners who relished the semi-public ambiance of fine restaurants.

From the royal court to the Parisian restaurants

The culinary identity of French cuisine was established with the grandiose feasts served at royal courts and civic banquets meant for kings. Gastronomy increasingly emerged as the vanguard of culinary art (Figure 12.1) as French cuisine gained from lucid formalized codes and practices early on, which proved an unequivocal advantage in the bid for culinary authority.

Louis XIV and the emergence of haute cuisine

Haute cuisine originated in 17th-century France, and the culinary cuisine transformed under the reign of Louis XIV at Versailles. Meals were part of the king's affirmation of power and were dramatic, orchestrated by a "maître d'hôtel," and used "service à la française" (French-style service). The culinary rules at Versailles were highly codified. Depending on the number of guests, at each service, the appropriate dishes were arranged symmetrically, with a center dish, four medium dishes, and four small and eight smaller dishes. It allowed diners to select from different dishes served simultaneously. The art of placing guests around the table and serving them meals symbolized the "etiquette" (unwritten rules) of Versailles, underlining their positions in the tiered pyramid of French society. For presenting the visual and aromatic pleasures, the table was arranged in a proportionate set to give it a harmonious and symmetrical appearance. Chef François Pierre La Varenne published the first true French cookbook *Cuisinier François* (French Cook) in 1651. It was the first book to specify clear rules for haute cuisine.

The Revolution and the establishment of French cuisine

Haute cuisine was originally meant to serve the court and the aristocracy. However, the French Revolution witnessed the exit of aristocracy, and chefs moved on to showcase their culinary talents to cater to the general elite public. The opening of new restaurants was easier than before as the guild system was abolished. This system controlled who could be a butcher, baker, or cheesemaker, and how they did their jobs.

A new class of consumers that enjoyed rich fine food emerged, which drew from the ancient practices of fine dining. The 19th-century gastronomic elite

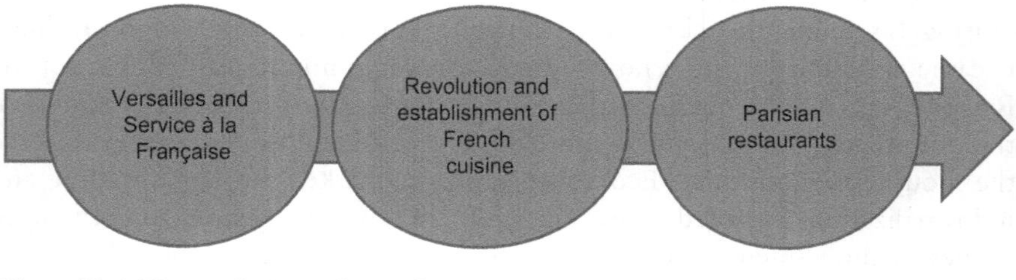

Figure 12.1 The evolution of French cuisine

were similar to the former aristocracy in affluence and taste but diverse as well. Grimod de la Reynière acquired fame as one of the first gastronomic reviewers who trained the wealthy post-revolutionary elites who had no classical education on how to host and dine as well as what and how to serve. His review of food establishments intended to regulate the culinary world and recommended the creation of more culinary institutions. Transformation in culinary art aided in the general movement of the post-revolution modernization of society, which was itself a function of both increasing control of production conditions and the developing international markets. The cuisine became "French," although the culinary arts were no longer associated with the aristocracy but soon formed a national identity. It is believed that the larger the market, the more identifiable the goods must be. For example, Camembert cheese that was sold from and within Normandy had little need for differentiation, but when it was sold in the Parisian market, the cheese needed to be reliable, identifiable, and attractive.

Universal Exhibition and Parisian restaurants

In late 19th-century France, new luxury hotels such as the Negresco in Cannes (1912) or Ritz in Paris (1898) flourished. Horses were replaced by automobiles, which allowed the bourgeoisie to easily discover regional culinary and artistic treasures. The French coasts were thriving with new palaces, casinos, and theatres where French cooks and *Maîtres d'hôtel* celebrated French cuisine. The bourgeoisie who previously ate in their private homes were welcomed by the restaurants in Cannes or Paris. The aspirations of both affluent and ordinary clientele of the Belle Epoque took wing when they were able to enjoy palaces and fine restaurants as public places that retained ostentatious and sophisticated references specific to the Versailles nobility and also avoided an expensive house brigade (Ory, 1998).

In 1889, the Universal Exhibition was held in Paris. It showcased French gastronomy to an international audience. In the French Pavilion, four restaurants with a capacity of 500 people were built. This included the renowned Restaurant de France. The Universal Exhibition has also hosted a culinary exhibition organized by the "Société des Cuisiniers Français" (Society of French Cooks) since 1883. A contest among chefs is conducted as part of this exhibition. The meals are displayed as masterpieces placed on large tables at the center of exhibition rooms, and guests are invited to view them before tasting. The Société des Cuisiniers Français aims to promote culinary art through such exhibitions. A gastronomic journal *L'art culinaire* (Culinary Art) was introduced to highlight its activities. This journal was considered prestigious in France at the time.

Culinary discourse in France

The role of discourse in establishing and enriching the reputation of French cuisine is discussed further. French cuisine was strengthened by the culinary discourse, which turned gastronomic aspirations into culinary practice transcending the realms of immediate culinary production.

Establishing French cuisine

The status of gastronomy as a general cultural practice remains uncertain as long as it remains word of mouth. Literature on cuisine would allow it to move out of the kitchen over to broader cultural arena. Discussions on cuisine changed the material into the imaginative, symbolic, and aesthetic and laid the foundation for cultural debates defining the gastronomic field. The spectacular development of a culinary discourse during the age of Enlightenment in France transformed the act of eating into an art linked to taste and refinement.

Grimod de la Reynière, Carême, and Brillat Savarin were the pioneers and essential contributors of culinary discourse. Their discourses were the textual basis to a specific set of culinary practices and became identified with the country as a whole and imposed standards. French culinary tradition was being identified with France mainly because of the literature that integrated food practice into a socioculinary tradition and a gastronomic code, which is due to the strength of the gastronomic field and affiliations with the literacy field.

Formalizing culinary practices

Critics establish and popularize a cultural hierarchy, helping ordinary customers to appreciate taste. Cooks are deemed to be unable both to arrive at a broader theorization of their own individual taste and to lack sufficient access to the public. Therefore, critical discourse acts as a mediator between producers and consumers of cultural objects and as a determinant of symbolic value (Lane, 2013). Critics judge the quality or merit of artistic work, which in turn produces a secondary discourse about cultural objects. They judge and rank cultural objects because of their vast experience and knowledge. They are well equipped to apply their knowledge widely and reliably to attain legitimacy.

Self-proclaimed founder of modern French cuisine, Marie Antoine Carême, developed several culinary treatises. By the late 19th century, he had worked in the kitchens of renowned European hotels such as Cesar Ritz. Present-day chefs often refer to his 1832 work *L'art de la cuisine française au 19ème* (*The Art of French Cuisine in the 19th Century*) as the "Old Testament" for cooking. George Auguste Escoffier's *Guide Culinaire* (Culinary Guide) published in 1903 became the "New Testament" with modern menus and a rationalization of the cooking tasks in the team. Classical cuisine became codified in terms of culinary practice and menus. Then, in the late 1960s and early 1970s, renowned chefs such as Paul Bocuse coined the term "nouvelle cuisine," which was characterized by lighter dishes, experimenting with ingredients and flavors. Often referred to as the "pope of French cuisine," Paul Bocuse was also a tireless pioneer and the first chef to blend the art of cooking with savvy business tactics. Their writings established French classical cuisine and remain to date the main training material for professional cooks (Mennell 1993).

Institutionalization of a gastronomic field

French gastronomy can be termed as a social and historical phenomenon that led to a distinctive cultural practice. Similar to other social practices, gastronomy drew on a combination of social, economic, and cultural conditions. This included abundant, various, and readily available foodstuff and experienced craftsmen (local producers and chefs) in a culturally specific site (the restaurant), both of which are supported by knowledgeable consumers (diners) and a secular culinary tradition (Ferguson, 1998). An institution is referred to as an observable form of collective practices, justified by a socially constructed norm shared by actors belonging to a given institutional field (Czarniawska, 1997). Institutional work has been defined as actions aimed at creating, maintaining, or disrupting such practices in an organization field (Dolbec and Fisher, 2015). These actions lead to "embedding and routinizing" practices and "infusing the normative foundations of an institution" into the daily routines of actors in the field (Lawrence and Suddaby, 2006). For an in-depth understanding of the emergence of a gastronomic field, five structural factors regarding French cuisine can be taken into account (Figure 12.2).

Figure 12.2 presents key elements that explain how French cuisine evolved as the epicenter of gastronomy.

First, "Terroir and food repertoire" is a unique concept that represents the unique confluence of land, culture, tradition, and climate. France boasts a very rich natural environment. Moreover, it has developed a set of rules on how to best use this richness to produce the finest cuisine. The natural resources of France represent a constant source of creativity, inspiration, and expertise around cooking

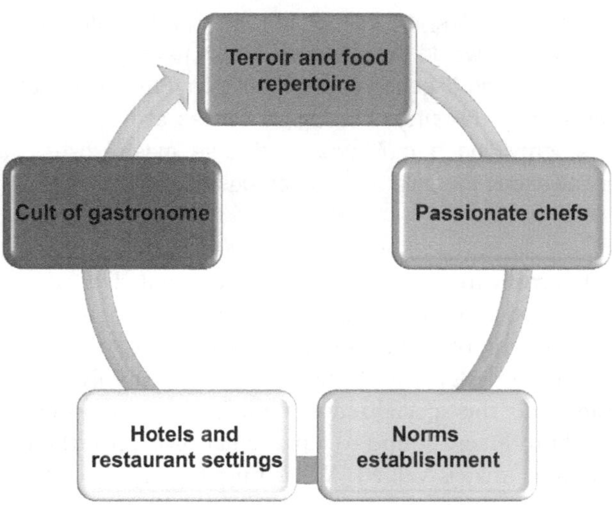

Figure 12.2 French cuisine historical heritage

practices. Chefs elevate cuisine into an art that respects natural products and transforms them into remarkable dishes. Professional guides generate norms to compare with and to appreciate the finest cuisines. Restaurants allow diners to enjoy meals as a social event. All these factors result in a cult of gastronomy at the national level, encouraging the tradition of flattering those who admire exquisite food and can be referred to as "sybarite," or those individuals having an epicurean approach and who are "bon vivant."

Terroir and food repertoire

There is no appropriate alternative English term for the French word *terroir*. Historically, *terroir* refers to a small region whose soil and climate imparts distinctive qualities to food products (Barham, 2003). Figuratively, terroir can also specify a region considered to have a marked influence on its inhabitants (Box 12.1). In this interpretation, products of terroir result from a long commitment to the same area and represent the interplay of human ingenuity and curiosity with the natural givens of place.

Box 12.1 Extract from interview with Guy Savoy, French chef of the 3 Michelin-starred restaurant La Monnaie de Paris

France is the country of gastronomy for geographical reasons. The diversity of the lands, seas, and climates has allowed the emergence of a very large variety of local productions. French craftsmen have then chosen to use their knowledge, expertise, and passion to transform natural richness into high cuisine. Through observation of nature and dedication to excellence, French producers and cooks created a unique heritage of French gastronomy. This is visible, for instance, with the Chardonnay wine: Passionate craftsmen observed that, depending on the climate, soil, and location of the land, a specific type of wine would best develop. Chefs have gained the knowledge through hard work and experience to benefit from French natural richness to create multisensory delights, arousing all senses at once. The richness of our markets, providing a multitude of diverse meats, fishes, fruits, and vegetables, awakens the palate of French customers.

Products of terroir are synonymous with cultural diversity, reflections of the evolution of a society, of its attachment to certain habits of consumption, but not the guardians of a culture that is fixed and turned on itself. The concept of an origin designation for a food product involves the unique roles of soil, climate, and the specialized knowledge that is associated with generations of food producers bound to a particular place; it is the raw material of the food ingredient that is valued. What might be unique about the French approach to terroir is the perspective that it is not the human actions that dictate what is produced and how, but rather that natural phenomena constrain human practices. Terroir is a given; it existed before human beings, who only revealed its potential. Food production becomes a complex dance with nature with the goal of interpreting or translating the local ecology, displaying its qualities to its best advantage.

Passionate chefs

A second key element of French cuisine revolves around passionate chefs. The concept of haute cuisine emphasizes the development of specific techniques by chefs who are passionate and motivated to constantly improve their art and provide emotions (Box 12.2). It celebrates chefs who possess those techniques (Ferguson, 2004) and who are willing to find ways to create culinary emotions (Figure 12.3). Pierre Hermé, well-known French "chef patissier" (pastry chef), explains that he developed a passion for "patisserie-boulangerie" (pastry and bakery) with his father who had always been in the field and with whom he learnt all the techniques. By observing his father and working with Gaston Lenôtre, the best pastry cook in Paris, he progressively developed a knowledge and rigor which were the foundations before adding some personal flair. Today, Pierre Hermé is guided by his strong desire to offer pastries which provide pleasure and emotions. To create new flavors and combine textures in an unexpected manner, he is often inspired by an ingredient and an emotion. This is how the "Macaron Citron Vert et Basilic" (macaron with lime and basil) or "Macaron Huile d'Olive et Vanille" (macaron with olive oil and vanilla) were born.

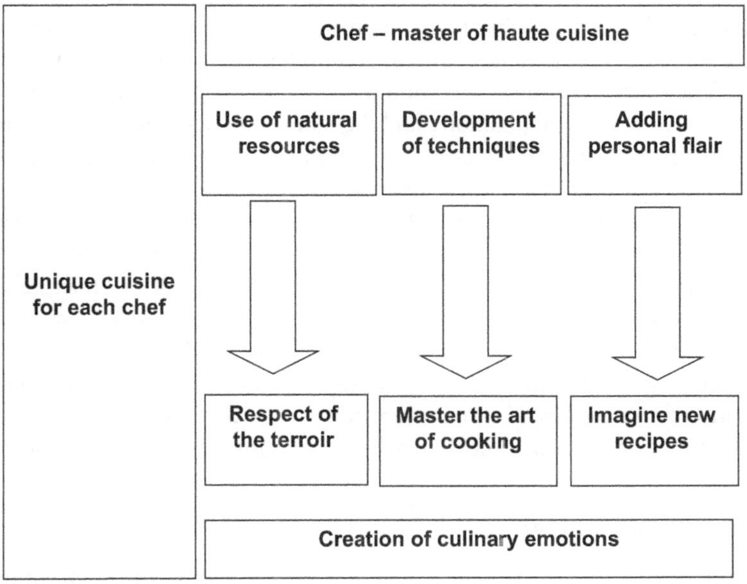

Figure 12.3 Haute cuisine process of creation

Box 12.2 Extract from an interview with Eric Frachon, chef of the famous Parisian hotel Le Bristol with 3 Michelin stars

A chef is responsible for evoking emotions that remain in the memory of diners. He must choose the best natural resources, know how to cook the products with perfection, and present dishes to make them beautiful. A chef works hard, constantly searching for this unique emotion when tasting a new meal, for something present in his memory but not exactly the same, revisited through his own sensitivity. He must provide an unforgettable moment and allow customers to enjoy authentic tastes of the natural products and original recipes. Each chef develops his/her own cooking philosophy and transmits it to his customers.

Norms establishment – the role of the Michelin Guide

A third element of French cuisine centers on norms and guides. The field of gastronomy is not self-regulated, and devices are needed to collect information that eliminates uncertainty as well as foster creativity. The standards of French cuisine have evolved progressively through guides providing criteria for judging excellence. The *Michelin Guide* system of restaurant ratings centralized symbolic power in the culinary field (Hansen, 2008). By writing guides with high circulation, reviewers provide access to the culture of haute cuisine to a wide audience. The authors aimed to systemize culinary knowledge and contributed to formalize the definition of French cuisine (Lane, 2013). Some reviewers claim to offer objective judgments, whereas others acknowledge their subjectivity and even claim to merely reflect readers' opinions. Elitist guides apply unified standards consistently to generate clear-cut ranking orders. The selection defines the common criteria to compare establishments despite the differences in regional traditions, and the ranking allows their classification.

Since 1926, the *Michelin Guide* has had anonymous reviewers visiting restaurants and awarding stars for fine-dining establishments. The gastronomic orientation of the guide was acknowledged from World War II based on bourgeois Parisian taste. The guide proposes a "triple operation of selection, comparison, and prioritization to make the individual decision easier" (Drucker-Godard et al., 2011). It addresses both the establishments and their customers. The *Michelin Guide* has long dominated French haute cuisine over much of Western Europe and over the United States metropolises. Its profound influence on chefs acts as a tastemaker, upholding the high status of French classical and modern cuisine. It is therefore responsible for what is still regarded by many as a highly complex, expensive, and therefore elite taste.

Hotels and public settings

A fourth element of French cuisine is its dissemination through hotels and public settings. The gastronomic field in the 19th century was marked by the public restaurant as the primary vehicle institutionalizing gastronomy as a social and cultural practice. Restaurants became a notable feature of the urban landscape. They became an ideal, semi-public venue for the display and affirmation of status in a bounded space that marked diners as members of the elite. Café de Chartres, Milles Colonnes, la Maison Chevet, la Maison Marion-Carême, and Café de la Paix are a few famous Parisian restaurants where diners gathered. Politicians, businessmen, journalists, writers, and artists flocked to the city and to its restaurants. The fluid population of a largely middle-class transient moving in and out and around the city stimulated the evolution of several types of eating establishments. Jean Anthelme Brillat-Savarin (1839: 324), a famous culinary critic, highlighted the intense competition between restaurants as it became clear that a "single, well-prepared stew could make its inventor's fortune." The range of Parisian restaurants was as important a factor in setting up the gastronomic field as the production of haute cuisine in a select few of them (Ferguson, 1998). The chefs who created their niche in the culinary market had an important contribution to the evolution of social order.

Cult of the gastronome

The last element of French cuisine is the national cult for gastronomes. The culinary term "gastronome" first appears in a poem from Joseph Berchoux in 1804 within a poem named "gastronomie": Gastronomy is the set of rules that define the art of good food. This art includes those, creative in some cases, collecting, adapting, or inventing recipes, selecting products, preparing dishes, and tasting them. Jean Anthelme Brillat Savarin thinks of gastronomy as a distinctly modern social practice. The derivative "gourmet" has come into use since his publication of "The physiology of taste": "Gastronomy is reasoned knowledge of everything that relates to human being as he eats." Brillat-Savarin further justifies the skill of the gourmand by dissecting the entire gustatory experience and by comparing eating to an art. Indeed, the perception of cuisine as a high art did not only develop out of the idea that the chef is an artist, but also that the eater is an artist. In the discord between indulgence and restraint, gastronomy held a specific position. A mental activity dealing with the senses, gastronomy relied on refined sensuality, but even more on intelligence (Pike, 2011). A glutton is an individual who eats eagerly and excessively. A gastronome is the one who loves and knows how to appreciate good food, and he could even be considered something of a philosopher-diner. This modern construction of culinary fervor sloughed off negative connotations, thereby securing for the gastronome a lofty position (Figure 12.4).

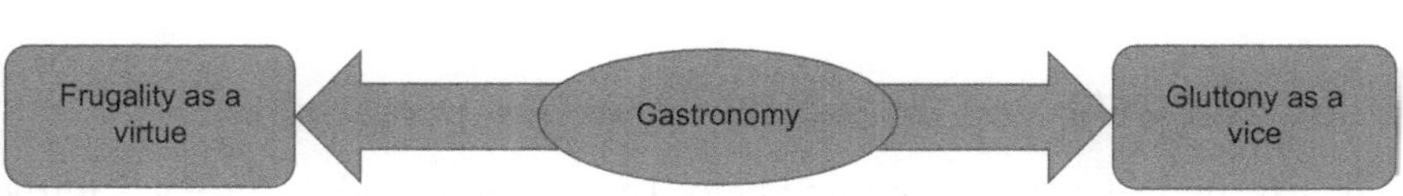

Figure 12.4 Gastronomy in between frugality and gluttony

This cult of gastronome could already explain part of the unique approach of French consumers to food and wellbeing. By considering eating as a highly positive activity, one may really feel good about it, as Jacques Pessis, director of the "Club des croqueurs de chocolat" (Club of chocolate bitters) explains in Box 12.3.

Box 12.3 Interview with the director of "Club des Croqueurs de Chocolat" - Jacques Pessis

Chocolate has recently become a cult product in France. As regards any other culinary category, when French craftsmen start a new food specialty, they do it with passion, rigor, a sense of detail, and love for it.

French "chocolatiers" only use the best cacao, limit the quantity of sugar, and innovate constantly to invent new recipes. French consumers love chocolate, and they know how to recognize the best chocolate, analyzing its color, its shine, its savors, and its duration of taste in the mouth. Club members are just like children who derive deep pleasure when fully enjoying the moment of eating their favorite chocolate.

A distinction can be made between the epicurean and visceral approach to food. Epicurean eating pleasure is described as the enduring pleasure derived from the aesthetic appreciation of the sensory and symbolic value of the food. Such pleasure is unrelated to impulses or relieving of an urge, and can be within people's volition. It cannot be summarized by its valence because it is intrinsically linked to differentiated aesthetic, sensory, and symbolic eating experiences (Cornil and Chandon, 2016). The French enjoy an epicurean approach to food through the art of cooking and the science of enjoying culinary delights. In summary, French gastronomy can be viewed from a social, cultural, and political view (Table 12.1).

Table 12.1 Overview of French gastronomy as asocial, cultural, and economic fields

	Social	*Cultural*	*Economic*
Vision	Gastronomy as an opportunity for being together and sharing	Gastronomy as a science and an art of delighting senses	Gastronomy as a source of wealth for a large set of stakeholders
Practice	Relationships built around French cooking practices and meals at the table	Transmission of French culinary heritage associating norms and creativity	Promotion of French haute cuisine and fine restaurants

Food and wellbeing in France – a unique perspective

The exceptional relationship that France has with food and wellbeing is further discussed. In contrast to consumers of several other nations, French consumers are highly scrupulous about eating and its role in their overall quality of life. Food wellbeing in France is measured in terms of enjoying high-quality, balanced meals with friends and family. This unique perspective of food and wellbeing has four dimensions: 1) harmony between the mind and the body, 2) a holistic sensorial and intellectual experience, 3) a quest for authenticity and discovery, and 4) a link between space and time. Finally, it is essential to assimilate the social dimension of meals, because French consumers consider eating with others an important part of deriving pleasure from life. This section discusses the French outlook on food and wellbeing, the four dimensions of the French perspective, and the importance of social dimensions.

Wellbeing as viewed by French consumers

Food wellbeing is defined as a positive psychological, physical, emotional, and social relationship with food at both the individual and societal levels (Block et al., 2011). It is influenced by the cultural, environmental, and legal factors that govern people's food attitudes and behaviors. Fischler and Masson (2008) compared "what it means to eat well" with consumers from the United States and France and found clear distinctions. In France, eating well is associated with notions of food variety and quality ("freshness" and "taste"). A balanced diet, through moderate intake of sugar, fat, and possibly salt, is considered as a significant feature of eating well. Moreover, for the French, "eating well" almost always leads to admiration about shared pleasure and "conviviality" associated with the time spent at the table as a family or among friends. In contrast, health is the first association with good eating practices in the United States. American consumers discuss meals in terms of health and nutrients (carbohydrates, fats, and proteins) and consider food as a personal affair that concerns each individual's responsibility (and also guilt feelings). Eating should be customized to the specific demands and requirements of each person's body. Rarely do Americans talk about sharing a table with others.

To explore this distinctness of French consumers, we interviewed Marie-Eve Laporte, associate professor at Sorbonne Graduate Business School and expert nutritionist. She claims that French consumers regard the multisensory aspects very highly. French gastronomes have a very strong sense of taste; they are interested in the ingredients and the way they are mixed to produce a unique experience. The French are meticulous about the food's sensory properties rather than the nutritional aspect. They are critical about the social aspect as well. French cherish the pleasure of sharing a meal as an opportunity for socializing. They sit down at the table with others. She explains the differences in the French and the Anglo-Saxon approach to food and wellbeing with the 4Ss as detailed in Table 12.2.

Table 12.2 Comparison between Anglo-Saxon and French approaches

The French approach to eating well	*Hedonic dimension of* ***savoring***	*Hedonic dimension of* ***socializing***
Anglo-Saxon approach to eating well	Functional dimension of **safety**	Functional dimension of **security**

The four dimensions of food and well-being in France

Gastronomy and wellbeing could be classified by French consumers' approach to what they eat, along with four key dimensions presented in Figure 12.5: 1) harmony between the mind and the body, 2) holistic sensorial and intellectual experience, 3) quest for authenticity and discovery, and 4) a link between space and time.

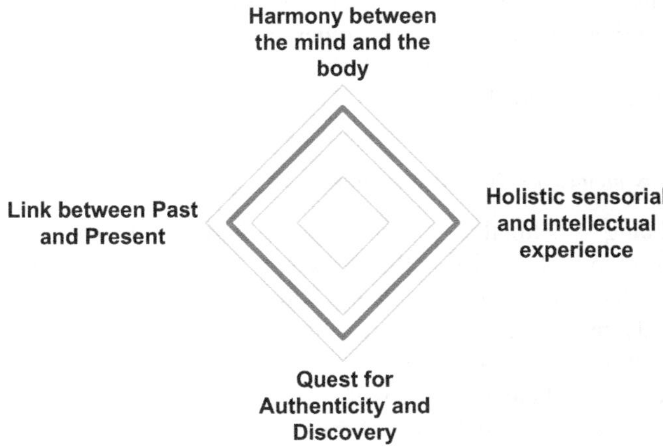

Figure 12.5 Dimensions of eating well in France

Harmony between the mind and the body

Food is supposed be good for the body and for the soul. Elizabeth Picchiottino, former marketing director at Sodexo and food expert with more than 20 years of experience in catering, explained how eating in France exceeds nutritional considerations. According to E. Picchiottino, the French have a holistic approach to food wellbeing. They prefer harmony in their life, and they believe that food plays a major part in this quest for a balanced life. The overall daily food balance is considered without necessarily evaluating each component separately. Priority therefore is given to quality and natural tastes over quantity. The joy experienced by eating arises from one's capacity to "savor" life, to choose the right food for one's own wellbeing, and to protect one's body and environment. The positive internal state is externally visible as one emits an image of joy and wellness. Meals are considered not only as food intake but also prominently as a pleasurable moment in the day. Epicurean aspects contribute to the pleasurable experience of eating by indulging in appreciation of food presentation, enjoying the rich multisensory information, and paying attention to the arousal of senses while eating.

Holistic sensorial and intellectual experience

In comparison with the purchase of material goods, hedonic activities bestow upon consumers an experience that fulfills aesthetic and autotelic desires

(Holt, 1995). They therefore provide pleasure and stimulation that are associated with experiential consumption (Holbrook and Hirschman, 1982). French gastronomy is designed as a full sensorial and emotional experience. It is not just about the food but also about the setting, service, company, and atmosphere (Box 12.4). The dimension of experience is vital. A meal is a whole experience, involving all the senses – not only hedonic but also with intellectual and symbolic dimensions.

Box 12.4 Extract from an interview with Christian Le Squer, 3 Michelin-starred chef of the restaurant Four Seasons Georges 5

When someone comes to my restaurant, it's not just any customer coming to eat. Diners search for a culinary experiment when tasting my cuisine. My responsibility is to create an exceptional experience which will provide joy and happiness. I draw on my strong sense of taste and aesthetic to produce something unique. Through dedication, hard work, love, and creativity, I generate outstanding meals. I create new alliances of flavors, just as a music composer. It is like becoming a creator of gastronomy.

Fine restaurants provide more than just food by means of the atmosphere, beautiful flowers, fine chinaware, impeccable service, and wonderful dinner; they reflect Paris and the French way of living (Figure 12.6).

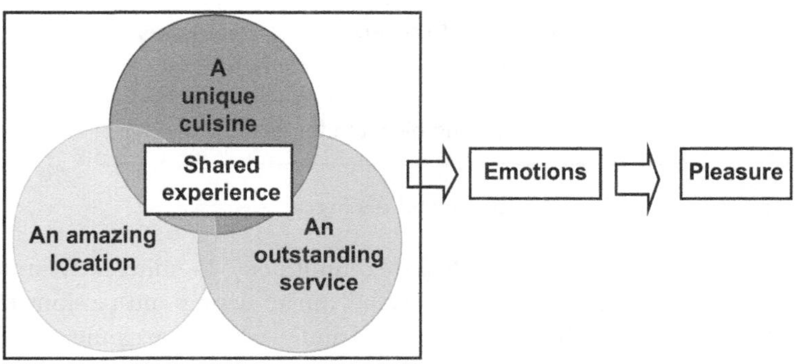

Figure 12.6 Generating a holistic experience with food

The quest for authenticity and discovery

Authenticity is a crucial factor in gastronomy. It can apply to French cuisine, which respects original recipes and the traditional norms of cooking meals. The co-founder and director of Epicery, an online platform selling fine high-quality food from local sellers, Elsa Ammal, explains that by "eating well," the French consumers refer to choosing authentic local food and organic products.

Consumers believe that by consuming local organic products, they savor authentic cuisine and behave responsibly, helping small producers and limiting transportation of products or use of pesticides. French consumers have the ethos to praise authentic high-quality food and are ready to pay a premium for such locally produced food purchased at gourmet caterers. To appreciate authentic cooking and distinguish it from inauthentic copies, French consumers appreciate accumulating culinary experiences and knowledge of variations of the same meal. Consequently, the French spend a larger part of their household income on food compared with their American counterparts. Such spending choices are associated with the positive feelings of making a better decision, for oneself, for local producers, and for the environment, which in turn enhances the self-esteem and the feeling that eating is part of an overall attitude in life. It is also a means of enhancing self-respect for making a conscious choice for high-quality food, which evokes positive feelings within. Authenticity is also relevant to the chefs who need to be innately passionate about their art, finding the right balance between hard work, passion, and creativity (Figure 12.7).

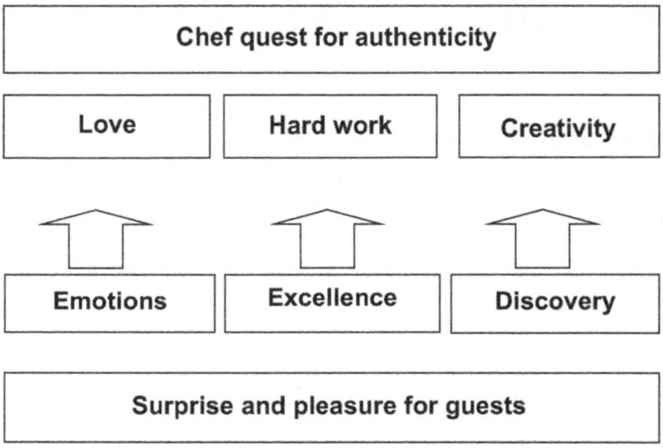

Figure 12.7 Chefs provide authenticity and discovery

Authenticity entails an individual's commitment to inherently motivated behaviors – those that arise from a person's innate desires and passions (Audrezet et al., forthcoming). These behaviors include "active engagement with tasks that one finds interesting" (Deci and Ryan, 2000). An authentic meal therefore is the outcome of a passionate chef, innately motivated by his or her art, using original recipes without the unnecessary addition of ingredients.

Links between space and time

With the notion of terroir and respect for local specificities, French gastronomy associates diners with the French regions. Guy Savoy, chef of the restaurant La Monnaie de Paris, explains how each village in France has its own local specialties with very clear, rigorous, and immutable recipes. He states that if gastronomy is the result of a multitude of expertise along with a variety of products, then France will always remain at the forefront. France has a deep link to the rural areas, which is also of great importance for him. For example, the "Poularde de Bresse" (poultry of Bresse) is absolutely unique because the climate, soil, and environment in the Bresse region create a perfect ecosystem for poultry to grow. Also, the concept of "Appellation d'Origine Contrôlée" (registered designation of origin) is associated with this idea of linking unique, natural, local characteristics and human knowledge.

For a consumer originally from France, eating specialties is a way of identifying with one's own country and situating oneself geographically. With the notion of national "Patrimoine" and historical roots, French cuisine is coupled to local and secular traditions and allows consumers to connect to their heritage. Culinary discourse helped the construction of a collective representation of the past through food. As French consumers abide by their traditional culinary practices, a set of rules tends to "regiment" eating practices, and it also reinforces the sense of national identity. For foreigners, eating French cuisine is a way to discover the country, its culinary tradition, and lifestyle. Parisian restaurants give tourists a feel of the French touch as the visitors savor products, discover recipes, and benefit from high-quality service and warm atmosphere believed to be unique and to represent French gastronomy. It is through cultural activities associated with gourmandizing that one, often unknowingly, plays out the rituals.

The social dimension of eating in France

The people of France sit down and leisurely prepare their food, dress a nice table, and enjoy the food. A meal is more than just a means to feed oneself. Most French people cannot eat a meal alone. It is a social time, something to be shared, a moment of conviviality. Thus, representations of "eating well" in France are planned around mealtimes and the concept of "commensality" conforms to rituals around food. Commensality is the practice of sharing food and eating together in a social group such as a family (Ochs and Shohet 2006: 37). It refers to human co-dependency, reciprocal commitment, and the social, political, and cultural aspects of eating together. Commensality is universally valued in France, and it implies that the host offers something of himself or herself and that the people seated together at a table are united in a feeling of communion.

Consumers often engage in hedonic activities with companions because companionship entails experiential benefits. Humans consider themselves as social entities and, thus, are innately driven to build and maintain relationships with others. Although several hedonic consumption activities can be performed alone, sharing them with a co-consumer augments happiness and gratification. "happiness shared is doubled" lies in the need to belong: Human beings are social actors with a universal desire for meaningful attachments to others. Sharing an already joyful activity further increases pleasure, because it offers the possibility of socializing through performing the activity together (Haumann et al., 2015). Shared consumption is one way of bonding, and the mere presence of a human affiliate tends to increase customers' happiness (Delre et al., 2016).

As regards the French, eating is a social affair and meals are considered an activity to be shared with others. One can see how the pleasure of eating can be enhanced. Communal dining is not merely eating but also quintessentially cooking for others and preparing a nice table to welcome guests. The French appreciate shared meals as an opportunity for building relationships while taking time out to converse with others, spend quality time, and pamper guests. Pierre Hermé associates his pâtisserie with a sense of conviviality and wants to offer a "pleasure to be shared."

For E. Picchiottino, French consumers never skip a meal and consider it an opportunity to be with friends, colleagues, or family members. The collective restaurants or on-site food services, especially at lunchtime, are more evolved in France. In other countries, going to a restaurant might be more for an occasional event for special occasions. French consumers tend to go every day, for lunch and dinner, to restaurants. Since expensive locations with lengthy service may not be feasible daily, a new trend named "bistronomie" emerged in France. To satisfy their desire to eat well at a nice table, a growing number of less expensive and more casual places named "bistros" have appeared, with menus ranging between 35 and 65 euros. Bistros differ from pubs and fine restaurants. It represents well the French approach to food and wellbeing as it provides occasions for sharing daily a quality meal in a nice setting.

The cultural dimension of eating in France

An individual's food selection and the capacity to appreciate varied culinary options are linked to opportunities for tasting a variety of food, the ability to differentiate them, and knowledge of their symbolism. Dining in France is therefore associated with training for developing one's taste and social approach to meals.

Definition of taste

Taste can be defined as the capacity to recognize and differentiate among various objects or experiences. Taste is an instrument of aesthetic sensitivity and intellectual discernment (Ferguson, 2011). Knowledge asymmetry is evident between buyer and seller, especially in the food industry, as the quality of aesthetic goods such as fine-dining restaurant food is not indicated by price alone but needs to be experienced and tested by a qualified analyst as well. Pierre Bourdieu (1986) claimed that every unique style of inhabiting a world originates in the internalized standards of a social milieu. Bourdieu locates taste in a specific social site and ties it to a social class. Discerning and discriminating taste can be taught at schools if meals are a quintessential part of children's education. In France, each year, a dedicated "Semaine du goût" (Taste Week) is organized to motivate youngsters to discover a large "palette" of savors by being served very different meals. Institutions can facilitate opportunities for learning and cultural environment can foster individual curiosity and willingness to appreciate good food. To make an educated choice, one must accept the effort to taste different options and discern his or her preferences. Guy Savoy, 3 Michelin-starred chef of the restaurant La Monnaie de Paris, underlined that if you have not tried eating a large variety of apples, you will never be able to appreciate the taste of a succulent one. One must have tried and discovered many different tastes to fully appreciate good food.

Cultural capital

Cultural capital refers to one's capacity to use taste in the sense of discrimination of sensory quality. Taste can be conceptualized as judgment power. It has different levels, and individuals can be distinguished on the basis of their tastes. Taste can be conceptualized in two ways, shown in Figure 12.8. In Bourdieu,

1. An endowment associated with higher social positions	2. A resource to win a struggle that is gained from exercise of taste
Sustains hierarchy and elevates select individuals over the mass. Judgment power and aesthetic discrimination between the laudable and the pedestrian	Device for affiliation between likeminded individuals which sequesters them from others with different tastes. A means to affiliate with a group and to signal that identification

Figure 12.8 Conceptualizing taste

cultured families exhibit different patterns of cultural consumption. If an individual was raised in a setting filled with paintings and sculpture, he or she would be endowed with a greater amount of cultural capital. They would have the capacity to exercise the sort of taste in cultural activities expected and respected among fellows who already held a high socioeconomic position (Box 12.5).

Box 12.5 Extract from the interview of Eric Frachon – chef of 3 Michelin-starred restaurant Le Bristol

We have a very wide culinary palette. I know few countries that have such a wide range of natural products, except perhaps China where there are many regions very typical in their cuisine but they still have a more restricted culinary repertoire. We can educate our palate to appreciate this wide variety of meals and tastes. If you make an effort to really taste products everything is not the same.

I have a son of 3 years and a half. I made him mono products, then mixed products, little by little, adding spices and condiments. People are less accustomed nowadays to eating pronounced tastes. I educate customers to recognize the true taste of natural products which is sometimes very pronounced.

You have to know a lot of products. It requires an education to enjoy our cuisine and the unique experience it provides. I cook what I like to eat and share.

The cultural dimension of "repas gastronomic": a national "patrimoine"

Experts from the United Nations Educational Scientific and Cultural Organization have considered that "le repas gastronomique à la française" (French gastronomic meal), with its rituals, could be included in the list of "Patrimoine culturel immatériel de l'Humanité" (intangible patrimoine of humanity) which includes practices, knowledge, expertise, and know-how that communities transmit from one generation to another, imparting a feeling of identity, contributing to advancing cultural diversity and human creativity. The country's gastronomy has achieved such a status for the first time. France strives to preserve its unique meal approach in order to preserve this "patrimoine." The "repas gastronomique" should start with an "apéritif" (appetizer) and finish with a "digestif" (digestive) with about four meals in between – a starter, a main meal, cheese, and dessert. Experts noted that meals in France are a "usual social practice aiming at celebrating important moments in the life of individuals and groups, such as births, birthdays, success and reconnections." They also reiterated the French way of enjoying company, practicing the art of taste, and the harmony between human and nature as "French people like to connect, drink well, eat well and celebrate as such." Moreover, the practice involves buying good food, preferably locally sourced, whose flavors blend well; a choice of a recipe from a large repertoire of options; association of meals and wines; the aesthetic dressing of the table; and conversation.

How food gastronomy contributes to food marketing and consumer wellbeing

Food gastronomy contributes well to food marketing. Indeed, in France, private and public institutions have ventured into developing the recognition of French expertise in the culinary arts. France promotes and encourages growth of its culinary arts through the "Meilleur Ouvrier de France" (best craftsman of France) award, created in 1924, to provide the winners with a recognition of their skills. The award gives the winner the privilege of wearing the colors of the French flag on the collar and establishes one's culinary expertise. In addition, in 1989, the French Ministry of Culture created the Conseil National des Arts Culinaires (National Council of Culinary Arts) with a mission of protecting French gastronomy by educating about the national palate. As part of its activities, children are imparted a taste education program and an official inventory of the culinary patrimony of each French region is maintained. Gastronomic expositions financed by city governments are held throughout France to familiarize people with foods from different regions. The "Salon Saveurs" (Savor Fair) in Paris, for example, is a biannual three-day affair that hosts 250 to 300 artisan producers of various food products (including many with labels and foie gras booths) and 25,000 visitors.

Institutionalization of French cuisine fosters an environment that rewards quality rather than quantity. The gastronomic approach can represent a positive approach to food marketing through self-expansion. Indeed, the experience of

French cuisine can cultivate a sense of self-growth, defined as broadening one's sense of self by acquiring new identities, developing new perspectives, enhancing capabilities, and gaining resources (De Kerviler and Rodriguez, 2018). Diners acquire knowledge and enhance their ability to appreciate fine food through education of tastes, the ceremony around dining, the link to one's national identity, and appreciating a chef's creativity. To prevent instances of obesity worldwide governments promoted a cultural approach to food through gastronomy as opposed to gluttony, which can help to generate better outcomes of health and wellbeing. Food marketing that focuses on educating customers on appreciation of rare gourmet pleasures creates an improved societal outcome. Marketers can therefore reconcile hedonism and ethics and contribute to positive consumer welfare.

Conclusions

French gastronomy is the result of a unique combination of historical, sociological, political, cultural, geographical, and social dimensions. A main challenge today is for French gastronomy to maintain its position and remain attractive for a wide global audience. For that purpose, it is essential for chefs and for French national cuisine to find the right balance between tradition and modernity as well as to uphold the link between French gastronomy and wellbeing. Chefs recognize French cuisine's long heritage and its links to the unique terroir of France. However, it is also important that gastronomy evolves with time and provides opportunities for creating new recipes and practices. Moreover, future generations of gastronomes will continue to evolve with edification of tastes. This demands a desire to continue motivating young people to appreciate the discovery of new dishes and the understanding of the value of authentic products. This is the condition that allows for having emotions and feelings through gustatory pleasures. Finally, the social dimension of French meals should be preserved to remain part of the national culture, even in the face of new growing trends of snacking and having lonely lunches.

References

Audrezet, A., De Kerviler, G., & Moulard, J. (Forthcoming). Authenticity under threat: When social media influencers need to go beyond self-presentation. *Journal of Business Research.*

Barham, E. (2003). Translating terroir: The global challenge of French AOC labeling. *Journal of Rural Studies*, 19, 127–121.

Berchoux, J. (1804). *La Gastronomie, ou l'homme des champs à table. Poëme didactique en IV chants.* Paris: Guiguet et Michaud, Imprimeurs-Libraires.

Block, L.G., Grier, S.A., Childers, T.L., Davis, B., Ebert, J.E., Kumanyika, S., & Pettigrew, S. (2011). From nutrients to nurturance: A conceptual introduction to food wellbeing. *Journal of Public Policy and Marketing*, 30(1), 5–13.

Bourdieu, P. (1986). The forms of capital. In J. Richardson (Ed.), *Handbook of Theory and Research for the Sociology of Education.* New York: Greenwood, pp. 241–258.

Brillat-Savarin, A. (1839). *Physiologie du goût ou Méditations de gastronomie transcendente.* Paris: Charpentier.

Cornil, Y., & Chandon, P. (2016). Pleasure as an ally of healthy eating? Contrasting visceral and Epicurean eating pleasure and their association with portion size preferences and wellbeing. *Appetite*, 104, 52–59.

Czarniawska, B. (Ed.). (1997). *A Narrative Approach to Organization Studies.* New York: Sage.

De Kerviler, G., & Rodriguez, C. (2018). Building relationships through stimulating brand experiences: The role of self-expansion, brand identification, and self-esteem. Proceedings of the 21st AMS World Marketing Congress, Porto, Portugal.

Deci, E.L., & Ryan, R.M. (2000). The "what" and "why" of goal pursuits: Human needs and the self-determination of behavior. *Psychological Inquiry*, 11(4), 227–268.

Delre, S.A., Broekhuizen, T.L., & Bijmolt, T.H. (2016). The effects of shared consumption on product life cycles and advertising effectiveness: The case of the motion picture market. *Journal of Marketing Research*, 53(4), 608–627.

Dolbec, P.Y., & Fischer, E. (2015). Refashioning a field? Connected consumers and institutional dynamics in markets. *Journal of Consumer Research*, 41(6), 1447–1468.

Drucker-Godard, C., Bouty, I., & Gomez, M.L. (2011). De la France au monde: Le Guide Michelin, vecteur du rayonnement de la marque France? *Revue Française de Gestion*, 37(218/219), 53.

Escoffier, A. (1903). *A Guide to Modern Cookery* (1st ed.). London: Heinemann.

Ferguson P.P. (1998). A cultural field in the making: Gastronomy in 19th-century France. *American Journal of Sociology*, 104(3), 597–641.

Ferguson, P.P. (2004). *Accounting for Taste: The Triumph of French Cuisine.* Chicago, IL: University of Chicago Press.

Ferguson, P.P. (2011). The senses of taste. *American Historical Review*, 116(2), 371–384.

Fischler, C., & Masson, E. (2008). *Manger. Français, Européens et Américains face à l'alimentation.* Paris: Odile Jacob.

Hansen, S. (2008). Society of the appetite: Celebrity chefs deliver consumers. *Food, Culture and Society*, 11(1), 49–67.

Haumann, T., Güntürkün, P., Schons, L.M., & Wieseke, J. (2015). Engaging customers in coproduction processes: How value-enhancing and intensity-reducing communication strategies mitigate the negative effects of coproduction intensity. *Journal of Marketing*, 79(6), 17–33.

Holbrook, M.B., & Hirschman, E.C. (1982). The experiential aspects of consumption: Consumer fantasies, feelings, and fun. *Journal of Consumer Research*, 9(2), 132–140.

Holt, D.B. (1995). How consumers consume: A typology of consumption practices. *Journal of Consumer Research*, 22(1): 1–16.

Lane, C. (2013). Taste makers in the "fine-dining" restaurant industry: The attribution of aesthetic and economic value by gastronomic guides. *Poetics*, 41(4), 342–365.

Lawrence, T.B., & Suddaby, R. (2006). Institutions and institutional work. In R. Stuart, C. Clegg, T. Hardy, B. Lawrence, & W.R. Nord (Eds), *The Sage Handbook of Organization Studies* (2nd ed.). London: Sage, pp. 215–254.

Mennell, S. (1993). *All Manners of Food: Eating and Taste in England and France from the Middle Ages to the Present.* Urbana-Champaign, IL: University of Illinois Press.

Ochs, E., & Shohet, M. (2006). The cultural structuring of mealtime socialization. *New Directions for Child and Adolescent Development*, 111, 35–49.

Ory, P. (1998), *Le discours gastronomique français des origines à nos jours.* Paris: Gallimard/Julliard.

Pike, J.E. (2011). Brillat-Savarin's occidentalizing of the oriental origins of French cuisine. *French Review*, 936–953.

13 Food shopping experience on the periphery of the supermarket

A social media-afforded quest for Whole30-compliant foods and wellbeing

Ana Babić Rosario

In 2009, the world renowned University of California Berkeley professor of journalism and bestselling food author Michael Pollan postulated a collection of "food rules" in his book *Food Rules: An Eater's Manual.* These rules were geared towards enhancing consumers' food experience while supporting their overall wellbeing. Among other things, Pollan (2009) advised his readers to not "eat anything your great-grandmother wouldn't recognize as food" (p. 7), to avoid ingredients "that a third-grader cannot pronounce" (p. 18), as well as to "shop the peripheries of the supermarket [where historically fresh foods such as produce, meat, fish, and dairy line the walls] and stay out of the middle [which is dominated by processed, imperishable food products]" (p. 28). Since 2009, these notions have caught wind and are nowadays frequent topics of discussion among consumers subscribing to a variety of "low-carbohydrate" and "ancestral" lifestyles such as keto(genic), gluten-free, grain-free, Wheat Belly, Whole30, Paleo, and Primal diets. This chapter deals with consumer behavior associated with shopping for meal ingredients. As noted by prior research, food shopping and consumption "is not just about product choice but also about social interaction and identity" (Gram, 2016: 55). Furthermore, understanding the effects of food consumption on health and consumer wellbeing has been identified as a topic of significance in recent years, both among scholars and food marketers (Raghunathan et al., 2006).

This study is primarily based on ethnographic accounts of the Whole30 dietary program in North America from 2015 to 2018. Secondarily, insights are informed by the author's longitudinal, interview-based investigation of North American consumers who subscribe to a variety of other gluten-free lifestyles mentioned above. Of specific interest in this chapter is the influence of social media affordances on consumers' shopping habits and sensemaking of marketplace discourses, as well as interactions with the various spaces of the market – in the supermarket and online. Additionally, attention is paid to food pleasure and ways in which consumers negotiate the meanings of hedonic food consumption. This chapter highlights the case of Whole30 because it is a good example of a consumer obsession with scrutinizing food ingredients while planning and shopping for meals. In the following account, food acquisition is seen as part of a structured effort to enhance food experience and overall wellbeing within a disciplinary micro society, and it will be of interest to a range of scholars exploring consumer behavior, new consumer technologies, and the sociology of food.

Background

Shopping for ingredients is often thought to be "located in the mundane … life of consumers faced with the diurnal task of provisioning for themselves, their family, and their friends" (Cappellini et al., 2016: 5). Extant consumer research has explored shopping for ingredients mainly as an individual-based decision-making process characterized by habitual, routinized, mechanic visits to the supermarket where consumers would walk the same route and grab the same goods from the shelf (Gram, 2016). However, as this chapter shows, this shopping task may be far less mundane, habitual, or individualized for consumers who subscribe to a disciplined, highly structured lifestyle.

From habitual practices (back) to rationalized, technology-mediated, networked processes

A meal is understood in this chapter as an assemblage of practices dispersed across places (Cappellini et al., 2016). Hence, food acquisition and consumption are seen as practices, so practice (e.g., Reckwitz, 2002; Schatzki, 1996) and assemblage theories (e.g., DeLanda, 2006; Epp et al., 2014) are used as enabling theoretical approaches that interpret lived experiences related to shopping for ingredients. Building on these theories, three aspects (or capacities) shape food acquisition and consumption practices: material, symbolic, and imaginative.

The material aspects of food consumption

The practice of food consumption contains material elements, as food is acquired, prepared, shared, and consumed in its very materiality. Thus, a holistic view of consumer practices across the meal-provisioning cycle (Cappellini et al., 2016; Goody, 1982; Marshall, 1995) is adopted in this research. Two aspects of materiality are of particular relevance here. One is the "unforgiving … materiality of food" (Mourad and Barnard, 2016: 224) that diminishes the shelf life of certain foods when they are prepared, such as peeled vegetables (Evans, 2011). Another is the materiality of the supermarket aisles as significant places wherein consumers reflect on their meals (Cappellini et al., 2016).

The symbolic aspects of food consumption

In 1841, the famous French gastronomy writer Jean Anthelme Brillat-Savarin (1841) penned: "Tell me what kind of food you eat, and I will tell you what kind of man you are." Since these early explorations of the symbolism of food, much consumer research has demonstrated that food is an integral part of consumer culture (Närvänen et al., 2013), and that it is never just about the biological process of eating (Bardhi et al., 2010; Rozin, 1999; Watson and Caldwell, 2005). Food carries significant symbolic properties in the lives of consumers (Douglas, 1972), so food consumption is central in defining who we are (Belasco, 2008; Fischler, 1988; McDonagh and Prothero, 2005; Thompson and Hirschman, 1995; Thompson and Troester, 2002). For example, a recent study exploring the identity value of food labels finds that consumers tend to choose low-calorie foods to signal competence (Oh and Huh, 2016). The importance of food consumption for identity work is one of the reasons why contradictory meanings related to food consumption make the choices – shopping-related and others – difficult for consumers (Leipämaa-Leskinen, 2007) and why they may need network support facilitated by technological affordances.

The imaginative aspects of food consumption

Recent studies find that 68 percent of consumers are interested in collecting information via online recommendations about food and beverages in order to make purchase decisions in the store (PowerReviews, 2017). At the same time, consumers are happy to share such information with others. Consider, for example, Kozinets, Patterson, and Ashman's (2016) study of collective consumer desire in the realm of food porn, which demonstrates that the global phenomenon of online food image sharing is afforded by the interrelation of material and technological objects in specific social circumstances. Contemporary eating culture is shaped by technology-mediated practices and technological affordances (Faraj and Azad, 2012; Heeter, 2000; Majchrzak et al., 2013). The concept of affordance (Gibson, 1979) refers to the idea that action possibilities of objects should be seen in relation to the actor, so that the environment – in this case, technology and social media – is incorporated in consumers' decision making. In other words, an affordance is not "a property of an object" as much as it is "a relationship between an object and the [actor] that is acting on the object" (Norman, 1998: 123).The proliferation of "social media platforms in the food world" has indeed become a particularly relevant aspect of food consumption (Rousseau, 2012; Truninger, 2016: 94) – and, as it is argued in this chapter, food acquisition. Specifically, I follow Truninger (2016) in conceptualizing shopping for meal ingredients as a meal-related practice, not as it is performed by individuals, but as it is co-created by a community of networked consumers who utilize contemporary technology such as social media (Kozinets et al., 2010) to perform a sequence of coordinated practices.

Research context

Whole30 is a trademarked 30-day dietary program proposed by Melissa and Dallas Hartwig in 2009. Their nutritional framework – based on eliminating certain food groups such as sugar, grains, dairy, and legumes – is detailed in a bestselling book *It Starts with Food* released in the United States in 2012. Since then, six additional books have been released, and the website offers free shopping and meal-planning resources, such as shopping lists and grocery guides, to assist with food acquisition and preparation. Much like Pollan's *Food Rules* from the introductory paragraph, this program strictly outlines which foods ought to be consumed and which ought to be avoided; if the consumer breaks any of the Whole30 rules during the 30-day period, the program needs to be restarted the following day. The program rules can be updated by the founders (e.g., since July 2014 "white potatoes are allowed on the Whole30 program"), who also occasionally feature "Whole30-approved" food suppliers and brands on their website. Since its inception, this radical lifestyle change has relied on technological affordances that facilitate a thriving Whole30 community on the official website forum as well as across social media. Consumers often use dedicated hashtags, such as #Whole30, #IAmWhole30, #Whole30Cookbook, #Whole30Recipes, and #Whole30Approved, and tag the Hartwigs in photos and posts. According to official sources, millions of consumers have completed this "short-term nutrition reset" in the last decade (Whole 30, 2018). In many ways, the Whole30 program and its networked consumers provide "authoritative reassurance about how best to eat" (Cappellini et al., 2016: xx). Thus, this rich context is highly fitting for exploring how consumers shop for ingredients in the context of an increasingly globalized and complex food economy (cf. Fischler, 1988; MacDonald, 2014).

Method and data collection

Prolonged ethnographic engagement with the focal topic in North America informs this inquiry. Over 13 years, I conducted online and in-person research which encompassed observational lurking (online and in the store) and participatory observation on a variety of sites centered on food consumption and founded by consumers (e.g., *Low Carb and Losing It*), authors of dietary books (e.g., *Against All Grain*), and medical practitioners (e.g., *The Zone*). I initially set out to understand the broader context around consumption politics and identity work related to long-term dietary changes. During this period, I observed, read, and archived selected posts, comments, and images from blogs, online communities, and Facebook groups and pages. I also participated by posting original content (including questions, calls to discussion, links to related websites, and images of self-prepared meals, meals enjoyed at restaurants, ingredients, and product labels). In addition to contributing in this fashion, I commented on other members' posts. Further, I participated in the Whole30 program for an extended period of time (four consecutive "rounds," i.e., four months) in 2016. Autoethnographic accounts were complemented by documentary movies on the sociology of food and the contemporary North American eating culture, such as *Fat Head, Food Inc., Food Choices, In Defense of Food, Rotten, The Magic Pill*, and *What the Health*.

Additionally, between 2014 and 2017 I conducted semi-structured in-depth phenomenological interviews (Thompson et al., 1989) with 25 United States and Canadian consumers who have adopted lifestyles centered on the elimination of gluten and grains. The informants were recruited through announcements in social media communities, as well as through snowballing (where they recommended friends and family members after our interview). Their ages ranged between early 20s to late 60s. The majority of informants voluntarily chose these lifestyles, but a small number disclosed that they or their family members have celiac disease. Two informants reported being part of the medical community (i.e., nurses) but were seeking alternative treatment through food consumption. The interviews lasted between 36 minutes and 4 hours, yielding over 1,000 pages of transcripts.

Following the recommendations of Kozinets (2015), a netnographic study of the Whole30 forum and Facebook spaces was conducted in 2015–18 in order to answer the following research questions: How do social media affordances influence consumers' shopping habits and interactions with market spaces (in the supermarket and online)? How do consumers make sense of marketplace discourses (e.g., food marketing and product labeling)? How do consumers negotiate food pleasure and wellbeing?

The chosen online sites they are enduring (thereby enabling longitudinal investigation); they focus on a particular form of consumption; they are heterogeneous with strong common features (dietary program and shared shopping and consumption rules); they have moderate barriers to entry and are generally very welcoming; they have a prominent collective belonging (i.e., active contributions by community members) (Thomas et al. 2013). At the time of writing this chapter, the official Whole30 Facebook page had over 667,000 "likes". While the overall data collection spanned micro, meso, and macro entities, the relevant units of analysis remained the practices shaped by activities, objects, and competencies (Epp et al., 2014; Schatzki, 1996), rather than individuals or macro-social objects (e.g., culture). A hermeneutical approach was used to analyze the data (Arnold and Fischer, 1994; Thompson, 1997). All informants' names reported here are pseudonyms, and netnographic narratives were rephrased to ensure the privacy of posters and protect their digital personae (Buitelaar, 2014; Kozinets, 2015; Markham, 2012). In examining the risks, the Whole30 group is not considered as "inherently vulnerable" (cf. Kozinets, 2015).

Findings

As the case of the Whole30 dietary program exemplifies, consumers modify their food-acquisition practices by (re)introducing rationalized, technology-mediated, networked processes. Habitual shopping through the center aisles laden with processed foods is transformed by a more thoughtful consideration along the peripheral walls of the store (cf. Gram, 2016; Warde, 1997). Limited processed foods that are "allowed" on the plan are dissected through the careful reading of product labels and online sharing of images, questions, concerns, and calls for help. Below, some central findings are presented to illustrate the community efforts – afforded by social media technologies – to shop for ingredients in the supermarket and to scrutinize food marketing.

Community sensemaking of marketplace discourses

The Whole30 community vividly resists costly food marketing efforts such as the $2 million for the United States Department of Agriculture's ChooseMyPlate initiative. In shaping their own consumption experiences and pursuing wellbeing, they regularly inspect and expose the dark side of food marketing, in particular food and nutrition labeling policies. Product labels satisfy consumer needs for information about how a specified ingredient or amount of a food contributes to a healthful diet (Block et al., 2011; Codex Alimentarius Commission, 2015). Consider, for example, the shopping experience of a consumer who explored a similar lifestyle for herself (before the brand name Whole30 gained awareness) while caring for a family member diagnosed with celiac disease:

> We buy things in the store. We buy it and we look at the label more than once, because they change their formulas in the store. So we'll look at the label, six months later, two months later, we might look at it again. Get it home, sometimes I look at it and it's never a no-brainer. It's a constant … We always read labels and I've pulled boxes out of the garbage [at a dinner party] to look at the ingredients. If somebody's made something that's a processed food, or has a list of ingredients, I'm reading it. Even if I have to pull a container out of the garbage. I do that and if it has gluten in it, nope.
>
> (Marigold, interviewee, mother of celiac patient)

In a disciplinary community such as Whole30, access to credible information of this sort is crucial as it enables consumers to adhere to social norms. Thus, consumers pull resources together and discuss individual products and brands in depth to scrutinize ingredients and make sense of food-marketing claims. Most of the time, consumers reach out for network support on the way to the supermarket or while standing by the product shelf. Highly interactive, real-time exchanges of knowledge in social media are made possible through technology capabilities. Consider, for example, these members' timely posts:

> My spouse is out shopping now; what almonds are compliant?
>
> (Heather, Facebook group member; wording rephrased)

> Trying to interpret the label on this beverage bottle … I see the sugar listed, but the website says there is very little of it remaining by the end of the manufacturing process. Am I safe? Is this compliant?
>
> (Flora, Facebook group member; wording rephrased)

In both cases, consumers have received close to 15 replies within a matter of minutes, and some of those included images of specific brands and product labels. For these consumers, the practice of food acquisition is thus mediated by technology in the form of an online community. In this respect, social media is seen as an "intermediary that opens up the possibility for thinking about meal practices in a particular way" (Truninger, 2016: 92) while adhering to a set of normative rules. The latter is critical because it serves to maintain a sense of unity with social peers (Kravets and Sandikci, 2014). In fact, as exemplified by the following account, consumers' sensemaking practices often spread from food to other product categories such as vitamins. Because the Whole30 program is highly detailed and prescriptive, anything that can be digested is to be subjected to scrutiny; in contrast, an exposure to profane ingredients (Douglas, 1972) may require the consumer to restart their rigorous effort. Marla's question below was accompanied by an image of a vitamin bottle label taken with a smartphone in the store.

> It's humorous how I read product labels to everything now, including supplements. It says sugar-free, but I thought sucralose is a sugar. Help?!
>
> (Marla, Facebook group member; wording rephrased)

Knowledge sharing and disciplinary practices via social media affordances

As discussed earlier, the Whole30 community relies heavily on disciplinary practices and guided shopping experiences. The program founders and online community administrators are particularly valuable in this process as they are afforded by the social media platforms to post and update resources – for example, by "approving" or "allowing" certain ingredients, products, brands, or retailers. The following warnings from one of the administrators illustrate this process:

> Please be cautious with grocery shopping lists that are available online. Some bloggers do not update their lists when the ingredients change or when the Whole30 rules get attuned … Lists from this group are correct, and when we need to change something, it is done within a day.
>
> We have seen that some supermarket chains have the same product with the same label but one store has compliant ingredients while the other store does not. So, a list won't help much. I recommend a [Facebook] group search for the store name to see what other members have posted.
>
> (Brandy, Facebook group administrator; wording rephrased)

Brandy's actions also exemplify how the practice of food acquisition and consumption get socially (re)constructed. In the latter case, when the administrator suggests a search of online knowledge repositories to better guide consumers in their shopping experiences, she demonstrates another affordance of social media that affects how consumers search for relevant, up-to-date content.

Negotiating food pleasure

Prior research offers mixed insights on food pleasure, i.e., eating enjoyment. For one, there is a philosophical view of "considering gustatory pleasure as animal and uncontrolled, pursued by brutes" (Cornil and Chandon, 2016: 52; Korsmeyer, 2002), and recent consumer studies indeed support the notion that the association between "unhealthy" and "tasty" operates at an implicit, visceral level (Raghunathan et al., 2006). Hence, one stream of research finds food pleasure to be quite problematic for consumer wellbeing. On the other hand, scholars have countered this understanding with "epicurean eating pleasure" – defined as pleasure derived from the multisensory, aesthetic, and symbolic aspects of food (Cornil and Chandon, 2016). The latter view supposes that food pleasure can be educated and refined (Kass, 1999).

In this chapter, food pleasure is juxtaposed with consumer wellbeing. Findings reveal that Whole30 consumers refine and negotiate the meaning of pleasure as they become more involved in the community and adhere to strict social norms. Two quotes below illustrate the varying – and evolving – views on food pleasure. Claire, for example, adopts the first view of pleasure as derived from tasty but unhealthy foods that are not "approved" by the Whole30 program. Norma's post exemplifies epicurean pleasure with single-ingredient foods like fruits and vegetables.

> Just remember that the minutes of pleasure you get from eating something non-compliant will eventually cause hours of disappointment. Not worth it.
> (Claire, Facebook group member; wording rephrased)

> You know you're on this dietary program when you eat a blueberry with a meal, and your brain's pleasure center brightens up like the summer sun.
> (Norma, Facebook group member; wording rephrased)

Understanding food pleasure is important for the present case because it governs shopping practices. This is, in fact, a common topic among consumers in social media. In terms of the Whole30 community, pleasure – an emic term here – is related to SWYPO (sex with your pants on), a catchy phrase proposed by the founders to remind consumers that remaking pleasurable food items, such as pizza and pasta, with Whole30-compliant ingredients may still be insufficient as it triggers them to give in to old habits and neglect the main goal of the program: a "nutritional reset." Facebook group administrators thus often post photos of products that seem fit for the program but are not (e.g., Trader Joe's cauliflower gnocchi).

Conclusions and the future

The present study finds that shopping for ingredients is not an individualized, routinized, habitual practice, but can rather be a networked, rationalized process mediated by social media technologies. Shopping experiences described herein are heavily regulated by social norms and corrected through an almost panoptical form of Foucauldian digital surveillance conducted by the all-seeing community administrators in a disciplinary micro society (cf. Foucault, 1995). Alas, in contrast to the unwilling subjects envisioned by Foucault, participants in the Whole30 program and related online communities bear greater resemblance to Zuboff's (1988) willing participants of the information panopticon.

This study further shows how consumers reinvent their food experiences and negotiate learned food pleasure. For many members of the Whole30 online communities, single-ingredient foods are reconceived as affordable health insurance that sustains the meal practice – more from a utilitarian than a symbolic or hedonic perspective. Pleasure exists, albeit on a smaller scale than before.

Finally, we see that the modern retailing environment has its fair share of concerns. As illustrated in this chapter, consumers are changing the way they shop for ingredients while using networked information to scrutinize food marketers. In addition, we have witnessed hundreds of retailers close their doors and drastically reduce brick-and-mortar presence. Whereas 90 percent of consumers are still purchasing groceries in a brick-and-mortar store (PowerReviews, 2017), online grocery shopping has become increasingly popular. Consumers following the Whole30 program, for example, report switching to online marketplaces such as Thrive Market, Primal Market, Barefoot Provisions, Amazon Prime Pantry, and various food blogger-linked Amazon stores. One consumer, for example, stated that "Whole Foods never has the stuff [she is] looking for and [she] find[s] grocery shopping time consuming and annoying so [her] first instinct is to buy online." Future research could explore this trend in more depth in the context of food consumption.

References

Arnold, S.J., & Fischer, E. (1994). Hermeneutics and consumer research. *Journal of Consumer Research*, 21(1), 55–70.

Bardhi, F., Ostberg, J., & Bengtsson, A. (2010). Negotiating cultural boundaries: Food, travel and consumer identities. *Consumption, Markets and Culture*, 13(2), 133–157.

Belasco, W. (2008). *Food: The Key Concepts*. Berg: Bloomsbury.

Block, L.G., Grier, S.A., Childers, T.L., Davis, B., Ebert, J.E.J., Kumanyika, S. … van Ginkel Bieshaar, M.N.G. (2011). From nutrients to nurturance: A conceptual introduction to food wellbeing. *Journal of Public Policy and Marketing*, 30(1), 5–13.

Brillat-Savarin, J.A. (1841). *Physiologie Du Goût*. Paris: Charpentier.

Buitelaar, J.C. (2014). Privacy and narrativity in the internet era. *Information Society*, 30(4), 266–281.

Cappellini, B., Marshall, D., & Parsons, E. (2016). Foreword. In *The Practice of the Meal*. New York: Routledge, pp. xxii–xx.

Codex Alimentarius Commission. (2015). *Guidelines on Nutrition Labelling*, CAC/GL 2–1985. Food and Agriculture Organization of the United States. Retrieved from: www.fao.org/input/download/standards/34/CXG_002e_2015.pdf

Cornil, Y., & Chandon, P. (2016). Pleasure as an ally of healthy eating? Contrasting visceral and epicurean eating pleasure and their association with portion size preferences and wellbeing. *Appetite*, 104, 52–59.

DeLanda, M. (2006). *A New Philosophy of Society: Assemblage Theory and Social Complexity*. London: Continuum.

Douglas, M. (1972). Deciphering a meal. *Daedalus*, 101(1), 61–81.

Epp, A.M., Jensen Schau, H., & Price, L.L. (2014). The role of brands and mediating technologies in assembling long-distance family practices. *Journal of Marketing*, 78(3), 81–101.

Evans, D. (2011). Blaming the consumer – once again: The social and material contexts of everyday food waste practices in some English households. *Critical Public Health*, 21(4), 429–440.

Faraj, S., & Azad, B. (2012). The materiality of technology: An affordance perspective. In P.M. Leonardi, B.A. Nardi, & J. Kallinikos (Eds), *Materiality and Organizing: Social Interaction in a Technological World*. Oxford: Oxford University Press, pp. 237–258.

Fischler, C. (1988). Food, self and identity. *Information (International Social Science Council)*, 27(2), 275–292.

Foucault, M. (1995). *Discipline and Punish: The Birth of the Prison* (2nd ed.). New York: Vintage Books.

Gibson, J.J. (1979). *The Ecological Approach to Visual Perception*. Boston, MA: Houghton, Mifflin, and Company.

Goody, J. (1982). *Cooking, Cuisine and Class: A Study in Comparative Sociology*. Cambridge: Cambridge University Press.

Gram, M. (2016). The supermarket revisited: Families and food shopping. In B. Cappellini, D. Marshall, & E. Parsons (Eds), *The Practice of the Meal*. New York: Routledge, pp. 55–66.

Heeter, C. (2000). Interactivity in the context of designed experiences. *Journal of Interactive Advertising*, 1(1), 3–14.

Kass, L. (1999). *The Hungry Soul: Eating and the Perfecting of Our Nature*. Chicago, IL: University of Chicago Press.

Korsmeyer, C. (2002). *Making Sense of Taste: Food and Philosophy*. Ithaca, NY: Cornell University Press.

Kozinets, R.V. (2015). *Netnography: Redefined*. New York: Sage.

Kozinets, R.V., de Valck, K., Wojnicki, A.C., & Wilner, S.J.S. (2010). Networked narratives: Understanding word-of-mouth marketing in online communities. *Journal of Marketing*, 74(2), 71–89.

Kozinets, R.V., Patterson, A., & Ashman, R. (2016). Networks of desire: How technology increases our passion to consume. *Journal of Consumer Research*, 43(5), 659–682.

Kravets, O., & Sandikci, O. (2014). Competently ordinary: New middle class consumers in the emerging markets. *Journal of Marketing*, 78(4), 125–140.

Leipämaa-Leskinen, H. (2007). Contradictions in food consumption. *International Journal of Consumer Studies*, 31(6), 597–602.

MacDonald, A. (2014). Negotiating “gastro-anomie”: Exploring the relationship between food, the body and identity in Halifax, Nova Scotia. Unpublished ms.

Majchrzak, A., Faraj, S., Kane, G.C., & Azad, B. (2013). The contradictory influence of social media affordances on online communal knowledge sharing. *Journal of Computer-Mediated Communication*, 19(1), 38–55.

Markham, A. (2012). Fabrication as ethical practice: Qualitative inquiry in ambiguous internet contexts. *Information, Communication and Society*, 15(3), 334–353.

Marshall, D.W. (1995). *Food Choice and the Consumer*. New York: Springer Science and Business Media.

McDonagh, P., & Prothero, A. (2005). Food, markets and culture: The representation of food in everyday life. *Consumption, Markets and Culture*, 8(1), 1–5.

Mourad, M., & Barnard, A. (2016). *"Don't waste the waste": Dumpster dinners among garbage gourmands*. New York: Routledge.

Närvänen, E., Kartastenpää, E., & Kuusela, H. (2013). Online lifestyle consumption community dynamics: A practice-based analysis. *Journal of Consumer Behaviour*, 12(5), 358–369.

Norman, D. (1998). *The Invisible Computer: Why Good Products Can Fail, the Personal Computer Is so Complex, and Information Appliances Are the Solution*. Cambridge, MA: MIT Press.

Oh, G.-E., & Young, E.-H. (2016). Judge me for what I eat: When consumers use low-calorie labels for signaling. *ACR North American Advances*.

Pollan, M. (2009). *Food Rules: An Eater's Manual*. New York: Penguin Press.

PowerReviews. (2017). 6 recommendations for meeting the expectations of today's grocery shoppers. PowerReviews. Retrieved from: www.powerreviews.com /blog/ 6-recommendations-for-meeting-the-expectations-of-todays-grocery-shoppers/

Raghunathan, R., Walker Naylor, R., & Hoyer, W.D. (2006). The unhealthy = tasty intuition and its effects on taste inferences, enjoyment, and choice of food products. *Journal of Marketing*, 70(4), 170–184.

Reckwitz, A. (2002). Toward a theory of social practices: A development in culturalist theorizing. *European Journal of Social Theory*, 5(2), 243–263.

Rousseau, S. (2012). *Food and Social Media: You Are What You Tweet*. Lanham, MD: Rowman and Littlefield.

Rozin, P. (1999). Food is fundamental, fun, frightening, and far-reaching. *Social Research*, 66(1), 9–30.

Schatzki, T.R. (1996). *Social Practices: A Wittgensteinian Approach to Human Activity and the Social*. Cambridge: Cambridge University Press.

Thomas, T.D., Price, L.L., & Jensen Schau, H. (2013). When differences unite: Resource dependence in heterogeneous consumption communities. *Journal of Consumer Research*, 39(5), 1010–1033.

Thompson, C.J. (1997). Interpreting consumers: A hermeneutical framework for deriving marketing insights from the texts of consumers' consumption stories. *Journal of Marketing Research*, 34(4), 438–455.

Thompson, C.J., & Hirschman, E.C. (1995). Understanding the socialized body: A poststructuralist analysis of consumers' self-conceptions, body images, and self-care practices. *Journal of Consumer Research*, 22(2), 139–153.

Thompson, C.J., & Troester, M. (2002). Consumer value systems in the age of postmodern fragmentation: The case of the natural health microculture. *Journal of Consumer Research*, 28(4), 550–571.

Thompson, C.J., Locander, W.B., & Pollio, H.R. (1989). Putting consumer experience back into consumer research: The philosophy and method of existential phenomenology. *Journal of Consumer Research*, 16(2), 133–146.

Truninger, M. (2016). Appropriating Bimby on the internet: Perspectives on technology-mediated meals by a virtual brand community. In *The Practice of the Meal*. New York: Routledge, pp. 116–130.
Warde, A. (1997). *Consumption, Food and Taste*. New York: Sage.
Watson, J.L., & Caldwell, M.L. (2005). *The Cultural Politics of Food and Eating: A Reader*. Malden, MA: Blackwell.
Whole30. (2018). *The Whole30® Program*. Retrieved from: https://whole30.com/new/
Zuboff, S. (1988). *In the Age of the Smart Machine: The Future of Work and Power*. New York: Basic Books.

14 Hungry eyes

How food porn affects wellbeing

Anthony Patterson, Robert Kozinets and Rachel Ashman

Say cheese, cheese!

> Later, another guest pulled out her phone to show me photos of every meal she had eaten in the last few years. "I don't know why I do this," she confessed, but there was evident joy and satisfaction on her face as she scrolled through the many moments of gustatory bliss.
>
> (Turow, 2015: 41)

Since everyone began staring at their phones as devoutly as an elderly vicar with a prayer book, humankind seems to have developed a similarly insatiable appetite for contemplating food matters (Rousseau, 2015). Cue the ever refreshing content on social media feeds where food discourse abounds. From clips of celebrity chefs made famous on TV, perhaps Gordon Ramsey artfully throwing insults, to adverts for the dystopian, experience-less, anti-food Soylent. From online restaurant review sites to flamboyant food vloggers waxing poetic about the joys of "the organic," "the local," "the vegan," "the sustainable," and inevitably, "avocado toast." From distressing stories about the cruelty of humanity's ingestion of animality to tales of how an obese person via extreme calorie control transmogrifies into someone thin. From tragic news of the millions of people, mostly children, who die every year from hunger to clickbait extolling diets discovered by housewives that are so miraculous that doctors are said to be baffled. This age of food is ever in the ether, waiting to be digitally digested and cogitated, and more often than not – since the sites themselves are built to maximize user engagement via the solicitation of new content, commentary, and likes – these gustatorial narrations are not passively consumed.

We have come a long way. For hunter-gather societies, regular food was little more than raw fruit and vegetables, but as Trifonas and Balomenos (2003: 100) note, "with the advent of formalised cultural cuisines, a hierarchy of culinary acrobatics accomplished by manipulating raw ingredients made the expectations of a meal much more complex." One firmly established consumer practice that is particularly immured in contemporary foodways and the building of "culinary capital" (Naccarato and LeBesco, 2012) is the sharing of food pictures on social media, often via the hashtag #foodporn. With a growing body of literature spanning many disciplines, coalescing to study the phenomenon, it is clear that Instagram and the like are teeming with amateur and professional "food porn" aficionados, so called because in creating their images they draw on the aesthetics and style of pornography (Greene, 2013; Lupton, 2018; McDonnell 2016; Spence et al., 2016). Via sophisticated smartphones equipped with photo and social media apps that make the process of selecting and enhancing exemplary images increasingly simple – even to the extent that apps now proactively suggest pictures to post with filters already applied – they regularly upload, share, and savour salivating "foodtography" of restaurant experiences and homemade food (Von Pape, 2018). And while sharing images of food on a social media platform is not, as Lupton (2018) recognizes, an explicitly political practice, making such posts communicates as much about the original poster (OP in popular abbreviated web parlance) as it does their food practices. If the established tenet of consumer research that "what you choose defines who you are" is true, then such practices are likely to digitally reflect an offline persona (Schau and Gilly, 2003). At the very least, as Roland Barthes (1979: 167) acknowledged 40 years ago, food is, "a system of communication, a body of images, a protocol of usages, situations, and behaviour." As one commentator recently quipped, "I'm turkey and Swiss on ciabatta with tzatziki, chipotle spread and a little basil pesto. That's who I am, dammit. My sandwich, my self" (Hingston, 2018).

This chapter presents a fresh take on the ethnographic, netnographic, and interview work conducted in the online space of the food and drink exhibition that we first utilized in our recent "networks of desire" project (Kozinets et al., 2017). We will explore the impact of such practices on consumer wellbeing, a term which has many competing and contradictory definitions and is recognized as "a nebulous, multifaceted notion" (Gillam 2018: 10). We collected and analyzed thousands of pictures, conducted 17 personal interviews, and set up a dedicated research webpage where dozens of people shared their "food porn" stories. We forgo providing a forensic discussion of our methodological approach, since it is detailed in depth in our paper (Kozinets et al., 2017). Therein we put empirical flesh on Deleuze and Guattari's (1983) energetic and connective theory of desire to develop a novel way of conceptualizing it in the digital age. Here among other theoretical anchor points, we utilize Lacanian theory to present the iMirror to explore how people seek self-development and the cultivation of their wellbeing through the practice of digital culinary voyeurism, vicariousness, and adventurism. We demonstrate, with some notable caveats, how a love of food porn, the ogling and sharing of often cheese-laden and funfetti edibles, can be used as a vehicle to flourish in the everyday and provide the impetus to lead a healthy lifestyle. We begin with a brief discussion of food and wellbeing.

Eat, drink, and be wary

Alongside water and air, we cannot live without food. It is the essential sustenance of life. Unless fasting, we eat several times daily. It enters our bodies by way of mouth. We taste, masticate, swallow, digest, then sometime later, by way of rectum, discretely defecate that which our bodies cannot absorb. This process is deeply rooted in the corporality of our biological being (Levy, 1981). Food also has organoleptic properties that titillate the senses such that eating is rarely a chore. According to Ruti (2018: 30), alongside "drugs, alcohol, television, spacing out, daydreaming about a better life," it is a pleasurable experience that makes living on this planet a little more bearable. Nonetheless, since the food choices heavily promoted by the processed food industrial complex often contain copious sugar, fat, and salt, it is all too easy for food consumption to be the harbinger of ill-being (Forgas and Baumeister, 2018). Consumers in the "First World" who purport to follow a healthy diet, and perhaps employ a personal trainer, do so because they understand the pernicious manner in which unhealthy food can affect the well-being of the embodied self (Gilman, 2010).

There was a time when fatness was an indicator of status and wealth, but today it is no longer a marker of distinction, since anyone can afford to gain weight through overeating (Banwell et al., 2012). Instead, with the obesogenic world in the grip of a "globesity pandemic" (Kline, 2011: x), the bodily preference today – the neoliberal ideal – espoused by hordes of body-beautiful Instagrammers and their followers, is to be slender, well-toned, and in control of one's appetite (Ashman, et al., 2018). It is perfectly acceptable to enjoy indulgent calorific foods, but such excess should not impinge on personal wellbeing or the stylizing of one's own body (Sassatelli, 2015). In effect, the seemingly impossible imperative is to "have one's cake and eat it," to somehow endlessly eat and still never gain weight. We assert, as we will soon elaborate, that being a food photo enthusiast actually makes this implausible idea realizable.

Nonetheless, recent studies on food porn, which have been widely reported in the media, hold that the posting, viewing, and sharing of appetizing and visually appealing meals on social media can adversely affect waistlines. Spence et al. (2016), for instance, suggests that our instinctual urge to forage for nutritious foods goes into overdrive when exposed to the endless array of virtual foods on social media, thus exacerbating our physiological hunger into an unnatural state of insatiability. More generally, scholars warn about the negative effects of spending too much time online. As Twenge (2014: 150) eloquently writes, "we're malnourished from eating a junk-food diet of instant messages, Facebook posts, e-mail, and phone calls, rather than the healthy food of live, in-person interaction." There is also mounting evidence to suggest that the constant firing up of our personal publicity machines on social media is associated with the cultivation of personalities that display narcissistic and egotistical tendencies (MacDonald, 2014). And given that, in the end, most individuals die of chronic degenerative illnesses caused by unhealthy lifestyles – such as a poor diet or physical inactivity – one might worry for one's wellbeing, especially if one spends long periods of time sitting still staring at a screen. These caveats in relation to wellbeing might well hold some truth, but, as we will now explain, by adopting a Lancanian take on food porn consumption, a more positive slant on the practice can also be taken.

Mirror theory

Lacan's (1977 [1949]) mirror theory of the self "holds that the autonomous self is constituted as an optical effect produced as a person tries to imagine inhabiting a landscape conceptualized as the field of other people's gazes" (Kozinets et al., 2014: 670) – in this case perhaps it is a field of hungry eyes, mouths, and stomachs. Yet like the consumers Kozinets et al. (2014) studied, our photo-sharing consumers use their social setting as a "stage to produce themselves in a world they desire, full of people who want them" and their food and food experiences "and who want to watch them" and their food and food experiences (p. 670), and perhaps eat with them as well. For eating together is a very social activity, and eating together creates a very communal place: a vast and virtual vicarious dining room we set and invite our friends and potential friends to join.

The visuality of this experience can lead simultaneously to a deeper identification of self with consumptive deserve as well as a disidentification with the physical that removes its natural limits. Brooklyn has this to say:

> If you're looking at food porn, it's just a visual pleasure. For me, I wouldn't be then like I've got to get there now, run out and eat that burger. It's just like "Oh My God" to show somebody something kind of spectacular, rather than something that I'm going to actually at any point necessarily eat. That's the difference, the end result. Pleasure for pleasure's sake, not pleasure because you're getting something at the end of it.
>
> (Brooklyn, food blogger, interview)

Brooklyn describes food porn as a visual abstraction, a perfect display of pleasure. She draws us to Bataille's (1988) spectacle, which Debord (1995) later transferred, helpfully, to the scopophilic age of screens. Brooklyn's desire exists as an abstract formulation, a cool principle and free-flowing channel. She is not all, "I've got to get there now, run out and eat that burger." No, Brooklyn is free from the need for actual embodied pleasure because she tells us in the interview, she has tasted great burgers before. Pleasure has become in some sense an abstraction, a ticked box, as well as something better shared, better consumed, through visual spectacle. Burgerless, Brooklyn seems destined to stay hungry, but aroused by her visual appetite for virtual food. And that, it seems, is exactly how she now likes it.

Why is this so? Also, according to Lacan's (1977 [1949]), mirror theory, the self-image of infants involves seeing themselves, their ideal ego, through a mirror that shows them themselves through others' eyes. This image becomes both divisive – separating ego from body, subjective from objective physical form – and charged with libidinous, some would say masturbatory, body image energy. Lacan's mirror theory thus suggests that we all get a little bit turned on when we turn our cameras on and turn them on ourselves, as one food photo enthusiast states:

> It tends to be, either food that looks the most amazing I have ever seen in my life, so might be really high standard food, or something quite dirty or something that is a guilty pleasure, for me, my guilty pleasures are terrible things like Reese's peanut butter cups, hideous amounts of cheese, yeah, really things, angel delight, that really gets me, yeah I love that, butterscotch or banana, I'm all over it, and that for me would be something, I think it's something that I would lust after the food, either that or something quite dirty like ribs or barbeque, or whether that is like Noma put out say. Just because it's unattainable and so beautiful, so achingly beautiful.
>
> (Miranda, interview)

The images we take, we make, and pose for are also often therefore images that simply make us feel good and enhance our wellbeing. The activity provides each one of us with an opportunity to regularly use our images to enhance our wellbeing through what we term the iMirror phenomenon.

The iMirror phenomenon

The iMirror phenomenon is the manifestation of repeated common acts whereby people use digital technology to visually reflect a combination of self, self-consumption, and desire in order to have the network reflect their image back to them. iMirror phenomena manifest consumption of the self to the self through the collective intelligence network of others; they teach consumers not only how to display their consumption and how to consume it, but where to consume, what to consume, what is good, what is bad, popular, hot, boring, and much more. The iMirror phenomenon works in tandem with a broadening public sphere that encourages (indeed depends upon) exhibitionism, voyeurism, narcissism, parasocial interaction, and vicarious thrills. Through the network of desire (Kozinets et al., 2017), people repeatedly cast consumptive desire outward into the iMirror and then reel it back in, hoping for a good catch of likes, comments, and kudos. For example, the posting of the not untypical burger image illustrated in Figure 14.1 engendered a tremendous amount of such interaction.

The iMirror depends upon the technology of the network of desire to both deinstitutionalize and reinstitutionalize consumption practices, identities, and characteristics. The resulting democratization of consumption is thus far more than a simple addition of voice to an existing process. The connections enabled by social media create entirely new demands for new self-presentational practices and work alongside increasing economic and social access to technology to

Figure 14.1 Typical #foodporn burger
Source: research-annotated image by one of our interviewees on Instagram. Reproduced with permission

channel, focus, code, and direct these practices. Although web technologies, according to the rhetoric at least, render an architecture of participation that engenders tremendous consumer empowerment (Constantinides and Fountain, 2008), we also must, following Weber's famous metaphor, see this as a type of "silicon cage of irrationality." When media is the marketplace, and when media is social, sharing images means that there is no escape from the gaze of the market. The implications for media scholar Henry Jenkins' (1992) notion of "participatory culture" are especially salient as they reveal how the constraints and limits of the online consumer crowd may serve to direct, dampen, undermine, quell, and redirect the potentially liberatory individual or collective initiatives (cf. Firat and Venkatesh, 1995). Emancipatory potentials are counterbalanced not only by marketplace hegemonies (Kreiss et al., 2011) but also through the wisdom of the crowd – or its inanity. Resembling a spectacle, throughout, the iMirror's representation of an insatiably hungry and always-eating consumer audience is always present, even when it is absent from life itself. Visualized and digitized, food consumption becomes an abstraction amplified through the network and reflected back through the network, to self, to network, to self, until, dissolved in the desire, distinctions blur and they are one and the same.

Food for thought

According to Lacan, prior to being aware of having a fleshy unified body with boundaries and limitations, the psychological growth of infants involves seeing the image they have of themselves, their ideal ego, through a mirror that shows, not themselves, but what they see of themselves through other people.

It is the desire to realize the unbounded image that they carry through with them to adulthood. Today's reflexively driven technological world provides them with an opportunity to do so through what we call the iMirror. It is not hard to understand then why inhabiting an online persona is a deeply alluring prospect for many of the perusers and purveyors of food porn. Through sublimation they can indulge their narcissistic imaginary projections, and in effect, become who they always wanted to be. And while they know their diminutive place in the grand scheme, amid social structure and assemblage, they are still free to invent an online persona which in the real world would be difficult, if not impossible to create. By dwelling, for instance, within an especially gluttonous online persona, consumers can become exaggerated, amplified caricatures of their real selves. Consider how Isobel, while comparing her online and offline personas, relies on the perception other people have of her, the iMirror, to make sense of who she thinks she really is, what she is really like:

> I'd say it's an extension of it but not directly part of it, the tweeting is, it's to a certain extent on all social media you create a caricature of yourself, it's not necessarily entirely who you are, although I have had someone turn around to me and say that you are exactly the same as you are on Twitter, and I take that as a compliment, I think on Twitter, to a certain extent I am a lot nicer than I can be in real life, because especially when you are writing a blog you want to come across as someone that people want to talk to, as someone that people want to listen to, so you don't want to come across as bitchy or nasty or any of the rest of it, yeh critical fair enough so long as you can be constructive in it, and say you know don't do this, do this and it may be a lot better, you know, and wording it right, something like that would be seen a lot better oh this was a tragedy … and I try and come across that way, but I have had people say oh, it is just like you, you are just the same, so, I don't think I am, but, there are bits that you have to keep to yourself, and so, whilst all of the food that I tweet photos of, I have either eaten, want to eat, or think looks pretty or whatever, it's not directly me, I think you have to keep a certain level of yourself back.
>
> (Isobel, blogger)

This perhaps explains why the people we encountered in the course of this study like to hang out in online spaces, "food-for-thought locations" (Greene, 2013: 102), where the other inhabitants share similar social values, why they instinctively gravitate towards others that mirror their food tastes. This like-minded collective reinforces their self-image and explains why they feel a pronounced desire to feel good about themselves, and to be arbitrators of other people's feel-good factors. Hence, they readily become part of social networks that retweet or like every digital utterance that they make. Its mutually reinforcing nature accentuates what they like and filters out what they dislike.

Digital double

Taking this further, we postulate that this mirroring process gives consumers good reason to create, in effect, a digital double, a better version of oneself. Amelia, for instance, who describes herself in real life as being "a grumpy loner who doesn't really like people," perfectly articulates how her participation in the world of food porn has enabled her to create a more dynamic and deviant digital version of herself:

> My friends, my very good friends who know me, who knew me way before my Twitter personality and before the blog, they know that I am very different, not very different but, my Twitter personality is almost like the ramped up version of me, so she is a lot more chatty and very social and nice, and more grumpy, and more you know, she is everything that I am but a lot more and she goes out a lot more than I actually do, you know, she is wild, she is a naughty girl, but then, so my actual friends who follow my Twitter, can be like well, you are not very much, you are like that, but it's kind of like an exaggeration, and they appreciate why, they appreciate it's a marketing tool and that I used to work in PR, I have this whole thing, coined this whole thing when I worked in PR, that there are two Amelias, the Amelia and the PR Amelia, and you know when PR Amelia comes out because she is very much like, oh hello, yes, how are you? Oh yes brilliant, and I, you know I just basically work the room.
>
> (Amelia, blogger)

Amelia clearly enjoys consuming this aspirational self-extension, this editable alter ego. She revels in the relational impact her digital double makes, even though she and many readers of her blog are aware that it is essentially a fiction. At one point, for instance, she speaks of forgetting that this virtual identity was supposed to be hyper-grumpy, so had to rewrite posts to more strongly reflect this self-imposed personality trait.

Others have found additional ways of consuming themselves while consuming food. They know that when they have eaten, that they will feel satiated and pleasured, but that soon after their desire ceases and only digestion commences until the next hit. To manage this, they have found ways to prolong reaching the climax of desire and of consuming their online personas, by adopting new practices of production such as taking pictures, editing and sharing photos/videos, conversing, and blogging in which their digital double appears. This transforms the eater's desire for food to other online personas before reflecting it back more strongly on themselves and their present moment, material consumption experience. These practices have become so deeply engrained that, for some at least, they are a part of their daily consumption. When dining with a friend, Pete's priority before eating anything is to snap artfully composed pictures of their food, edit, and post them onto a food-sharing social network.

> I will be sitting there, and I'll be like, "don't touch it don't touch it!!" And I'll be like … and I only every take pictures with my phone, I'm not, like, obviously, food bloggers do, are there with their proper, you know, zoom cameras and all that kind of stuff, I don't do that it's only ever with my picture, with my, my phone sorry, but um, yeah, it's kind of getting the right light, and it's really stupid because it is just a quick snap, but you do kind of, if you have made something, or you have gone out to eat something, and you know it's really good, and you want it to look really good.
> (Pete, blogger)

It is worth mentioning that rather than "breaking bread" with his friend, Pete, for a time at least, shares his meal not with him, but with others elsewhere. This practice alters communication between those who sit around the table and perhaps slightly frustrates non-photo-taking dinner companions who might resent is as a form of narcissistic self-aggrandisement or be annoyed that they have been temporarily restrained from consuming the food so that it can be photographed (see Figure 14.2). Nonetheless, we believe that such complaints about a fairly innocuous activity are overwrought and perhaps, to borrow a phrase, "The needs of the many outweigh the needs of the few." Throughout our research we encountered tales of many people who had discovered, say, a pop-up joint in Peckham, through the posting of a delicious-looking kebab on social media. These pictures

Figure 14.2 Glorious kebab (with irate friend just out of shot)
Source: research-annotated image originally posted on Twitter by interviewee, Pete. Reproduced with permission

engender conversation among wide varieties of friends who trade stories about their experience in said venue, which in turn encourages and facilitates further get togethers among these friends and the discovery of yet more shared experiences and taste sensations.

Haven't you had enough yet?

Our study shows that food photo fans gain almost as much nourishment from their practices as they do from eating the actual food. They enhance their wellbeing by catering to basic human needs to be involved in competition, collaboration, the tendency to gather in consumer tribes (Cova et al., 2007), and the universal appetite to be appreciated by peers for making valued contributions to that tribe. It is this network of relationships between food photo enthusiasts that sustains the infinite galaxy of food imagery. We also find that what motivates food photo devotees has more to do with being part of an encircling, inclusive community than with the actual currency of food imagery. As Chan (2003: 53) stated, with some prescience, the consumption of food porn's image taps "into our primal needs. We are all hungry for love, comfort, passion, gusto, and communal experiences." Moreover, by communicating such passion for food online its diffusion can potentially spread all over the world.

While it is well established that the augmentation of social capital, described above, is strongly linked to subjective wellbeing (Anielski, 2018), sexual wellbeing, though undeniably on the minds of many, somewhat surprisingly, is less discussed in the vast wellbeing literature. The link between food porn and sex is abundantly clear, not just from the moniker itself, but also in the literature which typically speaks of how "food porn evokes a more alluring rhetoric of excess that offers us myriad pleasures and delights, seduces us through the erotic, invites us to evolve into voracious gastro-sensualists, and ultimately propels us deeper into a realm of endless desires" (Greene, 2013: 89). Being propelled into a state of endless desire might seem like a condition unconducive to achieving a coveted sense of wellbeing. Logic, after all, might superficially imply that wellbeing depends on feeling full, satisfied, and contented. Nonetheless, true happiness is impossible without seeking new desires. While commenting on "the most fundamental formulation of the role of desire in human wellbeing," Belk et al. (2000: 114) adroitly note, "to be happy is to be able to desire. Just as we are in love with love, we desire to desire." As such, the ceaseless craving of desire is central to the cultivation and maintenance of human wellbeing.

Casual observers with Luddite inclinations, of course, may scoff at the notion that traveling into a digital world that fundamentally alters our identities and culture can somehow enhance wellbeing. Surely eating, singing, dancing, and reveling in the comfort of our fleshy bodies in the real world will always be a better option than shifting focus to the dematerialized abstraction of an online experience? Perhaps there is some truth in this, but we would suggest that both go hand in hand. As our analysis indicates, what happens in the online world compliments and enhances what happens in the real world. We note, for instance, how food bloggers frequently meet and enjoy the company of other bloggers as a consequence of their online interaction. Moreover, gazing at the iMirror we do not simply see ourselves reflected. Rather what is fascinating and enthralling about participating in social media, at least some of the time, is the effect of our reflection on other people. Whether we are liked, loved, noticed, ignored, or held in high esteem is there to be found out, daily. If our posts and comments are well received the impact on our wellbeing can be tremendously positive. Of course, the opposite can also be true.

In research that received wide media attention for its relation to food porn, Larson et al. (2014) experimentally found no satiation proceeding from consumers merely viewing photos of food, a finding which supports our contention that wellbeing is garnered from such stimulation. However, given the contradictory studies to date we still have no idea if viewing excessive food images or viewing food images in excess stimulate the appetite for actual (or impossible) food (see Spence et al., 2016). Do food photos increase extreme eating, or satiate appetites? Do they raise the bar on food preparation, stimulating demand for more refined cooking techniques, higher-cost purchases, more gourmet indulgences, better-rated restaurants and specialty food stores? Further research may be able to tease out some of these effects. What we do know is that food photo sharing and food porn lead to more food photo sharing and food porn. They stimulate desire for more visual, more virtual, more impossible food image consumption and consequently more realization of wellbeing. Technology consumption and networks of desire create free-flowing circulations of images and emotions that are, in many senses, boundless: They are freed both of traditional bodily food consumption and of material constraints. Their consumption moves food from the mouth and stomach to the eyes and imagination. Vicarious, uninhibited, elevated, fictionalized: We see enormous opportunities for other researchers to examine, develop, and refine our understanding of desire's relationship with food and wellbeing, and its relationship with many other important types of contemporary consumption, from sex, drugs, and violence, to fashion, home furnishings, and electronic goods.

References

Anielski, M. (2018). *An Economy of wellbeing: Common-Sense Tools for Building Genuine Wealth and Happiness*. Gabriola Island: New Society Publishers.

Ashman, R., Patterson, A., & Brown, S. (2018). "Don't forget to like, share and subscribe": Digital autopreneurs in a neoliberal world. *Journal of Business Research*, 92, 474–483.

Banwell, C., Broom, D.Davies, A., & Dixon, J. (2012). *Weight of Modernity: An Intergenerational Study of the Rise of Obesity*. London: Springer.

Barthes, R. (1979). Toward a psychosociology of food consumption. In R. Forster & O. Ranum (Eds), *Food and Drink in History*. Baltimore, MD: Johns Hopkins University Press, pp. 166–173.

Bataille, G. (1988). *The Accursed Share* (Vol. 1), trans. R. Hurley. New York: Zone Books.

Belk, R.W., Ger, G., & Askegaard, S. (2000). The missing streetcar named desire. In S. Ratneshwar, D.G. Mick, & C. Huffman (Eds), *The Why of Consumption: Contemporary Perspectives on Consumer Motives, Goals, and Desires*. New York: Routledge, pp. 98–119.

Chan, A. (2003). "La grande bouffe" cooking shows as pornography. *Gastronomica – Journal of Food and Culture*, 3(4), 47–53.

Constantinides, E., & Fountain, S.J. (2008). Web 2.0 conceptual foundations and marketing issues, journal of direct, data, and digital marketing practice. *Journal of Direct, Data, and Digital Marketing Practice*, 9(3), 231–244.

Cova, B.Kozinets, R.V., & Shankar, A. (2007). *Consumer Tribes*. New York: Routledge.

Debord, G. (1995). *The Society of the Spectacle*. New York: Zone Books.

Deleuze, G., & Guattari, F. (1983). *Anti-Oedipus: Capitalism and Schizophrenia*. Minneapolis, MN: University of Minnesota Press.

Firat, A.F., & Venkatesh, A. (1995). Liberatory postmodernism and the reenchantment of consumption. *Journal of Consumer Research*, 22(3), 239–267.

Forgas, J.P., & Baumeister, Roy F. (2018). *The Social Psychology of Living Well*. New York: Routledge.

Gillam, T. (2018). *Creativity, Wellbeing and Mental Health Practice*. London: Palgrave Macmillan.

Gilman, S.L. (2010). *Obesity: The Biography*. Oxford: Oxford University Press.

Greene, C.P. (2013). *Gourmands and Gluttons: The Rhetoric of Food Excess*. New York: Peter Lang.

Hingston, S. (2018). How millennials killed mayonnaise. *Philadelphia Magazine*. Retrieved from: www.phillymag.com/articles/2018/08/11/mayonnaise-industry-millennials/#yZlbIrTCsOvFZgjm.99

Jenkins, H. (1992). *Textual Poachers: Television Fans and Participatory Culture*. New York: Routledge.

Kline, S. (2011). *Globesity, Food Marketing and Family Lifestyles*. New York: Palgrave Macmillan.

KozinetsR.V., Sherry, J.F., Storm, D., DuhachekA., Nuttavuthisit, K., & DeBerry-SpenceB. (2014). Ludic agency and retail spectacle. *Journal of Consumer Research*, 31(3), 658–672.

Kozinets, R., Patterson, A., & Ashman, R. (2017). Networks of desire: How technology increases our passion to consume. *Journal of Consumer Research*, 43(5), 659–682.

Kreiss, D., Finn, M., & Turner, F. (2011). The limits of peer production: Some reminders from Max Weber for the network society. *New Media and Society*, 13(2), 243–259.

Lacan, J. (1977 [1949]). The mirror stage. In *Écrits: A Selection*, trans. A. Sheridan. New York: Norton, pp. 1–7.

Larson, J., Redden, J.P., & Elder, R. (2014). Satiation from sensory simulation: Evaluating foods decreases enjoyment of similar foods. *Journal of Consumer Psychology*, 24: 188–194.

Levy, S.J. (1981). Interpreting consumer mythology: A structural approach to consumer behavior. *Journal of Marketing*, 44(Summer), 49–61.

Lupton, D. (2018). Vitalities and visceralities: Alternative body/food politics in mew digital media. In M. Phillipov & K. Kirkwood (Eds), *Alternative Food Politics: From the Margins to the Mainstream*. London: Routledge.

MacDonald, P. (2014). Narcissism in the modern world. *Psychodynamic Practice*, 20(2), 144–153.

McDonnell, E.M. (2016). Food Porn: The conspicuous consumption of food in the age of digital reproduction. In P. Bradley (Ed.), *Food, Media and Contemporary Culture: The Edible Image*. New York: Palgrave Macmillan, pp. 239–265.

Naccarato, P., & LeBesco, K. (2012). *Culinary Capital*. New York: Berg.

Rousseau, S. (2015). Is sharing caring? Social media and discourses of healthful eating. In E.-J. Abbots, A. Lavis, & L. Attala (Eds), *Careful Eating: Bodies, Food and Care*. London: Routledge, pp. 45–68.

Ruti, M. (2018). *Penis Envy and Other Bad Feelings: The Emotional Costs of Everyday Life*. New York: Columbia University Press.

Sassatelli, R. (2015). Framing humanity consumerwise: Embodied consumer selves and their varieties. In A. Néstor & G. Martínez (Eds), *Being Human in a Consumer Society*. New York: Routledge, pp. 177–196.

Schau, H.J., & Gilly, M.C. (2013). We are what we post? Self-presentation in personal web space. *Journal of Consumer Research*, 30(3), 385–404.

Spence, C., Okajima, K., Cheok, A.D., Petit, O., & Michel, C. (2016). Eating with our eyes: From visual hunger to digital satiation. *Brain and Cognition*, 110(December), 53–63.

Trifonas, P., & Balomenos, E. (2003). *Good Taste: How What You Choose Defines Who You Are*. London: Icon Books.

Turow, E. (2015). *A Taste of Generation Yum: How the Millennial Generation's Love for Organic Fare, Celebrity Chefs and Microbrews Will Make or Break the Future of Food*. New York: McNally Jackson Books.

Twenge, J.M. (2014). *Generation Me: Why Today's Young Americans Are More Confident, Assertive, Entitled – and More Miserable than Ever Before*. New York: Free Press.

Von Pape, T. (2018). Living in the moment: Self-narratives of permanently connected media users. In P. Vorderer, D. Hefner, L. Reinecke, & C. Klimmt (Eds), *Permanently Online, Permanently Connected: Living and Communicating in a POPC World*. London: Routledge, pp. 97–106.

Index